Capital Cities: Varieties and Patterns of Development and Relocation

The issue of capital city relocation is a topic of debate for more than forty countries across the world. In this first book to discuss the issue, Vadim Rossman offers an in-depth analysis of the subject, highlighting the global trends and the key factors that motivate different countries to consider such projects, analyzing the outcomes and drawing lessons from recent capital city transfers worldwide for governments and policy-makers.

Capital Cities: Varieties and Patterns of Development and Relocation studies the approaches and the methodologies that inform such decisions and debates. Special attention is given to the study of the universal patterns of relocation and patterns specific to particular continents and mega-regions and particular political regimes. The study emphasizes the role of capital city transfers in the context of nation- and state-building and offers a new framework for thinking about capital cities, identifying six strategies that drive these decisions, representing the economic, political, geographic, cultural and security considerations.

Confronting the popular hyper-critical attitudes towards new designed capital cities, Vadim Rossman shows the complex motives that underlie the proposals and the important role that new capitals might play in conflict resolution in the context of ethnic, religious and regional rivalries and federalist transformations of the state, and is seeking to identify the success and failure factors and more efficient implementation strategies. Drawing upon the insights from spatial economics, comparative federalist studies, urban planning and architectural criticism, the book also traces the evolution of the concept of the capital city, showing that the design, iconography and the location of the capital city play a critical role in the success and the viability of the state.

Vadim Rossman is a social scientist and independent consultant. He has lived and taught in the United States, Russia, Israel, Southeast Asia and Central Europe. He is currently a Professor at the Higher School of Economics (HSE) in St Petersburg, Russia. Originally trained as a political philosopher and sinologist, he has published on a broad range of topics, including nation building, nationalism and ultra-nationalism, post-communism, geopolitics, European and Russian intellectual history, and urban studies. Vadim Rossman holds a Ph.D. from the University of Texas at Austin and Master's degrees from the Lomonosov Moscow State University and the McCombs School of Business. He is currently working on establishing a consulting practice in the field of capital city relocations to deliver strategic guidance to world governments and other stakeholders.

Routledge Research in Planning and Urban Design
Series Editor: Peter Ache
Radboud University, Nijmegen, Netherlands

Routledge Research in Planning and Urban Design is a series of academic monographs for scholars working in these disciplines and the overlaps between them. Building on Routledge's history of academic rigour and cutting-edge research, the series contributes to the rapidly expanding literature in all areas of planning and urban design.

Actor Networks of Planning
Exploring the influence of ANT
Yvonne Rydin and Laura Tate

Neoliberal Spatial Governance
Philip Allmendinger

Placemaking
An urban design methodology
Derek Thomas

Ideology, Political Transitions, and the City
The case of Mostar, Bosnia and Herzegovina
Aleksandra Djurasovic

Place and Placelessness Revisited
Robert Freestone and Edgar Liu

Sustainable Regeneration of Former Military Sites
Samer Bagaeen and Celia Clark

Politics, Planning and Housing Supply in Australia, England and Hong Kong
Nicole Gurran, Nick Gallent and Rebecca Chiu

Unfinished Places: The Politics of (Re)making Cairo's Old Quarters
Gehan Selim

Capital Cities: Varieties and Patterns of Development and Relocation
Vadim Rossman

Capital Cities: Varieties and Patterns of Development and Relocation

Vadim Rossman

LONDON AND NEW YORK

First published 2017
by Routledge
2 Park Square, Milton Park, Abingdon, Oxon OX14 4RN

and by Routledge
711 Third Avenue, New York, NY 10017

First issued in paperback 2018

Routledge is an imprint of the Taylor & Francis Group, an informa business

© 2017 Vadim Rossman

The right of Vadim Rossman to be identified as author of this work has been asserted by him in accordance with sections 77 and 78 of the Copyright, Designs and Patents Act 1988.

All rights reserved. No part of this book may be reprinted or reproduced or utilised in any form or by any electronic, mechanical, or other means, now known or hereafter invented, including photocopying and recording, or in any information storage or retrieval system, without permission in writing from the publishers.

Trademark notice: Product or corporate names may be trademarks or registered trademarks, and are used only for identification and explanation without intent to infringe.

British Library Cataloguing in Publication Data
A catalogue record for this book is available from the British Library

Library of Congress Cataloging-in-Publication Data
A catalog record for this book has been requested.

ISBN 13: 978-1-138-60153-6 (pbk)
ISBN 13: 978-1-138-83777-5 (hbk)

Typeset in Sabon
by Apex CoVantage, LLC

'A most impressive global history of capital city relocations.'
Göran Therborn, University of Cambridge

'A remarkable book that is both encyclopedic and expansive in ambition. By bringing together the history of dozens of capital cities in one place, Rossman offers a kaleidoscopic look at one of the core phenomena of urban life: the political capital. More than chronicling a number of separate stories disconnected by time and place, Rossman weaves together a single narrative that importantly offers several lessons. He goes beyond merely telling his story but tries to develop a framework for understanding the extent to which a new capital is a "success" or a "failure". At a time when regimes often consider moving their capital, Rossman's superb volume is an excellent reminder that such transfers are normal events.'
Blair Ruble, Director of the Woodrow Wilson Center's Urban Sustainability Laboratory

'Rossman has written an indispensable book on the timeless question of the correlation between power and space, particularly as evident in capital cities. With remarkable acuity and magisterial analysis, the author brings together the philosophical reflections, historical contexts, political ramifications, economic implications, and social consequences of the (re)construction, elaboration, (re)location of, and contestations over, capital cities in all parts of the world. *Capital Cities* is a tour de force.'
Wale Adebanwi, Professor, Department of African American and African Studies, University of California-Davis, USA, and Visiting Professor, Institute of Social and Economic Research, Rhodes University, South Africa

'Vadim Rossman is endowed with an uncanny ability to see systems in details, and details within abstract systems, and then also the connections between the two levels. Not to mention that he writes eminently readable prose.'
Georgi Derluguian, Professor of Social Research and Public Policy, New York University, Abu Dhabi

Contents

Foreword by Blair A. Ruble ix
Acknowledgements xi
Preface xiii

Introduction 1

Disciplines, contexts, and categories 1
Certain assumptions and hypotheses 6
Plan of the book 8

1 History and typology of capital cities 11

Preliminary definition 13
Functions of capital cities 14
Typology of capital cities 16
Historical types of capitals 22
History and arrangement of national capitals 32

2 Capital city relocation experience 51

Principles of capital city siting 51
Capital city relocation in empires 55
Disembedded capitals: despotic states of the ancient East 67

3 Capital city relocations and debates of this topic in different world regions 77

Generations of national capitals 77
Post-colonial nation-building in Africa 84
Post-colonial nation-building in Asia 99
Southeast Asia 99

South Asia 105
The Far East 112
The Middle East 119
Post-colonial nation-building in Latin America 127
Post-Soviet countries 140
Europe 151

4 Strategies of capital city relocations and their critics 173

The common themes in capital city relocations 173
Six integrative strategies for capital city relocations 177
Three strategies of an exclusive capital city 193
The budgets and the appraisals of the relocation total costs 200
Administration and timetables of capital city shifts 202
"The brilliant mistakes" at best: the critique of capital
  city transfers 203
Some counter-arguments in defense of capital city shifts 207
Success factors: the good, the bad, and the ugly 214

5 Three standards to assess the effectiveness
  of a capital city 224

Methodologies to assess the role and location
  of a capital city 224
Three standards to assess the effectiveness of a
  capital city 233
Capitals and global cities 255

Conclusion 271
Selected bibliography 278
Appendices 301
Index 313

Foreword

Vadim Rossman has written a remarkable book that is both encyclopedic in ambition and expansive in ambition. Rossman tells the remarkable story of how humans build capitals, why we build them, and then, why and how we move on to construct new capital cities. By bringing together the history of dozens of capital cities in one place, he offers a kaleidoscopic look at one of the core phenomena of urban life: the political capital. More than chronicling a number of separate stories disconnected by time and place, Rossman weaves together a single narrative that importantly offers several lessons for all of us alive at this historical moment.

The first of many lessons that Rossman conveys is that moving a capital city is a normal part of political life. As a Washingtonian I have been lured into thinking about capitals as somehow immutable. They are not, of course, and never have been. How many capitals has the United States had? At least nine since the process of secession from the British Empire began.[1] The process of contemplating further relocations continued well into the nineteenth century as advocates of Western expansion continuously argued for moving the capital from Washington D.C. to a city on the banks of the Mississippi River such as St. Louis.

As the American experience reveals, capitals move for many reasons. They might decamp to a nearby town for one night in response to military occupation by an enemy; they may shift in response to regional and political interests; they may emerge as physical expressions of new political regimes and ideologies. If this is the case in the relatively young United States, the impermanence of capital cities becomes amplified when turning to the centuries-old regimes of Europe and Asia.

The story Rossman tells is an ancient one. His discussion skillfully draws upon the transfer of the Roman capital from Rome to Constantinople as a way of setting out many of the issues swirling around capital cities that have occurred over and over again across the ages. As importantly, his broad knowledge incorporates Asian examples together with those drawn from the Americas, Africa, and Europe. In other words, Rossman argues forcefully that the transfer of a national capital to a new location is part of the natural sweep of history rather than representing a peculiar, singular, or unique moment in the life cycle of a political system.

Rossman's volume is noteworthy for a second reason. He goes beyond merely telling his story but tries to develop a framework for understanding the extent to which a new capital is a "success" or a "failure." Of course the criteria of success depend on the reason for transferring a capital in the first place. While reasons for moving and criteria of success may evolve over time, motivations invariably are political. Thus, as he argues, achieving political goals through the act of moving a capital rests in the end on the success or failure of the political system that is making the move. In other words, the act of moving a capital can't successfully address a list of political challenges on its own. It only can facilitate how a political system responds to those challenges. A capital city cannot succeed if the political system producing it fails.

At a time when regimes often consider moving their capital, Rossman's superb volume is an excellent reminder that such transfers are normal events in that they have happened hundreds of times throughout history. More importantly, his book reminds all who read it that moving a capital city in and of itself will not resolve the deep structural, political, demographic, and economic challenges any state faces at a given moment. The challenge is not simply building a "successful" new capital city (and there are dozens of ways in which we might measure success); the task is to develop and maintain a successful state in the first place.

Blair A. Ruble
Director, Program on Global Sustainability
and Resilience
Washington D.C.
January 19, 2016

Note

1 Philadelphia, Pennsylvania (September 5, 1774 to December 12, 1776; March 4, 1777 to September 18, 1777; July 27, 1778 to June 21, 1783; and December 6, 1790 to May 14, 1800); Baltimore, Maryland (December 20, 1776 to February 27, 1777); Lancaster, Pennsylvania (September 27, 1777 [one day]); York, Pennsylvania (September 30, 1777 to June 2, 1778); Princeton, New Jersey (June 30, 1783 to November 4, 1783); Annapolis, Maryland (November 26, 1783 to August 19, 1784); Trenton, New Jersey (November 1, 1784 to December 24, 1784); New York, New York (January 11, 1785 to December 5, 1790) and Washington D.C. (since November 17, 1800).

Acknowledgements

I am indebted to many colleagues, friends and students for all the stimulating and thought-provoking conversations we have shared over the past five years. First of all, I would like to express my sincere gratitude towards those colleagues and friends who have stimulated my interest in the topic of capital city relocations. Letter exchanges, critical comments and personal conversations with Sidney Monas, Blair Ruble, Nicolas Pujol, Irina Labetsky, Göran Therborn, Edward Schatz, Vladimir Nikolaev, Joseph Rossman, Boris Glazov, Yaroslav Shramko, and Olga Tuluzakova have broadened my knowledge, provided helpful suggestions and contributed towards shaping the thesis of this book.

Very special thanks go to Leonid Storch for his critical reading of the manuscript, many valuable suggestions and corrections that helped to improve the book and for many years of our friendship.

I am also thankful to Benjamin Payuk and Efim Shluger for their help with identification of articles related to the capital city relocation debate in Argentina, Brazil and Venezuela. I am most indebted to the extremely friendly atmosphere on both a professional and personal level at the International College for Sustainability Studies, Srinakharinwirot University, Bangkok, Thailand, and University of Economics in Bratislava, Slovakia. The colleagues there have created the congenial atmosphere to work on the manuscript of this book. The author is also thankful to Valery Anashvili, the Director of the Gaidar Institute of Economic Politics Publishing House in Moscow, for his abiding interest in the topic and his encouragement to produce the early version of this book that was published in Russian in 2013 but was substantially different from the current expanded edition. I am also highly grateful to Anna Rakitianskaya for providing me with hard-to-find journal articles.

This book was also produced in part by the capital cities themselves. The streets of Moscow, Tokyo, Beijing, Canberra, Ottawa, Jerusalem, Istanbul, Washington D.C., Vienna, Budapest, Prague, London, Paris, Rome, Stockholm, Madrid, The Hague, Berlin, Lisbon, Tbilisi, Bangkok, Helsinki, Kathmandu, Putrajaya, Phnom Penh, Vientiane, Saint-Petersburg, Naypyidaw, Bratislava, Astana, and many other cities and settlements have generously shared with me some of their secrets and presented me with new inspirations and fresh thoughts.

Finally, special recognition goes to my wife, Marina Besson, for her support, encouragement and patience.

Vadim Rossman
Bratislava, Slovakia
September 15, 2015

Preface

The purpose of this book is to study the problems of capital city relocations and provide a comparative analysis of them, as well as to review the issue of capital cities' functions and changing role in the present day world.

Despite popular perceptions that the practice of changing capitals is singular and rare, it is, as we will see elsewhere in this book, quite widespread and worthy of serious academic attention. Capital city relocation projects have emerged, and continue to do so, on all continents in countries with different levels of economic development and ruled by very different political regimes. Therefore, practices of this kind and the ideas on which they are based deserve much closer attention, both theoretical and practical, than hitherto given.

The few figures provided below unambiguously demonstrate the high occurrence of capital city relocations in the political life of modern states. Thus, over the past 100 years worldwide, capitals have been relocated every three to four years; factoring in smaller states and lesser capitals, this interval becomes even narrower, close to every two years (see Table 2). A historical view of the problem confirms such an observation. According to calculations made by the American urbanist Lawrence Vale, 74 percent of capital cities in the year 1900 were not capitals a century later.[1] Furthermore, over the past 100 years more than 30 relatively large states have successfully, or somewhat successfully, moved their capitals (Table 1, please note that all tables will be found in the appendices at the end of the book). Arguably the best-known examples include Turkey, Australia, Brazil, Pakistan, Nigeria, Kazakhstan, Germany, Burma, and Malaysia. The United Arab Emirates and Afghanistan have already initiated building their new capital cities. In 2015 Egyptian authorities also announced the beginning of a construction of a new capital. Several states, notably Iran, Japan, Indonesia, and Liberia, have committed to this undertaking in principle. While no final candidates for new capitals have been endorsed yet, and no final mechanisms for carrying out these plans have been selected, these countries are still working out details of their projects and continue to discuss various relevant options and possible scenarios.

In the course of detailing their plans or even after the constuction had already started, several countries encountered various problems – financial, legal or those caused by changes in political leadership and political continuity – and as a result the previously approved projects were suspended, halted, or frozen. Such were the cases of Argentina, Venezuela, Peru, South Korea, Mongolia, and some others. Nonetheless, political authorities of these countries periodically resume discussion of this issue, and it still remains on their national agendas.

In many states, the need for returning a capital city to its original location or rethinking the very function of the capital arose at the turning points of their history. To exemplify, after the fall of communism, Poland saw a debate of whether to move the seat of its government back to Kraków; South Africa, after the collapse of apartheid in 1994, raised the question of whether to replace the long-standing triple-capital system with a singular capital city;[2] and in the aftermath of the Second World War, in light of the changes in the international political environment, Finland faced the problem of moving its capital from Helsinki back to Turku.

Presently more than 40 nations of the world are debating the issue of capital city relocation. Debates have taken place in numerous Asian (China, Taiwan, Thailand, Nepal, and Bangladesh), South and Central American (Venezuela, Nicaragua, and Haiti), and African states (Zimbabwe, Kenya, Ghana, and Somalia). The establishment of a new capital has also been on the agenda of several post-Soviet states including Russia, Azerbaijan, Kyrgyzstan, Tajikistan, and Ukraine. While this topic has sparked a lot of discussions, the degree of intensity of the discussions may have been different in each country. This book will analyze the causes and paradigms of these debates.

The list provided here (Table 3) includes mainly the countries where the idea of a new capital has been enunciated by prominent government figures and leaders of major political parties and where the relevant debates have been conducted in parliaments and constitutional courts, thus making a strong public appeal.

However, the interest to this topic is not limited to these nations. In some countries, notably Australia, India, Switzerland, the USA, Italy, and Slovakia, the debates over capital city relocation are in the purview of a rather small group of politicians and intellectuals who fiddle with the idea. Thus, in the course of a recent debate, Geoffrey Blainey, recognized as the most prominent Australian living historian, opined that the country's capital should be moved to Perth, which would reflect an overall shift in concentration of Australia's key political and business activities from the Pacific Coast to the Indian Ocean.[3] Furthermore, several decades ago, Dr. B.R. Ambedkar, one of the authors of the Indian Constitution and leader of the untouchable caste, insisted on creating a dual-capital system in India and relocating some of the major capital city's functions to Hyderabad, closer to the geographical center of the country.[4] Today certain Indian politicians and followers of Ambedkar's legacy also repeatedly propose to shift the capital closer to the geographical center.[5] In Italy and Canada, some marginal political parties have launched campaigns to relocate the seat of the government. Thus, Lega Nord (North

League) and its leader Umberto Bossi have proposed to make Milan Italy's capital city instead of Rome, and the Rhinoceros Party in Canada has proposed to move the capital eastward, to the middle of the country. In the US Republican Senate, candidate Ben Sasses has proposed to move the capital to the geographic center of the country in Nebraska. Although these and similar marginal ideas are usually viewed by many as odd or unrealistic, they – along with the discussions presently having a limited audience – may eventually gain national publicity and develop into larger scale public debates.

Yet the importance and applied significance of the capital relocation subject are not limited to debates on the national-state level. Many principles of siting a national capital city are also, to a certain extent, applicable to the siting of subnational and supranational capitals or administrative centers. The debates over shifting a capital city are in progress in numerous provinces and member republics of nation-states, and the siting of the capitals of federal states, autonomies, provinces, regions, lands, prefectures, cantons, and territories has been widely debated (Table 4). While the locational logic of subnational capitals corresponds to that of national capitals, the former have been moved as frequently as the latter. Among the most representative examples of subnational capital relocations, one should mention those undertaken in such major countries as India, South Africa, Russia, Germany, and China. Notably, some of these subnational entities are larger in terms of territory than some European states. Since 1956 more than ten new states and union territories have been created in India, and ten new provincial governments have been created in South Africa,[6] in both cases, due to partition, consolidation, and reorganization of subnational entities. Most of the above examples have involved capital city relocation issues.

China's administrative units have some history of capital city relocations – e.g., the shifting of Inner Mongolia's capital in 1952. In Germany the capital of Thuringia was moved from Weimar to Erfurt in 1948. Furthermore, capitals of both union republics (e.g., Kazakhstan, Moldova, and Ukraine) and autonomous republics (e.g., Ingushetia and Karakalpakstan) were moved in the Soviet Union. Presently the possibility of capital relocation is being discussed in the Sakha Republic (Yakutia), Republic of Karelia, Transnistria, Gagauzia, and a number of major Russian regions. Some Indonesian, South African, and Canadian provinces, and US states have had similar experiences. Thus, a relocation of the capital of the State of Alaska has been under consideration for many years. A capital relocation is being considered in British Columbia, Canada, in Ras Al Khaimah, UAE, and in Ireland, UK (Athlone was proposed as a new capital).

Unfortunately, both the practical importance in understanding capital shifting processes and the need in criteria for the decision-making in this area have not yet been properly addressed by the academic community. To date, the phenomenon of capital city relocations has not been analyzed systematically in the literature on urban studies and political science. There is as yet no book-length study of this topic. There may be several reasons behind this.

Many historians and political scientists tend to believe that, driven by a combination of historical trends, capital cities are essentially sited randomly. Since the decisions on this matter are often made by individual rulers, one may be tempted to view the issue of capital relocation from the perspective of subjective and arbitrary decisions, which by definition have neither a roadmap, nor starting coordinates. As a result, some observers implicitly take a nihilistic position that no universal patterns, prescriptions, and conventional problem-solving models are applicable to this issue. They perceive the subjects of capital, metropolitanism, and capital shifting as something too broad, multifold, purely descriptive, and therefore unsuitable for generalizations and universal solutions.

It also must be noted that a study of various existing capital relocation models would hardly fit into a framework of a unidisciplinary and comprehensive research project. One of the difficulties associated with such a study is that it is multi-aspect, complex, and necessarily multidisciplinary in nature. A selection of a new capital often entails too many variables that are difficult to completely take into account.

As a result, from the standpoint of skeptics, capital relocation is gaining a reputation of a topic more interesting to and more easily approachable by poets and politicians rather than by scholars. What else, if not a metaphor or an inspiring call, can better grasp the will of the people, nation's dream of a new City, high-handedness of the tyrant, prophetic dreams of the dictator, charisma of the leader, elusive appeal of new yonder, and passionate flurries of national willpower which suddenly, as some romantic historians claim, drive people away from their long-inhabited homes to search for the Promised Land of the New Capital? How does one capture these impulses and their God-inspired moves with the plain numbers and dry lingo of scholarly abstractions? And even if we assume for a moment that all of these may be quantified and cataloged, how should the mechanics of relocation, after it has been quantified and verified, be returned to where it came from – the depths of the people's enthusiasm, the chemistry of the nation's imagination, the spontaneity of actions, and the flame of this idea, and the collective intoxication with it?

This book is based on the opposite premise, i.e., that the complex of relocation motives is unitary while the problems which the states seek to resolve by relocating their capital are quite universal. Although all decisions to relocate capital city are country-specific, they, nonetheless, are not solely driven by the unique problems of the country making this decision. It may be said that there exist universal models of capital relocation, generations of capital cities, and capital relocation cycles caused by new demands made by historical and political processes developing both internationally and regionally.

This book articulates the issues presented by modern political science itself. The objective of the book is at least to fill the gaps in our knowledge of capital cities and their patterns of relocation. First of all, these gaps involve practical issues related to intentional and unintentional consequences and implications faced by special committees' members, heads of states, expert consultants, and other policy-makers and decision-makers.

Here one can point at several groups of issues that appear most relevant:

Is capital city location a neutral factor or does it have a major or perhaps even determinant impact on the success of the state and its social and economic development?

What political strategies and state-building problems can capital relocation help to solve? How often in the past did capital relocations, once completed, lead to solution of the problems faced by the government?

Which of the problems believed to be solved by relocating the capital can be solved within the framework of the existing capital? Can the new technologies such as intra-city transportation solutions or high-speed intercity routes assist to overcome the problems that supporters of capital relocation seek to solve?

What are the long-term consequences of capital relocation for the economy and political life of different countries?

What are the main problems, both general and pervasive, encountered by capital relocation plans? What are effective steps to carry out these plans and in what order should these steps be taken?

What factors can help decide whether to relocate a capital city? What circumstances and conditions justify putting this topic on the national agenda and when is this topic a false concern? How much weight do speculations of futurologists or tactical maneuvers of politicians, armed with populist and demagogic slogans, have in the ongoing capital relocation debates?

In what case should operations of a capital city be considered effective and what are the methods of assessing its effectiveness? Does the size of a capital city have a negative impact on the development of the national economy?

What methods should be applied to assess feasibility of capital relocation projects and to select a location for a new capital? What decision-making procedures are most rational and what should be the correlation between the experts' evaluations and people's declaration of will?

While the answers to these issues may facilitate making an optimal decision, other factors – e.g., knowledge of relevant precedents and understanding of relevant facts, figures, budgets, motivations, and approaches – should be helpful too. This book contains a lot of such information and provides its comparative analysis. Furthermore, it proffers an explanation as to the causes of successes and failures of various capital relocation models, highlighting the lessons that can be learned from the experience of these models.

The issues enumerated above may hardly be fully appreciated and solved without addressing certain questions that are more theoretical in nature. These include matters pertaining to general history, general sociology, and general philosophy. Approaching the problem from the angle of more general and more abstract disciplines should facilitate choosing a more productive language, categories, and methods to be used for conceptualizing and proper understanding of the notion of a capital city. It is important to realize that addressing these general theoretical questions may also give an impulse and a system of premises for solving the issues and tasks we have set forth in this part of the book.

To what extent should the siting of a capital city be determined by the specifics or particularities of the proposed geographical location? Are "good sites" or natural seats of power really identifiable in the process of the search or are they socially constructed? Or perhaps they are formed by certain objective laws? What role does the concept of a capital city play in the genealogy of modern states?

To what degree do the assertions that the concept of a nation-state is declining and that global cities are rising conform to the importance of the role which many nations, by and through their leaders or governments, attribute to national capitals and nation-building?

To what degree is capital city relocation a new phenomenon in the political practice? Do modern capital relocations replicate causes and motivations of such relocations in the pre-modern world? When and how do capital cities emerge and what is their place in the nation-building process? Does the very concept of a capital city change in the course of time?

The author does not undertake to give a conclusive answer to all of the above questions. He does, however, hope that the proffered theoretical framework and historical narrative will help to better define these issues, providing a context where one may find the answers. While capital relocation debates are often accompanied with poetic metaphors and political slogans and speculations, this framework will also give an opportunity to see structural elements, strategies, and motives that are common to capital relocation debates in different countries and that may be relevant or irrelevant depending on the circumstances.

In addition to this, the understanding of general trends in the evolution of the concept of a capital city will make it easier to see the historical paths of different nations and to appreciate their sometimes existential choice of capital relocation, made at the turning points and crossroads of their national destiny. Last, this theoretical framework will allow the evaluation of relevant historical precedents in a systematic manner.

The practical and theoretical aspects of the capital relocation problem are barely separable. Nonetheless, the author hopes that by defining the relevant issues, it would be possible to break the deadlock of subjective and abstract approaches where the capital relocation problem has been caught, facilitating more constructive solutions to this problem. Although capital relocations may hardly become the subject of a rigid academic discipline, it may be useful and productive to lay out and discuss a theoretical system where this problem exists, as well as to determine what is at stake in the discussion of this problem and what its political, historical, and other implications are. This would avert a monologic, one-dimensional discussion of this subject within the tight boundaries of an academic field.

It should be stressed that one of the main issues to be addressed in this regard is the issue of the interplay between political regimes and capital city relocations.

The reasons for capital city relocations will be investigated in detail and illustrated with specific examples elsewhere in this book. However, it would be appropriate to highlight here, albeit briefly, some global development trends that both stimulate the growth of interest to this problem and call for its examination.

First, the problems related to capital cities have been becoming more and more topical because, since the beginning of the twentieth century, the international arena has seen the emergence of numerous new states. Thus, while there were slightly over 40 sovereign-state capitals in 1900, their number increased to 190 in the year 2000, more than quadrupling in 100 years' time. The emergence of new states necessitates the societal consolidation and the creation of new systems of intrastate communication, representation, and common symbols. Of course, the formation of a state assumes the choosing of a new political center with new symbols and new iconography reflecting the new identity of this state. Choosing a capital city is an organic and nontrivial part of this process. Even in the case when the seat of government remains in the same location, such a decision constitutes a rather definitive and nontrivial choice of several options. Over the past century, state unifications have been generally less frequent and less intense than state disintegrations; yet both of these processes have been putting the issue of a new capital on the agenda. A decision on this issue has a direct impact on the viability of a new state. Thus, Flemish nationalists insist on the establishment of two capitals in Belgium, one in Namur for the Walloons and one in Antwerp for the Flemish, whereas pan-Romanian nationalists call for the creation of a joint capital city for both Romania and Moldova.

Second, the process of urbanization has been such that capital cities have a tendency to a much faster growth than noncapital cities. Especially evident in the developing countries, this tendency further raises two sets of issues: 1) those of technological provisions of a new capital and 2) political and social issues.

The growth of capital cities poses the problem of whether new urban development technologies and standards can meet the demands of a particularly large and constantly expanding city. As the old capitals are becoming obsolete in terms of their engineering standards and urban technologies that they use to address the issues of security and sanitation, the uncontrolled growth of primate cities is creating overpopulation and traffic jam problems leading to additional costs for the whole national economy. Triggering an increase of migration to primate cities, this problem is particularly pressing in the developing countries. A primate city is defined as a city that is twice as big as the next city in the urban hierarchy and that plays a disproportional role in the life of the country.

The disproportionately fast growth of primate cities, which are usually capital cities, exacerbates many political and social problems including the problems of social justice, political equality, as well as proportional access to power and representation. In many nations, the privileged status enjoyed by the capital city and its residents in comparison with the residents of other cities may have a destructive impact on the degree of solidarity in the society at large. The privileged living standards of the capital city residents involve better money-making and investment opportunities, property, wealth, job-creation pace, etc., possibly casting a doubt on political stability in the nation and triggering unfavorable political and social consequences.

Last, one should mention here strong tendencies towards self-reproduction and self-perpetuation that are embodied in the hypertrophic role played by capital cities. Political centralism promotes a concentration of economic resources in a single city, further enlarging the gap between capitals and provincial cities in income and opportunities.

The accelerating growth of real estate prices in the capitals creates social polarization in general and negatively affects the availability of affordable housing for the middle class in particular, reducing the degree of social mobility. Also, the hypertrophic growth of the capital cities is often associated with the problem of quasi-urbanization, especially in the developing countries where migration to the large cities does not result in the growth of the actual urban occupations.

All of the above problems stimulate, in different states, debates on the new capitals. Supporters of a capital relocation believe that it may help to overcome the negative trends enumerated above and, thus, will unclog the streets of the old capitals, stop their seemingly uncontrollable growth, eliminate imbalances, as well as contribute to the solution of many social and political problems caused by the impact of large-city domination on the economy and the society at large.

Notes

1 Vale, L. "The Urban Design of 20th Century Capitals." In: Gordon, D. (ed.), *Planning 20th Century Capital Cities* (London: Routledge, 2006), 15.
2 Du Preez, P. *One Nation: One Capital, the case of Pretoria* (Pretoria: Adams & Adams, 1995).
3 Orr, A. "Move over Eastern States—Perth Could be Moving on Up," *WAToday*, October 26, 2012. www.watoday.com.au/wa-news/move-over-eastern-states—perth-could-be-moving-on-up-20121025-287z6.html
4 Ambedkar, B.R. "India and the Necessity of a Second Capital: A Way to Remove Tension between the North and the South." In: *Thoughts of Linguistic States* (Bombay: Ramkrishna Printing Press, 1955).
5 Anandan, S. "Make Mumbai Second Capital of India, city forum petitions PM," *Hindustan Times*, June 26, 2012; Gupta, H. "Pataliputra: The New Capital?", *Swarajya*, June 1, 2015, http://swarajyamag.com/ideas/pataliputra-the-new-capital/; Kumar, N. "Decapitate Capital tag from Delhi-Commemorating a century of Coronation," *Perspectives on Pan-Asianism*, Aug 29, 2009.
6 Mabin, A. "South African Capital Cities," In: Bekker, S & Therborn, G. (eds.), *African Capital Cities: Power and Powerlessness* (Cape Town and Dakar: HSRC Press, 2011), 147.

Introduction

Disciplines, contexts, and categories

As has been already said, one of the difficulties of the subject of capital relocations is its multidisciplinary character. Different aspects of the problem have been discussed in different fields of social sciences, notably history, geography, and political science.[1] Although the proposers of capital relocations by no means always rely on the results of academic analysis, very often they advance arguments following from certain forms of this analysis. To avoid the enthrallment with one specific disciplinary approach to the neglect of others, it is necessary to describe, albeit briefly, possible disciplinary approaches to the subject being addressed. This description will help us identify the categories and factors considered by said proponents and intended to identify a group of candidates for a new capital city. It will also allow us to define the place of these disciplinary approaches in our analysis and assess their relevance for our study. Identifying and selecting the most fundamental categories should make it easier to build a framework for the comparative analysis of capital relocations as we see it. Finally, this analysis will also assist us to develop the language describing the problem in question and to create proper analytical devices, patterns, and tools to be used in this book.

Political philosophy

First and foremost, the problem of capital cities is the problem of spatial localization of power and the problem of correlation between power and space.[2] Viewed from the more conventional disciplinary perspective, it is also the problem of interplay between politics and geography. Yet in addition to this, at the core of the capital cities problem are profound philosophical issues.

Most of the capital relocation debates are premised on the normative notions of state and nation, the idealistic understanding of state tasks, the perception of fairness, as well as on the boundaries and intensity of power. Both the very concept of capital and the proposals for capital relocation are often based on certain concepts of state and power.

2 Introduction

Furthermore, the concept of a capital city inevitably reflects normative characteristics of the authorities, state, and political regime benefited by this concept whereas characteristics of the capital stem from the normative perceptions of how the state should be ideally, or at least preferably, organized. Some political regimes are meant to broadcast and expand their power. Others tend to be characterized by efforts to limit their authority, and these efforts are embodied in the way a capital city is set up. Normative characteristics of power are also reflected in its geographical location, size, and inner workings, as well as in its symbolism and proffered forms of legitimation of power.

The subject of normative premises, which often are not even hinted at in relevant discussions and analytical articles, lies in the purview of political philosophy. Since these premises are implicit, explicating the ideas underlying the corresponding capital relocation concepts appears to be particularly important.

Geopolitics and military strategies

An important factor in siting a capital city has always been the security and defense capabilities of the state. At least, according to some interpretations, the siting of a capital city should take into account the possible expansion of the sphere of influence of the state and even the possibility of its spread beyond the national borders. The imperative of security necessitates that a capital city should be sited in such a way as to minimize the vulnerability of the state, safeguard its territorial integrity, and help it to gain a regional status guaranteeing its weight and importance in international affairs. This set of issues has been addressed in the works of some experts on geopolitics, military strategy, and international relations, although the author of this book is not familiar with any study specifically focusing on the issue.

In the research on geopolitics, the problem of the core and periphery has acquired not just a national, but also an international dimension. Today the location of a capital city takes into account not only the position the capital holds in the region but also its position in the global distribution of power.

Structural characteristics of capital cities

The problem of a capital city has been discussed in a number of publications on social sciences, economic geography, spatial economics, political science, demography, urban planning, architectural history, and other allied social sciences. Policy-relevant studies focus on capital cities' effectiveness and structural characteristics, viewing them from the perspective of the normative criteria to be met by states. The significance of these studies to the topic at hand is that they proffer various criteria and formulas for the evaluation of various capital cities' parameters and characteristics from the standpoint of their compliance with the normative tasks of the state. These studies examine the social and economic consequences, whether actual or possible, of having a particular city with particular characteristics as the capital. Very often they concentrate on the degree of correlation and interplay between certain characteristics of capital cities and the articulated normative expectations.

The causal relationships, important for our analysis, between the features of a capital city and the factors affecting the way it was shaped are further examined in many of these studies. Studies explaining the reasons why primate-city dominant capitals emerged in some states while small professional capitals emerged in others may serve as an example of this kind.

Such studies may be divided into two groups – those that are mainly economic and those that are mainly political in nature. While the former focus on the normative criteria of economic and public administration effectiveness, the latter relate to such normative criteria as fairness, social harmony, conflict resolution, and achieving civil peace.

Several studies on economic geography, spatial economics, demography, public administration, and urban planning pay a particular attention to economic and public administration effectiveness of capital cities. For example, they may point to the correlation between the capital city's size or proximity to the nation's demographic center on one hand and the level of corruption in the nation on the other. They may also examine such parameters as the demographic structure of a capital city, its ethnic composition, volume and rate of migration from the periphery to the capital city, distribution of economic resources between the capital and the rest of the country, and social and economic consequences of the above for the nation as a whole. By and large, at the heart of these studies is the category of capital city effectiveness as measured by the existing criteria.

Studies of the second group focus on how capital city characteristics affect possible settlements of regional, ethnic, religious, and internal tribal conflicts in various states. The studies that concentrate on such factors as political constitutions of states, the degree of social inequality, states' resistance to civil protests, and the possibility of social conflicts, examining these factors from the standpoint of capital city status and its internal organization, are particularly interesting to our topic. Unlike the studies of the first group, they investigate moral and political issues as opposed to the issues of effective governance.

Although many of these studies are only descriptive, their conclusions may be used as a basis of, or reason for, the recommendation to relocate or not to relocate a capital city. Understanding the structural and causal relations between the structure of a capital city and social consequences created by the way the capital city function is organized may certainly serve as an argument in favor or against the relocation of a capital city; the choice depends on the extent the existing conditions promote or hinder the desired social and political outcomes.

History

The problem of capital cities has also been discussed from a purely historical perspective in such disciplines as general history, archeology, theory and history of nationalism, symbolism studies, urban architecture studies, and some other disciplines related to the study of history and anthropology.[3] The authors discussing it reconstruct both the notion of a capital city and its main attributes as they existed in different historical periods, and explain the ever-changing role of capital cities in the life of states. The value of these studies is that they describe the various traditions, entrenched forms of existence, and historical requirements pertaining to the operation of capital cities.

Historical discussions of the problem of states' and nations' identities are particularly important to the objectives of this book. As we will see, the ideas expressed in this regard have played a major role in choosing a capital city. While the concept of national identity has been acquiring a special status in the context of the nation-building process, the places and cities related to the formation of this identity have often been proposed as candidates for a capital city.

Speaking of identity, one should at least touch on the problem of national perception of space. By no means is the concept of space universal, and there exist very culturally distinctive forms of capital city organization, administrative division, legitimation of power, and models utilized in the building of networks between capital cities, other cities, cores, and peripheries. Certainly, the elements of national spatial perception have an impact on choosing a capital. However, even the cultural forms that are quite nation-specific reveal certain universal features to be discussed in this book.

Miscellaneous problems of designing the capital city function

Some of the miscellaneous problems related to the organization of the capital city function include the problem of municipal governance in the capital, communication system arrangements both in the capital and nationwide, the built environment, as well as development of tourism in the capital. The status of a capital city during the civil conflicts, along with the capital city clauses in the constitutions of many countries, has been analyzed by experts in international and domestic law. The studies exploring the legitimacy of the claims for power are of particular importance to this subject.

While all of the above problems may be quite significant and far-reaching, they remain isolated problems for the purpose of our study. The auxiliary character of these problems is determined by the fact that they do not lead to a discovery of any fundamental normative categories, but rather, provide some kind of "technical support" to ensure the priorities stemming from more fundamental objectives of the state.

The four purposes of capital city

By analyzing the subject discussed in this book, we have identified four fundamental themes or normative concepts which underlie the choice of a capital city. In our opinion, these fundamental themes and normative concepts are as follows: (1) the theme of state's security, which also entails keeping its territorial integrity; (2) the theme of economic and administrative effectiveness; (3) the theme of fairness; and (4) the theme of identity. These four pervasive themes are interconnected with four distinct groups of issues: 1) Which capital city location will ensure the highest level of state security? 2) Which location will prove, economically and administratively, the most effective in achieving the state's goals? 3) Which location will prove the fairest from the standpoint of different parts and constituent units of the state? 4) Which location will be the most organic, authentic and compatible with both the identity and sovereignty of the nation that the state represents?

These issues pinpoint the spatial aspect of the problems pertaining to general philosophy and general sociology and involving pragmatics, morals, and ontology of communities and social groups in their relation with spatial categories. How are power, fairness, and identity embodied in space? How does the space advance or hinder the implementation of these practical or ideal elements in real social and political practices? Can a spatial location effectively promote social changes and make power more effective, fairness fairer, and identity more authentic?

The above four parameters may not necessarily be always successfully combined.

Furthermore, viewing one of them as a priority of economic or social policies and solely relying on it in choosing a capital city will certainly make the choice imperfect from the prospective of another normative criterion. These situations trigger tradeoffs, whereby some fundamental normative parameters are sacrificed for the sake of the others. Different stages of the development of the state call for different priorities. However, these priorities are driven not just by preferences, but rather, by the concerns for the viability and success of the state.

Thus, the most pressing tasks encountered by a recently independent state may be decolonization and the establishment of its identity and sovereignty. This situation would justify shifting a capital to the area which is deemed to reinforce the historical continuity of national history and emphasize the rootedness of the nation in a particular territory. In the case of a nation going through the process of modernization, the problem of reconstructing its identity, along with that of a new geopolitical positioning, may be more compelling. In yet another scenario, harmonizing various components of a state, coupled with building a capital city capable of balancing relations among different parts and constituent entities of the state, may present more importance.

While both the security and effectiveness of a capital city assume, first of all, the ability of the state government to organize itself rationally, the notions of fairness and identity are of direct relevance to the question of how legitimate both the power and emotional aspects of the nation's existence are.

In the context of the debates on capital cities, the issue of fairness manifests itself in several perspectives: first, whether the regions, constituent states, constituent lands, as well as the ethnic and religious groups, are represented in the capital; second, whether the capital-city benefits are available to the majority of the nation; and third, whether all relevant groups enjoy a virtual presence in the capital city not just in terms of political representation but also in the symbols and iconography of the capital. The government that does not take the factors of fairness and identity into account loses or weakens its own legitimacy.

Building a new seat of government in a city where the nation's cultural values were solidified and the key moments of its history took place emphasizes the nation's sovereignty even if the nation has been colonized or dependent for a long period of time.

Certain assumptions and hypotheses

Before we begin to analyze the history of national capital building and exemplify it with specific case studies, a number of hypotheses and assumptions should be postulated here since, to a substantial extent, they define both the research design and logic of material presentation in this book. These preliminary suppositions and hypotheses foreshadow and give a partial preview of the conclusions made in this study and clarify the ideas behind it.

Prospects of nation-building and state-building

The dominant perspective that defines our approach towards capital city relocations is the concept of nation-building and state-building. Many articles on the subject of capital relocation concentrate mainly on possible economic advantages that may be gained by such relocation. However, in our opinion, the broad publicity received by this subject and the support it has sustained internationally go far beyond the issue of mere economic gains.

Nation-building and state-building, whose objectives underscore the importance of our topic, are closely interconnected to the extent they become sometimes inseparable. For the purpose of this study, the term "state-building" means, first of all, foreign policy related factors of the state's existence, including the factors of state security and national borders. The term "nation-building" refers to creating state institutes and symbols based on the perspective of intrastate interaction among various communities. The range of issues pertaining to nation-building includes identity, political fairness, and relations among parts of the state. The author of this book believes that the success of capital city relocations largely depends on the extent the relocation meets fundamental needs and challenges faced by the country in each given stage of nation-building. This success is further determined by whether or not the relocation is capable of answering more than one of these challenges, and whether – in the long, strategic run – the new capital will combine important advantages for the development of more than one aspects of the building process.

Our analysis is also premised on the social constructionist interpretation of the capital city phenomenon and the notion of a nation. There are no "natural centers" for founding a capital city; rather, they are chosen from a set of various factors so that the choice becomes one of the most critical steps in forming a new nation. This choice has a great impact on the very concept of a nation since nations do not just emerge in the course of natural processes but deliberately build themselves, and the development of the concept of a capital city catalyzes these processes.

Capital cities and political regimes

One of the theses of this book is that different political regimes view the problem of capital cities differently, focusing on different aspects of this problem. In any given country, the existing urban hierarchies do not just embody its political nature and the history of its emergence but also solidify the principles that this country is based on. Liberal democracies, authoritarian and totalitarian regimes, as well as despotic states, create conditions for the development of various urban hierarchies, and in many cases the structure of the urban network stems from the degree of political centralization in the state. Every so often an oversized capital city is an indication that the country's political regime is particularly corrupt or that the pattern of corruption has been prevalent throughout its history. Such capitals monopolize the resources of the country and its international economic ties, hampering its political and economic development.

Capital relocation plans undertaken by different regimes reflect the goals and priorities of these regimes.

The fundamental principles of liberal democracies – separation of powers, system of checks and balances, principles of federalism, and societal control over activities of the state and corporations – are also embodied in the structure of cities and that of urban hierarchies. In such countries, capital relocations usually serve as a reinforcement of these political principles.

As a rule, autocratic and despotic states possess both better methods of mobilizing resources and a more effective leadership to carry out political projects of this magnitude and cost. Since these states are less constrained by the prospect of a change of power, they are more inclined to make long-term investments.

In the states governed by autocratic or despotic regimes, capital city relocations may also serve as a tool of keeping these regimes in power, solidifying exclusivity, centralism, the lack of transparency, and other antidemocratic principles. This said, some autocratic regimes may also pursue broader objectives such as nation-building and be less concerned with self-preservation. Since sometimes the goal of self-preservation may fully or partly coincide with the goal of nation-building, a capital relocation accomplished by such a regime may become an important starting point for the development, modernization, or political transformation of the state.

Therefore, under certain circumstances and regardless of the initial objective, a new capital city built by a despotic or autocratic state may very well develop into a viable nation-state capital. By and large, however, the successful political regimes are more effective in transferring their capital whereas the corrupt regimes are less effective.

The relocation of a capital city is not a panacea for all of the ongoing overcentralization problems; nor is it a lever for achieving certain social or economic objectives. It may advance a positive political transformation as much as a negative one, accompanying both social revolutions and modernization programs, as well as religious and conservative revolutions.

Plan of the book

Chapter 1 will provide a typological classification of capital cities, both from the historical point of view and in the modern perspective. It will also discuss the issues of what constitutes a capital city and what the normative content of this notion is. It will provide a brief historical insight into the history and genealogy of the modern idea of a national capital. This insight will help us to formulate certain patterns of capital city formation and evolution on one hand and to revise and supplement the existing definitions and typologies on the other.

Chapter 2 will provide a detailed description and analysis of capital city relocations in various countries, civilizations, and transcultural regions. It will identify the criteria for siting a capital city as determined by geographical, ecological, cultural, and other specific factors and will also illustrate the role capital cities played in the emergence of nations and nation-states. Among the issues to be addressed, the following are two of special importance: To what extent were capitals effective in solving problems of particular states? To what extent were the different types of capitals suitable for solving vital economic and social needs of particular states?

Chapter 3 will pay a special attention to the reasons, motivations, and arrangements for capital relocations, focusing on those in Turkey, Brazil, Malaysia, Germany, Nigeria, and Kazakhstan. It is the experience of these nations that has received the widest publicity internationally and had the strongest influence on the corresponding decisions made by other states. It will also present numerous case studies from different regions: Africa, Latin America, Asia, Europe, and beyond.

Chapter 4 will focus on the comparison of relocations from Chapter 3. Examining budgets, administration, and the outcomes of these projects, this chapter will also highlight critiques of the completed relocations, made by urbanists, sociologists, and economists, as well as provide a critique of these critiques and detailed balanced analysis of these relocations.

Based on the results of this examination, we will, first, identify six strategies that were used by the relevant countries; second, point to lessons that could be learned from these historical experiences; and, third, present a comparative analysis of these projects.

We will also study several success factors of such capital relocations and examine the public policy objectives that they satisfy. While understanding the concept and historical forms of capital cities allows us to understand the mechanics of and the motives behind capital city transfers, analyzing these transfers, likewise, ascertains and clarifies the objectives and functional role played by the capitals.

Chapter 5 will investigate methodologies and theoretical approaches towards capital city functions and decision-making models, including the concepts of spatial economics, growth pole theory, world-system analysis, and geopolitical analysis. It will also address the problem of what categories should be used to evaluate this experience and to plan out these actions, taking into account the existing scientific and managerial models. Specifically, we will discuss the issues of economic effectiveness of capital cities, their federative structure, symbolic adequacy, and other significant assessment criteria. As part of this discussion, we will touch upon the problems of iconography and architectural language of several newly built cities, as well as the interdependence of this language and nation-building. We will pay a particular attention to the analysis of the interplay of globalness, primacy, and capitalness and consider the advantages and disadvantages of combining all of these characteristics in one city.

Last, the Conclusion will summarize the results of the analysis made in this book, underscoring the causes and rationales that drive the governments to undertake these projects, concentrating on the interrelations between these projects and the general trends of political and economic development, and pinpointing the correlation between the nature of a political regime and the successfulness of its capital city relocation. We will also attempt to perceive to what extent the various aspects of the international experiences analyzed in this book are applicable to the analysis of the situation in the states where the issue of capital city relocation is in the process of being added to the agenda.

Notes

1 The pioneering theoretical studies in this field have been produced by the historian Arnold Toynbee and by a geographer Vaughan Cornish (Toynbee, A. "Capital Cities: Their Distinctive Features" and "Capital Cities: Melting-Pots and Powder-Kegs." In: *Cities on the Move* (New York and London: Oxford University Press, 1970), 67–78, 143–152; Toynbee, A. *A Study of History: Abridgement of Volumes VII-X by D.C. Somervell* (New York & Oxford: Oxford University Press, 1987); Cornish, V. *The Great Capitals: An Historical Geography* (London and New York: Methuen, 1923). Three other notable works are the collections of articles "Das Hauptstadtproblem in der Geschichte," published by Friedrich-Meinecke-Institut (Tübingen: Max Niemeyer Verlag, 1952); *Capital Cities/Les Capitales: Perspectives Internationales/International Perspectives*, edited by J. Taylor, J.G. Lengelle & C. Andrews (Ottawa: Carleton University Press, 1993); and Sohn, Andreas & Weber, Hermann

10 Introduction

(Hg.). *Hauptstädte und Global Cities an der Schwelle zum 21. Jahrhundert* (Verlag Dr. Dieter Winkler, 2000). Jean Gottmann has produced two important articles on this topic. Gottmann, J. "Capital Cities." In: *After Megapolisis: The Urban Writings of Jean Gottmann* (Johns Hopkins University Press: Baltimore, 1990); Gottmann, J. "The Study of Former Capitals," *Ekistics* vols. 314/315, Sept./Oct.-Nov./Dec. (1985), 541-546. Among more recent contributions are the papers by Géraldine Djament, Göran Therborn, Amos Rappoport, Scott Campbell, and Kenneth Corey (Djament-Tran, G. "Les scénarios de localisation des capitales, révélateurs des conceptions de l'unité nationale," Confins. Revue franco-brésilienne de géographie, no. 9 (2010); Therborn, G. "Monumental Europe: The National Years: On the Iconography of European Capital Cities." *Housing Theory and Society*, vol. 19, no. 1 (2002), 26–47; Therborn, G. "Eastern Drama. Capitals of Eastern Europe, 1830s-2006: An Introductory Overview," *International Review of Sociology—Revue Internationale de Sociologie*, vol. 16, no. 2 (2006), 209–242 ; Therborn, G. "Identity and Capital Cities: European Nation and European Union." In: Cerutti, Furio & Lucarelli, Sonia (eds.), *The Search for a European Identity: Values, Policies and Legitimacy of the European Union* (Routledge: NY, 2008), 65–70; Therborn, G. & Ho, K. C., eds. "Capital Cities and Their Contested Roles in the Life of Nations," *City*, vol. 13, no. 1 (2009); Rappoport, A. "On the Nature of Capitals and their Expansion." In: Taylor, John, Lengellé, Jean G., & Andrew, Caroline (eds.), *Capital Cities/Les capitales* (Ottawa: Carleton University Press, 1993); Campbell, S. "The Enduring Importance of National Capital Cities in the Global Era," University of Michigan, *Working Papers Series*, 2003; Corey, K. "Relocation of National Capitals," *International Symposium on the Capital Relocation* on September 22, Seoul, 2004: 43–107; Corey, K. "Planning and Implementing Capital Cities—Lessons from the Past and Prospects for Intelligent Development in the Future: The Case of Korea." In: Brunn, S. (ed.), *Engineering Earth: The Impacts of Megaengineering Projects* (Dordrecht: Springer, 2011). Valuable insights about the capital cities are found in the works by Edward Schatz, Michiel Wagenaar, and Andreas Daum (Daum, A. & Mauch, C., eds. *Berlin-Washington: 1800–2000: Capital Cities, Cultural Representations, and National Identities* (New York: Cambridge University Press, 2009); Schatz, E. "What Capital Cities Say About State and Nation Building," *Nationalism and Ethnic Politics*, vol. 9, no. 4 (2003); Wagenaar, M. "Townscapes of Power," *GeoJournal*, vol. 51 (2000); Wagenaar, M. "The Capital as a Representation of a Nation." In: Dijkink, Gertjan & Knippenberg, Hans (eds.), *The Territorial Factor: Political Geography in a Globalizing World* (Amsterdam: Vossiuspers, 2001).
2 Hirst, P. *Space and Power: Politics, War and Architecture* (Cambridge: Polity, 2005).
3 The following books studying the historical nexus between architecture and political power and the way power represents itself in the capital city are particularly notable: Minkenberg, Michael ed. *Power and Architecture: The Construction of Capitals and the Politics of Space* (Berghahn Books: New York, 2014); Parker, Geoffrey. *Power in Stone: Cities as Symbols of Empires* (Reaktion: London, 2014) and Vale, Lawrence. *Architecture, Power, and National Identity*. Second edition (Yale: Yale University Press, 2008). Another book focuses on the ways that planning in the capital cities has evolved: Gordon, D. ed. *Planning Twentieth-Century Capital Cities* (London: Routledge, 2006). Particular cases of capital city relocations also have been discussed in conference proceedings Konovalova, I. ed. *Perenosi stolits. Istoricheskii opit geopoliticheskogo proektirovania* (Moscow: Institut vseobschei istorii, 2013).

1 History and typology of capital cities

Until recently the problem of capital cities as a subject of *theoretical reflection* has not attracted enough attention from scholars, nor has it occupied a central place on the research agenda of the field of urban studies. Although numerous treatises and articles focusing on the history of specific capitals and addressing different aspects of city life have been published, capital cities have not made an especially popular topic for urbanists. The relevant research literature has been dominated by ideographic studies of metropolitanism and capital cities. Conducted within the framework of studies on national history or a particular city, they resembled a kind of biography of large capital centers. The historian Andreas W. Daum confirms this observation, noting that the study of capital cities constitutes a field of research that is still in an incubation phase.[1] The distinguished American geographer Scott Campbell also notes that "capital cities are an easily defined but poorly understood class of cities" and laments the lack of a single, explicit theory of capital city development.[2]

These assessments of the state of affairs in the discipline, however, should not be construed to mean that the extensive literature on *specific* capitals is characterized by a noticeable lack, or deficiency, of factual and historical material. On the contrary, critics sometimes expressed concern that as a result of the biases shown by journalists, historians, and tourist guidebooks, the image of a capital city would overshadow the image of the whole country. The topic of capital cities has remained unnoticed to the extent that to date it has not been integrated into a single discipline. The material pertaining to this topic is scattered in publications in different subject fields all of which have their own language, categories, standards, and models of explanation. Until recently only a few more or less general theoretical articles focusing on this subject were published.[3] Notably, the existing studies are also marked by pronounced Eurocentrism, as Andreas Daum has noted, and a global and transnational view of capitals has still never been developed.[4]

Clearly, a call for the creation of a new scholarly discipline, Capital City Studies, does not imply a mechanical, eclectic mixture of the data and methodologies taken from different disciplines; rather, it assumes the establishment of a new integrated field which, through comparisons, would create explanation models related to the emergence and functioning of capital cities and identify more universal standards of understanding of the changing role played by capitals in the modern global processes. This outlook of capital cities would allow to integrate a variety of the existing disciplinary approaches – economic, political, and geographical – overcoming their internal limitations and resolving the differences in the way they explain the growth or relocation of capital cities. Comparative analysis methods could serve as a foundation for this integrated approach.

Assessing the situation in the study of capital city problems, Daum and Campbell also acknowledge a conspicuous tendency, developed in the urban studies over the past two decades, towards analysis and description of global cities and urban networks. One may say that in addition to urban hierarchies, there also exists a hierarchy of knowledge both about cities and their evolutions, and our knowledge of capitals is far from being on the top of this hierarchy.

Many urbanists and geographers have adopted the economic methods of analysis and focused on the discussion of such important phenomena and concepts as a world city, or global city, agglomerations, and development clusters. However, neither these concepts nor theoretical paradigms of thinking are always fully applicable to the analysis of capital cities.

Furthermore, the belief that nation-states are declining, often relied on as a premise, albeit not always articulated, for many of these studies, implicitly assume that today, global cities and international corporations have become the main participants in the historical process and that capital cities are losing their role and former significance. Viewed in this theoretical paradigm, from a certain time on, capitals have been treated mainly as a place of localization of economic interests, their effectiveness being measured primarily on the basis of economic parameters. By the same token, the role of practically the only agents responsible for the formation of the existing urban networks and hierarchies has become attributable to the markets, whereas the role played by autonomous political factors and political exchange networks has been systematically underestimated.[5]

While economic models sometimes shed interesting and unexpected light on the ongoing processes, they can also distort the essence of many social problems. An exclusively economic approach to the problem does not factor in, among other things, the internal criteria of measuring the effectiveness of capital cities and assessing how they perform their tasks and functions. In recent years, there have been more studies focusing both on capital cities and the political networks forming them. It is noteworthy that not only do these studies examine modern cities, they also address the formation of medieval towns and other historical forms of urban networks.[6] The relatively new comparative turn in urban studies literature is particularly interesting and promising in this regard.

Preliminary definition

The most common definition of a capital is that it is a city where the seat of the country's government is located, although capitals of some modern states do not fully meet this criterion. The government of the Netherlands sits in The Hague, outside of the official Dutch capital city.[7] Furthermore, Sucre and Kuala Lumpur, the official capitals of Bolivia and Malaysia, respectively, are not the places where the governments of these nations are based. Such a mismatch between the nominal and the actual capital is, of course, an exception to the general rule.

The modern concept of a capital city is a relatively new political category, and it was not until the seventeenth century that it began to develop in its present-day form in Europe. Prior to this period, capitals had been either completely nonexistent in many societies or played a very limited role, fundamentally different from the role presently attributable to them. The rise of capitals stems from the emergence of nations caused by the processes described elsewhere in this book.

The main task of capital cities is to help the nation to visualize itself and to present the nation to the rest of the world. With this in mind, capitals represent the ideal image of the country and country's history, a miniaturized version of the nation, so to speak. Because of this representation function, capitals are sometimes perceived as the equivalent to the nation as a whole.

For this reason, the names of the capitals of some countries are based on the names of these countries, suffice it to mention Algeria, Tunisia, Mexico, Guatemala, El Salvador, Brazil, and Belize, where the name of the capital and that of the country essentially coincide, or did so in the past. Hitler planned to name the new capital of his proposed empire, which was also intended to become the capital of the world and to replace Berlin, Germania (*Welthauptstadt Germania*). Not only is this trend observable in the present, it is traceable back to the ancient world: Akkad, Babylon, Bactria, and Rome were all named after their capitals. Curiously, whereas ancient nations were known by the names of their capitals, this trend has reversed, and in the modern time, capitals are given the names of the nations and peoples.

Based on the same principle of *symbolic representation or symbolic substitution*, whole periods in the history of some nations have been named after their capitals – e.g., the Saint-Petersburg and Moscow periods of Russian history or Heian and Edo periods in Japanese history. Historiographers have often attempted to present the entire history of a people or country through the kaleidoscope of its successive capitals. Such attempts have been made with regard to the history of China, Persia, Japan, and the Arab Caliphate, among other countries.[8] Likewise, the Russian critic and historian Konstantin Aksakov viewed the whole history of Russia in the kaleidoscope of its various capitals, dividing it into the periods of Kievan Rus', Vladimir Rus', Moscow Rus', and Saint-Petersburg Russia.[9] This view had its appeal and justification; however, not every national history may be described using this framework.

The idea that being representative of the whole nation, a capital is its proxy or symbolic double is also reflected in various military strategies, many standard and accepted language practices (we commonly say "Washington or London has made a decision," referring to a whole nation), as well as formal or informal conventions of international law and international relations.

In the case of a civil war, decisions of international organizations often invoke a presumption that a belligerent exercising stable control over the capital is both the most legitimate representative of the nation (proxy) and bearer of national sovereignty although *de iure* there are no international law instruments establishing or confirming such recognition. Marika Landau-Wells highlights this fact in her recent article addressing decisions on the legitimacy of power in four African countries, rendered by various international organizations.[10] In the eyes of the international community, therefore, a *de facto* capital may often serve as a privileged locus of *sovereign authority* or sovereignty, especially during a civil war. This, by far, is only a tendency, not a rule.

Some classic works on military strategy also emphasize the importance of taking control over the capital of the enemy and even equate it with the victory in the war. This is pointed out by Friedrich von Bernhardi (1849–1930), a renowned military theorist of the past, in his fundamental treatise *On War of Today*.[11]

Military historians have also drawn attention to the fact that capitals had had a much greater significance in highly centralized or pre-modern states. In those states, seizing a capital often meant winning the war, as it could be illustrated by the examples of France and imperial China.

As it has already been noted, many capitals also perform a *symbolic representation* of the nation. While this point will be elaborated on in one of the following chapters, it should be stated here that in many countries, the toponyms of the capital represent a geographical map of the entire country, so that a small piece of space replicates a much bigger one as it was typical of many archaic religious centers. For example, Moscow still has neighborhoods that, through their streets and avenues, reflect the physical geography of the entire regions or member republics of the former Soviet Union, e.g., the Crimea or Ukraine, in the south of the city. The toponymy of many capital cities, both European and non-European, feature a similar geographical symbolization of their respective countries, replicating larger physical spaces.[12]

Functions of capital cities

Researchers have identified a number of fundamental functions carried out by capital cities. According to the historian Andreas W. Daum, the most important functions of a capital city include the following: (1) *administration*, (2) *integration*, (3) *performative, or symbolization*, and (4) *preservation* of cultural monuments, history, and national cultural values. The integration he refers to has two aspects – social and ethnic.[13]

The integrative function entails the ability of a capital city to capture and embody the elements and aspects of national unity, where the unity is often the result of a compromise. Among the most common and most important of these compromises, one should mention a compromise reached by two or more ethnicities, religious, or ethnolinguistic groups that compose the nation; those between the local and the national interests; those between or among the largest cities in the country, as well as those between the global and the national. Ideally these compromises are meant to make a capital city a temporary point of equilibrium among the different forces and interests that exist in the country; however, if certain groups do not have political, social, or symbolic representation, this equilibrium becomes fragile. Space, thus, is the form and locus of the embodiment of regulatory principles, both legal and moral. Not only does a capital city reflect the present and actual existence of the nation, it also represents its ideal image – the way the nation sees itself and what it would like to become, hence the multifaceted nature of the integrative function, performed by capital cities.

Carrying out its *performative function*, a capital city serves as a venue for national celebrations, mass processions, parades, rallies, and other events uniting the nation and essentially converting the claims of national identity into reality. Closely interrelated with the performative function, the *symbolic function* is reflected best of all in architecture and symbols of authority. Each national capital has a story reproducing a revised version of the national history. This story has its heroes, villains, coded references to national holidays and festivals, and images of the past and the future. This imaginary community comprises not only the living heroes, but also the epic and mythological ones, as well as founders and defenders of the nation.

At the outset, each nation builds itself using its *imagination* and seeking to visualize itself *in one particular city*; accordingly, a capital becomes a manifestation of this visualization. It is expected that eventually this ideal model will be extended to the whole country. The arrangement of a capital city, its architectural forms and ensembles, serves as construction materials for the creation of a nation just as national literature and music do, except the former process is more conscious and involves a much higher degree of participation on the part of the state.

While the above functions are universal, many other functions and tasks performed by capital cities are characterized by heterogeneity describable with anthropomorphic or anatomical metaphors. Thus, capitals of some countries function as the brain or the head of the state (this is even evidenced by the etymology of the word, which is derived from *caput*, the Latin for "head"), and serve as a sort of guiding force for the whole nation. In the countries that stress the cultural, spiritual, or religious significance of its capitals, a capital city functions as the heart or the soul of the state, playing mostly an observatory role. Accordingly, various authors have described capitals as the head, heart, face, or even eyes of the state (e.g., an Arab traveler referred to Baghdad as "the eye of Iraq"). Furthermore, while some capitals are turned outward (outward capitals), being the face of the nation, others are turned to the internal processes (inward capitals) and more likely serve as its heart.[14] Continuing the metaphor, one may say that generally cities form the skeleton of the nation whereas major market cities form its backbone.

Typology of capital cities, provided below, will explain some of the patterns in the composition and distribution of capital city functions in different countries.

Typology of capital cities

A popular typology of capital cities was proposed by the British geographer Peter Hall. He distinguishes the following seven types of capitals: *multifunctional capitals*, which play a combination of roles at the national level (Tokyo, Moscow, London); *global capitals*, which combine national and supranational functions (Paris, Geneva, Washington); *political capitals*, whose functions are reduced to national management (Lisbon, Kathmandu); *supracapitals*, which serve as the headquarters for major international associations and organizations (Brussels); *former capitals*, i.e., cities that have lost their formal role as capitals but continue to perform an important historical or religious function in the country; *former imperial capitals*, which used to serve as capitals of the entire empires; and *provincial capitals*, which only have a regional significance.[15]

Although often relied on by geographers, this classification, nonetheless, seems logically problematic since it divides concepts based on a comparison of incongruent grounds. We will attempt to make some adjustments and bring the division principles to a common denominator, supplementing this classification. The taxonomies proposed below take into account numerous characteristics of capital cities such as the level of scale they operate at, level of ambitions, historical and cultural forms, particularities of location, functional content, specific objectives, chronological cycles of their development, etc.

Viewing capital cities *in terms of geographical location and the tasks they serve*, one may distinguish *central, forward, retreat,* and *forward-thrust capitals*. *Central capitals* are typical for the states that are in the process of solving internal tasks of reconciling ethnic, confessional, or social group differences. *Forward capitals* are typical for the expanding empires or the states integrating new territories. *Retreat capitals* are a characteristic of the countries facing external threats or instability on the borders. Finally *forward-thrust* capitals are created in the states developing their hinterlands or interior areas. Change of a capital city may be driven by changes in the strategic position of these states, as well as their military victories or defeats.

In terms of the functions performed, capitals may be divided into administrative, military, cultural, business, religious, industrial, maritime, and transportation capitals (hubs).

In terms of the level of scale, we may distinguish regional, national, and transnational capital, as well as *supracapitals* (e.g., the capital of the European Union).

In terms of origin, urbanists often distinguish *evolved* and *designed capitals*, also referred to as *planned capitals*. The former include Paris, London, Tokyo, and Rome. It is believed that these cities became nation-state or imperial capitals, gradually evolving from important commercial, military, and religious centers and, thus, contain many historical layers.

Contrarily, *designed capitals* are built based on a specific plan and are intended for a specific purpose. This category includes, e.g., Washington, New Delhi, Canberra, Ankara, and Brasília. In contrast to evolved capitals, they are, so to speak, built of a single ideological concept and do not have historical layers, usually present in other types of capitals.

Designed cities are approximated by some evolved capitals – e.g., Berlin and Tokyo, where most of the historical center, which had been destroyed during the war, was rebuilt and reconstructed. It may be said that Madrid should also be considered part of this group since it was badly damaged by bombings during the Spanish Civil War. The same, incidentally, applies to many other evolved capitals. Thus, a military fortress and a small military settlement occupying the site of present-day Helsinki had been burned to the ground in a fire in 1809, and the new capital of Finland was essentially built from scratch.[16]

In terms of the level of spatial unity, *concentrated* and *distributed* capitals are distinguishable. The system of distributed capitals is associated with the separation of presidential, legislative, and judicial branches of power. In a number of countries such as Germany, the Czech Republic, Georgia, Russia, and South Africa, the constitutional court sits in a separate city: Karlsruhe in Germany, Brno in the Czech Republic, Batumi in Georgia, Saint-Petersburg in Russia, and Johannesburg in South Africa. In Chile, Georgia, and South Africa, a separate city has been designated as the seat of the legislature.

Some of the ancient states also had *spatially distributed capitals*, each of them performing a distinct function. For example, medieval Tungusic-Manchurian states – the Kingdom of Bohai (Balhae),[17] the Kingdom of the Khitans (Liao State), and the Kingdom of the Jurchens (Jin State) – located in the Far East and successively replacing each other, traditionally maintained five capitals each.[18] Some historians attribute this capital city system to the Chinese Concept of the Five Elements, *Wu Xing*.[19] China, however, never actually used the Concept of the Five Capitals, *Wu Jing*,[20] but it is not unlikely that the people of Bohai had borrowed the long-standing Concept of the Five Cities, *Wu Du*, and reformulated it into *Wu Jing*, which, in turn, was eventually borrowed from them by other nations.

Each of the capitals in the Tungusic-Manchurian states had its own jurisdiction and functioned as the medieval counterpart of modern ministries based in five different places. Their jurisdiction was divided into financial matters, matters related to money and iron, matters related to salt and iron, matters related to commerce and carriage, and the supreme capital.[21] Only one capital was considered supreme and, as a rule, also served as the residence of the prince or supreme ruler.

Spatially distributed capitals are contrasted with *time-distributed capitals*, although in some cases the existence of the latter had similar goals and led to similar results.

Many Asian states divided capital city functions on the basis of seasonality, maintaining both a summer and a winter capital. Examples include the cities of Mathura and Purushapura in the Kushan Empire, Ecbatana and Susa in Persia, Opis and Ecbatana in Parthia, Khanbaliq (present-day Beijing) and Xanadu in China, Kabul and Jalalabad in Afghanistan, and Thimphu and Punakha in Bhutan. Notably, in many cases these capitals were not just palaces located near the main city, but rather were separated from each other by hundreds of kilometers.

Sometimes this dual capital structure had an important religious significance. Thus, in Neo-Assyrian states, the period of the ruler's stay in Assur, both the winter capital and sacred capital, was scheduled in such a way that he could participate in sacral rituals while for the summer he would return to the political capital.[22]

Every six months the government (Durbar) of the Indian state of Kashmir changes its seat from Srinagar, the summer capital, to Jammu, located 300 kilometers away, and back again. This practice, inherited from the nineteenth century, costs the government approximately half a million dollars a year, but from the perspective of its supporters, aside from being a tribute to the tradition, it also furthers interests of the communities living in remote parts of the state since it allows them to participate in the political life more actively. A similar dual-capital system also exists in the state of Maharashtra and has been proposed in the state of Himachal Pradesh.

An even more exotic, tri-capital system – one for the summer, one for the winter, and one for the monsoon season – operated in the west of the British India in Bombay Presidency comprising several states of present-day India and Pakistan.

In terms of stability, one can distinguish *long-term capitals* as opposed to *short-term* and *provisional* ones. While capitals migrated quite frequently in some countries, they remained in the same location for a long time in others.

The Roman Empire was so closely connected with the history of Rome, and its position as the capital seemed so unshakable that many historians still view the transfer of the capital to Constantinople as the demise of the empire. In contrast, capital city relocations appeared much more natural for the Persian Empire, a country of a comparable size.

In Korea, in the period between the emergence of the Three Kingdoms (first century BC) and the rise of the Yi Dynasty (late fourteenth century AD), the capital was moved 22 times.[23] On the other hand, Constantinople, Kyoto, Cairo, and Anuradhapura, the ancient capital of Sri Lanka, served as capitals for close to a thousand years each. Baghdad, London, and Madrid also have been capitals for many centuries.

It is interesting to note, however, that the rise of highly stable capitals was often preceded by a long, and sometimes multiphase, process of searching for a suitable location. Thus, a number of transitional or test capitals were established in the process of relocating the seat of the empire from Rome to Constantinople. Similar tentative capitals, Harran and Anbar, were set up while the capital was being moved from Damascus to Baghdad. In Japan, the transfer of the capital from Nara to Kyoto was preceded by more than 20 intermediate capitals. Dordrecht had been the first seat of the government of the Netherlands before the capital was moved to The Hague. The high mobility of capitals is quite typical for the early stages of nation-building, and numerous cities had served as tentative capitals of the US before it was finally moved from Philadelphia to Washington.[24] The same holds true for the state capitals of the US.

Provisional capitals usually originate as a result of a threat posed to the main city of a country at war. To exemplify, during the Napoleonic wars, the capital of Portugal was moved overseas to Rio de Janeiro, while the capital of Prussia was transferred to Memel (Klaipeda). During the Second World War, most of the Soviet government was evacuated eastward to the city of Kuibyshev (Samara), whereas the Republican government of Spain was relocated to Valencia.

In terms of the degree of control exercised, hard and soft types of capitals are distinguishable. The Italian writer Umberto Eco spoke on this distinction in his speech on the concept, model, image, and framework of the new pan-European capital in Brussels.[25] *Hard capitals* – Eco called them "the Louis XIV type of capitals" – are characteristic of a larger, centralized state; they dominate most of the living environment, being rather cumbersome and combining multiple functions.

Soft capitals are more typical of smaller polycentric European countries such as Belgium or Switzerland and are usually characterized by compactness. Using a computer metaphor, one may say that soft capitals provide the state with software, whereas hard capitals serve as hardware, determining the totality of economic and social relations.[26] The same distinctions apply to states. Thus, prior to the French Revolution, as well as in the first half of the nineteenth century, there were six *alternating soft capitals* in Switzerland: Lucerne, Bern, Basel, Fribourg, Solothurn, and Zurich. After the religious civil war in 1847 and as a result of the 1848 revolution, the confederation became a single nation, with Bern as its capital.[27]

The criteria of hardness and softness have also played a significant role in the designation of the capital in many other countries. For example, in the 1864 debate over the new Italian capital, the Italian politician Ferrari spoke out against the hard model of a capital city: "The very idea of a preponderant capital has always been resolutely rejected by everyone. [. . .] We do not want an Italian Paris, we do not want an Italian London."[28] During that time when the debate was still in progress, the choice of Rome as a new capital of Italy was neither predetermined, nor obvious.

Nonetheless, not all European hard capitals, however gigantic and megapolitan they may be, are comparable with each other. Likewise, there are substantial substantive differences in terms of status between Anglo-Saxon capitals and continental European capitals.

This could be illustrated by a sharp contrast between London and Paris. Although both capitals are characterized by a high concentration of functions, Paris has always overshadowed London in terms of splendor and monumentality. Even the British Stuarts envied the metropolitan magnificence of Paris, Madrid, and capitals of some smaller continental countries.[29] The Stuarts were known to have made several attempts to turn London into a full-fledged royal capital using European princely baroque cities as a model; however, these attempts were not successful.[30]

The reason for this difference was that the state and political power in France played a much more prominent role, whereby the latter could centralize planning more effectively, mobilizing financial resources and building its capital at the expense of the provinces. As a result, the urban planning models of Paris became exemplary not only for England but also for the majority of other European countries.

In England, the capital city was under control of private interests. Municipal authorities of the British capital could not possibly afford reconstructing London in the classical monumental style, especially on the same scale, with the same magnitude, and with the same degree of splendor as it was done in the Paris of Georges-Eugène Haussmann, the Prefect of the Seine Department during the Second Empire. With this in mind, observers have pointed to what they perceived as a contradiction between the status of Great Britain as one the most powerful industrial and colonial nations in the world and the image of its capital, which was not in the position to compete with its continental counterparts.[31] This Anglo-Saxon concept of *an economical or parsimonious capital*, apparently, has been subsequently reflected in the concept of a low-key capital city developed in other Anglo-Saxon countries including the US, Australia, Canada, South Africa, and New Zealand.

Arguably, the Anglo-Saxon concept of an economical capital also gave rise to a distinctive municipal administration system. While London was governed through 33 city districts (*boroughs*), with an elected mayor playing the lead role in the process, governance of Paris was highly centralized and until recently concentrated in the hands of the prefect of the Seine.[32]

Jean Gottmann, an eminent French geographer, also proposed to distinguish between two models of capital cities, which he referred to as the *Platonic and Alexandrine models*.[33] Using another terminology, they could be also called the Continental and the Atlantic capitals.

The concept of the Platonic capital is rooted in the Plato's dialogue *The Laws*, where the Greek philosopher describes the proximity to the sea as a disadvantage for any city of the country.

> It is agreeable enough to have the sea at one's door in daily life; but, for all that, it is, in very truth, a briny and bitter neighbor. It fills a city with retail huckstering, breeds shifty and distrustful habits of soul, and so makes a society distrustful.
>
> (*The Laws*, VII, 705a)

The port-capitals following the Alexandrine model are distinguished both by the proximity to the sea and by the presence of commercial activity that corrupt cities by fostering love for money-making and by allowing close contact with foreigners. In contrast to the Platonic capitals, the Alexandrine capitals are cosmopolitan and combine politics with commerce.

The geographer Scott Campbell has proposed another interpretation of the Alexandrine model, construing it to include capitals of the states that have no single center. As the legend has it, Alexander the Great, when asked where he wanted to site the capital of his empire, presumably spread his hand on a map and used his fingers to point to several directions simultaneously. According to Campbell, if the Platonic model defines the modern capital, the Alexandrian defines the postmodern acentrism, a phenomenon which he attributes to the idea of a virtual de-centralized administrative network of capital city functions.[34] Albeit interesting and original, this interpretation, however, is factually and historically inaccurate. Alexander the Great is known to have dreamed of having a new seat of empire in the city of Babylon;[35] furthermore, linking Platonism to the concept of modern capital cities deprives the original distinction made by Gottmann of its value.

What is more significant in differentiating between these two models is their orientation and the way they position themselves: While the continental Platonic capitals are inward capitals, Alexandrine capitals are outward-oriented. Given this interpretation, Kabul, Madrid, and Moscow may be viewed as examples of the former while Constantinople or Stockholm may be considered examples of the latter.

Speaking of the Platonic and Alexandrine models, a short digression may be in order here. Aristotle, who was a student of Plato and the teacher of Alexander the Great, does not have a separate work discussing the issue of capitals. However, his *Politics* contains fragments that may be interpreted as direct recommendations in this regard. In a famous passage of the *Politics*, Aristotle defends cosmopolitan cities on the seas (Politics, Book VII), obviously alluding to *The Laws* of Plato, and aiming at Alexander the Great, who dreamed of a new capital in the East. Polemicizing with both Plato and Alexander, Aristotle seems to water down their intransigencies into a typical

Aristotelian compromise suggesting Crete as a new natural seat of power. This is how Aristotle describes this natural strategic center of ancient Greece.

> The island seems naturally situated to rule in Greece. It lies across the entire sea, and most of the Greeks are settled around the sea; it is not far distant from the Peloponnese on the one side and on the other from the part of Asia around Cape Triopium and Rhodes. Hence Minos established rule over the sea, subduing some of islands and settling others.[36]

Given that Greece has numerous island territories, the fact that Aristotle chose an insular capital appears logical and strategically justified. It is also important to realize that Crete was the historical center of the Minoan culture standing at the origin of the Greek culture. Besides, the island also had several strategic advantages – mainly a convenient geographical location, making it an important center that connected Africa, Asia, and Europe. This connection went beyond the advantages noted by Aristotle and enjoyed in other parts of the Greek world. Last, this idea entailed the possibility of creating a capital of the entire Mediterranean region centered around an island, a vision embodying the archetypal European spatial model.[37]

It is fair to say that in this passage Aristotle, to a substantial extent, reconciles the concept of Plato with that of Alexander. Like Plato, he keeps the capital within the historical boundaries of Greece, but contrary to Plato, like Alexander, he makes it a cosmopolitan center open to other civilizations. This is the *Aristotelian capital*, built on his principle of the golden mean.

The typology of capitals provided above is particularly important because it is based *on the different concepts of capital cities, existing in different countries or civilizations*. It will provide the reader a road map for further study of the subject and build a glossary required for further discussions.

It would be also appropriate to precede our further analysis by a short historical account illustrating the above listed types, determining the evolution of these cities, and outlining the trajectories of their development. All in all, six historical types of capitals will be discussed in the following chapters: mobile, sacred, royal, national, imperial, and disembedded.

Historical types of capitals

Mobile capitals

In the ancient times and the Middle Ages, i.e., approximately until the Westphalian system was formed, capitals as residences of the rulers had not played a critical role in the life of states. Strictly speaking, until the seventeenth century, capitals *in the modern sense of the term* did not even exist. In various languages, the word "capital" simply means a fortified city, fortress, royal residence (e.g., the Russian for *stolitsa*, "capital," stems from the word *stol*, a "table" or a "throne") or "mother of the cities."[38] Traditionally the mosaic of human settlements included military fortresses, notable and successful commercial centers, residences of princes and kings, as well as city-states, important religious centers, and places of worship. However, capitals in the modern sense were not known even in the major imperial states of antiquity, notably the Macedonian Empire.[39] They emerged in Europe as late as in the early modern period.

The mobile capitals are defined by the lack of permanent and single site for them. Two types of mobile or peripatetic capitals were identifiable in the pre-modern times: *itinerant capitals* and *wandering or roving capitals*.

Itinerant capitals were typical of many medieval states, where the "peripatetic" kings would move around their itinerant kingship, relocating from one city to another.[40] For example, the Capets moved mainly between Orleans, Paris, and Laon. Aside from maintaining an official residence in Dijon, rulers of the Burgundian Kingdom could be also stationed in one of the cities of Brabant (Mechelen and Brussels), in Paris, or in the Flemish (Ghent and Bruges) or French Flanders (Lille).[41]

Geographically speaking, itinerant paths of the German monarchs were much wider. Emperors of the Holy Roman Empire did not even maintain a permanent residence and headquarters, nor did they employ a regular staff of officials and recordkeeping clerks.[42] For example, Charlemagne spent most of his time in Aachen, but sometimes could be also stationed in Worms or in the Rhineland. Depending on the location of the emperor, the capital functions passed from one city to another, wandering from Worms to Nuremberg, Prague, Vienna, Rome, Berlin, Frankfurt, and Mainz. It was in Mainz where the coronation originally took place. Names of some of the renowned rulers of the Holy Roman Empire were associated with their favorite cities although these cities were not necessarily capitals. Thus, Bamberg was associated with the name of Henry II; Würzburg and Nuremberg, with Frederick Barbarossa; while Speyer, with Conrad III.[43] Outside of Germany, Toledo under Charles II and Prague under Charles IV and then Rudolf II were important and rather stable capital cities of the empire.

These traditions of the Holy Roman Empire may have laid the foundations of de-centralization and gave rise to the concept of capital pluralism and multi-centric polity at the time when the ancient unity of Europe was being formed. Nearly a decade ago, Romano Prodi convened a meeting with a number of notable figures to discuss the image of the European capital. An itinerant capital in lieu of Brussels was exactly what some of the invitees proposed. One of them was Bronislaw Geremek, a Polish dissident and expert on the history of the Middle Ages, eventually serving as Minister of Foreign Affairs of Poland and a member of the European Parliament. He supported his proposal with references to European feudalism and the experience of the Holy Roman Empire.[44]

Certain elements of this approach can be seen in the current distribution of capital city functions among some European cities beyond Brussels, e.g., Strasbourg, Luxembourg, and Frankfurt. It is noteworthy that an alternative,

24 History and typology of capital cities

monocentric US-modeled concept of European capital to be built on the artificial Europe Lake, on the border of France, Germany, and Luxembourg, was offered in the 1960s by the American architect James Miller.[45]

The phenomenon of itinerant capitals and their rulers was not confined to Europe. Like the emperors of the Holy Roman Empire, the Persian *shahs* also often moved from one capital city to another. Thus, a king of the kings usually spent the summer in his mountain residence in Ecbatana. Several months a year he lived near the healing springs in Susa, sometimes staying in Babylon but always celebrating the New Year festivities in Persepolis (Parsa), the religious capital centered on the Temple of Ormuzd.

While itinerant capitals had a more or less constant path of movement, wandering capitals did not. These capitals had been characteristic of the early medieval Japan until the first permanent capital was established in Nara. The idea that each new ruler had his own unique charisma necessitated frequent changes in the capital location, which essentially acquired a ritual character.[46] In the fifteenth through seventeenth centuries, wandering capitals also existed in Ethiopia, where they served as a strategic tool of waging a guerrilla war against the Muslim invaders. Functioning as a kind of temporary military headquarters, these capitals managed to remain important symbolic and intellectual centers.[47] Wandering capitals also existed in Rwanda and Uganda in Africa.

Itinerant capitals were also characteristic of many nomadic peoples. The residence of the Mongol rulers had been wandering since the seventeenth century, changing its location more than 20 times before settling at its present site in Ulaanbaatar in 1778. However, contrary to popular belief, many nomadic tribes, e.g., the Uyghurs, Khazars, and Bulgars, developed relatively stable political capitals.[48] Such political capital cities also emerged among the Scythians (Scythian Neapolis in the vicinity of Simferopol, Ukraine), Cuman-Kipchaks (Sharukan near Kharkov, Ukraine), and Tatars (Sarai Batu near Astrakhan, Russia). The Mongolian Ilkhanid dynasty in Persia established a capital Sulṭāniyya ("sultan's capital"), continuing the practice of seasonal migrations and staying there only in summer.[49]

Sacred and royal capitals played an important role in the ancestry of modern capitals, serving as both the precursors and antipodes of national capital cities. We will now try to trace the genealogy of sacred and royal capitals and their evolution path to national capitals.

Sacred capitals

In the context of the genealogy of modern capitals, the phenomenon of sacred, i.e., religious or ritual, capitals is particularly noteworthy. Many urban theorists, including such brilliant historians and anthropologists as Fustel de Coulanges and Paul Wheatley, have pointed to the *religious origins of urbanism*.[50] The most revealing in this respect is the book of the latter entitled *The Pivot of the Four Quarters: A Preliminary Enquiry into the*

Origins and Character of the Ancient Chinese City, which became a milestone in our understanding of urban history and anthropology. In one form or another, sacred capitals have developed on all continents: Teotihuacan in Mexico, Machu Picchu in Peru, Persepolis in Persia, or Great Zimbabwe, a ritual center of the ancestors of the Shona people in Africa, etc.[51]

Sacred capitals were essentially temple cities, established and spread around temple complexes. Containing main sanctuaries and repositories of the most revered holy relics, they also served as a residence for priests, clerics, and representatives of the pontifical power, and sometimes as the burial place of the kings and rulers or the venue for coronation ceremonies.

One of the main reasons determining the importance of sacred capitals was that they were perceived not only as an instrumental part of the social order of the state but also as a part of the cosmic order of the universe, whereby their governance function was viewed as a continuation of the world-creating function of the gods and the ancestors. The significance of these cities was not as much in their geographical centrality in ancient states, but in the cosmic centrality, in their role as a link between Heaven and Earth, a connector between the divine order and the human order of the universe.

For instance, once Marduk, a leading deity of the Babylonian pantheon, put the chaos in order, he proceeded with erecting the sacred and primeval city of Babylon, which would serve as a dwelling for him and other gods.[52] Sacred cities were built as a model of the universe, imitating a larger space on a smaller scale and linking the corners of the world. Traditional cosmographical images modeling sacred cities after Heaven reinforced the legitimacy of the ruler's power. Such cosmographical schemes and forms of spatial organization are found in the civilizations of Egypt, Babylonia, and ancient China.[53]

The American anthropologist Clifford Geertz describes the sacred Hindu capitals of Indonesia in the thirteenth and fourteenth centuries as exemplary centers, noting that many of their traits have survived in much later periods:

> The capital city was at once a microcosm of the supernatural order – "an image of . . . the universe on a smaller scale" – and the material embodiment of political order. The capital was not merely the nucleus, the engine, or the pivot of the state; it was the state. In the Hindu period, the king's castle comprehended virtually the entire town. A squared-off "heavenly city" constructed according to the ideas of Indic metaphysics, it was more than a locus of power; it was a synoptic paradigm of the ontological shape of existence. At its center was the divine king (an incarnation of an Indian deity), his throne symbolizing Mount Meru, seat of the gods; the buildings, roads, city walls, and even, ceremonially, his wives and personal staff were deployed quadrangularly around him according to the directions of the four sacred winds. Not only the king himself but his ritual, his regalia, his court, and his castle were shot through with charismatic significance. The castle and the life of the castle

were the quiddity of the kingdom, and he who (often after meditating in the wilderness to attain the appropriate spiritual status) captured the castle, captured the whole empire, grasped the charisma of office, and displaced the no-longer-sacred king.[54]

Sacred capitals were seen as the promised or *chosen cities*, singled out from the rest of the natural and social worlds. Therefore, their symbolism emphasized not only the governance component but also the cosmic one, making them a part of the cosmological chronology and mythological narratives. Not only was a sacred capital believed to be located in the center of the state, it was also perceived as the center of the world and described as the navel of the earth or the *Axis Mundi*.[55] For example, according to the ancient Inca, the ritual capital of Vilcabamba was located at the intersection of the four cardinal points of the universe.

Religious legitimization of the status of the ruler played an important role in all the states whereas the concept of spatial organization served as an important instrument of political control and propaganda. Ancient states were a kind of theocracy, with their supreme ruler described as a descendant of gods (Egypt), Son of Heaven (China), or Son of the Sun (Inca). Nevertheless, different civilizations have developed different models defining the relations between political and religious centers within a country.

Ancient states of Mesopotamia, as well as ancient Israel and Greece, developed a sort of division of labor between their religious and political centers. Ceremonial centers or spiritual capitals played a crucial role in the cultural integration of various tribes and peoples, remaining a neutral territory, relatively autonomous in relation to a political center. They often emerged in a situation where political power was fragmented or where a federation to protect against common enemies was being created.

Examples of this could be Delphi in Greece, Shiloh in ancient Israel, and Nippur in ancient Mesopotamia, which served as *the main religious centers* of the pan-Hellenic, pan-Judaic, and pan-Sumerian civilizations, respectively. At that time, each of these peoples constituted a confederation of city-states, clans, or tribes. In the Era of the Judges (thirteenth through eleventh centuries BC), Shiloh was where the Tabernacle of the Covenant (Joshua 18:1) was kept and where high holidays of the Israelites were celebrated, while Delphi was the site of the Oracle, a prophet equally important for all Greek *poleis*.[56] None of the entities composing the confederation claimed a monopoly on these religious capitals; hence the neutrality of these religious centers and their role in the intertribal integration and resolution of intertribal conflicts.

Ancient China also knew a period when a sacred capital was separated from the centers of political power. Thus, in the ninth through eighth centuries BC, at the outset of the Zhou Dynasty, there existed the sacred capital of Qixia in the west of the country, with the administrative capitals operating elsewhere.[57] In the article focusing on capital relocations during the Zhou era, relying on an in-depth analysis of the relevant texts and archaeological data, Marina Khayutina, a sinologist and expert on this period of Chinese history, shows that, despite the rise of the new administrative capitals, the ancient city of Qixia (or Qishan, so named after the sacred Mount Qi) continued to serve as the sacred capital of the Zhou state. Having the main altar of the Zhou rulers, it was a site where the holy relics of their clan were kept and where the Mandate of Heaven to rule was revealed to them through the phoenix and the red crows.[58] Qixia was similar to the sacred capital of both the Greeks and the Jews, separated – as Delphi and Shiloh – from the centers of political power. While the main relic of the Israelites was the Tabernacle, the main relics of the ancient Chinese were the Nine Tripod Cauldrons that embodied the nine regions of China and afterward served as the symbol of power of the emperor.[59]

Eventually the rulers of these ancient states tried to acquire a monopoly on the religious legitimacy of their power by transferring the symbolism of the sacred capitals to the political centers. This transformation took place, for example, in Babylon under King Hammurabi and in ancient Judea during the reign of King David. In the third millennium BC, the rulers of Babylonia and Assyria transferred the characteristics of the city of Nippur's cosmic centrality, primalness, and sacredness to their political centers, so that the characteristics of Enlil, one of the Nippur's supreme deities, were applied to the Babylonian Marduk, as well as the Assyrian Ashur; Nippur's topographical elements and the system of its temples were reproduced in the political capitals.[60]

However, despite the few cases where the political capital and the sacred capital were merged into one entity, the division of powers continued to persist in many Mesopotamian and Middle Eastern states. For example, while Assur remained the sacred capital of Assyria, its political capital was migrating. For a long time, Nisa served as both the sacred capital of Parthia and the main religious center of the Saka tribes, as well as the coronation venue for the Parthian kings. A distinct separation of the sacred and political capitals was typical of Armenia, where King Yervand IV (Orontes IV) simultaneously founded both a political capital, Yervandashat, and a religious capital, Bagaran. After Petra, the old capital of the Nabataean Kingdom, had lost its function as the political center, it preserved its role as the sacred one. Petra remained a city-temple and a city-tomb in contrast to Avdat, located in the present-day Israel, and Bosra (present-day Syria), which in different times served as political capitals of the Nabataeans. After the Greeks had destroyed Persepolis in 330 BC, the sacred capital of Persia,[61] the city of Istakhr became the spiritual center of Zoroastrianism, accommodating its main fire temple and the repository of the Avesta. Neither Mecca, nor Medina ever functioned as a political capital of the Arab Caliphate.

In contrast, in a number of other states, political capitals were much more closely linked to the religious cult and sacredness. Exemplified by Egypt, Byzantium, Russia, and Hindu kingdoms of Southeast Asia, these states tended to be more centralized, having a less developed commercial system, urban culture, and intercity network.

In ancient Egypt, the status of the capital city entailed a strong association with religion. The rise of the specific *nomes* and cities where capital functions were transferred to was accompanied by the rise of religious cults peculiar to these entities. Thus, Heliopolis was known for its cult of the god Ra; Memphis, for the cult of Ptah; Thebes and Amarna (Akhenaten), for the cult of Amon and Aton, respectively. It can be inferred from the consolidation of political power with religious cults that in Egypt the nexus between state and religion was closer than in the Mesopotamian states.[62]

The consolidation of religious and secular elements was also typical of capitals in the Caesaropapist Byzantine Empire. Similarly to ancient Egypt, where priests were in fact officials of the pharaoh, pontifical power in Byzantine was subordinate to political power. The system of *pentarchy* that developed here comprised five Orthodox patriarchates, those in Constantinople, Alexandria, Antioch, Jerusalem, and Rome. Rather than being viewed as sacred centers of their own, they were mainly perceived as extensions of the administrative authority exercised both by the Byzantine emperor and the Ecumenical Patriarch of Constantinople, his seat being in the Hagia Sophia cathedral. The nonreligious, administrative nature of the division among the five patriarchates is exemplified by the fact that initially the Church was dominated by the Alexandrian and Antiochian patriarchates while Jerusalem, despite being the cradle of Christianity, was merely afforded the status as a diocese, upgraded to a patriarchate only as late as in 451 AD. The final word in the election of the patriarch and the five major patriarchal officials belonged to the emperor.[63]

A similar trend existed in Russian history, traditionally characterized by the merger of the religious and secular capitals. In Russia, the ancient religious center in the Kremlin, which still has the appearance of a church complex, evolved over the centuries into a center of political power. During the pre-imperial era, the dominant model of relations between Russia's sacred and political centers was essentially the Caesaropapist model. Thereafter, in the imperial period, Moscow was stripped off its status as the political capital and functioned mainly as a religious center. Paradoxically, when in the post-imperial period it became the political capital again, the pre-imperial pattern was restored, and nowadays the patriarch of the Russian Orthodox Church still resides in Moscow.

Certainly, religious centers of the modern world are not sacred in the sense they were in the ancient times. Nonetheless, the tendency to separate religious centers from political capitals, persisting in the present-day Europe, is to some extent reminiscent of the historical experience endured by ancient Greece and Rome. The role of Rome as the pan-European religious center was somewhat consistent with the role played by Delphi in Greece, and the division largely determined the nature of the relations between the secular and clerical authorities within nation-states.

Numerous European cities became *religious centers, physically separated from the centers of political power*. The list includes Canterbury, England, where St. Augustine's Abbey operated; Toledo, Spain, where the residence of the primate was located; Reims, France, where the ceremonial anointing of the French kings took place; the Vatican, Italy; Mtskheta, Georgia; Etchmiadzin, Armenia; Gamla Uppsala, Sweden; Niš, Serbia, serving as the residence of the Metropolitan of the Serbian Orthodox Church; Gniezno, Poland, the traditional seat of the Primate of Poland and Archbishop of Gniezno; Trnava, Slovakia, where the Archbishop of Trnava resides; Esztergom, Hungary, where the seat of the primate is situated, etc. Every so often the old political capitals were converted to religious centers. Some of the examples of this practice, extremely common to both European and Asian states, include Toledo, Gniezno, Mtskheta, Nara, and Kyoto.

Given the realities of the modern world, the argument that the sacred status of a city warrants making it the official capital is a clear anachronism. Nonetheless, such an idea has been expressed in the debates on capital city relocations. Thus, the appeal to recognize Jerusalem as the political capital, whether of Israel or the Palestinian state, has been often justified by its status as a sacred city.[64] Likewise, many conservative groups discussing the problem of moving the capital of Russia argue that the purported sacredness of Moscow affords it a unique and indisputable right to be the capital.[65] In today's world, such arguments are rather rare examples of the view that *a political capital must necessarily have the attribute of holiness.*

One should note parenthetically that in many traditional civilizations, the designation of a holy place or sacred city was a much more pragmatic and arbitrary act than it may appear to modern historians and commentators. Historically the selection was always made from a huge pool of qualified sacred areas. The analysis of the location of major ancient religious centers – Delphi, Mecca, and Jerusalem, to name a few – shows that their heavenly status was conferred on them for very earthly reasons including considerations of pragmatism and political profit.[66] In fact, today many fundamentalists seem to be more religiously motivated in their attempts to reinstate the old sacred centers as the official capital or to establish control over them.[67]

Royal capitals

Although monarchical power has manifested itself in diverse forms in various societies, capitals of the monarchies share distinct common characteristics allowing to classify them as a separate group that we will term *royal capitals*.

In ancient and medieval times, capital cities were, so to speak, inseparable from the body of the king or emperor. Royal or princely capitals were usually cities where the royal family resided (*sedes regni*, "the seat of the king"), which made them more mobile in comparison with sacred capitals. The examples of royal capitals include Burgos, Toledo, Segovia, and Valladolid in Spain; Newcastle, Irving, Stirling, and Perth in Scotland; Clichy, Tours, Blois, and Fontainebleau in France; and Płock, Kraków, and Poznań in Poland.

For the purpose of establishing a royal capital, the presence of the ruler was more important than the geographical location of the ruler's residence. In some cases, the royal residence may have also served as the sacred center of the state, whereby aside from fulfilling government tasks, the king could also perform various religious and ritual functions.

Often located in the immediate vicinity of the largest cities in the country, the royal power was not always sufficiently rooted in these cities and sort of stayed away from them, as if vaguely feeling their hidden hostility. In France, Spain, and England, the countries that still remain highly centralized, the royal capital and the court, albeit located in the proximity to major cities, never mingled with them and were often in conflict with their interests. It took a long time for the political power to settle firmly in the largest and main city of a particular country.

The history of relations between the royal court and the main city was characterized by a confrontation between the crown and the urban classes. According to Jean Gottmann, it is this confrontation that, among other reasons, laid the foundations of modern democracy.[68]

In Paris a collision between the crown and the urban classes began as early as in the Middle Ages. As a result, the University of Paris on the Left Bank of the Seine managed to obtain a special charter from Rome, granting it self-government privileges. On the Right Bank, the court was opposed by merchants, and to ensure a better control over them, the royal palace was removed there. However, ever since the sixteenth century, the court would rarely stay in the capital, migrating from one royal *château* in the Loire Valley, Saint-Germain, and Fontainebleau to another. Stationed in Blois in the era of Marie de' Medici, the court made two moves in the seventeenth century: first to Saint-Germain-en-Laye and then to Versailles. Practically the only reason the King would visit the Louvre was to give a formal audience.[69]

A similar confrontation between the crown and the main town was also characteristic of England. The attempts of the English kings to "tame" London and turn it into a royal capital failed. In the thirteenth century, the Treasury moved from Winchester to Westminster, which gradually became the capital and headquarters for the royal administration. At that time, Westminster was a small town near London, the commercial center of the country. Only in the beginning of the seventeenth century did Westminster and London merge into a single entity, and yet despite the persistent efforts of the first Stuarts, the English kings did not succeed in making it a full-fledged, continental-style capital. A series of conflicts and the civil war, which in fact was not as much a war between the King and the Parliament as it was a war between the King and the city, completely destroyed the royal ambitions and plans related to London.[70]

In Spain the relations between the authorities and the cities were somewhat analogous to those in England. The antiroyal opposition and the Revolt of the *Comuneros* in Toledo and Valladolid aimed at the protection of municipal rights were largely responsible for provoking the Spanish court to move from Valladolid and Toledo to Madrid (1561), from Madrid to Valladolid (1601), and then back to Madrid (1606).[71] Located in Escorial, 50 kilometers northwest of Madrid, the royal capital of Spain – as the Spanish historian David Ringrose puts it – was perceived only as some kind of "an optional addition to the court," a theatrical stage to demonstrate its splendor. Madrid's role as the capital was essentially confined to hosting processions and ceremonies legitimizing monarchical power. Ringrose stresses that before 1561 the Spanish kings did not have a fixed court, and it was not until the rise of the Bourbons in the eighteenth century that monumental royal buildings began to appear in Madrid. The fact that the Habsburgs – Philip II, Philip III, and Philip IV – always consistently and deliberately avoided this city was no accident.[72]

All of the above examples illustrate what Jean Gottmann refers to as "an obvious will to separate the big city from the center of political power that could not be entrusted to the turbulent metropolis...."[73] "This arrangement," he notes further, "lasted a century. One of the first acts of the Revolution of 1789 was to bring the king and court back from Versailles into the city. To make the central city safer for the government after the troubles of 1848, the Second Empire supported the huge urban renewal directed by Haussmann."[74]

Thus, regardless of whether the royal palace was located inside or outside of the capital's boundaries, political power was not an *integral part of the capital*.

With the royal capitals in existence, the monarchical power and the city were divided and opposed to each other so that the city, given its cellular memory of the Magna Carta and medieval forms of self-government, presented an alien and often hostile environment for the localization of power. However, the royal court and the city were growing to meet each other, and eventually, with the emergence of nation-states and new national identities, political power became consolidated in capital cities.

One has to admit that in some European countries the very growth and ambitions of royal capitals were a precursor to nationalist movements. With their power mobilization resources, their practice of income redistribution between the core and the periphery, and their tendency towards overcentralization and bureaucratization of political power, the absolutist regimes of Europe laid the foundation for the emergence of national capitals and nation-states. The monarchs' attempts to bring their grace to the cities led to an eventual nationalization of the monarchies. What the kings and queens failed to accomplish was finally accomplished by the nations, a new subject of history.

As it will be shown in the following chapters, national capitals owe many of their most important forms and ideas to their predecessors, sacred and royal capitals. The next several sections of this chapter will examine *various aspects of the history and arrangement of national capitals*. The other two forms of capital cities, imperial and disembedded capitals, which we have already mentioned above, will be discussed in chapter 2, mainly in the context of their relocations.

History and arrangement of national capitals

On the wealth of capital cities: seventeenth century

In the seventeenth century, it was capital cities that enjoyed particularly high growth rates compared to all other European cities. While in the previous periods all European cities had been growing at a more or less equal proportion and pace, the seventeenth century, however, saw a transition from the domination of the *world-economies* centered around mercantile cities such as Genoa, Venice, and Antwerp, for example, to the rise of major national economies, concentrated in the capitals. In his treatise on the history of European capitalism, Fernand Braudel was the first to point out this fact.[75] While some modern historians call this view and the related observations "impressionistic,"[76] the relatively recent studies on urban dynamics – the works of Jean de Vries, in particular – have provided a reliable quantitative substantiation of Braudel's "impressionism."[77]

According to the historians of European urbanization, *one third of the total growth of European cities* in the sixteenth through seventeenth centuries fell on the capital cities.[78] Economically dependent on the expansion of the royal courts and state bureaucracy, the influx of large landowners, and the development of the luxury items industry, capital cities became international centers of fashion and role models, setting standards in clothing, lifestyle, architecture, manners, leisure activities, and methods of material goods consumption.

From 1600 to 1700, the urban population in England grew from 8 percent to 17 percent. During this period, the share of London in the total population of the country increased from 5 percent to 11.5 percent, while the percentage of London residents in the urban population of England went up from 60 percent to 67 percent.[79] Such a dynamic growth of the city was of concern to King James I, who ironically remarked that "with time England will only be London, and the whole country will be left waste."[80]

The case of London, however, was consistent with general European trends, and in continental Europe, the growth rate of capital cities was equally high. Thus, the population of Paris grew from 200,000 inhabitants in 1590 to 550,000 in 1700; Madrid showed an increase from 40,000 in 1560 to 170,000 in 1630; and Berlin, from 10,000 in 1650 to 170,000 by 1800. Other European capitals with the population more than doubling over the same period of time included Copenhagen, Dublin, Stockholm, Vienna, Lisbon, and Rome.[81]

As we know, Adam Smith called his opus magnum *The Wealth of Nations*. The acclaimed American social urban theorist Jane Jacobs made a significant amendment to Adam Smith's theories; from her point of view, the real historical beneficiaries of growth and wealth are not nations, but rather cities. Therefore, she opines, due to the uneven economic development within national borders, it would be much more accurate to juxtapose the rich and the poor cities (or regions), rather than the rich and the poor nations.[82] As it follows from the above figures, however, in terms of the seventeenth century, it would be even more accurate to speak not of the wealth of the cities but of *the wealth of the capital cities* since it were the capitals where in this period practically all resources and capabilities of each given country were concentrated. Accordingly, the concentration of the wealth in the capital cities largely determined the trajectory of the further development of Europe.

Many economic historians have traditionally attributed the dramatic growth of European capitals primarily to market development, viewing them merely as sprawling commercial centers. From the perspective of these historians, the key economic centers inevitably turn into political centers, converting their economic power into political power. Thus, to them, the market network structure explains the broad integration of the seventeenth century urban market and political spaces, which replaced the old fragmented urban systems and networks.

According to David Ringrose, this explanation is rooted in the disciplinary prejudices of economic historians. Ringrose believes that it was political factors, not economic urban networks, that created preconditions for growth of major European capitals, which eventually became the engines of economic development of both their countries and Europe as a whole.[83]

Describing the system of supplying capital cities, Fernand Braudel explains the mechanism of this process as follows: the development of major capital cities would always reach a point where the local, medieval-style agricultural markets could no longer satisfy the economic needs of capital cities. The standard supply zone for medieval cities covered an area within a radius of 40–50 kilometers of the city,[84] not enough to provide for the rapidly growing population of the capitals. This situation led to the development of long-distance trade and the rise of large business structures capable of maintaining it. It was in their capacity as consumption machines that capital cities contributed to the consolidation of the capitalist system, intensifying activities of large retail chain suppliers. In this regard, Braudel sarcastically observes that the greatest credit for innovations must be given to the stomachs of London and Paris, which revolutionized the supply and manufacture of food products, carried out by big sellers.[85]

Following Braudel, David Ringrose further emphasizes that the growth rate of capital cities was driven by the industries that were economically low efficiency. The demand for luxury goods and exotic goods consumed by the royal courts and delivered by the sea and by land formed the configuration of global markets. All these processes redistributed wealth in favor of capital cities, where the royal court sat and where the demand for these products was localized, impoverishing and neglecting the cities and other areas adjacent to the capital.[86]

Centralization and the concept of nation: advantages

Centralization processes in Europe were accompanied by abrupt social changes, considered unfavorable by many theorists and affecting the nature of relations between the core and the periphery, as well as those between the capital and the provinces. For example, as noted by Alexis de Tocqueville, the centralization process in France, which had begun as early as in the time of Richelieu, i.e., the era of absolutism, gradually transformed the country into a system of provinces, similar to the eastern satrapies.[87] Although this trend often caused distress to the provinces, it gave important advantages to the state at large.

In terms of economy, a major centralized state served as a political sponsor for national merchants and provided for a formation of a larger domestic market ensuring, in its turn, a more successful trade on international markets. In addition to this, since the new projects, where innovations were playing an increasingly important role, required a narrow specialization and the availability of substantial capital, the larger states were receiving a competitive economic advantage over the old commercial city-states. Venice, Genoa, and Florence, which had dominated the European economy in the Renaissance, were not in the position to develop the level of long-term specialization necessary for large-scale industrialization.

Large capital cities were part of this economic success, as the agglomeration of population in one city led to spatial consolidation of demand, reduction of transportation costs, and expansion of business structures supplying these cities.

In terms of the ability to resolve internal conflicts, large centralized states also had a number of advantages. Thus, they had the ability to exercise a tighter control of civil and religious conflicts and tensions, minimizing the level of violence in the country and maintaining stability and strength of the domestic market. This ability was one of the main reasons why the idea of a strong state power gained a tremendous popularity in the seventeenth century.

In terms of military capacity, these states had the most essential and decisive advantages, as they were able to effectively mobilize financial capital to wage a war. As many historians have opined, it was primarily military advantages that determined the transition from an absolutist state to a nation-state.

Compared to a nation-state, an absolutist power with its monarchical system of personal dependence was much less effective in waging wars. As the basis of the new notions of identity and social solidarity, the concept of a nation was more suitable for meeting new historical challenges. With major economic changes occurring in the society, the three pillars of loyalty that had grown up in the womb of feudalism – cities, religion, and vassalage – sustained major damage and no longer met the interests of the states. The new idea of a nation, which replaced the old forms of identity, carried out administrative and military tasks more efficiently. Nation-states became more effective as "war machines" and less vulnerable to external enemies. While in pre-modern – especially despotic – states, the fall of a capital as the center of power usually meant defeat in the war, in European countries of the modern age, the concepts of citizenship and nationalism made states more stable, significantly reducing the probability that the seizure of a capital would necessarily entail defeat in the war.

Originated as an ideological trick, the concept of a nation was gradually taking possession of the minds of the masses until it finally turned into a solid political reality. The nations, which had been brought to life by calls to defend the motherland and engage in hostilities, reached a point when they perceived themselves as real agents of history and began to create their own political institutions. In large centralized states of Europe, the nations built themselves through opposition to religions and monarchies, with the growth of civil consciousness accompanying this process. Ultimately, the nations "nationalized" the states themselves, including the economy, religion, and system of political power.

Capitals and the nation-building process

Unfortunately, to date, social theorists have not fully understood or articulated the role capital cities played in the formation of the idea of the nation and the other processes mentioned. Even the fathers of the theory of the nation-state – Benedict Anderson, Ernest Gellner, Eric Hobsbawm, and Anthony Smith – are almost silent on this subject. Thus, while discussing the role of the newspapers, cartography, and European novels in the construction of a new identity, Benedict Anderson practically makes no mention of the capitals.[88] However, the role the European capitals had in the emancipation of people from the interests of religion, aristocracy, and monarchy, as well as in the process of constructing a new identity, has been equally important, if not crucial. The capital city became a true center of national unity and a visual *laboratory of national imagination*.

To engender itself, a nation needs a center that can unite various disparate groups and create symbols legitimizing the current regime and providing it with a broader social base. Such centers, as we have seen, began to emerge as early as during the period of absolutism. However, they were not yet sufficiently effective since their urban nature did not allow them to become a reliable stronghold of the monarchical authority. The rise of the nations changed this situation.

National capitals emerged as a *new model of localization of power*, an alliance of the nation, cities, and political power. Such an alliance was made possible only by the creation of a new national identity.

Given these developments, the capital became a state agent of its kind, entrusted by the state with mobilizing the population and distributing political power throughout the whole country. It evolved into a very special city, which was not closed on itself, but rather, was actively engaged in reorganizing the state economy at large, as well as the very relationship between the political authorities and the people, and becoming *a mediator between the state and the nation. Being the physical body and the engine of governance, the state found its soul and legitimacy in the face of the nation* whereas the nation received its visual representation in the capital, which became a collective propagandist and a collective organizer, to use the Lenin's expression applied to the press.

Before national capitals emerged, political power embedded in the royal court had migrated around the country or been situated in the vicinity of the main city. In nation-states this power was localized in the main city or urban network, which had been previously alien or even hostile to it, and in many cases the location of a capital was fixed by the constitution. Pre-modern states with their amorphous frontier borders were being replaced with modern states that had strict borders and fixed capital cities, and multiple capitals were becoming a rare exception.

With a progressively larger share of population concentrating in capital cities, and the population of capitals growing rapidly, these cities were becoming more insistent on positioning themselves as representatives of the interests of their entire country.

In addition to the above changes, as a result of increased social mobility, capital cities became "a melting pot of the nation."[89] Pulling people from different regions and provinces of the country, capitals were symbolically replacing the face-to-face interaction, which was the basis of social solidarity in physical communities, with a new type of social ties and interaction, thereby nurturing the idea of an imaginary community.

The alliance between the state and the city, however, was being made based on mutual concessions.

The strengthening of centralized states, along with the rapid expansion of capital cities, created problems that were much greater than the resources in the possession of the capitals. This prompted the state machine to actively intervene in the capital's life, stripping it of its traditional urban functions and turning it into *something other than just a city*. As a result, not only did the capital come to embody the urban spirit as such, it now represented the spirit and interests of the whole country. This transformation caused profound changes in the system of loyalty so that the key determinant of the people's identity became loyalty to the state or the nation, superseding that to the city.

Likewise, alterations affected the social image of a capital city. The rise of capitals consolidated the rise of social classes other than the aristocracy and clergy. In a traditional society, each class had its own space: the king had the palace, the clergy had the church and monastery, the aristocracy had the castle, the peasants had the village, while the bourgeoisie and artisans had the city. The rise of the absolutist state and the subsequent birth of national capitals led to the emergence of a new class, state bureaucracy, i.e., administrative and civil servants, with whom the old urban classes were forced to share their living space. The servants of both the king and god had to give way not only to the bureaucracy but also to other growing urban classes and professional communities. In this regard, of a particular interest is a description of the rapidly developing Madrid, which was attracting officials, king's messengers, patronage seekers, lobbyists, and royal guards from across the country.[90]

This compromise started a new far-reaching process that was destined to transform the state itself so that it would eventually cease to be absolutist and gradually give way to the prerogatives of the parliament and all the social classes who were seeking representation in the parliament and in the capital.

In the course of time, many of the privileges enjoyed by townspeople were extended to the rest of the residents of the territorial states. As the city-states were being replaced with the *state-cities*, urban forms of self-government, self-identity, and even certain day-to-day activities were transferred to the whole country. As a result, the entire population became to some degree townspeople, that is, citizens, and this significantly expanded loyalty to state power.

The Israeli sociologist Shmuel Eisenstadt noted that the emergence of national capitals was one of the most important results of the nation-building process.[91] It would be much more accurate, however, to view national capitals as *one of the most important catalysts and instruments of nation-building*. Preparing the ground for national revolutions and transformation of the state, capitals of the absolutist states served as the tools that the nations used in the cities, religion, and vassalage to create or reinvent themselves, as well as to present themselves visually through their architecture; these capitals became a sort of *a screen on which the nations would project images of their identity*.

As a material for utopian art and architectural experiments, one single city was quite rewarding and easy to use. Imitating the great utopians Tommaso Campanella and Thomas More, nations attempted to build their own *social utopia in a single city*, its size commensurate with the objectives of this utopia. Initially, a nation presented itself in urban forms of the capital, where the alienation of urban life could be removed with the metaphor of the "imaginary community." The capital city became the national laboratory of creativity, testing the ideas generated by the nation and analyzing its visions of the past and the future. Like midwives, capitals were bringing to life the imagination of the nation.

Thus, the capital united the three previously disparate elements – *political power, reverence, and urban environment* – which gave rise to new forms of the collective consciousness spreading throughout the country. It was this combination that determined the might of the nations, their viability and sustainability, as well as the cardinal features of the capital as a distinct urban category.

Sources of architectural and other forms

Separation from both religion and royal power, as well as (in the case of colonized and dependent states) from external political dominance, became the main launching pad for the process of shaping the image of national capitals. Dynastic and religious forms of identity, which traditionally had been more universal in nature, were striving to compete with or challenge the new national identity. Despite this confrontation, however, both the nations and their new capitals were actively adopting the old forms and ideas from the cultural reservoirs and repertoires of the royalty, aristocracy, and clergy. These old forms became construction material for national substance, iconography, and architecture. As it is often the case, the victors imitate the vanquished, and, thus, rejecting old identities, the national capitals came to imitate the royal courts and sacred capitals.

Louis Mumford sees the origin of national capitals in the seventeenth century baroque capitals.[92] Certainly, some elements of the royal court's way of life, traditions, and design were transposed, albeit in a modified and heavily exaggerated version, to national capitals.

Architectural forms of the national capital are reminiscent of *an inside-out palace* stretched along the entire length of the capital city's central avenues and squares. The royal theater gave birth to the national drama theater, opera, and concert hall; the royal and aristocratic art and curiosities collections gave rise to the national museums, while the royal parks and menageries engendered the public landscape parks and zoos, respectively.[93] The classic Latin of royal architecture evolved into the vernacular of the capital's streets and shopping districts. In a sense, the court had unintentionally tested and endorsed all the major urban functions and elements of the urban experience, which subsequently became classic expressions of the capital city's *ethos*. The squares of the transformed capitals absorbed the splendor and the spirit of the royal parks, palaces, and mansions. Finally, the newly emerged nations came to mimic the aristocracy by displaying (or perhaps only pretending to do so) excessive concerns over the issues of their origin, ancestry, and pedigree in recording their national history. Thus, by and large, all the substantive elements of royal and aristocratic culture were gradually nationalized and democratized.

Developing their ritualistic forms, the nations increasingly imitated sacred capitals, modifying the old rites and ceremonials and creating the new, civil cults, along with numerous symbols, paraphernalia, and ceremonies intended to substitute their religious predecessors. Terence McGee aptly calls national capital cities "modern *cult centres*," acknowledging their role as symbolic theaters of nationalism.[94] Indeed, the design elements and ceremonial components of sacred capitals became building blocks in the devising of the iconic forms of holidays, solemn processions, parades, festivals, and the very cult of both the nation and national history, around which they were formed.

In the newly constructed pantheon, the old Christian saints and martyrs were replaced with the new characters, i.e., victims of the struggle for national liberation and national unity, immortalized in mournful memorials. Temples of national fame were built across the countries, commemorating new national saints, especially writers and poets who had usually died young. Majestic monuments glorified the sacrifices these heroes had made to ensure that the triumphant sun of glory would shine on the nation. One may say that the central squares of the capitals were turned into *inside-out churches featuring the national iconostasis*, monuments to the heroes of the struggle against foreign oppressors and invaders, religious dogmatism, or absolute power of the king. These heroes were perceived as the atoning sacrifice on the altar of the national cause.

Aside from explicitly adopting old forms, national-states were also creating new forms and shifting the emphasis in the structural composition of capital cities. Thus, the center of capitals gradually drifted from the main cathedral and main palace to the stock exchange and parliament. After fortresses had lost their military significance and status as the protector of the city, they were transformed into symbols of military might, embodied in the grandeur of the capital city, albeit sometimes cyclopean in form and size. Symbolization and exaggeration of military power, thus, replaced actual military fortifications. Production, exchange, and consumption were allocated between different parts of the capital city.

The narrative of national history also changed. Transformed by the imagination, *chronos* of this narrative streamed into the visual *topos* of the capitals, forming sinkholes of national achievements represented with victory squares and monuments to the heroes of liberation movements. The capital city became a national history book in miniature format where the old symbols of royal or imperial power were adapted to the new realities and presented as chapters or decorative elements of the new historical narrative.

The ideology of nationalism was shaped in the process of opposition, whether it was the opposition to the royal power, religion, foreign invaders and colonizers, or local separatism, and all these emphases and aspects of nationalism were reflected in the iconography of capital cities.

As observed by Michiel Wagenaar, planners of the nineteenth century European capitals were seeking to create "open-air national museums,"[95] subjecting old meanings and symbols to mandatory *museumification*. Accordingly, not only did the capital city function as the display of the national time, it also served as the map of the national space so that iconography and toponymy of the capital reflected the variety of parts and constitutive elements of the nation. Authorities used the capital to sing the praises of their own greatness and glory. As a result, metaphorically speaking, the capital city became the national anthem, its streets and squares full of military-band bravado.

To summarize, nationalization of capital cities ended the process of nation-building. *State power, religious reverence, and urban environment – the three previously disparate and spatially separated components – were finally united in the capital city*. Emerged shortly before the rise of the nations, the capital allowed the nations to consolidate, perceiving themselves as something real and unified and condensing their ideas and symbols.

Philosophical reflections on national capitals

In the seventeenth through eighteenth centuries, two traditions of intellectual reflection on capital cities originated in the works of the leading philosophers of that time. While the first tradition presents a sort of apologia of the capital city, the second one is a romantic reaction to this apologia.

Describing the functions of the capital in his treatise entitled *La Métropolitée* (1682), Alexandre le Maître was probably guided by Thomas Hobbes' ideas of the absolute state as well as by the geometrical preoccupations and sensitivities of his century.[96] If the cities and settlements constitute the body, then, in relation to them, the capital must act as the head. It must also be the absolute capital of the society, playing the leading role in carrying out all state functions including those in the fields of economy, politics, morality, and intellectual developments. The capital should be the center of commerce and the richest of the cities since the economy cannot function normally unless it is directed by the suzerain. The capital gives to receive and receives to give away. Thus, the provinces supply the money to the treasury; in return, the capital gives greatness and glory to them, protecting them and serving as the guarantor of the fairness in the state.[97]

Jean-Jacques Rousseau represents the opposite, romanticist approach towards the rise of capital cities, pointing out the burden that the very existence of capital cities imposes on the rest of the state and state's population. He also calls attention to the problem of unequal distribution, inherent in the interaction between the capital and the provinces.

> The more our capital cities strike the vulgar eye with admiration, the greater reason is there to lament the sight of the abandoned countryside, the large tracts of land that lie uncultivated, the roads crowded with unfortunate citizens turned beggars or highwaymen, and doomed to end their wretched lives either on a dunghill or on the gallows. Thus the State grows rich on the one hand, and feeble and depopulated on the other . . . .[98]

Rousseau equates each site where a palace is erected to a desolate wasteland. In his mind, capitals, as exemplified by the Paris he disliked heartily, are a much greater source of degradation and decay than any other city.

As an alternative to the dominance of capitals, Rousseau, in *The Social Contract*, suggests "to allow no capital, to make the seat of government move from town to town, and to assemble by turn in each the Provincial Estates of the country."[99]

It is most likely that this idea was inspired by the six-rotating-capital system, which had been implemented in his native Swiss Confederation long ago. It is interesting to note that in France Rousseau's ideas continuously influenced the concept of territorial development for centuries, even as late as the twentieth century, and were relied upon in laying out a number of plans for downsizing Paris. The Rousseauistic resentment against large capital cities also has often fostered the argument and the feeling that small towns are the most appropriate venue for capitals.

Stein Rokkan's theory

The theory developed by the Norwegian sociologist Stein Rokkan (1921–1979) provides the answer to the question as to why "hard" political capitals emerged in some countries while "softer" capitals emerged in others.

As it has been noted above, two types of capital cities may be distinguished in Europe: (i) those that are characterized by a complete dominance over the national urban system; and (ii) those that may yield to other cities – j for example, in terms of economic supremacy. Following Umberto Eco, we term these types as "hard capitals" and "soft capitals," respectively.

Stein Rokkan offers a novel explanation of the reasons for the difference between the countries having *a monocephalic urban structure* and those having *a polycephalic structure*. According to him, this difference is determined by whether a given country occupies a peripheral or central position in relation to the continental urban epicenter, where the density of cities is particularly high and where trade routes and commercial cities are traditionally concentrated.[100]

Rokkan points to the North-South axis in Central Europe, which housed the most important trade routes linking its northern part, the Hansa, with Italy and the Mediterranean, calling this axis *"the belt of cities."* Today this belt still encompasses the cities of Belgium, the Netherlands, Germany, Switzerland, northern Italy, and southern France.[101]

The farther from major trade routes a political center leading the state-building process is, the more dominant and significant a capital city it becomes, both in terms of population concentration and in terms of the role it plays in comparison with the rest of the country. Worded differently, the closer major trade routes are, the less dominant a capital city is.

Another thesis Rokkan sets forth is that the denser the networks of cities in a given country, the lesser the role of the capital city, and the higher the chances of forming a polycephalic urban structure. Conversely, the thinner the network of cities, the greater the role of the capital city. According to Rokkan, the development of the territories to the east and west of the belt of cities was driven by the strong urban centers involved in the state-building process, distant from the established trade routes, and having no serious competitors among the cities close to those routes.

Following this pattern, centralized monocephalic states such as France, Spain, Portugal, Great Britain, and Scandinavian states emerged west of the city belt[102] while the area lying east of the belt saw the emergence of Austria, the Ottoman Empire, and Russia, all of which were also centralized and monocephalic.

Of all the states formed to the west of the city belt, Great Britain was by far the most centralized one. This led its capital city, whose supremacy had a long historical tradition, to reach a very higher degree of primacy. Arguing that this primacy was deeply rooted in the historical past of the country, the British historian John Morrill compares London with other European cities:

> Paris, the largest city in France, had 350,000 inhabitants in the mid-seventeenth century. The second and third largest cities were Rouen and Lyons with 80,000–100,000 inhabitants. In Europe, there were only five towns with population of more than 250,000, but over one hundred with more than 50,000 inhabitants. In England, however, London had more than half a million inhabitants by 1640 or 1660; Newcastle, Bristol and Norwich, which rivalled one another for second place, had barely 25,000 each. London was bigger than the next fifty towns in England combined.[103]

In contrast to the fragmented economies of autonomous commercial cities, large centralized states transformed into nations and were industrialized much faster. This allowed them to participate in large-scale industrial and commercial projects, as exemplified by business activities of such a corporate giant as the English East India Company.

Rokkan did not analyze operations of urban networks outside of Europe. However, many countries of the world had their own trade routes and their own "belts of cities" defining their international trade, affecting their level of centralization, and influencing their urban structures. Aside from the Silk Road, the examples of the international trade routes that gave rise to the belts of cities include the Grand Trunk Road in India, the Armenian trade routes in the Middle East and Asia Minor, and many others. Although the topic of configuring non-European political spaces in the context of the size of their capital cities is highly promising, it, nonetheless, requires a separate analysis.

The Westphalian system and non-European countries

The Westphalian system formed the basis of the concept of a *territorial state*, defining the boundaries of state authority. At the heart of this concept was the idea that jurisdiction of state authority is determined only by territorial borders, and not by other factors such as religious denomination or the ruler's relations with his subjects. In modern states, modern territory replaced bounded political space that was characteristic of the supremacy system in pre-modern states.

The concept of the territorial state was naturally complemented with the new concept of the nation. From that moment on, the identity of the state's population would be determined neither by religious concepts, nor by ties with the royal dynasty, nor by association with a particular city, but rather, by association with a particular nation. National capital cities became an instrument allowing to mobilize a nation and creating a locus of identification for the population of a given territory.

Edward Schatz offers an innovative hypothesis that without the historical experience of the Westphalian systems, the non-European capital cities in their capacity as agents of the state interests were less effective than their European counterparts.[104]

In the case of Europe, the Westphalian system merely gave a legal recognition to the then existing actual situation. Leading to the emergence of a new system of loyalty, the processes of state-building and nation-building preceded the creation of a modern state. In contrast, outside of Europe, the processes involving both nation-building and the formation of a new loyalty system achieved their peak after the rise of independent states, although by the time these states gained independence, they had already been recognized as nations within the meaning of the international legal system formed on the basis of the Westphalian system. Peoples of the majority of non-European countries had yet to develop into a nation in the European sense of the word.[105]

Schatz believes that under these circumstances, European capitals served as much better instruments of establishing political and territorial control. According to him, post-colonial non-European states were predisposed to capital city relocations because they were attempting to create more effective national capitals similar to their European prototype.

Albeit quite interesting, this hypothesis needs some extra assumptions and modifications. Schatz' analysis is based on the concepts of nation-building and state-building, and he rightly excludes capital city relocations in pre-modern states from it. However, such states as the US, Australia, and Canada fit into this analysis quite well. Furthermore, they have introduced an important alternative form of nation-building that has become wide-spread and attractive to many other countries. Contrary to the European model of national capitals, which was premised on a highly centralized model of the state, federal capitals were more suitable for a de-centralized model. In the mid-nineteenth century, many Latin American countries were seriously considering the concept of a neutral federal capital as one of the possible scenarios of their development. By and large, the nation-building process in Latin America was also much closer to the experience of European countries than to that of Asian and African countries.

It is noteworthy that some European peoples did not quite develop into full-fledged nations. Thus, many historians have concluded that the pace of the nation-building process in Russia has been delayed and too slow compared to the level of its development as a state.[106]

It should be also emphasized that non-European countries often lacked not only the concept of a nation but some other notions that they also had to adopt and that were closely related to it, e.g., the citizenship and the city.

The most fundamental categories of a European political consciousness have been traditionally based on the normative concepts related, whether logically or linguistically, to the notion of the city. Some of the examples include the concept of citizenship (derived from the word "city"), politics (derived from "*polis*," the Greek for "city"), civilization, civism, and civics (derived from "*civis*," the Latin for "city-dweller" and related to "*civitas*," Latin for "community"). The very concept of the European state originated from the idea of the city; furthermore, the modern state was modeled after the city, *made in its image, after its likeness*. The city-related norms of political life – first and foremost, the concept of self-government – were gradually spreading among all the people living in the state and turning them from mere residents into city-dwellers, that is, citizens.

Many plans for the construction of new capitals in non-European countries may have taken into account the gaps in the historical experience of these countries. The new capitals were intended to compensate for the lack of a developed urban system and to foster the formation of new political institutions. Even building just one city was highly important to the states where there were but a few economically prosperous cities and where the economy was strongly dependent on agriculture. In these cases, the state, by and through the capital city, had a particularly vital need to penetrate the periphery, where political loyalty often remained rudimentary.

As it has been shown, in most of the European countries, the change of political regime or the conquest of independence was accompanied by a rather radical change of the capital city's iconography. For non-European countries, such a change was often insufficient. The geographical location of the capital city played a more important role than in Europe, which had a substantial historical experience of nation-state building. Proximity to the territories where loyalty to the nation-state had not yet been formed was more essential for non-European countries.

To illustrate and to test the above theses, chapter 3 will look at capital city relocation plans and scenarios that have been set forth in different parts of the world.

Notes

1 Daum, A. & Mauch, C., eds. *Berlin-Washington: 1800–2000: Capital Cities, Cultural Representations, and National Identities* (New York: Cambridge University Press, 2009), 4.
2 Campbell, S. "The Enduring Importance of National Capital Cities in the Global Era," University of Michigan, *Working Papers Series*, 2003, 3–4.
3 Eldredge, H. *World Capitals: Toward Guided Urbanization* (New York: Anchor Press, Garden City, 1975); Hall, P. "The Changing Role of Capital Cities: Six Types of Capital City." In: Taylor, J., Lengelle, J.G., & Andrew, C. (eds.), *Capital Cities/Les Capitales: Perspectives Internationales/International Perspectives* (Ottawa: Carleton University Press, 1993); Campbell, S. "The Enduring

History and typology of capital cities   45

Importance of National Capital Cities in the Global Era," University of Michigan, *Working Papers Series*, 2003; Gottmann, J. "The Study of Former Capitals," *Ekistics*, vol. 314/315 (Sept./Oct. –Nov./Dec. 1985), 541–546; Tyrwhitt, J. & Gottmann, J. eds. "Capital Cities," *Ekistics*, vol. 50 (March/April 1983) [Oslo, Warsaw, Rome, Tokyo, and Washington, D.C.].

4 Daum, A. & Mauch, C., eds. *Berlin-Washington: 1800–2000: Capital Cities, Cultural Representations, and National Identities* (New York: Cambridge University Press, 2009), 10.

5 Ringrose, D. "Capital Cities, Urbanization and Modernization in Early Modern Europe," *Journal of Urban History*, vol. 24, no. 2 (January 1998), 155–183.

6 Ibid.; Daum, A. & Mauch, C., eds. *Berlin-Washington: 1800–2000: Capital Cities, Cultural Representations, and National Identities* (New York: Cambridge University Press, 2009).

7 In the case of the Netherlands, this situation was created by a post-revolutionary compromise between the House of Oranje, whose residence was traditionally located in The Hague as the royal capital of the state, and the Amsterdam patriciate favoring this richest and economically developed city of the country. Today the constitutional position of Amsterdam as capital is honorific.

8 Hitti, P. *Capital Cities of Arab Islam* (Minneapolis: University of Minnesota Press, 1973); Fiévé, N. & Waley, P. *Japanese Capitals in Historical Perspective: Place, Power and Memory in Kyoto, Edo and Tokyo* (London: Routledge, 2003); Geil, W.E. *Eighteen Capitals of China* (Philadelphia: Lippinkot Co., 2005); Cotterell, A. *Imperial Capitals of China* (Woodstock, NY: Overlook Press, 2008).

9 Aksakov, K. "Znachenie stolitsy." In: *Moskva-Petersburg: Pro et Contra. Dialog kultur v istorii natsionalnogo samosoznania* (Saint-Petersburg: Russkii khristianskii gumanitarnii institut, 2000).

10 Landau-Wells, M. "Capital Cities in Civil Wars: The Locational Dimension of Sovereign Authority," *Crisis States Occasional Papers*, London School of Economics, April 2008.

11 Bernhardi, F. *Sovremennaya voyna*, vol. 1–2 (Sankt-Peterburg: V. Berezovsky, 1912), 196.

12 For examples, see Radović, S. "From Center to Periphery and Vice Versa: The Politics of Toponyms in the Transitional Capital," *Bulletin of the Institute of Ethnography*, vol. 56, no. 2 (2008), 53–74.

13 Daum, A. & Mauch, C., eds. *Berlin-Washington: 1800–2000: Capital Cities, Cultural Representations, and National Identities* (New York: Cambridge University Press, 2009), 5–8.

14 Shevryev, A. "The Axis Petersburg-Moscow: Outward and Inward Russian Capitals," *Journal of Urban History*, vol. 30, no. 1 (2003), 70–84.

15 Hall, P. "The Changing Role of Capital Cities: Six Types of Capital City." In: Taylor, J., Lengelle, J.G., & Andrew, C. (eds.), *Capital Cities/Les Capitales: Perspectives Internationales/International Perspectives* (Ottawa: Carleton University Press, 1993), 176.

16 Kolbe, L. "Helsinki: From Provincial to National Centre." In: Gordon, David (ed.), *Planning Twentieth-Century Capital Cities* (London: Routledge, 2006), 73–87.

17 The Kingdom of Bohai (698–926) included the territory of modern Russia's Primorsky Krai and the Amur River region, North Korea, and most of Northeast China (Manchuria).

18 Longli, Ye. *Istoria gosudarstva kidanei*. Translated by V. Taskin (Moskva: Nauka, 1979), ch. 22.

19 Zadvernyuk, L. & Kozyrenko, N. "Migratsia stolits v Kitae i fenomen pustogo goroda," In: Zabiyako, A. (ed.), *Rossia i Kitay na dalnevostochnyh rubezhah*, vol. 6 (Blagoveschensk: AmGU, 2002), 154–159.

46 *History and typology of capital cities*

20 In China, during the West Han period, the Concept of the Five Cities, *Wu Du*, which represented the five largest cities in the country – Luoyang, Handan, Linzi, Wan, and Chengdu – in addition to the capital, probably corresponded to the five elements in Chinese natural philosophy.
21 *The History of the Khitan State (Qidango zhi)* describes the five capitals as follows: Yan Capital had the three financial departments, Western Capital–Administration of the Chief of Carriage, Middle Capital–Bureau of Accounts and Finances, Upper Capital–Administration of Salt and Iron; and Eastern Capital–Money and Iron Administration of the Department of Finance (Ye Longli, 1979, ch. 22).
22 Maul, S. "Die altorientalische Hauptstadt—Abbild und Nabel der Welt." In: *Die Orientalische Stadt: kontinuitat. Wandel. Bruch*. 1 Internationale Colloquium der Deutschen Orient-Gesellschaft. 9.-10. Mai 1996 in Halle/Saale. Saarbrücker Druckerei und Verlag (1997), S.109–124.
23 Yoon, H.-K. *The Culture of Fengshui in Korea: An Exploration of East Asian Geomancy* (Lanham: Lexington Books, 2006), 332.
24 Fortenbaugh, R. *The Nine Capitals of the United States* (New York, PA: Maple Press Co., 1948).
25 Therborn, G. "Identity and Capital Cities: European Nation and European Union." In: Cerutti, Furio & Lucarelli, Sonia (eds.), *The Search for a European Identity: Values, Policies and Legitimacy of the European Union* (New York: Routledge, 2008), 70.
26 European Commission & Belgian Presidency. Brussels, Capital of Europe. Final Report, October 2001, 10–11.
27 Therborn, G. "Identity and Capital Cities: European Nation and European Union," In: Cerutti, Furio & Lucarelli, Sonia (eds.), *The Search for a European Identity: Values, Policies and Legitimacy of the European Union* (New York: Routledge, 2008), 63.
28 Djament, G. "Le débat sur Rome capitale," *L'Espace Géographique*, Tome 34, no. 3 (2005), 376.
29 As James Robertson notes, a piece of advice for appraising a seventeenth century town included . . . "estimat[ing] the largeness of the Bird by the Nest" (Robertson, 2001: 38).
30 Robertson, J. "Stuart London and the Idea of a Royal Capital City," *Renaissance Studies*, vol. 15, no. 1 (2001), 38–41.
31 Wagenaar, M. "Townscapes of Power," *GeoJournal*, vol. 51 (2000), 5.
32 Röber, M. & Schröter, E. "Governing the Capital—Comparing Institutional Reform in Berlin, London, and Paris," *Working Paper PRI-8* (2004), 10.
33 Gottmann, J. "Capital Cities." In: *After Megapolisis: The Urban Writings of Jean Gottmann* (Baltimore: Johns Hopkins University Press, 1990), 67.
34 Campbell, S. "The Changing Role and Identity of Capital Cities in the Global Era," *Paper presented at the Association of American Geographers*, Pittsburgh (2000), 18.
35 Boiy, T. *Late Achaemenid and Hellenistic Babylon* (New York: Peeters Publishers, 2004), 97.
36 Aristotle. *Politics*. Translated by Carnes Lord (University of Chicago Press: Chicago & London, 2013), 53.
37 Russian sinologist Artemiy Karapetyants has contrasted the Chinese model of the country and the universe as the land surrounded by the four seas to the predominant European model of the universe where the sea (Mediterranean) is surrounded by land (Karapetyants, A. "Kitaiskaia tsivilizatsiia kak alternative Sredizemnomorskoi," *Obschestvennie nauki i sovremennost*, no. 1 (2000), 132–138.)
38 Emet, C. "The Capital Cities of Jerusalem," *Geographical Review*, vol. 86, no. 2 (1996), 233–234.

History and typology of capital cities   47

39 Unlike many capitals of the ancient states, which were named after their royal founders, Alexandria, founded by Alexander the Great, was not intended to serve as a new capital of his empire. Jean Gottmann, a French geographer, writes about an attempt to build Megalopolis (Big City), a joint capital for all of the Greek city-states, undertaken by Epaminondas (410–362 BC), a Theban general and a Pythagorean. Epaminondas began to build the new capital in Arcadia in southern Greece, but his plans for the unification of the country were destined to fail (Gottmann, J. "The Study of Former Capitals," *Ekistics*, vol. 314/315 (Sept./Oct.-Nov./Dec. 1985), 67).

40 Boucheron, P., ed. *Les villes capitales au Moyen Âge. XXXVIe Congrès de la SHMES (Istanbul, 1–6 juin 2005)* (Paris: Sorbonne, 2006).

41 Maizlish A. "V konkurentsii s Parizhem: Burgundskie goroda v borbe za rol politicheskogo tsentra." In: Konovalova, I. (ed.), *Perenos stolitsi* (Moscow: Institut vseobschei istorii, 2013), 81–84.

42 Berges, W. "Das Reich ohne Hauptstadt." In: Friedrich-Meinecke-Institut (ed.), *Das Hauptstadtproblem in der Geschichte* (Tübingen: Max Niemeyer Verlag, 1953), 2–29, 1–30.

43 Although some authors still erroneously view the Holy Roman Empire as a largely fictitious, artificial formation that played a nominal role in the political destinies of Europe, addressing it in this context is relevant and important due to the essentially federal nature of the empire. The nihilistic assessments largely consonant with the well-known formula of Voltaire ("It was neither holy, nor Roman, nor an empire") are somewhat witty but hardly accurate since they rely heavily on the clichéd idea of empires as extremely rigid political formations. Many modern historians consider the Holy Roman Empire the herald and precursor of the European Union, maintaining that the legacy and mission of Austria-Hungary in European and international politics and diplomacy was a direct continuation of the mission of the Holy Roman Empire (Nedrebø, T. "City-belt Europe or Imperial Europe? Stein Rokkan and European History," *Europæus norvegicus*, vol. 30. mars 2012 (originally published in Nervegian at *Nytt Norsk Tidsskrift*, no. 3, 2012). Brussels, located not far from Aachen, carries on the legacy of the empire and, to a substantial extent, is based on its values.

44 Wise, M. "A Capital of Europe?," *New York Times*, March 2, 2002.

45 Miller, J. M. *Lake Europe: A New Capital for a United Europe* (New York: Books International, 1963).

46 Wheatley, P. & See, T. *From Court to Capital: A Tentative Interpretation of the Origins of the Japanese Urban Tradition* (Chicago & London: University of Chicago Press, 1978), 242. See also *Journal of the Royal Asiatic Society*, vol. 111, no. 2, 181–200; Goethem, E. von. *Nagaoka: Japan's Forgotten Capital* (Leiden: Brill NV, 2008).

47 Horvath, R.J. "The Wandering Capitals of Ethiopia," *The Journal of African History*, vol. 10, no. 2 (1969), 215.

48 Durand-Guédy, D. *Turko-Mongol Rulers, Cities and City Life* (Leiden & Boston: Brill, 2013), 7.

49 Blair, S. "The Mongol Capital of Sulṭāniyya, 'The Imperial'," *Iran (British Institute of Persian Studies)*, vol. 24 (1986), 139–151.

50 Coulanges, F. de. *The Ancient City* (Kitchener: Batoche Books, 2001); Wheatley, P. *The Pivot of the Four Quarters: A Preliminary Enquiry Into the Origins and Character of the Ancient Chinese City* (Chicago: Aldine Publishing House, 1971).

51 For a detailed review of Asian sacred capitals, see an article by Surinder Bhardwaj (Bhardwaj, S. "The Concept of Sacred Cities in Asia with Special Reference to India," In: Dutt, Ashok (ed.), *The Asian City: Processes of Development, Characteristics and Planning* (Dordrecht: Kluwer Academic Publishers, 1994). An interesting discussion of the sacred capitals of Indonesia and the Hindu

48 History and typology of capital cities

sacred capitals as a whole is presented in a book authored by the famous anthropologist Clifford Geertz (Geertz, C. *The Interpretation of Cultures: Selected Essays* (New York: Basic Books, 1973), 223–230).
52 Eisenstadt, S. *The Origins and Diversity of Axial Age Civilizations* (New York: SUNY Press, 1986), 186–187.
53 Meyer, J.F. *Peking as a Sacred City* (Taipei: Chinese Association for Folklore, 1976), 109; Westenholz, J.G., ed. In: *Capital Cities: Urban Planning and Spiritual Dimensions* (Jerusalem: Bible Lands Museum, 1998).
54 Geertz, C. *The Interpretation of Cultures: Selected Essays* (New York: Basic Books, 1973), 222–223.
55 Rossman, V. "Misteria tsentra: Identichnost i organizatsiya sotsialnogo prostranstva v sovremennykh i traditsionnikh obschestvakh," *Voprosy filosofii*, no. 2 (2008), 42–57.
56 Iannaccone, L., Haight, C., & Rubin, J. "Lessons from Delphi: Religious Markets and Spiritual Capitals," *Journal of Economic Behavior & Organization*, vol. 77 (2011), 333–334.
57 Khayutina, M. "Did the first Kings of the Zhou Dynasty Relocate Their Capital? The Topos of the Central Place in Early China and its Historical Contexts," *XVII Conference of the European Association of Chinese Studies*, 6–10. August 2008, Lund; Khayutina, M. "Zur Konstruktion der imperialen Hauptstadt im frühen China," *Workshop "Metropolen" of the interdisciplinary project "Comparison of Empires" at the Ruhr-University Bochum*, 2. February 2007, Bochum.
58 Khayutina, M. "Did the first Kings of the Zhou Dynasty Relocate Their Capital? The Topos of the Central Place in Early China and its Historical Contexts," *XVII Conference of the European Association of Chinese Studies*, 6–10. August 2008, Lund.
59 Ibid.
60 Maul, S. "Die altorientalische Hauptstadt—Abbild und Nabel der Welt," in *Die Orientalische Stadt: kontinuitat. Wandel. Bruch. 1 Internationale Colloquium der Deutschen Orient-Gesellschaft. 9.-1 0. Mai 1996 in Halle/Saale.* Saarbrücker Druckerei und Verlag (1997), 109–124.
61 Cut off from the economic life of the rest of the country, Persepolis was situated in the middle of a rocky plain, in a barren terrain dependent on food supplies from other regions (Perrot, J. "Birth of a City: Susa," Westenholz, Joan Goodnick (ed.) In: *Capital City: Urban Planning and Spiritual Dimensions*, Westenholz, Joan Goodnick (ed.), (Jerusalem: Bible Lands Museum, 1998), 83–97. While this factor approximates Persepolis to political *disembedded capitals*, discussed in Chapter 2, its role, nonetheless, was more ritual than political.
62 In his book entitled *Memory and the Mediterranean*, Braudel juxtaposes the nature of urbanism in Egypt with that in Mesopotamia. While the Mesopotamian cities were quite autonomous and primarily commerce-oriented, the Egyptian cities functioned mainly as religious centers. This difference is partly explained by the dead-end geographical location of Egypt, contrasted with a greater market exposure of the Mesopotamian states, which lay on the major trade routes. The economy of ancient Egypt was predominantly rural, and therefore, writes the French historian, its main urban potential was centered around the capital cities controlled by temples and priests. In contrast, Mesopotamia was more deeply rooted in commercial activities and even saw the development of a kind of urban patriotism as reflected, for example, in the Epic of Gilgamesh. According to Braudel, these differences were determinative in shaping the Mesopotamian economy, making it more dynamic and more diverse than its Egyptian counterpart (Braudel, F. *Memory and the Mediterranean* (New York: Knopf, 2001), 66–69). Babylonia, located in the southern part of Mesopotamia,

History and typology of capital cities 49

featured the most extensive and most densely populated urban network in the area (Eisenstadt, S. *The Origins and Diversity of Axial Age Civilizations* (New York: SUNY Press, 1986), 186–188).

63 For a discussion of some aspects of the Byzantine urbanism and capitalness, see the book *In Search of the Fourth Rome* (Rossman, V. "In Search of the Fourth Rome: Visions of a New Russian Capital City," *Slavic Review*, vol. 72, no. 3 (2013), 505–527.) focusing on capital relocation debates in Russia.
64 Melman, Y. "Israel Should Give Up Jerusalem as Its Capital," *Haarez*, December 6, 2009.
65 Rossman, V. *V poiskakh Chetvertogo Rima* (Moskva: Vysshaia shkola ekonomiki, 2014), 140–141.
66 Joffe, A. "Disembedded Capitals in Western Asian Perspective," *Society for Comparative Study of Society & History*, vol. 40, no. 3 (1998), 549–580.
67 Pipes, D. "The Muslim Claim to Jerusalem," *Middle East Quarterly*, September, 2001.
68 Gottmann, J. "Capital Cities." In: *After Megapolisis. The Urban Writings of Jean Gottmann*, (Baltimore: Johns Hopkins University Press, 1990), 69–71.
69 Ibid.
70 Robertson, J. "Stuart London and the Idea of a Royal Capital City," *Renaissance Studies*, vol. 15, no. 1 (2001), 44–48.
71 In 1208 the royal court had moved from Burgos to Valladolid, the city that in 1492, with the completion of the Reconquista, became the capital of the unified Spain. Thereafter, Toledo, which had been the capital of the Visigoths in the fifth through eighth centuries, also served, albeit sporadically, as the residence of the Spanish kings.
72 Ringrose, D. *Madrid and Spanish Economy: 1560–1850* (Berkeley: University of California Press, 1983), 232–233.
73 Gottmann, J. "Capital Cities," In: *After Megapolisis: The Urban Writings of Jean Gottmann*, (Baltimore: Johns Hopkins University Press, 1990), 68.
74 Ibid., 70.
75 Braudel, F. *Afterthoughts on Material Civilization and Capitalism* (Baltimore & London: John Hopkins University, 1977).
76 Ringrose, D. "Capital Cities, Urbanization and Modernization in Early Modern Europe," *Journal of Urban History*, vol. 24, no. 2 (January 1998), 155.
77 Vries, J. de. *European Urbanization, 1500–1800* (London: Methuen, 1984).
78 Clark, P. & Lepetit, B. *Capital Cities and Their Hinterlands in Early Modern Europe* (Cambridge: Scholar Press, 1996); see also Hohenberg, P. & Lees, L. *The Making of Urban Europe, 1000–1950* (Cambridge: Harvard University Press, 1985).
79 Vries, J. de. *European Urbanization, 1500–1800* (London: Methuen, 1984), 64.
80 Cited in Robertson, J. "Stuart London and the Idea of a Royal Capital City," *Renaissance Studies*, vol. 15, no. 1 (2001), 37–58(22).
81 Ringrose, D. "Capital Cities, Urbanization and Modernization in Early Modern Europe," *Journal of Urban History*, vol. 24, no. 2 (January 1998), 177.
82 Jacobs, J. *Cities and the Wealth of Nations: Principles of Economic Life* (New York: Random House, 1984).
83 Ringrose, D. "Capital Cities, Urbanization and Modernization in Early Modern Europe," *Journal of Urban History*, vol. 24, no. 2 (January 1998), 156, 181.
84 Fields, G. "City Systems, Urban History, and Economic Modernity," *Berkeley Planning Journal*, vol. 13 (1999), 110–112.
85 Braudel, F. *Afterthoughts on Material Civilization and Capitalism* (Baltimore & London: John Hopkins University, 1977), 22.
86 Ringrose, D. *Madrid and Spanish Economy: 1560–1850* (Berkeley: University of California Press, 1983), 177; Ringrose, D. "Capital Cities, Urbanization and

Modernization in Early Modern Europe," *Journal of Urban History*, vol. 24, no. 2 (January 1998), 155–183.
87 Tocqueville, A. de. *The Old Regime and the Revolution* (New York: Harper & Brothers, 1856).
88 Anderson, B. *The Imagined Community* (London: Verso, 1991).
89 Toynbee, A. "'Capital Cities: Their Distinctive Features' and 'Capital Cities: Melting-Pots and Powder-Kegs'," In: *Cities on the Move* (New York and London: Oxford University Press, 1970), 67.
90 Ringrose, D. "Capital Cities, Urbanization and Modernization in Early Modern Europe," *Journal of Urban History*, vol. 24, no. 2 (January 1998), 179.
91 Eisenstadt, S.N. & Shachar, A. *Society, Culture, and Urbanization* (Newbury Park: Sage, 1987), 178. Charles de Montesquieu attributed a more active role to the capitals: "It is above all a great capital which creates the general spirit of a nation; it is Paris which makes the French . . . " Montesquieu, C. *My Thoughts (Mes Pensées)*. Translated, edited, and with an Introduction by Henry C. Clark (Indianapolis: Liberty Fund, 2012).
92 Mumford, L. *The City in History: Its Origins, Its Transformations, and Its Prospects* (New York: Harvest Books, 1968), 356, 380, 391–392.
93 Ibid., 381.
94 McGee, T. *The Southeast Asian City: A Social Geography of the Primate Cities of Southeast Asia* (London: Bell & Sons, 1967).
95 Wagenaar, M. "The Capital as a Representation of a Nation." In: Dijkink, Gertjan & Knippenberg, Hans (eds.), *The Territorial Factor: Political Geography in a Globalizing World* (Amsterdam: Vossiuspers, 2001), 350.
96 Le Maître, A. *La métropolitée, ou De l'établissement des villes capitales, de leur utilité passive et active, de l'union de leurs parties, de leurs anatomie, de leurs commerce* (Amsterdam: B. Boekholt, 1682).
97 Cited in Roche, D. *France in the Enlightenment* (Cambridge UP, 1997), 641–642.
98 Rousseau, J.-J. *The Social Contract* (JM Dent & Sons: London & Toronto, 1913), 245.
99 Ibid., 13.
100 Rokkan, S. *State Formation, Nation-Building, and Mass Politics in Europe*. edited by Peter Florida (Oxford: Oxford University Press, 1999); Rokkan, S. "Dimensions of State Formation and Nation Building: A Possible Paradigm for Research on Variations Within Europe." In: Tilly, Charles (ed.), *The Formation of National States in Europe* (Princeton: Princeton University Press, 1976); Rokkan, S. "Territories, Centers and Peripheries: Toward a Geoethnic, Geoeconomic, Geopolitical Model of Differentiation Within Western Europe." In: Gottman, Jean (ed.), *Centre and Periphery: Spatial Variations in Politics* (Sage: Beverly Hills, 1980).
101 Rokkan, S. *State Formation, Nation-Building, and Mass Politics in Europe*. edited by Peter Florida (Oxford: Oxford University Press, 1999), 128, 145, 156.
102 Ibid., 159.
103 Morrill, J. *Stuart Britain: A Very Short Introduction* (Oxford: Oxford Paperbacks, 2000), 87.
104 Schatz, E. "What Capital Cities Say About State and Nation Building," *Nationalism and Ethnic Politics*, vol. 9, no. 4 (2003), 3–4.
105 Ibid.
106 Hosking, G. *Russia and the Russians: A History from Rus to a Russian Federation* (London: Allen Lane, 2001).

2 Capital city relocation experience

Principles of capital city siting

So far this book has focused on the history of different types of capital cities, leaving aside the issue of their siting principles. However, it is mainly these principles that give rise to capital city relocations, and, therefore, identifying them would certainly help to better understand the motivations behind these relocations. One of such principles appears to be the implicit principle of centrality, often appealed to today by the supporters of capital relocations.

Intuitively, this principle seems quite logical since the central location allows a capital city to control both the population and the territory of a given country more effectively. Furthermore, such an arrangement seemingly stems from common mythological concepts based on the mythologem of the Center. As it has been demonstrated above, some systems of national mythology perceived capitals as the center of not only the state but also the whole world.[1]

The idea that geographical centrality is a norm for the state-building process dominated even state theories of the modern age. Thus, Alexandre le Maître in his *La Métropolitée* prescribes a centrally located capital city. Likewise, in Thomas More's *Utopia* the capital is sited in the very center of the island.

A central location also appears to be most rational from the perspective of general economic principles. The economic theory generally predicts that a capital city should be centrally located to maximize tax revenue or improve governance.[2] To select the most optimal location for their headquarters or a production facility, corporations must analyze a whole complex of factors, e.g., the availability of raw materials, power supply, qualified labor, transportation network, and potential markets for the products to be produced; the proximity of end-users; the distance to competitors; and the possibility of effective communication among the participants in the processes of production, sales, and management. In many cases, this is the logic of a transportation hub serving customers in different parts of an evenly populated and relatively homogeneous area. If one applied production facility siting principles to the task of selecting a capital city, the most decisive principle would be the proximity to the end-users, that is, proximity to the citizenry consuming public benefits produced by the capitals. Ideally these benefits would have to be equally available to all the citizens, thus justifying the idea that a capital city should be sited in the center of the state.

However, for modern states, centrally located capitals are an exception rather than a rule. State territories are rarely homogenous, and sometimes the very question of what constitutes the center of the state becomes problematic too.

Although many capitals were originally sited based on the principle of centrality, boundary changes caused by territorial losses or gains often turned centrally located capitals into peripherally located ones. This phenomenon is illustrated by the cases of Vienna and Istanbul, both of which, as a result of major territorial losses, found themselves situated at the very edge of Austria and Turkey, respectively. Moscow was once located in the center of the European part of the Soviet Union but, after the union collapsed, moved much closer to the western periphery of present-day Russia. Paris also lost its original central location as the capital of the Capetian possessions in northern France but did so not as a result of losses, but rather, as a result of territorial expansion of the state.

Despite its shortcomings, the principle of centrality represents an important ideal model and as such is helpful for the purpose of our study. This model may serve as a reference point to determine the degree of deviation of modern capitals from the ideal center.

In the course of history, capital city siting has been affected by a set of diverse factors, not all of which can be easily identified today. However, four groups of factors – geographical, military, cultural, and political – appear to be of utmost significance. Not always determinative in selecting the optimal site, they have always imposed constraints on capital city siting, often leading to deviations from the principle of centrality.

Geographical factors

Physical geography – including *the landscape and climate conditions* – has always played a greatly important role in placing a capital city, affecting the nature of the populating process and creating the geometry that gives meaning to the concepts of centrality of intermediacy. In the countries where the ecumene significantly differs in size from their total territory – e.g., Russia, Australia, or Algeria – the central location of the capital does not necessarily imply its geographical centrality.

Capital cities were often sited in the locations where food supplies from the outside storehouses could be easily delivered using natural transportation routes. In this regard, rivers linking the capital with food suppliers were of particular importance. Sometimes a capital city could be built at the intersection of different landscape types, for example, the forest and the steppe, the mountains and the plain, or the desert and the oasis. The natural nodality of the city was always taken into account.

These natural geographical reference points and physiography often went through some sort of a symbolic adaptation, and the intersection areas could acquire a special meaning if they coincided with the natural boundaries of composite ethnicities or other groups.

In many countries, capital city relocations were directly caused by natural cataclysmic events such as an earthquake, diversion of the river channel, or even climatic changes. Thus, in 1598 the capital of Khwarezm was moved from Gurganj (now Urgench) to Khiva because the Amu Darya river channel diverted from the old river bed. Furthermore, a diversion of the Euphrates led to the relocation of the capital from Babylon to Seleucia-on-the-Tigris. Also known as the New Babylon, the latter had been founded by the Seleucus I Nikator, a former general of Alexander the Great, and located in a short distance from the old Babylon. Climate changes – e.g., general climatic cooling – could also lead to the relocation of a capital city.[3]

Last, the availability of construction materials, most notably building stone, associated with the notion of power, was also one of the factors affecting the siting of capital cities.[4]

Military factors

Throughout the centuries, military considerations have been the biggest factor causing the deviation of capital cities from the geographic center.

Certain geographical factors played a vital role in state defense. Thus, elevated locations surrounded by natural water reservoirs or ravines provided ideal natural fortifications.

The British geographer Vaughan Cornish, whose theory will yet be discussed in more detail below, believed that the eccentric location of most of the imperial capitals are explained by military factors. As a rule, capitals were situated on the frontier which served as a springboard for further expansion of the state or, contrarily, which was exceedingly susceptible to external attacks.

For example, no capital city of China has ever been located in the center of the country. Historically, practically all of the campaigns to reunify China have started in the north where the borders were extremely vulnerable and frequently invaded by various northern nomadic tribes, the Mongols, Turks, and Tungus, to name but a few. Due to this factor, most of the prominent Chinese capital cities were sited on the dangerous northern frontier despite the fact that, as early as the tenth century, the economic center of the country had shifted to the south, the Yangtze River Valley.[5] Some historians have opined that siting China's capitals near the northern border, at the gateway to the steppe, was justified by the need to control the army and its generals, who would have otherwise organized a coup d'état and taken the power in the country. This logic, however, was hardly universal since many other states, both ancient and modern, have tended to do exactly the opposite, moving their capitals away from the border to less vulnerable locations.

Cultural factors

Cultural factors that may affect capital city siting are not inferable from or solely explained by the geographical location of the country. Although geography certainly affects them, it does not exhaust their content. Relevant cultural factors include first of all, *fundamental orientations, values, visions, religious beliefs, and spatial organization schemes*. This list may be supplemented with numerous other factors such as the symbolic meaning of the cardinal points, proximity to religious centers, nature of economic activities, level of universal or global ambitions of a given state or civilization, etc. The capital's location with respect to the sea and the model of a land-sea relationship may also play a significant role defining the difference between land and maritime empires.

The Chinese Empire had a convenient access to the ocean and the seas, and its coastline was well suited for navigation and sea-port siting. It is interesting to note in this regard that regardless of these geographical advantages, *none of the numerous China's capitals except Lin'an* (present-day Hangzhou), *the capital of the Southern Song Dynasty (1127–1279), was located on the sea coast*.[6] Many sinologists believe that this situation stemmed from the fundamental continental orientation of China, lengthy historical period of isolation from the outside world, and the lack of world domination ambitions.

The Russian sinologist Artemiy Karapetyants explains the differences between the European Mediterranean and Chinese civilizations by fundamentally conflicting spatial models underlying these civilizations. While the European political space was centered around the Mediterranean, surrounded by various lands and countries, China saw both itself and the whole civilized world as a piece of land washed on all sides by four seas.[7] Karapetyants maintains that this opposition also gave rise to two different types of primary civilizing activities defining these cultures: (i) irrigation in the case of Europe and (ii) land reclamation from the water bodies in the case of China. Accordingly, the efforts of the Mesopotamian and Egyptian civilizations were focused on irrigating land and providing water supplies whereas, by contrast, the Chinese civilization, as exemplified by its mythological and cultural heroes, strived to conquer the element of water, reclaiming land from the seas and the oceans.[8] These spatial perceptions, along with other factors, made the siting of China's capital cities in the coastal area undesirable and unlikely.

Some historians attribute the decline of the Ming Dynasty to the fact that its capital, Beijing, was located in the extreme north of the country. Such a location made the cost of supplying Beijing very high, resulted in a loss of influence in the southern regions, and prevented China from developing a successful maritime geostrategy.[9]

Many countries and regions have had distinctive cultural practices associated with the relocation of a capital city. Thus, China and some other oriental cultures developed the concepts of corporeality and energetic "fullness" of space. Geomancy, a branch of science studying these problems allowed to identify the most favorable sites for cities and, of course, capital cities. The geomantic approach to this topic will be discussed in more detail in one of the following chapters. In some African countries the royal villages were founded on selected and sanctified sites, and there were some rules and rituals that governed their selection and symbolic organization.[10]

Speaking of cultural practices, one should also mention capital relocation concepts based on religious beliefs. Various states have had mythologies grounded in covenants related to capital city siting. Sometimes the notion of chosenness stemmed not from religion, but rather, a protective *genius loci* associated with a capital city. The concept of sacred space or "the natural capital," albeit appearing anachronistic today, continue to influence the ongoing capital city relocation debates in many states and affect decisions on the shifting of capital cities.

When siting a capital city, the above mentioned factors were always taken into account although they were not always in harmony. Furthermore, one should realize that because different political regimes favored different siting and relocation logics, these factors did play the identical role in the respective processes.

Unquestionably, the siting of a national capital city tended to take geographical, military, and cultural factors into consideration; yet, by and large, it was based on political reasons which we will analyze below. For empires and despotic states, military effectiveness and retention or strengthening of political power were more decisive parameters of capital city relocations.

The next two sections will discuss two logics of capital city relocation, the first of which is characteristic of empires and is primarily concerned with military confrontations while the second one involves despotic states and is intended to establish a new balance of power and authority within the state affected by internal political confrontation brought about by political factions. The goal of these despotic regimes was to create new technologies of governance, legitimizing their own political dominance.

Capital city relocation in empires

The British geographer Vaughan Cornish and the British historian Arnold Toynbee have attempted to analyze the principles of capital city siting and relocation followed by great powers and major empires.

Examining how *great powers* sited their capitals, Cornish introduces the concept of a *forward capital*. According to Cornish, the siting of capitals of great powers was determined by three basic elements: (i) Storehouse or production zones supplying food and human resources to the state; (ii) Crossroads, which ensured the delivery of these supplies; and (iii) Strongholds, which served as protection devices ensuring the safety of this delivery. In most cases, the location of the state's Storehouse determined the location of both the Crossroads and Strongholds. Usually imperial capitals were sited on the states' most active and at the same time most vulnerable frontier that dictated its foreign policy.

The geographical center of the state was an extremely unusual location for imperial capitals; usually they were situated either inside the production zones or near the frontier, at the forefront of protecting the access to the Storehouse. Changing the state borders led to the search for a new site ensuring that the position of the capital with respect to the three fundamental elements would remain the same. If the borders did not undergo changes, the geographical location of imperial capitals was stable; sometimes, however, they migrate, in a very conservative way, within the boundaries of a single strategically important region.

Cornish illustrates his theory with numerous historical examples. Thus, most of the capitals of India were located in the Delhi area, a vulnerable northwestern region which conquerors from Central Asia and Afghanistan frequently used as the gateway to invade India. The Indian capitals often migrated within this strategically important region but did not leave it, since doing so would have greatly increased the risk of the country's being conquered.

Likewise, nearly all of the capitals of China were sited in the north, where the main threat to the security of the empire, nomadic invasions, was particularly high. Migrations of the capitals were confined to a small northern region, while "the rice bowl of China" – the rice-producing areas – was centered south of Beijing, in the plains between the Huang He and the Yangtze rivers.[11] Following the same patterns, the location of Ctesiphon, the capital of Persia, reflected the western orientation of the country while providing a connection between Persia's demographic center with the Mesopotamian Delta, which served as the granary of the empire. Another example involves the Roman Empire, where the throne was moved from Rome to Byzantium. Cornish attributes this move to the new, eastern orientation of the empire, as well as to the need to ensure protection of this vulnerable area from the barbarians.[12] It might be added that with their southern border constantly threatened by the Persians and by the Greeks, and finding their northern enemies far less formidable, the Armenian kings entrenched themselves strongly in the south by siting most of their capitals there. Furthermore, the cases of the Austro-Hungarian, British, French, and Inca Empires, according to Cornish, reveal similar trends in placing their forward capitals.[13]

In his treatise entitled *A Study of History*, in the section studying "universal states," Toynbee formulates a principle providing that both the siting of a new capital and the direction of the shifts in political power essentially depended on who the builders of the empire were – alien invaders, barbarians, marchmen, or metropolitan inhabitants[14] The litmus test of his classification is the origin of ruling dynasties that built capital cities of *universal empires*. Toynbee points out that the dynasties of foreign extraction sited a capital city in near proximity to their original point of invasion to facilitate a reinforcement of men and a replenishment of food supplies. He substantiates his thesis with the examples of the capitals of barbarian dynasties in north China, those of the Arab and Greek conquerors in the Middle East (Damascus and Antioch, to be precise) and the Parthians in Babylonia; and the capital of the Hyksos in Egypt.[15] Toynbee further develops and details this theory in his later book, reaching conclusions similar in many ways to those made by Cornish.

Relying on the motives that led to the foundation of a capital, Toynbee also proposes an alternative classification of capital cities, wherein capitals are distinguished by the motives leading to their establishment: geographical convenience, considerations of prestige, and strategic reasons.[16] This classification, however, does not seem to be sufficiently accurate and logical. For example, considerations of convenience include excessively numerous and sometimes conflicting factors, both economic and political in nature. "Capitals of prestige," as described by Toynbee, encompass cities whose sacredness and significance transcended the borders of a specific state and specific time, cities that played a unique and special role in the history of their state, and cities that retained their capital status merely by force of historical habit, e.g., Rome of the late Empire.

Overall, both Cornish and Toynbee, in a very informative, colorful, and interesting way, illustrate and detail the principles that they believe to be crucial for understanding the subject. Both present their concepts not as normative descriptions, but rather, empirical laws of capital city relocation and capital city functioning. However, real historical geography has many cases that do not confirm their principles, and the universality of their analytical schemes is not always convincing. For example, while Spain undoubtedly meets the definition of a "great power," the central location of its capital, Madrid, refutes the universality of the concept of a forward capital. Sometimes the principles proposed by Toynbee sink in the details that do not even support his generalizations. It was in part for these reasons that the well-known Indian sociologist G.S. Ghurye strongly criticized Toynbee's analysis of the migration of India's capitals.[17]

Interestingly enough, the empirical laws Toynbee discovered did not prevent him from making two unsuccessful predictions on capital city relocations. Thus, in 1935 he claimed that in accordance with these laws, the capital of China would never be returned to Beijing.[18] In the period between the two world wars, China's capital was located in Nanjing; however, after the communists came to power in 1949, it was safely moved back to Beijing. In another instance, during the Greek-Turkish war of 1919–1922, Toynbee, who then was serving at the British Foreign and Commonwealth Office, predicted the relocation of the Turkish capital to Izmir. In fairness to him, it

58 *Capital city relocation experience*

should be admitted that at that time he had not yet completed formulating his laws of capital relocation.

The direction of imperial capitals relocation is determined not as much by who founded the empire, but rather, by general direction of the expansion and the need to consolidate territorial gains, or, on the contrary, by territorial vulnerability and the need to locate a firmer social and political base, loyal and committed to the existing governance system. Transferring capitals in the empires was driven by the *logic of empire-building*, and within this logic one can distinguish several distinct objectives.

The first logic is the logic of absorption and incorporation, represented by imperial states in the phase of stability and military expansion. To facilitate the military command process, supply of the troops, and communication system, these states often moved their capital closer to the frontier, to the forefront of their conquest and expansion.

An example of this type of logic is Prussia, which in 1648, after the Thirty Year's War, moved its capital from Königsberg to Berlin, in parallel with its expansion westward.

The first capital of the Norwegian kingdom was located in Trondheim, in the center of the historical ecumene of the Vikings, north of Sognefjord. However, when the Vikings began their penetration into the south, conquering the British Isles and Normandy, Trondheim became too distant from the targets of the conquest, and the capital was transferred to Bergen, which was much closer both to the these targets and to the theater of military operations.[19]

In 77 BC the Armenian king Tigranes the Great moved the capital from Artashat (Artaxata) in the east to a newly founded city of Tigranakert (Tigranocerta) located in the southernmost region of Armenia, close to the border with Mesopotamia, into which his kingdom was expanding. He forcibly resettled residents of the Greek cities and other frontier areas to the new capital.[20]

This capital relocation strategy, illustrated by the above examples, was described by Ibn Khaldun (1332–1406), an Arab historian and sociologist. Exploring the anatomy of political power, he wrote in his fundamental treatise *An Introduction to History*:

> Each nation must have a home, (a place) . . . from which the realm took its origin. When the realm expands and its influence grows, it is inevitable that the seat of government be amidst the provinces belonging to the dynasty, because it is a sort of center for the whole area. Thus, the (new seat of government) is remote from the site of the former seat of government.[21]

A more radical, albeit quite common form of the same strategy, is the *transfer of a capital city directly to the territory of the recently annexed states*, not yet fully integrated into the empire and still alien to it, whether ethnically, religiously, or both. The type of capital cities created by such a relocation may be termed as *incorporated capitals*.

King David moved his throne to Jerusalem, situated on the land that had been recently seized from the Jebusites.

In 762 the Arabs shifted their capital to Baghdad, the area that had previously belonged to the Persian Empire and was located not far from Ctesiphon, the summer residence of the Persian *shahs*.

Expanding to the west, the Ottoman Turks were also transferring their capitals. Since around 1300 their first capital was Yenişehir; then they moved from Yenişehir to Bursa (1335–1363) and then to Adrianople, Thrace, in 1363, renaming it to Edirne; and later to Constantinople, which after the fall of the Byzantine Empire, became Istanbul.[22]

As the Persian Empire was growing westward, the *shahs* often founded new capitals on the territories recently taken from the conquered peoples. The list included Ecbatana, the former capital of Media; Susa, the former capital of Elam; and Ctesiphon, the former capital of Parthia and Babylonia. These relocations were respectively effectuated by the Achaemenids – in 550 BC and 521 BC – and the Sassanids in 227 AD (notably, the capital of Parthia was seized in 224 AD). Perhaps, the unusual mobility of the ancient Persian capitals should be attributed to the nomadic past of the Persians.

The Parthian capitals were also moved east to west: from Nisa, located on the territory of present Turkmenistan, to Dara; then, in 216 BC, to Gekatompil, eventually renamed to Mitridatkert; thereafter, in the middle of the first century BC, to Ecbatana, and finally, in the middle of the first century AD, to Ctesiphon. Enlarging their territorial possessions, the Yuezhi, the founders of the Kushan Empire, transferred their capital from Linshi, located near modern Dushanbe, to Kushania in Sogdia; then to Bagram, a district of modern Kabul; and then, for a short period of time, to Taxila in the northwestern part of modern Pakistan. In the heyday of the Kushan Empire, its capital was Purushapura, situated on the territory of modern Indian State of Peshawar.

Alexander the Great followed a similar logic. According to the testimonies of the ancients, he planned to site a future capital of his Hellenistic state in Babylon, thereby seeking to consolidate his territorial acquisitions and integrate the East into the Macedonian state.[23] This plan probably reflected both the influence and strength of the view presenting Babylon as the axis of the world, a widely accepted concept in the ancient East.

Political reorganization of the Mongol Empire pursued the same objectives. Kublai Khan, grandson of Genghis Khan, moved his throne from Karakorum to Beijing in China, thus integrating this huge territory into his empire and absorbing China's population, culture, and state administration technologies. At a later time, the Manchus, after they had conquered China, followed the example of the Mongols and moved their capital from Mukden (Snenyang) to Beijing.

Another example illustrating this political power technique involves the Empire of Turan. In 1369 Tamerlane moved its capital to Samarkand,

60 *Capital city relocation experience*

located on the newly conquered land that had been previously dominated by the Persians, Khwarezmians, Kara Khitans, and Turkish Karakhanids. Prior to Tamerlane, in 1212, the Khwarezmians had done the same, and after defeating the Kara Khitans, transferred their capital city from Gurganj (Urgench) to Samarkand.

In 969 AD, the Fatimids (909–1171) conquered Egypt and built a new capital of Cairo far from their ancestral lands while in 1170 the Almohads (1121–1269) transferred the seat of the caliphate to Sevilla. Thereafter, the Berberian Arab empires of North Africa, which absorbed both the Fatimid Caliphate and the Almohad Caliphate, also sited their capitals far away from their Algerian or Tunisian homeland.

In 1161 the Afghan conquerors Ghaznavids moved the capital from Ghazni in southern Afghanistan to Lahore, located in the Indus Valley, on the territory of modern Pakistan.

In 1485 Hungarian king Matthias Corvinus captured Vienna and made the city his capital.

In 1712 Russia's Peter the Great transferred the capital of Russia to Saint-Petersburg, sited on the territory seized from Sweden, an act that by nine years predated the official recognition of the annexation of this land.[24] In the tenth century, the Russian Prince Svyatoslav, who had defeated the Khazars, was entertaining the idea of turning Preslav (Pereyaslavets), the old capital of the Bulgarian khans on the Danube, into a new Russian capital. In the letter to his mother, Princess Olga, he described his plans as follows: "I do not care to remain in Kiev, but should prefer to live in Pereyaslavets on the Danube, since that is the centre of my realm, where all riches are concentrated; gold, silks, wine, and various fruits from Greece, silver and horses from Hungary and Bohemia, and from Rus' furs, wax, honey, and slaves."[25]

Following the same strategy, in 1832 Said bin Sultan moved the throne of the Sultanate of Muscat and Oman thousands of kilometers away to East Africa's Zanzibar, which had been colonized by the Omani Arabs.[26]

Following his vision of Great Britain's future as represented in his novel *Tancred*, the British Prime Minister Benjamin Disraeli insisted on transferring the capital of the British Empire from London to Delhi and strongly recommended that the Queen and the entire imperial administration also move there. The new location was meant to reflect the new nature of the state as the true world capital and underscore the special role that the East was playing in its imperial structure and political design.

Similarly, the program of many Russian imperial ideologists and pan-Slavists called for the transfer of the capital of the Russian Empire from Saint-Petersburg to Istanbul. According to them, Russia as the rightful heir of the legacy of the Byzantine Empire had to revive Constantinople as the capital of this empire. In the nineteenth century, Fyodor Tyutchev, a poet and diplomat, and Nikolai Danilevsky, a historian, emphasized the need in consolidating Russian conquests and Russian Orthodox identity in the southern part of the Black Sea and advocated the unification of the Slavic peoples under the Russian emperor. Notably, the plan to relocate the throne to Constantinople had been formulated earlier, in the eighteenth century, by Catherine the Great.[27]

Friedrich Ludwig Jahn (1778–1852), a German nationalist writer, claimed that the geographical position of Vienna made it not very suitable for the role as the capital of a vast empire. "Vienna, which is one of the causes of the decay of Austria, is not a central point to the provinces of the empire."[28] He believed that the capital of the Austrian Empire would be much better sited in Belgrade or Semlin, that is, in Serbia or Poland. The formation of one federal empire from these provinces could be carried out more effectively if it were accompanied by the change of the capital city.

In "A Secret Plan of Government" produced in 1798 by Honda Toshiaki, a prominent political economist and a polymath, had a provision to move the capital city of Japan to Kamchatka belonging to Russia to colonize the northern territories, to break away the isolation and to develop an empire. Although these daring, fanciful plans never became a reality and appear to be historical curiosities, the proposal of Disraeli, the intentions of Catherine the Great, as well as the ideas of Jahn were quite consistent with the capital siting concepts typical of many strategies of empire-building.

The state-building strategy presented in the above examples and involving capital city relocation to the newly conquered territories was formulated as early as by Niccolo Machiavelli, who wrote in his treatise *The Prince*:

> When states are acquired in a country with a different language, different customs and different institutions, then there are problems; great good fortune and great abilities are required in order to keep such states. One of the best and most efficacious solutions would be for those who acquire them to go and live there. This would make their possession more secure and lasting; and this is what the Turks have done with Greece: even if they had used every other method of keeping hold of that state, they could not have held onto it without going to live there.[29]

He proceeds, noting general governance considerations behind this strategy.

> In addition, the province is not looted by one's officials; and one's subjects are happy to have immediate recourse to their prince; consequently, those who wish their prince well have more reason to love him, and those who do not wish him well, more reason to fear him. Any potential external aggressor will think twice, for he who lives there can only be dislodged with extreme difficulty.[30]

Associated with *high risks*, sometimes this tactic of empire-building led to vulnerability of the empires having a capital city of this sort. For example, to build a new seat of empire on alien lands, the Persians had to leave their stronghold in the mountains and descend to the valleys, a move that left their ancestral lands unprotected and ultimately resulted in their loss. The legend has it that as early as the sixth century BC, Cyrus the Great warned the future Persian *shahs* of this danger.[31] The history of both Greek Bactria and Parthia reveals the same pattern of losing the original land base due to imperial expansion.

Similar strategies – at least in the form of political statements and slogans – can be seen in the modern world. Today's radical Islamists of the Mursi-led Muslim Brotherhood that recently were in power in Egypt dream of restoring the Arab Caliphate (of the United Arab States). They envision Jerusalem as the capital of this new political entity and believe that siting the capital in Jerusalem will allow the caliphate to absorb the entire territory of Israel.[32] Another example worth mentioning in this regard entails the political programs of radical Albanian nationalists with their plans of creating Greater Albania on the territory of Kosovo, Macedonia, Serbia, and Montenegro. The maps of Greater Albania show Skopje, capital of Macedonia, as the capital of the united pan-Albanian state.

Driven by the unfavorable political climate in the empire, the opposite type of logic led to the establishment of a *retreat capital*.

Under the onslaught of the Muslims, the capital of the Khazar Khaganate was gradually shifting from the south to the north, to the safe haven of the regions far away from the southern frontier. First, it was moved from the original capital of Balanjar, situated in a dangerous proximity to the border, then to Samandar, in the coastal area of Dagestan, and therefrom to Atil (Khamlij), located in the Volga River delta, just above the modern Russian city of Astrakhan.

Around the same time, under the onslaught of the Muslims advancing from the seacoast, the capital of the Kingdom of Axum, precursor of today's Ethiopia, began to shift from the coastal region to the inland. Once a rival of the Byzantine Empire, this Christian state even developed some sort of special tactic of guerilla war against the far superior forces of the enemies, whereby it was constantly moving its capital around the country. It was not until the end of the nineteenth century that, with the foundation of Addis Ababa in the far south, at the maximum distance from the coast, the state finally stabilized.[33]

The 1126 Mongol invasion of China triggered the relocation of the throne from Kaifeng to Lin'an (presently Hangzhou). This move marked the beginning of the Southern Song Dynasty.

In the fifteenth through sixteenth centuries, yielding to the advance of the Siamese forces, the rulers of Cambodia were moving their capital southwest, to the inland—from Angkor Thom, destroyed by the Siamese, to Phnom Penh, therefrom to Longvek and Udong and then, at the end of the nineteenth century, back to Phnom Penh.

Similarly, under the onslaught of Dai Viet, a Vietnamese state that had recently freed itself from the yoke of China, the capitals of the Hindu Kingdom of Champa, located in the central and southern regions of Vietnam was gradually relocating southward. From the northern city of Hue, which eventually became the capital of Vietnam, the seat of the kingdom was successively transferred to My Son, Indrapura, Vijaya, and a number of other cities until it finally reached Cha Ban, the last site of the Champa Kingdom.

Under the offensive of both the Hindus and the Tamil Muslims coming from the north, the capital of the Buddhist Sri Lanka was shifted to the south. The main goal pursued by the Sinhalese was to preserve the sacred relic of the Buddha's Tooth kept in the capital city.

In 1563 King Setthathirat, ruler of Lan Xang, a country that was the predecessor of present-day Laos, moved his throne from Luang Prabang to Vientiane, fearing an advance of the Burmese from the north.

In the eighteenth century, pressured by the advance of the Afghan troops, the capital of Persia was relocated. After the liberation from the control of the Safavid Dynasty, the Afghans attempted to reign in Persia and, seizing one city after another, even established an Afghan dynasty in the country. As a result, the throne was moved from the centrally located Isfahan, where it had been since 1598, to Shiraz in the south (1766–1791) and then to the safe haven of Tehran, near the Caspian Sea. The Tehran area was primarily inhabited by the Turkic peoples, which was an additional factor in winning the loyalty of this area to the Qajar Dynasty, Turkic in origin (See Table 5).

In the fifteenth century, pressured by the expansion of the Ottoman Empire, the capital of Montenegro was transferred from Žabljak to the better fortified town of Obod and therefrom to Cetinje. By the same token, due to the expansion of the Ottoman Empire in the early sixteenth century, the capital of Hungary was moved from Buda to Pozsony (present-day Bratislava, Slovakia).

This defensive logic is comparable with some capital city transfers in Poland, effectuated to strengthen its defense capability against the aggression of German principalities.[34]

Another fairly common principle of capital city siting, characteristic both of empires and despotic states, was a search for *more reliable and loyal centers of state power*. Empire-builders sought to consolidate their authority by gaining support of the most loyal region in the country. The task of a new capital city was to neutralize or weaken the influence of hostile or competing social and religious clans, factions, families, and elites. This logic drove the transfer of the capital of the Arab Caliphate from Medina to Kufa in 657. At that time, during the civil war, Kufa was the only city supporting Ali, who was fighting against the rebels.[35] Likewise, in Japan, the objective to secure support of the area most loyal to the ruler led to the relocation of the throne from Nara to Nagaoka.[36]

Loyalty to the metropole was an important criterion for capital city siting in colonies or dependencies. Furthermore, geographical proximity to the metropole constituted an additional favorable factor in the siting process.

After Russia had conquered Finland from Sweden, the capital was moved from Turku to Helsinki. Because anti-Turkish sentiment was widespread among the Romanian *boyars*, i.e., aristocrats, in the old capital of Târgoviște, and due to the proximity of Bucharest to the Ottoman Porte, the capital was transferred to Bucharest. Norway's increasing dependence on Denmark shifted the center of the country's political life to Christiania (Oslo), and the city's proximity to Copenhagen played a decisive role in this process. In the Hellenistic period, the Greek conquerors of Egypt moved the capital from Thebes to Alexandria. In 1887 the Japanese relocated the seat of the administration of Taiwan from Tainan to Taipei because the latter was located closer to the metropole in Japan.[37]

In sum, it may be said that there existed two most common tactics of imperial capital siting, the one contrary to the other. The first tactic entailed a search for a more loyal base for building a capital city in a period of domestic political instability, while the second one was aimed at the siting of a capital city in a potentially separatist area, least loyal to the empire, in a period of stability. In both cases, military and strategic considerations played the decisive role in the process.

Other important factors included the proximity of food supplies, sources of manpower reinforcement, and transport systems. In the empires that were expanding and seeking to annex new territories, capital cities were usually sited *on the forefront* of the expansion, ensuring an effective mobilization of military resources for the use on the border and beyond.

From Rome to Constantinople: reasons

Given the tremendous and unique influence exercised by the Roman Empire both on the formation of the European urban system and the nature and logic of the European imagination, it is appropriate to examine, in a separate section, the specifics of the Roman metropolitan life and analyze the reasons leading to the *transfer of the capital from Rome to Constantinople*.

Rome was the first in Europe to discover the idea of centrality, that is, a state's concentration in a single city, and this idea has defined certain features of the entire European history. While the capitals of Persia, the most powerful empire of the ancient East, were often moved, the stable capital city location was a major characteristic of the Roman state. Playing with the words *urbis* and *orbis*, Roman poets and politicians sometimes equated a city to the world, and in the mind of numerous notable personalities and ideologists, Rome was synonymous of the whole state. The City was so central to the identity of the empire that many perceived the fall of this city as the demise of the entire state, although in actuality the Roman Empire did not vanish, but rather, just shifted its center of gravity. In retrospect, it would be accurate to say that Rome failed to resolve the contradiction between the city and the citizenship and perished, unable to handle this strategic dissonance.

Transferring the throne from Rome to Constantinople, Constantine the Great was driven by weaknesses of the former and *military and strategic strengths* of the latter, which was less vulnerable to the attacks of the invaders and situated deep in the interior. Indeed, compared to Rome, Constantinople had significant and obvious advantages both in terms of defense capabilities and topography, which was subsequently proved in the course of many military campaigns.[38]

Centuries earlier Rome had enjoyed the advantages of being located on the Apennine Peninsula, which facilitated military operations on land. In the course of time, however, these advantages became less obvious as the Roman state developed maritime power, started sea wars against Carthage, and gradually conquered the entire Mediterranean basin. The control over the mouth of the Tiber River and the adjacent areas ensured both a success in land military operations and a stable delivery of food supplies from Central Italy.

However, over the centuries, this location became less convenient. First, with the development of trade and new technologies, marine vessels grew bigger in size; second, the Tiber shoaled, and its waterway was heavily silted up. As a result, navigation of larger warships and merchant vessels was no longer possible. To transport goods to Rome, suppliers had to reload them on smaller boats and barges, which highly increased the total cost of the goods. The artificial harbor built on the Tiber did not solve all the problems completely.

When the entire Mediterranean perimeter fell under the direct or indirect control of Rome, the main resources of the empire had already been concentrated not on the Apennine Peninsula, but rather, in the Levant, which encompassed Egypt, Syria, and Asia Minor, and which became the principal industrial and commercial engine of the empire. *However, these three key regions were located much closer to Constantinople than to Rome.*

Much earlier, Julius Caesar and Octavian Augustus had already been contemplating building a new capital in the East. During the visit of Cleopatra to Rome, rumors of the capital transfer to Alexandria began to circulate around Rome, and Troy was seen as another possible candidate for the new capital. These two cities provided control over the Aegean Sea and the Dardanelles, which were the key transit points on the way from Europe to Asia. By the time Constantine assumed the throne, the main route from Europe to Asia had already shifted to the Bosporus, thus making Byzantium an important hub between the Aegean and the Black Sea. Another reason why Byzantium was preferable to Alexandria was that the former had a massive natural harbor, Golden Horn, protecting it on both sides. Thus, the topography of the city was highly favorable for both the deployment of the fleet and the anchoring of merchant vessels, giving the area a tremendous advantage in resisting the attacks of the barbarians.[39]

It should be also noted that contrary to some present-day views, by the time the new capital was established, the economic advantages of Byzantium had already diminished to some degree. When the Greek city-states dominated the region, Byzantium was an extremely important trade center, linking these cities with their colonies on the north coast of the Black Sea.

Supplying Greece with grain, these colonies served as a major market for Greek industrial and artisanal products. According to some historians, it was the trade with the Black Sea region that triggered the economic revolution in Greece, which ultimately led to the transition from the agrarian economy to the industrial and commercial economy.

At the time the new capital was founded, this *grain route* had already been in decline, and eventually, as a result of the Goths' invasion into what is now Ukraine, ceased to exist. Afterward, Byzantium was supplied with grain from Egypt and other areas that were supplying Rome itself. As to the other economic advantages Byzantium presumably had, they were quite ephemeral.

Roman historians and writers talked about the burden of the second, "parasitic capital" imposed on the empire: Constantinople had to be fed with "bread and circuses" at a very unfavorable moment, when the empire's cost of maintaining the military dramatically increased. The capital transfer coincided with an immense economic crisis that hit the Roman Empire in the fourth century. All of this indicates that the main and only motives for moving the capital were military advantages of Constantinople, as well as the new strategy of the state, rather than economic causes or reasons related to the change of religion.

This is not to say, however, that the new capital did not have any other significant advantages. This area did have a certain volume of internal resources to ensure provision of food supplies and various communication needs, functioning as a natural connection link between different regions. Jean Gottmann notes in this regard:

> The capital is not only the hinge between the country it governs and the outside, but a pluralistic hinge, articulating the various sections, networks, and groups of interest within the territory. Constantinople was to be a hinge between Europe and Asia, Mediterranean and Pont, Romans and Greeks, land and sea power. That was probably why it remained for so long a great capital under very different regimes.[40]

It is interesting to point out that *de facto* Rome had lost its status as the capital long before the relocation, when the actual center of the empire shifted towards the Balkans and Asia Minor. As early as the reign of Diocletian (293–305), the empire had been divided into four prefectures with administrative centers in Trevorum (Trier), Antioch, Mediolanum (Milan), and Nicomedia. This system of government became known as the *tetrarchy*. Being the head of the tetrarchy, Diocletian moved his throne to Nicomedia in Asia Minor; thus, Constantine merely continued the reform initiated by his predecessor, extending its vector east of Rome. It should be noted, however, that neither the siting of the new capital nor the relocation path was a predetermined matter, and prior to the foundation of Constantinople, Constantine had tried many other sites, successively transferring his residence to Trevorum, Mediolanum, Sirmium, and Serdica (Sofia). Thus, over the span of one century, the empire had a roving capital city, the situation approximating the one in the Holy Roman Empire.[41]

Constantinople did not become the capital immediately after Rome; even after the foundation of the former, it was still unclear whether it would remain the long-term capital of the empire. With the demise of Constantine the Great, Trevorum, which became the residence of his son, Constantine II, began to rise. Calling it *Roma Secunda*, the Romans rightly regarded it as their capital north of the Alps. Constantinople temporarily lost its status as the "second Rome," and under the reign of Juliane the Apostate, Constantine's nephew who attempted to revive the cult of pagan gods, the actual capital city of the empire became Antioch. By making his quest to the East, he apparently hoped to fulfill the dream of Alexander the Great, whom he identified himself with, and establish a new capital in Babylon (Ctesiphon). It was not until after Constantine's grandchildren ascended to the throne that Constantinople's status as the capital was restored, to be retained for centuries.

Disembedded capitals: despotic states of the ancient East

The so-called *disembedded capitals* constitute a distinct category of capital cities.

This term originated in the depths of archeology – more specifically, in publications related to excavation of the ancient cities of the New World, Mesoamerica (Monte Albán), in particular. Initially, it was mainly used to describe *a special type of administrative capitals located in some distance from major economic centers and excluded from direct economic activities and product exchange processes*. Subsequent excavations revealed, however, that Monte Albán was in fact a commercial center, supplying itself with agricultural products and, thus, did not meet this definition. Accordingly, archeologists rejected this term as unsuitable and abandoned its use in reference to administrative capitals of the Mesoamerican cultures.

Alexander H. Joffe, an American archeologist and expert on ancient Middle Eastern civilizations, has attempted to rehabilitate and to recycle this term by demonstrating its more accurate applicability to ancient and medieval capitals of Western Asia – Egypt, Assyria, Babylonia, and Arabia. He showed, among other things, how the newly emerged disembedded capitals of Mesopotamia and Egypt, created from scratch, developed into centers of power for the new elites and functioned as *institutional alternatives* to wandering capitals and provisional capitals.[42]

According to Joffe, the main purpose of disembedded capitals was to acquire competitive advantages in the internal factional struggle, incubate new elites, and consolidate state power.[43] It could be said that in contrast to the more common integration strategies, royal founders of disembedded capitals were pursuing *strategies of disintegration and alienation* from the existing centers of power.

68 *Capital city relocation experience*

To illustrate his thesis, Joffe gives three groups of examples from the history of Egypt, Mesopotamia, and Arabia, respectively.

1   The primary examples of disembedded capitals in Egypt are Memphis and Amarna (Akhenaten). Seeking to integrate the various lands along the Nile River, the rulers of Egypt developed a system of common rituals intended to adopt local deities into the official state religion. To secure a better access to trade routes and resources of Lower Egypt, the Upper Egyptian elites established Memphis in the north. Amarna was located between Memphis and Thebes and built by Akhenaten (1379–1362 BC), a pharaoh of the 18th Dynasty. Its foundation was triggered by the religious reform of Akhenaten, who had introduced a worship system centered on Aten, the Sun, and stressed the divine origin of the ruler. For the reform to take effect, it was necessary to isolate the new capital from the older generation of priests.
2   Capitals of the Akkadian Empire fall into the same category. In 2300 BC, the Akkadian ruler Sargon the Great moved his throne to the city of Agade. After Tukulti-Ninurta I, an Assyrian conqueror reigning from 1244 to 1208 BC, had destroyed and deserted Babylon, in fear of the revenge of the conservative part of his subjects, who believed that the destruction of Babylon was a sacrilege (the Assyrians revered the Babylonian gods), he moved the capital and the cult statue of the god Marduk to the newly built city of Kar-Tukulti-Ninurta, several kilometers away from the ancient Assur. Shortly thereafter, as a result of a plot organized by his outraged subjects, the king was imprisoned in his own palace and subsequently murdered.

    In the ninth century BC, another Assyrian ruler Ashurnasirpal II (reigned in 883–859 BC) moved his throne to Kalhu (Nimrud), a small and previously unknown city 65 kilometers north of the old capital. In the eighth century BC, Sargon II transferred the capital therefrom 20 kilometers northeast, to Dur-Sharrukin (Fortress of Sargon). After he had been killed during one of his military campaigns, his son, Sennacherib shifted the capital to the ancient city of Nineveh, located between Kalhu and Dur-Sharrukin.
3   The next group of disembedded capitals involves the Arab Caliphate and includes Baghdad, Raqqa, and Samarra. In 762 the Abbasid Caliph al-Mansur founded Baghdad to broaden the support of his reign. Unlike the Umayyads, the Abbasids were attempting to create a universal empire and integrate the Persians into it. To forestall tribal wars, Harun al-Rashid transferred his throne to the city of Raqqa in Syria. In 835 his son al-Mu'tasim founded Samarra. Deprived of the support of Baghdad, he relied on the army of Turkish slaves, as well as the doctrines of Mu'tazilism. The new disembedded capital was meant to become the stronghold of the new religious teaching and distance itself from commercial, cosmopolitan Baghdad.

Joffe provides yet other examples of disembedded capitals that emerged in this region. Speaking of their common features, he points to their short lifespan caused by the very nature of their origin.

> Because the legitimacy and efficacy of a capital were so closely tied to a particular individual or dynasty, successors often found it necessary to break away and recreate new capitals. With such an urban pattern in full play, disembedded capitals were often extremely short-lived and highly unstable, not to mention expensive to build and operate. . . . Only a developed urban society could shoulder the various costs involved but the option created conditions that necessitated more expensive and extractive policies which often undermined other processes . . . . [T]he needs of cities frequently run counter to those who comprised the society in them. In most cases it appears that disembedded capitals were short-term solutions and long-term burdens. Their instability and degrees of spatial and social artificiality are reflected in their ultimate fate, which minimally and almost invariably included the loss of status as capitals and, at the extreme, complete abandonment.[44]

The concept of the disembedded capital is quite interesting and provides a valuable synthesis of the experience of Western Asian civilizations. Nonetheless, Joffe's explanation of the phenomenon is inconclusive, and this concept requires important qualifications.

The examples Joffe gives are somewhat contradictory. Noting that a short lifespan was a common feature shared by all disembedded capitals, he puts into this category the cities of Memphis and Baghdad, each of which served as the capital of Egypt and the Arab states, respectively, for centuries. Although he does state that in some cases disembedded capitals could be *reembedded* into the social and economic system of the country, both Memphis and Baghdad are still clearly distinguishable from the rest of his examples not only by virtue of being long-standing capitals but also by virtue of having a completely different task assigned to them. This task was to create a new format of the state as opposed to isolating the old elites. In the case of Memphis, this was intended to be achieved by integrating Upper and Lower Egypt, while in the case of Baghdad, by integrating new cultures and newly acquired lands, most notably Persia, under the authority of the Abbasids.

Furthermore, Joffe unreasonably limits the region where disembedded capitals emerged to Western Asia. Interestingly, however, most of the cases he describes involve political regimes situated far beyond the region. Although according to Joffe, the type of capitals in question was specific to despotic states, prevalent in the ancient East, examples of these capitals may be found in the history of China, Russia, and the Middle East. In ancient China, disembedded capitals were represented by the new capital of the Qin State, Xianyang, established by the vision of Shan Yang (390–338 BC), a famous philosopher of the Legist School. The city faced the task of weakening the influence of the old clan elites. After King Zheng of Qin unified the Chinese states under his control and proclaimed himself Emperor Qin Shi Huang, the city of Xianyang became the capital of the new empire. In Russia an example of a disembedded capital was Alexandrov Kremlin, the sixteenth century *oprichnina* stronghold of Ivan the Terrible. In Parthia the city of Vologesocerta (Valashabad) functioned as a very short-term disembedded capital founded to eliminate the influence of the Hellenized elites of the state.

To some extent, Joffe dilutes the very concept of a disembedded city, drawing parallels between it and some modern designed capitals, notably Washington D.C. Apparently, the basis of the comparison is that like some disembedded capitals, these capitals were built from scratch and, in a sense, were disembedded from the economic life of their countries and distanced from their economic centers. The main difference between disembedded capitals and modern designed capitals, according to Joffe, is that disembedded capitals were "designed as tools of factional competition" *while modern designed capitals were designed to balance different factions and political forces*.[45] However, these two types of capitals also have other equally important differences, the most significant of them being the methods of their creation and the nature of the identity they epitomized.

Many of the above enumerated disembedded capitals were constructed in a way typical for the despotic states of the East (the German historian Karl A. Wittvogel calls them "hydraulic civilizations") – using the labor of numerous foreign slaves.

Furthermore, while the modern capitals attempted to reflect identities of various ethnic and other groups, the new capitals of the despotic states, by contrast, sought to diminish or neutralize the old historical and particularistic identities. Very often disembedded capitals tried to win greater loyalty by destroying local identities or by incorporating sacred symbols of the subdued or conquered states. Another common tool used by despotic rulers was their special demographic policy of massive resettlements of particularly recalcitrant tribes and residents of other kingdoms. This tactic was followed by Emperor Qin Shi Huang, who drove members of the most prominent families from the newly conquered states to his capital Xianyang.[46] Likewise, Armenia's Tigranes the Great resettled numerous Greeks living in the kingdom and inhabitants of the areas he had conquered to Tigranakert (Tigranocerta), his new capital.[47]

Thus, despotic regimes built disembedded capitals mainly to isolate themselves from most influential political and religious elites, as well as to create new forms of loyalty required of the state subjects.

Interestingly enough, the process of relocation to such a capital was often accompanied by both fundamental religious reforms and the rise of heterorthodox and heretical movements. The Egyptian cult of the Sun, the construction of the new Babylon in Assyria, and the ideas of Mu'tazilism in the Umayyad Caliphate led to the formation of the new forms of power legitimation for the rulers and marginalized the old elites of the old political and religious centers. These elites – the Theban priesthood, old clan nobility of the conquered Chinese states, the Persian elite (aristocracy of Khorasan) in the court of the Abbasids, and major *boyar* families of Russia – were to be replaced by the new servicemen elites, which built from scratch a base of loyalty to the new regime. In the cases where the relocation to a new capital was not associated with religious reforms, it was often meant to emancipate the regime from undesired cultural influences and use new cultural grounds to create new elites. For example, by moving his throne to a new capital, Tigranes the Great sought to Hellenize his kingdom and do away with the influence of the Persian culture. Likewise, by building a new capital in Raqqa, Harun al-Rashid intended to emancipate the country from the influence of the Persian elites in Baghdad.

Most of the disembedded capital projects failed. The reason for their failure was the disproportionate scale of the goals (mostly tactical ones) to the tools used by the rulers to achieve these goals. Tactical tricks and moves of the rulers were made by using strategic and very expensive instruments.

The concept of a disembedded capital is extremely important as a capital-building strategy different from the capital city model of universal empires. Erecting a new capital gave a despotic ruler an opportunity to establish a new base of loyalty, to develop his own special identity and language of symbols, and to surround political power with an atmosphere of mystery and secrecy. Certainly, it is not always easy to draw a clear distinction between the strategies used by empires and those used by despotic states. Thus, Tigranes the Great built his capital on the far edge of his territories to ensure control over the conquered lands in accordance with the above imperial strategies. At the same time, it was established as a disembedded capital with the use of despotic methods and tools. Nonetheless, in most cases the difference between strategies of despotic states and those of empires was quite obvious: The former were based on domestic political considerations whereas the latter were centered on foreign policy considerations.

The list of examples set forth by Joffe may be supplemented with several more examples of the despotic states of the East, illustrating how unfavorable the results of such relocation projects could be.

In Japan the 794 transfer of the capital to Kyoto was preceded by 25 unsuccessful attempts. In 645 the emperor's residence was shifted from Asuka, to the seaport of Naniwa, near Osaka. Seven years later, however, it was moved back to Asuka since temples, monasteries, and influential clans had refused to relocate. In 667 the seat of the empire was transferred to Otsu, only to be returned to its previous location. In 710 it moved to Nara, modeled after the then capital of China, Chang'an (presently Xi'an). However, the extraordinary influence of the Buddhist monasteries and clans in Nara destabilized the position of the emperor. To strengthen his loyalty base, in 784 Emperor Kanmu erected a new capital in Nagaoka, Yamashiro region, which was his mother's native area, but the assassination of the city's chief builder was deemed a bad omen. As a result, despite the ten years of hard

72 Capital city relocation experience

work (784–794) and the expenses equal to the whole country's annual budget, the project was abandoned.[48] Finally, with the financial support of the Chinese immigrant weavers, the capital was moved to Kyoto. To neutralize the monastic influence, only a few of the monasteries were permitted to relocate to the new capital.[49]

Subsequent periods of Japanese history saw similarly problematic and ill-considered capital city relocations. The epic *Heike Monogatari* (*The Tale of the Heike*) contains an important narrative describing the unsuccessful transfer of the capital from Kyoto to Fukuhara undertaken in the twelfth century by Lord Kiyomori, the head of the Taira (Heike) clan at the peak of its prosperity and glory. Bypassing the legitimate heir, he enthroned his minor grandson and attempted to put an end to the influence of the opposition Buddhist clergy in the old capital of Kyoto. Furthermore, Fukuhara was located on the lands owned by the Taira clan, and the relocation was intended not just to provide Kiyomori with a stronger loyalty base but also to generate lucrative profits from leasing out the Taira lands. The epic represents the moving of the throne to Fukuhara as yet another link in the chain of crimes committed by Kiyomori:

> Most splendid and auspicious was the Ancient Capital [of Kyoto] . . . . But now few wagons plough their way over the deserted roads, and but an occasional passer-by is to be seen in some lowly equipage. The houses of the city that formerly jostled each other for room are now daily becoming fewer and more ruinous; broken up and made into rafts . . . and the furniture and possessions of their owners are piled up on boats and brought down to Fukuhara. Ah, how sad to see the Flower Capital thus turn into an expanse of rice fields.[50]

Within several weeks Kyoto was turned into a ghost city, scattered groups of paupers and vagrants eking out a meager existence on its wrecked streets. The temples and palaces were dismantled, most of the houses were untiled, and the income of monasteries plummeted. The aggrieved were petitioning for the return of the capital, and the popularity of the Taira clan began to decline. A few months after the beginning of this unsuccessful project, the throne was moved back to Kyoto.

Another interesting example of this kind is an attempt to transfer India's capital from Delhi to Daulatabad (also known as Devagiri), made at the beginning of the fourteenth century by Sultan Muhammad bin Tughluq. In the opinion of the sultan, Daulatabad had a number of obvious strategic advantages, lying roughly equidistant from Delhi, Gujarat, Lakhnauti, Telingana, and other important centers of medieval India. Striving to isolate the Hindus, who often provoked riots and uprisings in Delhi, as well as to strengthen both the Muslim presence and missionary activities in the south of the country, the sultan believed that the Muslim clergy would be able to convert huge masses of the Hindus living in the Delhi empire, especially the poor and the members of the lower castes. For this reason, among those who were required to move to the new capital, there were a lot of Islamic mystics, the most successful preachers of Islam at the time. Sultan Muhammad Salman Khan Tughluq also took a series of reasonable preparatory actions; thus, he built a broad road to Daulatabad, planted shady trees on both sides of the road, and established a regular postal service between Delhi and the new capital. Since the residents of Delhi did not wish to relocate, he ordered a forcible resettlement of the Muslim elites, *ulemas* (Islamic scholars), and civil servants. Since the relocation was carried out during the hot summer months, many people died on the way.[51]

This move greatly damaged the sultan's popularity. The Mongol invasions in the north and possible revolts of the Hindus put the country in a dangerous situation because now its capital was too remote from the northern regions. Realizing his mistake, the sultan initiated the transfer back to Delhi. Many of those who had survived the first relocation did not survive the second one. As a result of these events, Delhi fell into decay, losing its wealth and splendor. Although thereafter the sultan attracted new men of letters, merchants, and traders to the city, a substantial part of it remained desolated. Many Muslim graves at Daulatabad cemeteries keep the memory of these sad events alive.

A possible lesson to learn from the above examples is that even the unlimited power and resources of the despotic rulers were not always sufficient to compensate for the lack of a reliable strategy. While building disembedded capitals was tremendously costly, they tended to destabilize both the state political course and the very political regime, often remaining the capitals only for a very short period of time. As we will see below, some modern rulers have repeated these mistakes.

Notes

1 Rossman, V. "Misteria tsentra: Identichnost i organizatsia prostranstva v sovremennih i traditsionnih obschestvah," *Voprosy filosofii*, no. 2 (2008), 42–57.
2 Olsson, O. & Hansson, G. "Country Size and the Rule of Law: Resuscitating Montesquieu," *European Economic Review*, vol. 55, no. 5 (2011), 613–629.
3 Hsu, S. "From Pingcheng to Luoyang—Substantiation of the climatic cause for capital relocation of the Beiwei Dynasty," *Progress in Natural Sciences*, vol. 14, no. 8 (2004), 725–729.
4 Parker, G. *Power in Stone: Cities as Symbols of Empires* (London: Reaktion, 2014).
5 Turchin, P. "A Theory for Formation of Large Empires," *Journal of Global History*, vol. 4, no. 2 (July), 2009, 2–3.
6 Eisenstadt, S.N. & Shachar, A. *Society, Culture, and Urbanization* (Newbury Park: Sage, 1987), 132–134.
7 Karapetyants, A. "Kitaiskaia tsivilizatsiia kak alternative Sredizemnomorskoi," *Obschestvennie nauki i sovremennost*, no. 1 (2000), 133–134.
8 Ibid.
9 Grygiel, J. *Great Powers and Geopolitical Change* (Baltimore: John Hopkins University, 2006), 142–145.

74 Capital city relocation experience

10 Kuper, H. "The Language of Sites in the Politics of Space," *American Anthropologist*, vol. 3, no. 74 (1972), 416.
11 Cornish, V. *The Great Capitals: An Historical Geography* (London and New York: Methuen, 1923), 23.
12 Ibid., 46.
13 Interestingly, Baron de Montesquieu has made an observation about Paris that attests well to the idea of Cornish: "France's strength consists in the fact that the capital is closest to the weakest border. That makes her pay more attention to that which demands more, and enables her to send aid there more easily." Montesquieu, C. *My Thoughts (Mes Pensées)*. Translated, edited, and with an Introduction by Henry C. Clark (Indianapolis: Liberty Fund, 2012). Fragment [561]
14 Toynbee, A. *A Study of History: Abridgement of Volumes VII-X by D.C. Somervell* (New York & Oxford: Oxford University Press, 1987), pt. VI, ch. XXV.
15 According to world system theorists, this pattern of development often takes place in so-called "semiperipheral marcher states," where the older core cities lose dominance to semiperipheral cities due to the rising centrality of the former semiperiphery. The Akkadians, the Assyrians, the Persians, and the Islamic Caliphates are often cited as cases of semiperipheral marcher states.
16 Toynbee, A. "'Capital Cities: Their Distinctive Features' and 'Capital Cities: Melting-Pots and Powder-Kegs'." In: *Cities on the Move* (New York and London: Oxford University Press, 1970), 67–70.
17 Ghurye, G.S. *Cities and Civilization* (Bombay: Popular Prakashan, 1962), 182–186.
18 Kedourie, E. "Foreign Policy: A Practical Pursuit." In: *The Crossman Confessions and other Essays in Politics, History, and Religion* (London: Mansell, 1984), 34.
19 Tarkhov, S.A. "Perenosy stolits", *Geografia*, no. 5–6, 2007.
20 Mommsen T. *Istoria Rima*. vol. 3. Ot smerti Sully do bitvy pri Tapse. Translated by I. Masyukov (OGIZ: Moskva, 1941), 44.
21 Khaldun, I. *The Muqaddimah: An Introduction to History*. Translated by Franz Rosenthal (Princeton University Press, 1967), 4, 19.
22 Parker, G. *Power in Stone: Cities as Symbols of Empires* (London: Reaktion, 2014), 57; Toynbee, A. *A Study of History: Abridgement of Volumes VII-X by D.C. Somervell* (New York & Oxford: Oxford University Press, 1987), VI, XXV.
23 Boiy, T. *Late Achaemenid and Hellenistic Babylon* (New York: Peeters Publishers, 2004), 97.
24 Contrary to common belief, Saint-Petersburg did not rise on the uninhibited banks of the Neve, "a wave-swept shore, remote, forlorn" as the great Russian poet Alexander Pushkin described; rather, it was sited on the location of the Swedish fortress Nyenschatz (Nyenskans) and the town of Nyen that controlled the edge of the Swedish territory near the mouth of the Neva River. In 1610, after having taken control of the Neva River delta, the Swedes built a fortress here, reconstructed in 1644. In the middle of the seventeenth century, according to some estimates, the population of this area reached 2,000 people. Kotilaine, J.T. *Russia's Foreign Trade and Economic Expansion in the Seventeenth Century* (Leiden: Brill, 2005), 41. Note that as early as the fourteenth century, the Swedish fortress Landskrona was erected on these lands.
25 The Russian Primary Chronicle. *Laurentian Text*. Translated & edited by Samuel Cross and Olgerd P. Sherbowitz-Wetzor (Massachusetts: Cambridge, 1953), 86.
26 Plekhanov, S. *Reformator na trone* (Moscow: Mezhdunarodnie otnoshenia, 2003).
27 Rossman, V. *V poiskakh Chetvertogo Rima* (Moskva: Vysshaia shkola ekonomiki, 2014), 86–89.

28 Jahn, F.L. "An Essay on Capital Cities," In: *Essai sur les Moeurs, la Littérature, et la Nationalité des peuples de l'Allemagne* (Paris: J.B. Nichols & Son, 1832). The Gentleman's Magazine, vol. 103, (Jul-Dec), part 2 (1833), 228.
29 Machiavelli, N. *The Prince*. Translated by J.G. Nichols (London: Alma Classics, 2009), 7–8.
30 Ibid., 8.
31 Toynbee, A. *A Study of History: Abridgement of Volumes VII-X by D.C. Somervell* (New York & Oxford: Oxford University Press, 1987), VI, XXV.
32 In his informative and well-reasoned article, Daniel Pipes, an American historian and expert on the Middle East, explains that *by and large the idea of Jerusalem in Arab history has been politically motivated*, whereby the narrative of the religious significance of the city has been manufactured or adjusted to accommodate political ambitions of the Arab rulers. He points out that political campaigns of various Arab dynasties periodically led to a sharp rise of interest in Jerusalem, while during the periods of political hiatus when the city fell into decay and disrepair, this interest disappeared. Not even once is Jerusalem mentioned in the Qur'an or any Muslim prayers, nor did it play any role in the earthly life of Muhammad. Religious passions about Jerusalem flared in the Muslim world each time the city became politically important to the Muslims, whether it was in the Umayyad period, during the wars against the Crusaders, under the British administration, or during the so-called "occupation by Israel." For example, in the seventh century, confronted by the Mecca-based rebels, the Damascus-based Umayyad rulers strived to aggrandize Syria at the expense of Arabia, seeking to glorify Jerusalem, make it equal of Mecca, and possibly transform it into their administrative capital (Pipes, D. "The Muslim Claim to Jerusalem," *Middle East Quarterly*, September, 2001).
33 Horvath, R.J. "The Wandering Capitals of Ethiopia," *The Journal of African History*, vol. 10, no. 2 (1969), 205–206.
34 Tarkhov, S.A. "Perenosy stolits", *Geografia*, no. 5–6, 2007.
35 Hitti, P. *Capital Cities of Arab Islam* (Minneapolis: University of Minnesota Press, 1973). Many historians attribute idealistic or ideological motives to the actions of Ali, Muhammad's cousin and son-in-law, and claim that he sought to protect Mecca and Medina from the corrupt political and cosmopolitan influences or perhaps wished to preserve the integrity of both the language and way of life of Muhammad's time. According to this interpretation, giving political status to these cities would have inevitably undermined their status as sacred cities and the cradle of Islam. Notwithstanding this argument, considerations of loyalty appear to be a more plausible reason for the relocation. As it is known, neither Mecca nor Medina supported Ali in his military confrontation with the opposition. It is noteworthy that, probably following the example set by Ali, none of the Abbasid caliphs dared to use Mecca and Medina to pursue political goals (Carmichael, J. *The Shaping of the Arabs* (New York & London: Macmillan, 1967), 194).
36 Goethem, E. von. *Nagaoka: Japan's Forgotten Capital* (Leiden: Brill NV, 2008).
37 Wang, J. & Huang, S. "Contesting Taibei as the World City," *City*, vol. 13, no. 1 (2009), 103–104.
38 Dagron, G. *Naissance d'une capitale. Constantinople et ses institutions de 330 à 451* (Paris: Presses universitaires de France, 1974).
39 Dagron, G. *Naissance d'une capitale. Constantinople et ses institutions de 330 à 451* (Paris: Presses universitaires de France, 1974); Mango, C. "Constantinople: Capital of the Oikoumene?" Presented at *'Byzantium as Oecumene'* Conference, Athens, Greece 2001. Published by the *Institute for Byzantine Research*, Athens, 2005.
40 Tyrwhitt, J. & Gottmann, J., eds. "Capital Cities," *Ekistics*, vol. 50 (March/April) [Oslo, Warsaw, Rome, Tokyo, and Washington D.C., 1983], 89.

41 Mango, C. "Constantinople: Capital of the Oikoumene?" Presented at *'Byzantium as Oecumene'* Conference, Athens, Greece 2001. Published by the *Institute for Byzantine Research*, Athens, 2005.
42 Joffe, A. "Disembedded Capitals in Western Asian Perspective," *Society for Comparative Study of Society & History*, vol. 40, no. 3 (1998), 549–580.
43 Ibid., 543.
44 Ibid., 573.
45 Ibid., 574.
46 Lewis, M.E. *The Construction of Space in Early China* (New York: SUNY Press, 2006), 191.
47 Mommsen T. *Istoria Rima*. vol. 3. Ot smerti Sully do bitvy pri Tapse. Translated by I.Masyukov (Moskva: OGIZ, 1941), 44.
48 Toby, Ronald P. "Why Leave Nara? Kammu and the Transfer of the Capital," *Monumenta Nipponica*, vol. 40, no. 3 (Autumn, 1985), 338–340.
49 Southhall, A. *The City in Time and Space* (Cambridge: Cambridge University Press, 1998), 160–161.
50 Heike, Monogatari. *Transactions of the Asiatic Society of Japan*, vol. XLVI, Part II (Tokyo: Keiogijiki, Mita, 1918), 182.
51 Ernst, C. *Eternal Garden: Mysticism, History, and Politics at a South Asian Sufi Center* (Minneapolis: Lerner Publications, 2003), 111–114.

3 Capital city relocations and debates of this topic in different world regions

Generations of national capitals

It would be a mistake to view the selection of capital cities and their relocations separately from the international processes and to consider them to be only a result of domestic decision-making. International developments have always had a significant impact on the ways in which capital cities were understood and chosen. Therefore, it is important to distinguish several generations of capital cities that emerged as part and parcel of the cycles of formation of nations, nation-states, and nationalisms. It must be noted that membership in a particular generation of capital cities has greatly influenced the choice of urban iconographies, architectural styles, and urban solutions for the newly formed capital cities.

Conceptually, there were three main paths of nation-formation. Following the first path, nation-states emerged in England and France in the course of opposition to the Crown and to the Church. The second type of nation-states emerged when fragmented territories were brought together under one leading center. This path was characteristic for Netherlands, Switzerland, and Germany. The third type of nation-states emerged in opposition to the foreign princes and to foreign rule in general. In many cases following this path, the nation asserted itself not only against the foreign rule but also against other ethnic groups.[1] Most of the presently existing countries of the world have developed their nationhood in the course of the third type of development.

Remarkably, the nation-formation process in many countries represented the combination of two paths. For instance, the Italian nation asserted itself both against the foreign rule of the Austro-Hungarian Empire and against the fragmentation and separatist trends. In a similar vein, the American nation was formed in opposition to the British rule and to the separatist tendencies of southern US states. The Dutch nation has asserted itself against the Spanish domination in the course of the Eighty Years' War and against the trends of feudal fragmentation.

Under the first path of nation-formation, the selection of the new capital city was not a matter of great concern, and the seats of government were typically preserved in old capital cities.[2] On the other hand, under the second path, the choice of the new location was an essential element and the milestone in the formation of a nation. For instance, Germany did not have a permanent seat of power in the pre-modern period, and Berlin was by no means the only choice. Curiously, the concept of a new capital city was already contemplated in the nineteenth century long before national unification in the Bismarck era, when some prominent German nationalists and intellectuals pondered this issue. Friedrich Ludwig Jahn (1778–1852), a German nationalist writer, insisted that the new capital city of the united Germany should be situated near the Elbe River, in a district equally distant from Geneva and Memel and from Trieste and Copenhagen. Jahn attributed the idea of such a well-defended Prussian capital on the Elbe, the middle river of the north of Germany, to Frederick the Great. He proposed to name this new capital city Teutona.[3] In the Netherlands and in the United States the choice of the capital cities was an important part of the formation of a new nation. The 17 states of Netherlands and the 13 colonies in the US had identified a neutral place for this role. Amsterdam and in some measure Philadelphia remained loyal to the Spanish/Burgundian empire and to the British Crown respectively, and it made these cities unsuitable for the seat of government of these emerging nations.

Even more important the issue of a capital city was for the countries that have followed the third path. The majority of modern nations were formed in the course of the fight for independence against the British, French, Spanish, German, Ottoman, Austro-Hungarian, and Russian empires. The nationalisms in these newly-emerged nations were more ethnic and cultural rather than civic in nature. The establishment of the new seat of power was often a critical element in the identity formation of these new nations. Accordingly, in Italy and Greece the first capitals Turin and Nathplion were later replaced by Rome and Athens.

Chronologically, the following historical developments served as important milestones in the course of the new nations' formation. The establishment of the Westphalian system in 1648 has established the legal groundwork for the development of the concept of the modern territorial state that was defined by the national capital and its borders. It has replaced the pre-modern concepts of the royal seat of power and the frontier. The Dutch nation was forged at this period, gaining its independence from Spain in 1648 and establishing its capital in The Hague. The end of the Napoleonic wars and the formation of the Vienna system in 1815, the end of the First World War (1919) and the Second World War (1945) have determined the process of new states' and nations' formation and stimulated the emergence of new capital cities. Accordingly, several generations of capital cities were formed that were united by common themes, symbols, common elements of their nation-building plans, and their concepts of a capital city. The iconographies of these capital cities and their choice of heroes and monuments were influenced by the time period when they were selected.

After the Napoleonic wars in the nineteenth century, many new nation-states emerged, establishing their capitals in Brussels (1830), Bern (1848), Athens (1834), and Kragujevac (1818). After the Russian Empire conquered Finland from the Swedish empire, the Finnish capital Turku was transferred to Helsinki in 1812, closer to the new metropole.[4] Approximately at the same time, due to the demise of the Spanish dominance on the continent (1810–1826), Latin American countries gained independence, and some of them started to reconstruct their capital cities and contemplate the possibility of moving them elsewhere (such ideas were floating in Brazil and Argentina). Italy, Bulgaria, and Romania gained their independence a little later, establishing their capitals in Rome, Sofia, and Bucharest. Berlin, the ascent of which was the result not of emancipation from foreign control but rather national consolidation of German principalities, has closely followed this generation of capitals.

The First World War precipitated the collapse of the four land empires, the Austro-Hungarian, the German, the Russian, and the Ottoman. As a result, newly independent states and the third generation of national capitals had emerged in the Near East, in the Balkans, in Eastern Europe, and in the Baltic region.[5] In 1920, in Albania, the capital was relocated from Durres, a port city on the coast of the Adriatic Sea, to Tirana. Dublin, the capital of the Irish Republic, which gained its independence in 1919, also belongs to this generation of capitals. In the aftermath of the war the capitals of the majority of modern Arab nations were also formed.

The next generation of capitals emerged after the Second World War, when Asian and African states gained their independence in 1945–1954 and in 1960–1975 respectively.

Finally, the last generation of national capitals emerged in Eastern Europe and Eurasia after the demise of communism, the collapse of the Soviet Union, and the fall of the Berlin wall. These were mainly capitals of newly emerging post-Soviet republics and the capitals of the former Yugoslavia, as well as Bratislava, the capital of Slovakia. Berlin and Astana as the new capitals of Germany and Kazakhstan respectively also emerged as a result of these processes.

In the colonial countries of Africa and Asia, the capitals were typically sited in port cities and former trading posts, which funneled the agricultural products, timber, minerals, and other raw materials out into world markets.[6] Prior to colonization of these countries, most of these sites were small settlements that did not play an important role in their political life. The main factors determining the choice of such cities as administrative capitals were the considerations of logistics and transportation system. The colonial capital cities, fairly cosmopolitan both in their demographics and attitudes, linked the agrarian hinterlands of these countries with global trade and industrial centers. Calcutta, Karachi, Kuala Lumpur, Manila, Batavia, Dakar, and Lagos are illustrious examples of this type of cities. Not surprisingly, after gaining national independence, the establishment of their own administrative centers in the interiors of these countries often became a priority issue for these nations. The debates about the need to transfer the seats of government of these post-colonial countries were often motivated by the need to liberate these newly independent states from the colonial heritage.

This type of motivation was less evident in Latin American countries, since Spain kept the administrative capitals of most of its American colonies in their pre-colonial political centers. In those rare countries where coastal colonial capitals were established, the issue of moving them inland was contemplated and debated in the post-independence era as we will see below.

It must be noted that decolonization was only one of the reasons to move capital cities, among others. There are at least four other reasons that have motivated these decisions and the debates – the changes in the capitalist system and the improvement of the transportation infrastructures, the issues of large metropoles, the diminishing role of military considerations, and ethnic problems.

The coming of the post-colonial era coincided with the introduction of the new means of transportation and forms of communications that contributed to the breakdown of hub-and-spoke transportation systems inherited from the colonial times. With the advent of new transportation systems, the highways and the higher-speed railways, along with the development of air transport, the administrative capitals located in the port cities (*entrepôt*) largely have lost their logistical and communication advantages. More centrally located capital cities have promised to provide more effective administration of the countries and enhance their communication infrastructure.[7]

The coastal capitals also created a host of social problems. Due to the low level of urbanization in most of the colonial countries, their capital cities have attracted large migration inflows that led to their uncontrolled expansion, increasing social polarization in these cities, creating a misbalance between the core areas, and stagnating and declining the rest of these countries.

The development of new military technologies, specifically the ballistic weapons, and the changes in the character of modern warfare has vastly reduced the importance of the geographical factors in military success or failure. Additionally, the development of international law and the rise of international organizations that warrant additional security to nation-states have also contributed to the reduced importance of capital city location in terms of security. Certainly, military-strategic rationales for siting the capital cities are not becoming completely irrelevant and obsolete. However, the weight of such considerations was largely reduced in the last several decades.

The issues of ethnicity also played a tangible role in the debate. In many cases one ethnic group that was dominant in the region which was chosen by the colonial administration as a capital had significant perceived advantages over other groups. Yoruba in Nigeria, Tutsi in Burundi and Rwanda, Barolong in Botswana are good examples. In the aftermath of independence, the underprivileged ethnic groups were seeking to establish the capital in a more neutral place. Relatedly, in many regions of the world after independence, the various ethnic minorities different from the titular nation were dominant or constituted a sizable part of the capital city population, vastly disproportional to their share in the total population of the country. We will see below that this type of situation was not exceptional but was rather typical for many colonized and dependent countries in Southeast and Central Asia, the Caucuses, the Balkans and Central and Eastern Europe. In some cases the nationalist leaders who promoted nationalism along ethnic lines perceived this situation as a serious problem. The most notable examples of this phenomenon were the Chinese in Southeast Asia and the Jews in Central and Eastern Europe.

In the colonial period the titular nation was not a majority or was not economically dominant in many capital cities in the countries in Southeast Asia, including Malaysia, Vietnam, Indonesia, and Thailand. In these countries the Chinese often served as quintessential outsiders and the intermediaries between the colonized populations and the metropoles, constituting the majority or disproportional share of population in the capital cities of these countries. The Chinese population of Kuala Lumpur was close to 80 percent of the total at the end of the nineteenth century. The Chinese population in Batavia (present-day Jakarta) was about 20–25 percent of the total; however, if the slave laborers are excluded, this number would be close to 50 percent. In 1749 the Chinese population of Manila, the capital of Philippines, was more than 60 percent, 40,000 of the total population of 60,000.[8] During the French colonial period, estimates of the number of Chinese residents of the Saigon-Cholon area were upwards of half of the total population. At the time when Saigon became a capital of South Vietnam, it was still close to 30 percent.[9] Only at the turn of the twentieth century the Thai population approximated the number of the Chinese in Bangkok.[10] In 1919 in Mongolia, shortly before the declaration of independence, the Chinese population in the capital city of Urga (present-day Ulaanbaatar) was 70 percent). After India gained independence the Muslim population of Delhi was at least 40 percent. In East Africa the Hindi and Arabs often played the role of global intermediaries between the colonialists and the indigenous population.

Such an ethnic situation in the preeminent cities of these countries was often perceived as a matter of concern by many nationalist leaders at the time when these countries had gained their independence. There were two options to address this situation – to alter the ethnic balance in the capital in favor of the titular nation or to transfer the capital to a new city. We will see below that such a motivation for transfer of the capital of a country was very important, for example, in Malaysia.

In many countries of Central and Eastern Europe, as well as in the post-Soviet countries, the problem of the ethnic make-up of a capital was also a matter of concern. The indigenous population of Central-East European countries was mainly rural. Perhaps, not surprisingly, in many of these countries the ethnic minorities – the Jews, the Germans, the Poles, the Russians, the Greeks, or Muslims – often dominated in their largest cities that were also their capitals. For example, in Sofia there were more Jews and Muslims than Bulgarians. The Romanian capital Bucharest was to some degree a Greek city.[11] Belgrade was founded by Bulgarians; a Serbian writer Milan Milićević recalled that "it was part Turkish, part Greek, part cosmopolitan and less of all Serbian, and had an appearance of a typical Levantine city with Ottoman architecture." The population in the Baltic capital cities, Tallinn (Revel) and Riga, as well as in Prague, was predominantly German or at least German-speaking. Up until 1875, the majority of the population of Buda (Ofen) was German, though the city remained German-speaking even after it became predominantly Hungarian. In 1910, in Bratislava, the current capital of Slovakia, the Slovakian population did not exceed 15 percent, while the aggregate German and Hungarian population was more than 80 percent. Bratislava also served as the capital of Hungary for more than two centuries, and even in the early twentieth century the Hungarian language dominated as the spoken language in the city. In Warsaw, a third of the population was Jewish (in 1917–1918 almost half), and the city was ruled in Russian. At the turn of the twentieth century more than half of the population of Minsk (52 percent), the capital of Belarus, was Jewish (census of 1897), and Yiddish was a dominant language there. That year the Lithuanians in Vilnius constituted no more than 2 percent of the total population, while the Jews accounted for nearly half of the city's residents. In Kyiv there were 2.5 times more Russians than Ukrainians.[12] In Chisinau, Moldova, in 1897 the share of Moldovans was no more than 18 percent, the Russian population was 29 percent, and the Jewish population was 47 percent.

The ethnic minorities were also dominant in the capitals of Trans-Caucasian and Central Asian republics that were part of the Soviet Union, that is Georgia, Azerbaijan, Armenia, Kazakhstan, Kyrgyzstan, Uzbekistan, Turkmenistan, and Tajikistan. In 1897, Tiflis was predominantly Armenian, while the Georgian population of the capital of Georgia was a mere 26 percent of the entire population of the city. In 1913, the share of Turkish Muslims in Baku, the capital of Azerbaijan, did not exceed 21 percent.[13] In 1897 in Yerevan, the capital of Armenia, the number of Azeri and Armenians was almost equal at 43 percent. However, prior to the Russian military forces entering the capital of Armenia in 1827, the number of Armenians in Yerevan was no more than 20 percent.[14]

A similar picture can be seen in Central Asian countries. In Samarkand, the capital of Uzbekistan, Tajiks made up the majority of the population. Ashgabat, the capital of Turkmenistan, was a Russo-Persian city with practically no Turkmen population, though with a significant number of ethnic Armenians and Azeri. In Frunze (currently Bishkek) the Kyrgyz people made up only 23 percent of the population. In Alma-Ata the Kazakh language was considered native by only 22 percent of the population. Even in 1959 the share of Tajik people in Dushanbe, the capital of Tajikistan, did not exceed 20 percent.

The ethnic considerations, however, motivated capital city shifts and the discussion of this topic only in some countries. We will see that such considerations played an important role in the decision made in Malaysia and in the current debates in Central Asian countries. In 1930 the capital of Uzbekistan was moved from Samarkand to Tashkent ostensibly in part because of the Tajik majority in Samarkand. Another curious example of the discussion motivated at least in some measure by ethnic considerations was the proposal in the 1920s to move the capital city of Lithuania to Memel; this intriguing example will be discussed in more detail in due course. Although this proposal was never realized, the emergence of such proposals indicates that this motivation was not unfamiliar to European countries. In Slovakia there were also some proposals to move the capital closer to the center of the country, which would better reflect its ethnic identity.[15]

Perhaps, the scarcity of such precedents in Europe can be explained by several factors. Culturally the Central and Eastern European countries have been much better integrated into the rest of Europe, and the location of their capitals was never determined by the considerations related to the export of raw materials. These countries were much more ethnically homogeneous in comparison with the countries of Africa and Asia, and their developed urban systems did not produce an excessive concentration of population in one city.

It is quite possible that capital city relocations would be more prevalent in Europe if the historical transformations of the Second World War period did not take place. The forced migrations of some ethnic groups, the ethnic cleansing and the genocide of the Jewish population living in the preeminent cities of these newly-formed nations during the second world war have dramatically changed the demography and ethnic make-up of their capital cities. Such measures were also taken in some Balkan countries. As a consequence, their capitals have become much more ethnically homogeneous.

In the East-Central European countries the large-scale reconstructions of the capital cities and drastic changes of their iconography consistent with the new visions of their national identity were much more prevalent compared to capital city relocation plans. In his perceptive review of 17 capital cities of East-Central Europe, Göran Therborn has described their gradual architectural and symbolic adaptations to the changing ideologies.[16] The iconography of these capital cities has changed, adopting first to gaining independence, then to the advent of communism and later on to de-communization after the fall of the Berlin Wall. The choice of heroes to be commemorated, the toponymics, and the historical memory of the capital cities reflected the changes of ideologies that were chosen by these nation-states.[17]

The relevance of the concept of the generation of capital cities is underscored by the fact that the plans to relocate the capital city drew heavily on the regional models deemed to be successful. The models of the countries that have relocated their capitals had an appeal for many countries in the same region or belonging to the same culture. As we will see below, the neighborhood effects played an important role in the decisions made in different countries of the same mega-region. The countries of Latin America were more receptive to the model of Brazil. The British Commonwealth countries have used Washington D.C. as their model. The Abuja concept in

Africa and the example of Astana in the post-Soviet sphere also have been used by the African countries and by the post-Soviet countries respectively. Understandably, the countries in the same mega-region often faced similar problems of nation-building and learned from the experiences of each other. Not infrequently, the countries also drew on overseas models that emerged in response to the same cycles of development.[18]

Needless to say that the character and the specific features of the capital cities were never completely determined by the historical period in which the capital cities of the same generation were established. They have followed the models that resonated with their political systems, sense of identity, and were consistent with their stage of nation-building and national development. There were also factors of cultural affinity. The capital cities of Canada, New Zealand, South Africa, and Australia drew heavily on the model of Washington D.C., although they had been established much later. In building Astana, Kazakhstan drew on the Ankara model, although the latter was established much earlier. Although Ankara, Brasília, Putrajaya, and Astana emerged in very different historical periods, their urban plans and architectural styles are typologically similar, and one can clearly see some signs of influence of the first two on Astana.

In the pages below I will provide brief descriptions of capital city relocations in the last 100 years and explore their rationales, focusing on the particular patterns and features specific to each continent and mega-region. I will also discuss the debates in the countries that have mulled this issue, especially in the parliament setting. The patterns of discussion in these countries are no less interesting and valuable for our analysis than actual relocation cases because they will help us to see the reasons that drive the interest in this topic. The presented case studies will also facilitate our understanding of the factors that determine the success or fiasco of these projects and will elucidate the trajectories of development of the national self-consciousness of different nations and their strategies of nation-building. After the presentation of these case studies, we will summarize the results in the next chapter, showing that all discussed cases exemplify one of the six strategies and that some of these strategies were more prevalent in specific continents and meg-regions. I will also highlight the broad themes that are articulated in the urban plans of different regions.

Our survey is based on both the academic studies of this topic and the articles in newspapers and magazines, most of which are informational rather than analytic in their character.

Post-colonial nation-building in Africa

Africa is a continent where capital city relocations were happening most often in the course of the last century. In the last 100 years the seats of government have been moved already in 10 out of 54 African states or in 18 percent of all African nations. Presently, serious discussions on this topic take place in another 10 African nations. Capitals have been relocated in several African countries before independence, notably in Côte d'Ivoire (1896, 1934), Togo (1897), Mozambique (1902), Rhodesia (now known as Zambia) (1935), and Guinea-Bissau (1942), among others. However, in contrast to more recent precedents, these older cases were motivated primarily by the convenience of colonial administration and by economic reasons and not by the considerations of nation-building, the principal topic of the current chapter.

The prevalence of capital city relocations on the African continent can be explained by several reasons that gave them specific character.

Most importantly, the decolonization of the continent gave rise to the emergence of newly-formed nation-states that aimed to break with and dissociate themselves from the colonial legacy. A geographer Gamal Hamdan has famously named Africa "the continent of eccentric capital cities."[19] Before independence most of the African capital cities were located in the coastal cities that served as *entrepôts* in the peripheries of these countries. Most of the time, the capital cities of the landlocked countries of the continent (Chad, Democratic Republic of the Congo, Central African Republic, Malawi, Zambia, among others) were also placed in the peripheral parts of these countries due to the structure of colonial communication and transportation system. The peripheral location of the continent's capital cities also reflected and reinforced the exterior orientation of the economies of African countries and contributed to the low level of intra-African connections.

This peculiar situation of post-colonial geography has challenged the new African nations in several ways. Economically and geographically the African countries were poorly integrated both at the national and at the continental level – therefore, the integration of their interiors was the most urgent task. Some African countries such as Mauritania and Botswana did not even have their own capital cities within their territories. Consequently, their new capitals, Nouakchott and Gaborone, were established out of necessity. The colonial cities did not reflect the identity of the newly-emerging nations. To use the expression of Gamal Hamdan again, they were "the most evident fingerprints of Europe on African life and the most solid palimpsests of colonial history."[20] The defenders of relocations believed that capital city moves conceived in the context of decolonization will help to address these problems.

Curiously, the attempts of decolonization of African capitals took place already in the nineteenth century. In 1885 after the liberation of Sudan from Ottoman-Egyptian rule, the leaders of the Mahdi revolution immediately destroyed Khartoum, the colonial capital, and started to build a new capital city of Omdurman on the western part of the Nile, across the river from the former capital, according to their thoroughly anti-colonialist program of development. The new city was constructed based on the ascetic and unpretentious needs of the dervishes. Omdurman survived only for a very short period of time until 1898 when the British forces took it over. They moved the capital city back to Khartoum, rebuilding it according to the principles of European urban planning.

86 *Capital relocations in world regions*

Central to many capital city relocation projects that we will describe in more detail below (in Nigeria, Tanzania, Côte d'Ivoire, and elsewhere) was the idea of moving the seat of government from the coastal port cities inland. In case of landlocked countries such as Malawi and Rwanda, where the colonial capitals, Zomba and Butare (then known as Astrida), were sited in the peripheral locations, more central locations for the post-colonial capital cities, Lilongwe and Kigali, were later chosen. In both cases they were given preference over more economically developed but less centrally located cities of these countries.

The urge to remove the colonial legacy that defined the politics of many African countries also manifested itself in the renaming of many capital cities of the continent. Léopoldville named after Belgian king Leopold became Kinshasa (Congo), Salisbury was renamed into Harare (Zimbabwe), Lourenço Marques into Maputu (Mozambique), and Pretoria into Tswane (South Africa).[21]

As noted earlier, decolonization was not the only issue at the center of capital city debates in Africa. Another trend relevant for our topic was the exponential capital city growth in many of the African nations. This trend was especially pronounced in Lagos (Nigeria), Conakry (Guinea), Harare (Zimbabwe), and Abidjan (Ghana) where the capital cities were showing double digit annual growth over extended periods of time. The high level of primacy of many African capital cities can be explained by the low level of urbanization of the African continent, the least urbanized of all the continents.[22] The proposals to move the seats of government are still often motivated by the interest in development of the territories and the interiors of African countries. The supporters of this measure believe that the excessive primacy of the capital cities in Africa impedes the national economic development and the development of Africa as a continent. They believe that new capitals with better infrastructure will be better places to absorb the migrants and to contribute to the de-centralization of the skewed urban system of these countries.

Another important reason for the prevalence of capital city shifts in Africa is the very high level of ethnic diversity on the African continent. Some social scientists have pointed to a high degree of correlation between the ethnic diversity of the region and the propensity to change capital cities.[23] Indeed, the considerations of diversity were central to the capital city relocation decisions in Africa and the debates thereof, as many countries of the continent sought to consolidate different ethnic groups via construction of the new capital cities as their integrative national center. The nation-building needs of newly-emerged independent states required the construction of the new identity of the diverse ethnic groups. The case in point is Botswana where the capital city was moved in 1969 from Mafeking, which was the traditional base of *barolong*, one of the most influential tribes of the country, to Gaborone, which traditionally served as a meeting point and congregation place for different tribal chiefs. Moving the political power closer to the city in the sphere of influence of six out of eight main tribal groups, the government was aiming to reach political compromise.[24]

It must be noted that in spite of all the important and noble reasons cited above – balanced development, de-colonization, and the like – many of the leaders of post-independent Africa pursued their own agendas unrelated to nation-building. Thus, in reality the selection of the capitals were often influenced by their paternalistic interests, the attempts to strengthen their power base, and to establish new loyalties and new forms of allegiance. Hence, not infrequently, the capital cities were moved or proposed to be moved to the birthplace of the rulers, notably in Côte d'Ivoire, Malawi, Senegal, Zimbabwe, and Libya. Mobutu in Democratic Republic of Congo, Bokassa in Central African Republic, and Ahmadou Ahidjo in Cameroon also have turned their home village into flights of fancy. Notably, Ahidjo had intended to move the capital to Garoua, his home village, but it has never been endowed with this status.

Finally, another important reason for more frequent capital relocations in Africa was the availability of the external funds for these projects immediately after independence. At the time many nations in Africa have embarked upon large infrastructure projects, financing them by external borrowing and domestic inflation. In the 1980s, however, the Western banks and other international financial institutions took a less lenient attitude towards the debts of these countries and imposed "structural adjustment programs." These programs made it more difficult for African nations to consider capital relocations or large-scale reconstructions of their existing capital cities.

Most of the above applies only to the countries of sub-Saharan Africa. The countries of Maghreb were more commercially developed and were much better integrated into the global systems of politics and commerce. Consequently, their urban systems were much better developed and more polycentric compared to the countries of sub-Saharan Africa. They had important urban centers beyond their coastal lines. Their urbanities were also much more influenced by Arabic architecture and urban planning. The case in point is Morocco where there were four imperial capital cities – Rabat, Fes, Meknes, and Marrakesh – that served at different periods as the capital cities of the country and preserved their role of important regional economic centers. The coastal Rabat, where the French colonial administration moved the capital in 1912, remained the seat of government after the country was granted independence.[25] But the proposals to move the capital back to Fes are still occasionally debated. In Egypt and Libya the proposals to move capital cities were motivated not so much by the new identity considerations and emancipation from the legacy of colonialism but more by the concerns about overpopulation in these cities and by the need to reach a compromise in the rivalry between different regions.

Below I will describe several of the most representative and high-profile cases of capital city relocations in African countries.

Côte d'Ivoire

In 1983 the president of Côte d'Ivoire and the father of the nation Félix Houphouët-Boigny moved the capital city of the country from the large coastal city Abidjan to Yamoussoukro. The capital city move was realized at the time of the fifth reelection of the president, who led the country from 1960 to 1993 and who was one of the most tenured post-colonial rulers in the continent. Prior to relocation, Yamoussoukro was a little village in the tropical swamps in the center of the country and the place of birth of the president.

The movement of the seat of government was intended to emphasize the independence of the country, its new aspirations, and its economic prosperity. The decision was made at the peak of "the Ivorian miracle," that is the economic boom of the 1970s that was a result of the high agricultural commodities prices (cacao, coffee, and cotton). Apparently one of the tasks of this project was the better integration of the Muslim agrarian north of the country. Boigny believed that Christianity is a more modern and more progressive religion. Accordingly, the Christian identity of the country was to be highlighted in the key construction projects of the new city. For that particular reason the Basilica of Our Lady of Peace was built in the center of Yamoussoukro. It is still considered the largest Christian cathedral in the world that imitates in its shape and architecture the Cathedral of St. Peter in Rome. Another key building of the city is the President's Palace surrounded by an artificial lake and guarded by the totemic crocodiles, a gift from the president of Mali. Reportedly, crocodiles play a role in the mythology of the ethnic group to which Boigny belongs.[26]

Many opponents have vehemently criticized the capital city relocation project in the Ivory Coast, claiming that the new capital city did not help to integrate or pacify the Muslim north of the country. The rise of the rebel movement in the north, which was strengthened by the labor migrants from the neighboring Muslim countries, led to the protracted civil war. The construction of the poorly attended basilica did not make Christianity a more popular religion in the country and only doubled the country's debt. Furthermore, in the late 1980s the country had lost its economic velocity and, consequentially, the financial means that had made the establishment of the new city possible.

Nigeria

In Nigeria, which liberated itself from the colonial control of Great Britain, the capital city was moved from Lagos, once the biggest slave port in West Africa and the largest city in the country, to Abuja. The general, Murtala Mohammad (1938–1976), who came to power as a result of the coup d'état and who was soon assassinated by the rebels, was the person who inspired this idea. His successor Shehu Shagari, the second president of the country, carried on his cause and moved several ministries from Lagos to Abuja. However, it was only the next president, General Ibrahim Babangida, who made several more decisive steps on the path of his predecessors in 1985. The oil revenues were used to finance this project.

One of the purposes of this decision was to ease the congestion and overpopulation in Lagos and to improve its living conditions. Describing the catastrophic situation, the acclaimed Nigerian geographer Mabogunje has called Lagos "the area of disaster that took the form of a city." The population of Lagos almost trebled in the decade preceding 1963 and continued to grow at a pace of 11–15 percent a year in the 1960s. The estimated population of greater Lagos rose from 1.14 million in 1963 to 3.55 million in 1976 and 4.07 million in 1982.[27] Obviously, this growth has created challenges for housing and transportation, overloading the urban infrastructure of Lagos, which could not withstand such pressure.[28] Abuja was built based on the growth projections, and its land size was twice larger than that of Lagos, which had limited room for expansion.

However, the most fundamental problems that the new city was intended to address were political issues. The new capital was intended to strengthen the central political power and to alleviate the North-South divide of the country with its religious, ethnic, and economic aspects.

The shift of the seat of government was expected to move the center of political power closer to the geographic center of the country. Such a central position would lay the groundwork for better administration of the territory and for political engagement of the tribes and ethnic groups that were not participating in political life, being geographically remote from the political and commercial center of the country. Historically Lagos was dominated by the Yoruba, and its dominance has evoked dissatisfaction from other ethnic groups and tribes. The ethnic and geographic conflicts also had a religious aspect, the cleavage and confrontations between the Christian south and the Muslim north. Most of the Yoruba ethnic group members were Christian. Hence relocation promised to rebalance and mitigate religious and ethnic tensions.[29]

One of the factors that also might have influenced the decision was the proximity of a new capital to the centers of one of the oldest cultures on the African continent, the Nok culture (1000 BC—300 AD). The most valuable artifacts of Nok culture were found in a Taruga archeological site that is located 60 km from Abuja. In addition to other reasons, the relocation was expected to solidify and reconnect the Nigerian culture to its ancient ancestral roots.

The official government declarations emphasized the advantages of the central location of Abuja in the context of complicated ethnic relations. Abuja was presented as a neutral city on the border between the Muslim and Christian populations of Nigeria.[30] The move promised to integrate other ethnic minorities that populated the middle belt of the country, which served as a sort of a buffer zone between the south and the north.

In 1990 the incentive to move the capital city faster was provided by the coup d'état attempt in Lagos that was initiated by the southerners and the ethnic groups of the middle belt. Although this coup has failed, Ibrahim Babangida started to move government functions to Abuja and significantly increased the funding of this project. Under the rule of his predecessor Muhammad Buhari, the construction was going slowly and all government functions were still lingering in Lagos. Ibrahim Babangida built for himself a presidential villa that was fortified almost like a castle and was equipped with underground tunnels and bomb shelters in case of civil war or consequent attempts of coup d'état. In 1993 he cancelled the results of the elections and transformed himself into a military dictator of Nigeria.[31]

The Abuja project attracted a lot of criticism and revealed the corrupt nature of the Nigerian political regime. Notably, the term "Abuja contracts" became a synonym for corruption. The substantial funds dedicated to the project were embezzled by the government officials, developers, and subcontractors that were close to the government.[32] The prices for projects were inflated, and kickbacks were taken on contracts awarded to multinational firms. Contracts for administrative buildings, housing projects, and other sundry contracts were handed out to political cronies and party members who handed kickbacks to politicians (Akam, 2011). According to some economists, in the case of Abuja the extra expenses associated with corruption were estimated at 25 percent of the cost of the project. These estimates were based on the cross-country price comparison in sub-Saharan Africa.[33]

The political and social outcomes of the project were also problematic. Lagos remains an overpopulated city plagued by many problems of a large metropolis.[34] The prospects of reaching the ethnic harmony and of overcoming inter-religious and inter-ethnic conflicts, which were declared the main drivers of the project, also remain weak and remote. Some experts even claimed that the new capital might have exacerbated some of the existing tensions.[35]

Hausa, the northern tribe, has received significant advantages over other tribes as a result of switching the capital. The Islamization of Abuja, manifested in the architectural style of many public buildings, also did not contribute to religious harmony. The ruling elites from the north have tried to present the obvious Islamic imagery in the architectural plan of the city as eastern decorative elements common to the countries of the Orient. However, the dome of the National Assembly is unmistakably reminiscent of a mosque. "No-man's-land", as Abuja was described at the time of the promulgation of shifting the capital, turned out to be not a neutral place but an expansion to the northern sphere of influence.[36] The Muslim population has become the demographic majority of the country due to higher reproduction rates, and Abuja only reinforced the Muslim political and cultural dominance. Therefore, many critics have complained that the leadership of the Muslim elites did not make Abuja an inclusive capital as it was promised. Not surprisingly, many Christians and members of minority groups have perceived the project as an attempt to marginalize them and push them out of the political life of the country. This situation has undermined the moral foundation of the project.

Another strand of criticism has found the public places of Abuja inefficient both from the standpoint of the ideals of democracy and from the standpoint of inclusivity. The main public spaces of the city, such as The Three Arms Zone that houses the presidential complex and the National Assembly and the Square of the Eagle that was designed for the large-scale national ceremonies, are not accessible for the public beyond the participation in the official state demonstrations and holidays.[37] On regular days these public spaces are surrounded by barbed wires and are tightly guarded by soldiers.

The capital city relocation project also did not help Babangida to achieve his personal goals of preserving political power. In 1993, shortly after the capital city relocation, amidst a round of strikes and protests, he declared that he was stepping aside as head of the military regime.

More recently, there were some more positive assessments. With the arrival of democracy in 1999, the new capital became more relevant, housing two legislative houses. Abuja has grown to almost 4 million people, up from 800,000 in 2006, redirecting some of the development from Lagos. Reportedly, it is still not the most attractive city to live, but it is becoming more livable and is overcoming its original sterility.

Tanzania

The plan to move the capital city to Dodoma was initiated by the president of the country, Julius Nyerere, one of the architects of African socialism in 1973. The special Agency for the Construction of Capital City was tasked to develop and realize this plan. The construction of a new capital city, it was expected, would take 10 years and the new capital would be completed in 1986.[38] The National Assembly was moved to Dodoma in 1996. However, to date the government is still run from both Dar es Salaam and Dodoma.

Dodoma was selected as the most centrally located site, equidistant from the centers of the major tribes. The town was also a crossroads of communication with main national roads. The new capital city was expected to harmonize the interests of 120 ethnic groups that populate the country. Dodoma region was also a place that needed economic development. The region was lagging behind other regions, plagued by drought and famine, and the new capital was seen as an impetus for regional growth. It was also necessary to de-centralize the country, as all business activities were concentrated in Dar es Salaam, the colonial capital city.[39]

The construction of the new capital also was ideologically motivated. Nyerere's national development project known as *ujamaa* ("extended family") aimed to remove all entrenched social divisions in Tanzania and to establish a new social system based on the idealized view of traditional pre-colonial African community. In pursuit of this goal, Nyerere aimed to undermine the traditional tribal rule and to regroup the rural population of the country into larger units through a compulsory policy which came to be known as "villagization." This policy was intended to create stronger national identity in the country, on the one hand, and to break the colonial era dependency and promote self-reliance, on the other. Dodoma was meant to become a Chief Village in the country of villages and to promote a model African city, without skyscrapers or superhighways but instead a rural city, produced and lived in by peasants.[40] This vision was strongly influenced by Maoist ideology that emphasized the confrontation between the peasant countryside and the capitalist urban path of development. The new type of capital city was also designed to eliminate the gulf between the rural peasants and the government elite.[41]

Nyerere did not have enough time to realize his plans: he relinquished power in 1985. Since the 1980s the country does not follow the socialist model of development, and the idealistic ideas that have animated the Dodoma project have long been abandoned. Dar es Salaam remains *de facto* political capital, and the embassies of other countries are still located there. As for Dodoma – the infrastructure is not ready yet to assume the capital city role.

Some of the problems that prevented the implementation of the vision were clearly financial. In those years when the construction took place, no more than 1 percent of the state budget was devoted to the project instead of the 10 percent that was promised and approved.[42] Government grants from 1973 to 1986 provided only 39 percent of the sum required for implementing its first five years and less than $3 million (T.Shs. 5.3 billion) was granted from 1987 to 2002.[43] In the 1980s some corruption scandals associated with this project have also ensued.[44] In spite of the government incentives and tax breaks, very few businesses have moved to Dodoma.

Even more importantly, there was no unity within government ranks and no real commitment to "the Cause." In fact, some politicians argued to rescind the relocation decision as the transportation system has improved regardless. Nevertheless, the successive presidents of Tanzania have invariably pledged their commitment to the Dodoma project. But the implementation is still going extremely slow and more needs to be done to improve the infrastructure and services to the required standards. Questions continue being raised about funding and the timeline within which the government will execute the move.

The Dodoma project is rightfully recognized as the most problematic and unsuccessful capital city relocation project so far. However, many politicians in Tanzania still see a need for the new capital city that was envisaged by Nyerere and call for the resurrection of his "grand idea." Some urban planners also have praised the master plan of the city that has many "brilliant physical planning ideas." Among other things, it includes the city-region plan, people-centered transportation system, provisions for urban agriculture, mixed densities, and residential social mix; it also addresses some important inter-regional and intra-regional problems. This group believes that proper resource allocation and strong political will can help this important project to become more successful in the future.[45]

Malawi

In 1975 the capital of Malawi was moved from Zomba in the south of the country to the already existing city of Lilongwe. This relocation was motivated first and foremost by the need to establish an independent center for this new African nation in the core area of the country. Although Mali does not have any access to the ocean, the capital city in the south was part and parcel of the colonial economic and communication system – the epitome of its dependency both on its British metropole and more economically developed neighbors – and reflected the export character of its economic life.

The new capital city was also tasked to stimulate the economic development in the north and in the core regions of the country. It was expected that the new capital would become a new economic and demographic growth pole, which will balance the economic development in the south and particularly counter-balance the business capital in Blantyre.

So far the students of Malawi find little evidence that Lilongwe has become a veritable growth pole of the country. Critics also accentuate the personal nature of the presidential motives. Lilongwe is located close to the core areas of the Chewa ethnic group to which President Hastings Banda (serving from 1963 to 1994) belonged. The project was at least to some extent self-serving, as it assisted the president in strengthening his own base of loyalty.[46]

Senegal

In Senegal the seat of government was moved in 1958 to Dakar from Saint Louis, which was the capital since 1872. The initiative to move the capital belonged to Mamadou Dia, the prime-minister of the country, whose decision was supported by the majority of the parliament. During the colonial period Dakar served as an administrative capital of the whole of Afrique Occidentale Française. When the plan to establish the federation uniting eight former French colonies was put forward, Dakar was envisaged as a city that had a much greater integrative potential compared with other candidates. However, this emerging federation quickly fell apart (1960), and Dakar's role as a capital was reduced back to Senegal only. It is remarkable that, contrary to all other African precedents, after independence the new capital city of Senegal stayed in the coastal area and moved to a larger city.

Presently, the issue of capital city relocation is still debated in Senegal in the context of the overpopulation and congestion problems in Dakar. Being located on an isthmus in the Atlantic Ocean, Dakar does not have any place for further expansion and natural growth. With the highest density of population in the country and the highest concentration of industry (75 percent) the city is beset by traffic and sanitary problems. Due to all of the above, in 2007 Abdulla Wade (serving from 2000 to 2012), the president of the country, renowned for his large infrastructural projects, unveiled plans to relocate the seat of government to the coastal village of Lompoul, 150 km to the north of Dakar. Notably, this village was close to the president's place of birth.

Lompoul was promulgated as an ultra-modern futuristic city in the sand dunes on the Atlantic coast. Olivier-Clement Cacoub, the French architect known for his construction of African Versailles for the ruler of DRC (Democratic Republic of Congo), was already charged to draft the blueprint for the new city. Dubai World and its partners promised to fund the construction and then to lease buildings for up to 50 years to the state and businesses. The city described as the "New African Dubai on the Atlantic" was expected to be built on 25 hectares of land. Its cost was estimated at $30 billion. According to the original plans, the project was to be completed in three years.[47]

Critics expressed concerns about the feasibility of this project against the background of high unemployment and poverty in the country. However, the financial crisis and the end of the presidential term of Wade have put a natural end to the plan. Meanwhile, the debates about a possible change of capital city in Senegal go on.

Libya

After getting independence from Italy, Libya declared itself a federal monarchy – United Kingdom of Lybia, with three provinces and a rotation of the capital city between Tripoli and Benghazi. Initially, the key capital city functions were consolidated in the royal palace of King Idris, close to Benghazi. Then the construction of the new federal capital in Bayda (Jebel Akhdar, Green Mountains area) was started in the 1950s, and most of the necessary government buildings were erected there. However, later the plan to move the capital from Tripoli to Bayda was cancelled, as in 1963 the federative constitution of the country was discarded and Libya became a unitary state. Most of the capital city functions were moved to Tripoli, which has been endowed with the status of the first national capital.

In 1987 Muammar Gaddafi unveiled his plans to de-centralize Libya and to distribute capital city functions between different cities of the country. This policy was motivated both by nation-building and security considerations. The US Air Force attack on the residence of Gaddafi in Tripoli in 1986 revealed the vulnerability of the country from the sea. Sebha and Benghazi were the capitals of the two out of three provinces of the Libyan federation (Tripolitania, Cyrenaica, and Fezzan), and moving some of the ministries there was intended to facilitate the integration of the country. The distribution of different capital city functions between cities was also geared to stimulate the economy of other regions and to free Tripoli, where a third of the Libyan population resided, from overpopulation. Gaddafi stressed the need of the country to abandon the conventional concept of a capital city; in his perception it was closely tied with the concepts of the bourgeois state and bureaucracy that hindered the development of the Libyan revolution.[48]

Although the full scope of planned de-centralization could not be accomplished, most of the ministries were indeed relocated. Tripoli retained only part of its functions associated with international affairs. The majority of the administrative functions and government departments, however, were posted to Sirte, the birthplace of Muammar Gaddafi, which became a de facto capital city. The sessions of Libyan General National Congress were held in Sirte, where the palaces, squares, parks, and other attributes of capital city have been built. Besides considerations of security and loyalty, the choice of Sirte was determined by its central location relative to the three provinces of the country, equidistant from their historic capital cities. In the course of the 2011 uprising, Sirte was destroyed and the essential activities, including the sessions of the parliament, were transferred to Cyrenaica in the west, which was the springboard of the revolution.

Proposals and debates in other African countries

The plans to relocate the capital city are currently being discussed in 10 other African countries. In several of them, the principal decisions to transfer a capital city have been already made and the construction of new capital cities have commenced.

As a tendency in West Africa (Liberia, Ghana, Senegal, and Equatorial Guinea), most projects were motivated by overpopulation and physical characteristics of their capital cities that limit their expansion and create security concerns.

The proposed transfer of the capital city of **Ghana** is motivated by the fact that Accra, the current capital and the second largest city in Western Africa, is overpopulated and congested and is naturally constrained for its growth by the sea. Accra is also located in the seismically active zone. The proponents of the capital city transfer also stress the importance of de-centralization of the country and separation of its economic and political capitals.[49]

The three contenders for the role of a new capital city are Kintampo, Atebubu, and Dodowa. Dodowa was proposed by the previous political administration of Ghana as an administrative capital and is only one hour drive from Accra. Kintampo is centrally located and has stronger ties with the national identity of the Ghanaians, as it has in its proximity the archeological site associated with the Neolithic culture of the same name. Atebubu is another location in the interior of the country that is also considered to de-centralize the country.

In 2012 Theodoro Obiang, one of the longest serving presidents of **Equatorial Guinea**, have unveiled his plans to abandon the coastal capital in Malabo and commenced the construction of the new capital city in the jungle in the barely settled eastern part of the country. A small city of Oyala was chosen as a new capital. The necessity of the capital city transfer is explained by the considerations of security and the threat of the invasion of the country from the sea. Being the third country in sub-Saharan Africa in terms of oil production, the project is funded from its oil revenues. It is planned that a quarter of the population of the country, that is 200,000 people, will reside in the new capital city. It is also envisaged that the University in Oyala will be a pan-African center of education.

The critics warn that the more urgent needs of the citizens such as the shortage of drinking water, meager incomes at $2 a day, and paucity of roads and schools make the ambitious plans of the president very ill-timed and injudicious.

In **Liberia** the plans to move the capital city were mulled already by the 20th president of the country, William Tolbert, who was assassinated in the course of a coup d'état in 1980. He proposed Gbarnga in central Liberia for that role. This old idea of Tolbert's was recently recycled by Ellen Johnson Sirleaf, the current president. In 2012 she said that due to the rise of the sea level and the possible threat of flooding, the capital city should be moved from Monrovia to a centrally located city on the border of several counties. Her candidate for this role was the city of Zekepa. The oil revenues of the country, she claimed, will be sufficient to fund this project.[50] In 2013 a small task force had been set up and charged with conducting the research, technical analysis, master planning, and design that will be necessary for the comprehensive development plan for the proposed city of Zekepa.

East African countries (Somalia, Kenya, Uganda, and South Sudan) experienced more political turbulence, civil wars, and ethnic and clan strife, and new capital city proposals there focused more on the new institutional arrangements for ethnic or clan reconciliation, including federalization. Curiously, the current discussions of the establishment of a new East African Federation that would unite five principal Swahili speaking countries (Tanzania, Kenya, Uganda, Burundi, Rwanda) and possibly South Sudan also involve proposals to create a common capital city of this federation. The proposed capital is the Tanzanian city of Arusha, almost on the border between two most powerful members of the proposed federation, Tanzania and Kenya.

In **Somalia** the debates about a new capital started in 2004. The reasons cited were the congestion and overpopulation in Mogadishu, which was reduced to a pile of bullet-pocked bricks by the protracted civil war and has a very high crime rate. Besides that, the proponents of this measure claim that the control of the city by the Hawiye clan creates unfavorable conditions for peace-making and nation-building efforts, giving dominance to the south. The new capital city should address the anomalies of development of the country and offer the basis for reconciliation between many clans that represent extended family networks. Some of the analysts and political leaders, including the vice-mayor of Mogadishu, insist that a smaller centrally located city will be much more suitable for this role and will facilitate the efforts to federalize the country. Many proponents believe that after major reconstruction, Mogadishu should remain the commercial hub of the state.[51]

The end of the protracted civil war in Sudan in 2005 led to the independence of South Sudan; the idea of establishing a new capital city for the youngest nation on the African continent emerged almost immediately. The new capital city was supposed to emphasize the sovereignty of a new nation. In 2011 the cabinet of ministers of the country approved a $10 million budget for the new project.

There were several contenders for the role of the new capital city. Originally there was a proposal to radically transform and rebuild Juba in the shape of a rhinoceros, the pan-African symbol.[52] However, there was a vocal opposition and strong arguments against Juba, the old regional capital of South Sudan, and the Juba region in general, as many people considered it unsuitable for the new role.

First off, Juba did not have appropriate infrastructure for the capital city of a new nation. As a result of the civil war and the influx of refugees, the population of the city grew tenfold from 100,000 to 1 million people.[53] Moreover, the clan warfare in the city and its high crime rates created security problems for the future government residing there. Second, the Bari tribe members owning the lands in the Juba area and constituting only 10 percent of the population of the country were concerned that if Juba will be a capital of the new nation, they will lose control over their own tribal territories due to the preponderance of the Danka tribe members in the government and in the ruling Sudan People's Liberation Movement.[54] Third, the ascent of Juba as the capital of South Sudan was originally linked with the Muslim elites from the north and was associated with painful memories. Therefore, its historical connotations made it an undesirable candidate after the independence.

The candidacy of Ramciel was regarded as more realistic as it is located much closer to the geographic center of the country. The larger agripastoral ethnic group of Dinka that owned these lands was much more enthusiastic about the prospect of siting the capital city on their lands. However, later there emerged other proposals to move the capital city further north to the city of Wau, which was considered more neutral and also loyal to the present government.

The skeptics have questioned the rationality of the decision to relocate the capital, as Juba has a large international airport and a more developed transportation and communication system connecting the country with Uganda and other neighboring countries. They also believe that such large resources could be deployed more acrimoniously for other vital projects important for the new nation.[55] Nevertheless, many analysts recognized the need for a new capital city and consider it an important aspect of the survival and political viability of a new nation comprising around 60 indigenous ethnic groups.

In 2009 several ministers from the government of Uganda convinced the president of the country, Musaveni, to consider plans to relocate the capital city from Kampala to Nakasongola and do all the necessary research and preparations.

While the primary motivation of this decision stems from the congestion and gridlocks in Kampala, this project also has important federalist aspects.

In the past Uganda was a federalist country. However, the new constitution abolished several of the traditional kingdoms and included Kampala into the territory of the neighboring kingdoms. While some politicians of the country are trying to strengthen the unitary concept of the country and insist on expanding the territory of the capital city at the expense of other kingdoms, others insist that the country needs to develop as a federalist state and that for this reason it needs a new capital city. Hence the topic of capital city relocation became important in the national presidential election campaigns. Following the federalist agenda, in 2010 Abed Bwanika, the presidential candidate from the People's Development Party endorsed by several opposition parties, pledged to move the capital to Nakasongola.

This topic is not new in Uganda politics. After independence in 1962 the president of the country, Milton Obote, proposed to move the capital to Mbrara, the city that is still considered for this role today.

In Kenya the overpopulation and fast growth rates in Nairobi are most often cited reasons to relocate the seat of government. The defenders of the new capital also stress the importance of development of the north of the country to balance the country's economy. The centrally located small city is advocated as the most suitable concept of the capital city that should both help to better integrate the northern regions and to create a neutral ground for the different ethnic groups of Kenya.[56] Some of the proposals have called for the conversion of Konza Techno City that is being built by the Kenyan government as a "silicon savannah," into a new capital city. The government is spending $14.5 billion on this city that lies 60 km from Nairobi and plans to complete this project by 2019. Some of the politicians reason that a dedicated technology city is not as essential and urgent for the needs of the country as the need for a new capital. In 2007 the Association of Architects of Kenya also prepared the blueprint of the new capital and specified a number of requirements for it, including seismic resilience of the new construction, and referenced Nigeria, Tanzania, and South Africa as the models for de-centralization of the country.

The proposals to switch current capital cities also emerged in the south of Africa, notably in Zimbabwe and in Zambia.

In 2012 Robert Mugabe, the president of Zimbabwe, has unveiled plans to move the capital from Harare to a small settlement at Mount Hampden in the Zvimba region, which is the place of his birth. For many years Harare was considered one of the least livable capital cities in the world, having precarious water supply and excessive congestion. It was also noted that the city was doubling in size every 14 years. Several members of the government criticized this plan, noting the poverty of the country and lack of funds in the budget for such projects. They also stressed that the currently envisioned capital city will benefit the wealthy elite of the country and will not contribute to the welfare of other citizens and other cities that have very poor infrastructure. However, in spite of criticism, Mugabe continued to carry out his plans and signed a contract with a Chinese firm to commence the construction of the new city in 2016.

In Zambia there were many proposals to move the capital from Lusaka to a more central and a better planned place to de-centralize the country and to de-congest Lusaka. The candidacies of Chisamba, Kabwe and a new designed capital have been proposed.[57]

Post-colonial nation-building in Asia

In this section of the book we will review the peculiar features of capital city relocations and the debates thereof in several distinct regions of Asia: the Far East, Southeast Asia, Middle East, and South Asia. Each region has exhibited specific patterns of relocations and emphasized different rationales to move their capital cities.

Similar to Africa, the countries of Southeast Asia and South Asia were aiming to de-colonize the countries and to move them inland from their coastal locations.[58] In contrast to African countries, the countries of these regions are on average less ethnically diverse, and many of them were more concerned about promoting their own status within regions and about region-building in general.[59]

In the Far East the central problems that the shift of the seat of government was supposed to address were the problems of the misbalances in the economic development of the regions. The de-centralization goals figure prominently in the political agendas of these countries. These problems haunted China, Japan, South Korea, and Taiwan.

In the Middle East the needs of de-colonization in the choice of capital cities were also less articulated. The fall of the Ottoman Empire has led to national consolidation and the relocation of the capital city only in Turkey and Jordan. The current debates in Iran, Afghanistan, and Egypt are stimulated mainly by the problems of oversize capital cities. The debates in Yemen are motivated primarily by the needs of national reconciliation. Central to the UAE debates was the concept of a federalist capital city.

The variations and differences represent the tendencies of development, the differences of a degree rather than the differences of a kind, as the continental membership of particular countries did not determine all the features of relevant relocations as we will see below.

Southeast Asia

Malaysia

The official decision to move the capital city of Malaysia was made in 1993, and in 1997 the new administrative capital city of Malaysia was already built in Putrajaya, 25 km from Kuala Lumpur, the old capital. In 1999 the new city was open for corporations. Kuala Lumpur remains the *de iure* capital of the country, while both the parliament and the prime-minister have their offices in Putrajaya, which serves as *de facto* seat of government. This project turned out to be one of the favorite projects of Mahathir Mohamad, the charismatic and the longest serving prime-minister of the country. It is remarkable that the state oil monopoly Petronas has served as the largest investor, developer, and builder in the process of construction of the new capital.

The official reasons to construct the new administrative capital city of Malaysia were the periodic flooding and congestion in Kuala Lumpur.

Another reason, some critics claim, is the colonial and ethnic history of the country. Similar to other countries of SEA, Kuala Lumpur became a capital city of Malaysia because it was an important colonial port of the British Empire. Being founded in 1857, it turned into a capital of British administration in 1880, replacing the royal capital of Klang in Singalor state.

The colonial Malaysia was characterized by the ethnic division of labor. While Malaysians were primarily rural people, employed mostly in agriculture and in military service, the ethnic Chinese were dominant in commerce, having important international connections. Practically all larger cities of Malaysia – Kuala Lumpur, Malacca, and Georgetown – had a predominantly Chinese population. In 1891 the population of Kuala Lumpur was 80 percent Chinese.[60] The spatial structure of the cities reflected the ethnic division of labor described above: the houses of the officials of British administration and of the merchants were located in the center of the city, the Chinese commercial quarters were in the middle, and the houses of the ethnic Malaysians were located on the outskirts. The political life of the country also reflected the confrontation and opposition of the Chinese cities and Malaysian periphery, which has intensified after the Second World War and especially after independence in 1957. The nationalist leaders of Malaysia were concerned that the economic dominance of the Chinese can also manifest itself in the political sphere.

Under the circumstances the post-colonial nationalist leaders started to pursue the politics of "economic nationalism" that was geared to alter the class structure of the Malaysian society along the ethnic lines. The goal was to create Malay capitalists and the middle class more generally. In the framework of this politics, the state has promoted ethnic Malay businesses and given them large state monopolies and large infrastructure construction projects. Mahathir Mohamad who became the prime-minister in 1981 adopted this politics. The construction of Putrajaya to a large extent was a manifestation of this politics, as it led to the creation of a Malay urban class and nationalization of business ventures. Putrajaya has laid the foundations for the concept of an ethnically Malay city that was intended to serve as an incubator for the creation of a Malay urban class, as the absolute majority of the civil servants there are Malay. Ross King dubs this phenomenon counter-colonization and even counter-urbanization, as it was directed against the Chinese dominance in the historic cities of the country.[61]

The urban and architectural plan of the new capital city reflected the new orientations and sentiments of the Malay political elite. The dominant architectural styles adopted in Putrajaya represent not so much the endogenous artistic forms and styles but the Middle Eastern, Indian, and Central Asian architectural influences. Most government buildings are supplied with stylistic elements of Islamic architecture that make them look like mosques rather than government offices. This style was intended to reinforce the religious components of Malay national identity contrasted with Chinese elements and identity of the historic cities of the country. King keenly observes that this eclectic pan-Islamic architectural style betrays the new elements of self-colonization.[62]

Besides the above mentioned Islamic elements, the architectural plan of the city contains certain political programs and emphasizes the global aspirations of the Malaysian nation. The office of the prime-minister rather than the parliament occupies the central place in the ceremonial and symbolic space of the capital city. Putrajaya also exhibits the ambitions of the nation to become an important global center of modern civilization. The modernist elements of the architectural plan include symmetrical forms and an artificial lake with seven bridges over it. These global and technological ambitions are stressed through the proximity of Ciberjaya that was built at the same time to become the Silicon Valley for Malaysia and for SEA in general.

In general the realization of the plans of the new capital city was praised both by the urban planners and politicians. The city was built quickly in the middle of a plantation of palm trees. Some critics have lamented about some sterility of the city, which does not have the vitality, ethnic diversity, and chaos of the great world metropolises. In this vein and in the spirit of Michel Foucault, Ross King contrasted the utopia of Putrajaya to the heterotopy of the real big cities with their antagonisms, conflicts, and cosmopolitanism.[63] However, this type of criticism is common for most other planned cities.

Putrajaya still has some vacant spaces and land that are waiting to accommodate the embassies of different nations that has so far chosen to remain in Kuala Lumpur.

Indonesia

The current debates in Indonesia about the change of capital city have a long history.

Between 1945 and 1949, at the time of the struggle for independence, the capital city was in Jogjakarta. Jakarta resumed its capital function after independence. Sukarno, the founding father of independent Indonesia, started the construction of a new capital city in the geographic center of the country in Palangkaraya on Kalimantan Island. Sukarno believed that the establishment of a new capital would help to mitigate ethnic conflicts in the country; Kalimantan was also considered a safer and less tectonically precarious place. However, Sukarno did not have sufficient financial resources to complete this large-scale project.

In the 1990s Suharto, the general and the military ruler of Indonesia, reintroduced this topic to the public debates, proposing Jonggol, 50 km from Jakarta, as an alternative location.[64] The two locations were associated with two different concepts of the capital city. While Jonggol was probably inspired by the model of Putrajaya in Malaysia, the concept of Palangkaraya that is currently debated, is more reminiscent of Brasília.

The current discussions initiated in 2010 by Susilo Bambang Yudhoyono, the president of the country, owe much more to the original concept of a new administrative capital introduced by Sukarno rather than to that of Suharto. He has established a special group of experts and analysts who continue to study the feasibility of this project.[65] The current debates are motivated by several groups of reasons.

First, the main problems of the current capital are the frequent floodings, especially in monsoon period, the high population density, and the vulnerability for earthquakes. Considering that Jakarta is located in the most seismically active zone of earth, the current capital is most vulnerable to earthquakes that will definitely bring a high level of human casualties.[66] Lying at the western part of Java Island, this metropolis has already merged with its satellite towns to form a humongous agglomeration. Only the official estimates put the population of the capital at 12 million people, while most experts believe that it vastly underestimates the real number. Most independent experts agree that the real population of this city is double this number at 25 million. In combination with high rates of urbanization, this population size causes many serious problems, from the infamous Jakarta traffic and gridlocks and the average speed of traffic at 10 km per hour to the subsiding of the city lying on the banks of the Java Sea under the heavy weight of the skyscrapers. Most of the territory of Jakarta already lies below the sea level.[67] The underdeveloped public transportation system, the shortage of highways and roads,[68] the 10 percent annual growth of the number of personal automobiles magnify and exacerbate all the above problems. The economic cost of the gridlocks on the national economy is estimated at $3 billion a year.[69]

Another important reason and another significant aspect of the debate is the international standing of the country in the transnational region of SEA that can also be measured by the quality of its capital city. Indonesia strives to promote itself as an economic leader of the Pacific; it is also a personal ambition of its president to establish a reputation as an important regional reformer.[70] The headquarters of the ASEAN are located in Jakarta, and the city expressed ambitions to become the Brussels of Southeast Asia. The size of the country and the dynamics of its development give some basis for this supranational status. However, the capital city of Indonesia is considered by many as substandard, being inadequate even for domestic and national needs, which became especially evident after the construction of the new capital city in Malaysia. Hence the new capital city project is viewed by some politicians as a chance for the country to strengthen its leadership role and make a statement about its new economic and political standing.

The government of Indonesia has recruited experts and established research centers that study different options and alternatives. Indonesia 2033 Vision Team, one of such groups, was formed to explore different possible scenarios.

Most of the experts support the candidacy of Palangkaraya ("Great Sacred Place"), considering the central location of Kalimantan Island relative to the archipelago of Indonesian islands as a significant advantage and recognizing the need of accelerated economic development of this region to balance the national economy concentrated in Java. They also see some demographic benefits in the migration of part of the 130 million Java populations to Kalimantan. It should also balance the ethnic dominance of Javanese and help to overcome the separatism in Irian Jaya, Aceh and other regions.

Besides Palangkaraya there are two other contenders for the role of the capital city on Kalimantan: Pontianak that is located on the western edge of the island and Banjarmasin on the south of the island. While the advantages of Pontianak are associated with its proximity to Singapore and the potential for better integration into Pacific economies and for improvement of the country's nodality and connectivity, the advantages of Banjarmasin stem from its role of a communication and transportation center connecting the new capital with the islands in the Java Sea. It was estimated that the establishment of a new capital city on Kalimantan will draw about 75,000 officials and 125,000 members of their families.

Thailand

Thailand is the only country of SEA that never served as a colony of another country. However, its capital city migrated from the inland areas closer to the coast where active sea trade took place, following the pattern and general logic in the colonial countries.

The flooding of Bangkok in 2011, which transformed the city into a zone of national disaster propelled the debates into the national discussion about the possibility of a capital city transfer to one of its provinces in the heartland. 20 MP from the ruling *Pheu Thai Party* (*PTP*) in the parliament led by Sataporn Maneerat have submitted a motion to move the capital city. A special commission to study the options and alternatives was established. The proposed candidates included Nakhon Nayok and Phetchabun to the east and northeast of the current capital.[71]

Concerns about flooding were dwarfed by the preoccupation among many Thai scientists and engineers with the subsiding issue. It is estimated that parts of the city may be permanently under water within two decades. Bangkok is sinking at a rate of 1cm a year due to subsiding land. Bangkok and adjacent provinces are only 50cm to 2m above sea level, which is rising 4mm every year. It was also predicted that due to the combination of rising water and subsidence Bangkok will be submerged within the next 30 years.[72]

The debate about flooding and subsiding has brought into sharper focus the monocephality problem. The second largest Thai city has only 200,000 citizens and thus is 40 times smaller than Bangkok. Therefore the level of primacy of the Thai capital is probably the highest in the world for the countries of similar size. Besides that 80 percent of all investments go to Bangkok and around half of the GDP of the country is generated in the capital.[73] Such concentration of resources in Bangkok fuels social problems and political agitation in the country and contributes to political instability. The Red Shirts protesters mainly represent rural and provincial Thailand, while the current ruling party represents mainly Bangkok. Capital city transfer, the defenders of the new capital believe, will facilitate political stability and appease the people in the countryside. The relocation of the capital city will diminish the pressure on the urban infrastructure, will slow down the sinking process, and will redirect the economic energy to regions that require more serious attention.

Remarkably, the plans to move the capital of Thailand have been mulled before much earlier in the history of the country. Field Marshal Plaek Piboonsongkram, the first prime-minister of the country, insisted on the transfer of the capital city to Phetchabun.[74] Some members of the government under Thaksin Shinawatra also contemplated the candidacy of Nakhon Nayok, which was considered to be less vulnerable to earthquakes. One of its merits is that it is located close to the international airport Suvarnabhumi. The Bureau for National and Social Development was tasked to research this issue further.

Philippines

In 1948 the capital city of the Philippines was moved to Quezon City based on the initiative of Manuel Quezon, the president of the country, who founded this planned city. The main reason for the transfer was associated with the military vulnerability of the Manila Bay for the attacks from the sea. Until today many bodies of government are located there, including the House of Representatives. However, officially the capital city was moved back to Manila in 1976 by Ferdinand Marcos, the president of the country, who also considered several other places as candidates.

The congestion and overpopulation of Manila brought the issue back into the realm of public and parliamentary agenda in the last couple of decades. Manila is considered the most densely populated city in the world at 43,000 people per square kilometer and is poorly designed to accommodate its residents.

The need to consolidate the discontiguous territories of the country better is another reason for the debate. In pursuit of this goal, Gloria Arroyo, the former president of the Philippines (serving from 2001 to 2010), urged to move the seat of government to Cebu City, the oldest city in the country. The most important advantage of this island, she claimed, is its central location relative to the whole archipelago of the Philippine islands. Another contender is Fort Bonifacio, the candidacy of which was discussed under the president Fidel Ramos and Clark.[75] There are also proposals to move the seat of government back to Quezon City, which already has the necessary infrastructure for capital city functions.

Under the initiative of Senator Antonio Trillanes IV, a special commission was set up in 2013 to study the possible scenarios for capital city relocation and to conduct feasibility studies to solidify knowledge of the available options. According to Trillanes, "Metro *Manila* is a capital which could hardly stand proud in the ranks of national capitals throughout the world." This rationale has its parallel in Indonesia, where the capital city is sometimes looked at as a political prestige item that should assert the influence and prestige of the country within the mega-region.

South Asia

India

In India the capital city relocation from coastal Calcutta to Delhi took place at the time of colonial rule in 1911. Originally the choice of Calcutta was determined by the considerations of more effective colonial control as it was better placed to project power both over the coast of the Indian Ocean and over Burma. Calcutta also served as a classical *entrepôt*, allowing entrance to the heartland of the Indian subcontinent through the Ganges.

The original impulse for moving the seat of government probably came from the circumstances of anticolonial protests in Bengal, of which Calcutta was a capital. In 1905 Lord Curzon divided Bengal into two parts, western and eastern. The Hindu western Bengal was wealthier and more economically developed compared to Muslim eastern Bengal. It was assumed that the division of Bengal would weaken the protest movement. However, this measure only aggravated the situation, and the Bengalis united against the British rule. The demonstrations against the division of Bengal, the creation of the secret societies, the guerilla warfare, the assassinations, and the boycott of British goods were a part of the protest. The protest movement reached its peak in 1905–1911. In response the British Empire reunited Bengal but decided to move the seat of government from the rebellious province. Unlike Calcutta, Delhi and the northern Indian princedoms were much more loyal to the British raj at that time.

Nevertheless, the reasons to move the capital city were not limited to the internal warfare and protests. The Brits had chosen the city not in the middle of the country but a place that was recognized as the center of Indian state and culture by the wide public of India. The neighborhood of Delhi had resonated with the sense of identity of the Indian people. Historically Delhi was the most important pre-colonial center of country. "The Seven

Cities of Delhi," seven distinct fortified capitals built by kings and emperors before the seventeenth century, including Qila Rai Pithora, Siri, Tughlqabad, Jahanpanah, Firozeabad, Deen Panah, and Shahjahanabad,[76] lie on the territory of today's Delhi. In the ancient Mahabharata epic, the half-mythical Indraprastha ("City of Indra") sited in the neighborhood of Delhi was the capital of the kingdom led by the Pandavas. The other seats of power of the Moghuls such as Agra and Fatehpur Sikri were also built relatively close to Delhi. During the 1857 war of independence, the sepoys proclaimed the last Mughal emperor, Bahadur Shah Zafar, the emperor of India since he ruled from Delhi. It was also in Delhi where three successive durbars took place, including the last and most opulent one where the construction of the new capital of India was announced and the first stone was laid in its foundation.

By returning the seat of government to the capital of the Great Moghuls, the Brits intended to split the nationalist movement in India, marginalizing Bengali nationalists and making a compromise with the all-Indian nationalist movement. While in the early twentieth century the center of protests moved to Bengal, Delhi was still recognized as a protest center and moving the capital there was a concession to Indian nationalism.

In spite of the clearly imperialist architecture of New Delhi, the transfer of the capital was already laying the groundwork for de-colonization due to its very location close to the heartland of historical Hindu civilization. Inside India the decision about the movement of the capital to the north was perceived as an invitation for a more open and confidential relationship with the metropole. Indeed there were some plans to make the governance of India more open for local people and to establish joint Hindi-British administration of the country.

There was still another reason that reflected the geopolitical interests of the British Empire and was no less important. By the beginning of the twentieth century the goals of control over Burma and the territories in the east of the Raj had been sidelined or lost their significance. The western gates into India in the mouth of the Ganges came to be more important than the eastern gates in the delta.[77] The protection of the entrance to India from Afghanistan and the control over territories in the north became more critical. Though, ostensibly, the Big Game with the Russian Empire was formally finished with the signing of the Anglo-Russian convention of 1907 that demarcated the spheres of influence of the two empires, the threat of invasion of India through Afghanistan was still a possibility. Afghanistan was not a reliable ally as it typically attempted to play both sides of the conflict for the best deal and failed to keep in check the tribal leaders. This threat was later materialized in the third Anglo-Afghan war (1919). The relocation of the capital strengthened the control over this strategically important region, helping to prevent the advent of the Russian army or Afghan tribes. It was consistent with the historical role of this region from where invaders have been best able to assert their control over the rest of the subcontinent.

The architectural layout of Delhi still preserves the symbolism and atmosphere of a colonial British capital. Notably, the presidential residence is located in the Viceroy's House of India. After independence Indians have removed many monuments of British imperialism, and many of them have been converted or resignified into national monuments of Indian history. However, the colonial atmosphere deeply ingrained in the built environment of Delhi still persists, as the city was constructed "not to be Indian, nor English, nor Roman, but to be Imperial," to use the words of Herbert Baker, the designer of the key government structures.[78] Not surprisingly, occasionally the proposals to replace Delhi with more national post-colonial capital city have been made.[79] Consistent with the patterns in many other countries, the supporters of the new seat of government suggest to move the capital city to a more central location or to disperse capital city functions between two or more other Indian cities. In this context the candidacies of Hyderabad, Mumbai, and Pataliputra have been proposed by several important politicians and intellectuals.[80]

Pakistan

In 1959 the government of Pakistan made a decision to relocate its seat of government to the north to a planned city, Islamabad. At independence the capital city was in the coastal Karachi. The plan to build a new capital in the mountain valley surrounded by the spurs of the Himalayas was approved in 1960 and completed in its main forms in 1963. Rawalpindi, 15 km from Islamabad, became the interim capital of the country, and the seat of government moved there already in 1958.

The transfer of the capital can be explained by several important reasons.

First, the new capital was located in the immediate proximity to the contested territory of Kashmir, allowing Pakistan not only to maintain its positions in northern Kashmir but also to lay claims to the whole of Kashmir. Moreover, the transfer of the capital to the north solidified the control over the northwestern Pashtun tribes showing separatist tendencies and aspiring to establish their own state of Pashtunistan, uniting their tribesmen from both Pakistan and Afghanistan.

The internal reasons were no less important – the need to develop the northern regions to balance the historical commercial and industrial dominance of the coastal south. In the first years of independence Karachi almost doubled in its demographic size mainly due to the influx of migrants (muhajirs) that soon formed the majority of the Karachi population. Besides that, Ayub Khan, the military leader of Pakistan, has tried to balance the different political and ethnic forces of the country, including Western and Eastern Pakistan. Moving some legislative functions to Dhaka and the political capital to Islamabad was a part of this de-centralization plan.

The Pashtun ethnic origins of Ayub Khan might have played a role in his choice of a capital as he located it in the proximity to Peshawar and the residence of most Pushtuns simultaneously expanding his loyalty base. It is hardly an accident that initially his choice was Abbotabad, located quite close to Islamabad and the place of his birth. However, later it was discovered that Abbotabad is located in a seismically active zone.[81]

The intention to isolate the capital city from the mass protests in Karachi was not less significant in the relocation plans. The ethnic conflicts between Sindhs and Muhajirs, the anti-government manifestations of the students and working classes in Karachi created an unsafe environment for the military regime that had acquired political power beyond the conventional election system. Not surprisingly, the city was sited close to Rawalpindi, the garrison town of the Raj period, which had relatively good infrastructure and available military units to suppress possible mutinies. It is noteworthy that for many years after the capital was founded, the military outnumbered the civilians in the population of Islamabad. The proximity of the garrison town and the lack of strong political identity in the region also contributed to this choice.

Adnan Rehmat notes in his article on the topic that contrary to the declared goals, the city was "tailor-made for friendly military takeovers and khaki rule. It is difficult to imagine a military power based in the densely populated and short-tempered Karachi or Lahore or Peshawar to both seize the city and hold it virtually indefinitely as Islamabad has proved." Its distance from large metropolises, proximity to the military base, and lack of self-government made Pakistan an ideal place for military coups, which were characteristic for the subsequent political life of the country.[82]

Islamabad has offered many benefits to its residents. It is located in the valley with pleasant climate and good water supply. It is roomy, clean and well-planned, and is rightfully considered one of the most comfortable places to live in the country. The plan of the city that merges the elements of the European architectural planning, Muslim traditions, and national Pakistani style was developed by the Greek architect Alexander Doxiadis who aimed to recreate the human dimension in architecture lost in modernity; Le Corbusier and John Stone also contributed to the development of its urban plan. The capital city is divided into 8 parts: diplomatic, administrative, business, educational, industrial, and residential and others. The Constitution Avenue, serving as the center of the administrative part, houses the Parliament, the National Assembly, and different ministries. Some critics lament that the residents of Islamabad are much better off compared to the rest of the country due to higher income and better quality of life.

Myanmar

In 2005 the ruling generals of Myanmar have decided to move the capital city from Rangoon to a new designed capital known as Naypyidaw (The Royal City of the Sun) located in the remote region of the country 320 km away from Rangoon. The decision was made already in 2001. The transfer of the capital was accomplished in only one day when the bureaucrats of the country were instructed to pack their luggage and move to a new capital city in a specially selected and astrologically felicitous day and hour. The exact time when the relocation started was Sunday, 6:37 am, March 27, 2006.

Today the population of the city is close to 1 million residents and it is one of the fastest growing cities in the world. The area of the city is 4,000 square kilometers, six times bigger than New York.

The transfer of the Burmese capital turned into a subject for jokes in the international media primarily because of its astrological inspirations of the necessity of this transfer and unfounded concerns of the rulers about the possibility of invasion of the country by the US and NATO. The new capital was often portrayed in the media as a lifeless ghost town built under the instruction of the ruling junta led by Generalissimo Than Shwe.[83] After visiting the city in 2007 one Indian journalist dubbed it a "masterpiece of urban planning designed to defeat any putative 'color revolution' – not by tanks and water cannons, but by geometry and cartography."

However, more sanguine and careful analysis reveals much more solid and rational reasons for this relocation. In his analytic review article Russian geographer Sergey Rogachev reveals more substantive reasons in the transfer of Burmese capital, considering references to astrology only as a cover for superficial journalists. The study of the logic and geography of this move points to at least several valid concerns that underlie this decision.

> The settlement pattern of the country in the Irrawaddy valley has high density of the population producing extremely negative effects on the country. The new pole of growth that is built in Naypyidaw half way between Irrawaddy meridian in the west and the Salween meridian in the east is moving the population concentration away from Irrawaddy valley to the smaller Sittaung River. The valley of Salween squeezed in the mountains is much less settled and developed compared to a larger alluvial plain of Irrawaddy. The translocation of the capital city further from Irrawaddy and closer to Salween can be viewed as a geographical signal and as an economic stimulus for the development of the eastern Salween regions of the country.[84]

The other rationale is the establishment of a balance between the largest and most important cities of the country, between north and south of the country, and between the territories settled by different ethnic minorities.

> The shape of the territory of Myanmar is far from the ideal circle or the rectangular pattern with easily definable center. If we try to identify the center of gravity of this complex figure, we will see that the location of Naypyidaw is the closest to the geometric ideal. Its location is in close proximity to two points with the highest population densities – in the mid- and downstream of Irrawaddy – and is creating a balance between them.[85]

Rogachev observes further that Naypyidaw is also located between the coastal colonial capital Yangon and Mandalay, the capital of the north. It is sited in the middle of the triangle formed by three major urban agglomerations of the country, Yangon, Mandalay, and Moulmein, the historical capital of Mon state. Hence it is a point balancing the three main social and economic masses of population.

The ethnic map of the country provides more clues about the advantages of the new geographic position of the capital city, supplementing the picture. The capital forms a hinge between the settlement areas of the three major ethnic groups: the dominant Burmese in the west, the Karens of the southeast, and the Shans in the northeast of the country. Forming the periphery of all three ethnic groups, the area of Naypyidaw has a potential to become a common center of these three groups.[86]

It also can be observed that the more central location of the capital – with stronger military and governmental presence – helped the government to better control the adjacent Shan, Kayah, and Kayin states and provide more stability to those chronically turbulent and not well-managed regions.

This analysis demonstrates that in their decision to transfer the capital, the authorities of Myanmar were trying to achieve a balance between the most important urban centers and ethnic groups and to distance themselves from the colonial capital following the experience of other countries of Asia and Africa. The reporting on Myanmar, however, is showing a tendency to inflate and overemphasize the astrological and military motivations at the expense of the above mentioned more rational and practical reasons.[87]

The relocation of the capital can also be better understood in the context of the pre-colonial history of Burma, where capital city relocations took place quite often. The interesting and detailed analysis of the precedents in Burmese history was presented by a Thai historian, who has demonstrated that in the past the decisions to move the capital also had astrological justifications although reasons could be different.[88] Notably, the Naypyidaw was established in the Dry Zone, the cradle of Burmese civilization where all pre-colonial capitals of the country were sited.[89]

Bangladesh

The capital city relocation debate in Bangladesh is stimulated by one of the highest population concentrations in the world, the highest concentration of all economic and material resources in one city, the gridlocks that paralyze the traffic, and a gamut of urban infrastructure issues. The population density in Dhaka is reaching 28,000 residents per square meter.

Some Bangladeshi politicians and analysts believe that such overconcentration of resources leads to corruption and is prone to self-perpetuation. The change of capital city is expected to jumpstart the program of large-scale social transformation from technical innovations to the liberation from corruption. The ideal place for a new capital is seen as a place with low population density, relatively close to Dhaka, and remote from the border and the plains that are flooded in certain seasons.[90]

Nepal

The environmental problems of Kathmandu, its uncontrollable growth, the influx of internal and external migrants, and the poor urban infrastructure of the city has brought the topic of capital city relocation to the political agenda in Nepal. Although the population of the agglomeration is only two million people, the peculiarities of the landscape and topography of the city do not allow any further expansion.

The need to move the city was more than once debated by the Constituent Assembly of Nepal. Such measure was also suggested by Hari Prasad Shestra, the political analyst who served as an advisor to two prime-ministers of the country. In 2012 the ruling Maoist party proposed Chitwan, 200 km from the current capital in Kathmandu, to serve as a new capital. The new city is supposed to create the conditions for the federalization of the country. The central location of Chitwan and its equal accessibility from different regions of the state would facilitate these goals.[91] In the aftermath of the earthquake in 2015, making most buildings in Kathmandu uninhabitable and unsafe, this issue was brought again to the center of public attention. It was suggested that Kathmandu should be rebuilt as a cultural capital and that Chitwan needs to assume capital city functions, at the same time helping the country to restructure for federalism.

Bhutan

In 1955 the king of Bhutan moved the capital city from Punakha to Thimpha in the course of his reforms directed at the modernization of the country. The separation of civil and religious authorities of the country was a part of this plan. As a result Punakha, the former winter capital, was turned into the Buddhist center of the country, the religious capital. Meanwhile, Thimpha has become the political capital, being located in between Punakha and the city of Paro, where the most important military castle and one of the two airports of the country is located.

Sri Lanka

In 1982 Sri Lanka moved its capital city from Colombo to Sri Jayawardenepura Kotte, 11km from Colombo, following the policy of counter-urbanization and de-centralization. The new city was named after the first president of the country.

While Colombo was founded by the Portuguese as a trading post, Kotte was the last capital city of the centralized Singhalese state that united the island in the fifteenth century. In the sixteenth century the kingdom was split into several warring states. Therefore the relocation of the seat of government had an important symbolic sense in the context of Singhalese history and identity politics. It is noteworthy that Colombo remains the premier city of the country in terms of the concentration of business activities. Apart from the legislation, many government decisions are still made in Colombo.

The transfer of the seat of government did not put a stop on the continuing ethnic confrontation between the Buddhist Singhalese and the Muslim Tamils. Tamils believe that the north and the east of the country where most of them reside do not receive the benefits enjoyed by the Singhalese residing in the central regions of the country.[92] The Tamils are also not represented sufficiently in the symbolism of Kotte.

The Far East

Japan

The idea of relocating the functions of the central government was first floated in Japan in the 1960s. During the so-called bubble period of the late 1980s, land prices in Tokyo were absurdly high, and it was thought that moving at least some of the government would spread the wealth around. The main idea that inspired the advocates of New Capital national movement, who managed to enlist support of some influential politicians, was not the development of some specific regions in the hinterland but the necessity to relieve Tokyo, which had become uncomfortably large and too expensive to live.

Although Tokyo was recognized as one of the most effectively planned megacities in terms of its urban infrastructure, which includes a fast speed transportation system, high-rise and underground construction, many Japanese politicians still believed that high concentration of resources in one place created hurdles and inefficiencies for the Japanese economy and for the governance of the country.

In 1990 on the occasion of the centenary of the Diet, Japanese lawmakers adopted the resolution to relocate the seat of government from Tokyo. The resolution provided that not only the Diet but also other government branches and ministries will be transferred to a new city. The goal was to create a "Washington D.C." in Japan and to allow Tokyo to maintain itself in a manner similar to New York.[93] A bill was approved by the Diet in 1992.

After three years of deliberation and intense debates and conducting more than 30 conferences dedicated to this issue, the Roundtable Committee on the Promotion of Building a New Capital City has published a report that identified three possible sites for the new capital. All of them were located not too far away from Tokyo in central or northeastern prefectures of the country. These sites were selected based on the assessment of 16 parameters of these regions such as seismic security, transportation accessibility, the conditions of purchasing land from its current owners among others, and their total scores were calculated. More than 70 experts participated in the collection and summarization of the results. The results of the debates within the Roundtable Committee were also taken into account. As part of this approach, which integrated different insights, the total scores for each contender were counted.[94]

The relocation of the capital city functions was expected to stabilize the urban development of Tokyo and facilitate the economic self-reliance and independent cultural life of each Japanese province in the framework of the general de-centralization strategy.

However, when the economy cooled later in the 1990s so did the discussion about relocation. In 2000 the ruling parties of Japan have decided to freeze or postpone this project due to the unfavorable economic situation. The debate though had several other tides. In 2005 the Diet resumed the process of proper place identification. There were again three contenders for this role: Nasu (Tochigi Prefecture), 300 km to the north from Tokyo; Higasino (Nagano Prefecture) in central Japan; and Mie, close to Nagoya, 450 km to the west from Tokyo. However, since that time the analysis and the decisions of the Roundtable Committee were never disclosed publicly to prevent possible land speculation in the contender cities.

After the tragic events in Fukushima the interest in the subject was rekindled and led to the formulation of several alternative decisions. The scenario of establishing several auxiliary capitals that can take over if Tokyo is hit by a major natural disaster or terrorist attack was most carefully discussed. If in the 1990s the potential of an earthquake in Tokyo was only one of the motivations, since 2012 the seismic threat became central to the debates.

The problem of overconcentration of political and economic resources in the Tokyo region also remains topical. The population of the capital city region is more than 30 million people. Hence, 63 percent of the population is concentrated only on 3 percent of the territory of the country in its six largest cities, that is Tokyo-Yokagama-Nagoya-Kyoto-Osaka-Kobe. It should be noted that such concentration resulted not only from poor economic planning policies but also from the peculiar landscape of Japan.[95]

The idea of moving the capital also has its enemies and the metropolitan government of Tokyo is one of them. Shintaro Ishihira, once the governor of the Japanese capital, has called the concept "an attempt to desecrate the history of Japan." Some other opponents point out the paucity of arable lands in Japan and believe that the new construction will reduce the amount of available land that is already in deficit.[96]

China

In China the proposals to move the seat of government have been suggested since the 1980s. However, since the middle of the 2000s this debate has acquired new proportions and started to appeal to wider audiences. The problems of Beijing urban infrastructure and the misbalances in the economic development of the country served as the motivation of the debate. While most of the proposals about relocation were introduced and justified by the scholars, they were also often supported by prominent politicians. In 2006 almost half a thousand representatives attending the National People's Congress, the legislative branch of the Chinese government, moved the joint motion, requesting the shift of the Chinese capital city.[97]

The environmental situation in Beijing, especially the smog, sand storms and subsiding is a matter of special concern in China. The high population density in the city, the traffic gridlocks that take place beyond peak hours, and the extremely expensive supply of water into a city form a part of the background that explains the topicality of the issue. The persistent incidents of larger sandstorms and the long all-city traffic jams each time have triggered new cycles of these debates.

The tension between the Mandarin North and commercial South has defined the historical geography of China. However, more recent economic development trends made the divide between the developed coastal east of the country and the underdeveloped west more topical. The gap between these two regions is increasing every year. The eastern part of the country occupies only 13 percent of its territory but it has a 60 percent share in the GDP of China and 41 percent of its population. The western part occupies 60 percent of the territory but its share in GDP is only 14 percent and its population is 23 percent of the total.[98] Many Chinese scholars believe that under the circumstances the government needs to provide the economic stimulus to the hinterland in the west and have proposed a capital city transfer as one of the tools to provide such a stimulus. Others believe that China's economic core also should be shifted from the east to the midwest.

In 2010 Shen Hanyao, the president of the Wharton Economic Institute in Shanghai, has proposed to move the capital city closer to the south of the country. He has suggested the candidacy of Xinyang in Henan Province and Yueyang in Hunan Province. Both of these cities have abundant water resources and convenient transportation systems. Their location on the flat plain is described as their additional advantage.[99]

In 2008 two Chinese scholars Qin Fazhan and Hu Xingdou co-authored a long article, in which a concept of "one country, three capitals" was put forward. In their plan Shanghai will serve as an economic capital of the country, Beijing will remain its cultural capital, and a new planned city in the midwest closer to the center of the country will perform the functions of the political capital.[100]

The suggested names for the new capital aim to reinforce the continuity of Chinese history and to announce a new stage in its development. Beijing, Nanjing, Xi'an (Chang'an), and Kaifeng have served as the northern, southern, western and eastern capitals of China respectively. The new capital city should be named Zhongjing, the central capital, to signify both its location and to embed it into the fabric of Chinese history.[101]

The concept of the capital in the hinterland of China bears comparison with the paradigm of debate in some post-colonial countries that have shifted their capitals from the coast inland.

Taiwan

In 2006 70 MPs of the Taiwanese parliament urged the transfer of the seat of government of Taiwan to the south. The proposal was motivated primarily by the sharp divide between the wealthy and developed north of the country and its poor and underdeveloped south. Most of the support came from the Democratic Progressive Party whose power base is in the south of the country. The advocates of this proposal argued that Taipei receives a disproportionately large share of the benefits associated with capital city status. The Kuomintang party whose support base is in Taipei and in the north in general decried this proposal.[102]

The capital city transfer was also recommended by a number of scholars who have emphasized the threat of flooding of Taipei due to the global warming of the oceans. Taipei would be flooded, they claim, if sea levels rose by 6 meters, which is not unrealistic.

The candidacies of the cities in the middle of the country have been also proposed. The candidacy of Taichung, located close to the center is especially popular. It was supported by some prominent politicians (e.g., by Lin Chia-lung, the mayor of Taichung and the ex-minister of information of Taiwan), businessmen, and local authorities of Taichung.[103]

There were also some calls for unorthodox capital city arrangements. One of the ideas was to make Taipei a nominal capital city, while siting the *de facto* capital in the south of the country. The concept of an itinerant capital when the capital city oscillates between the north and the south every two years was also introduced. Finally, some politicians have proposed to split capital city functions between three cities. In the latter case the presidential power will be located in Taipei, the legislative power in Taichung, and the judicial power in Kaohsiung.[104]

In 2012 the president of the country, Ma Ying-jeou, has formed a special working panel from the members of his cabinet for the study of this issue.

South Korea

In 2002 Roh Moo Hyun, the president of South Korea (2002–2008) urged the transference of the government seat to Sejong, 120 km from Seoul. The parliament of South Korea has approved this bill almost unanimously: 158 MPs have approved the transfer of the government functions while only 13 MPs disapproved. It is remarkable that both the ruling Uri Party and the opposition Grand National Party (GNP) have converged on this issue.

The main official reason for the transfer was to balance the development of the country. Remarkably, more than half of the total population resided in the capital city region that occupies only 12 percent of the territory of South Korea. The capital city region housed 56 percent of all manufacturing companies, 95 out of 100 largest Korean corporations, and 20 of the best universities (65 percent).[105]

The decision to move the capital was also justified by the proximity of Seoul to the North Korean frontier, lying only 35 km from the city, and the threat of invasion from North Korea.

Based on these reasons, Sejong offered several important advantages. It is separated from North Korea by a larger distance. The city has a symbolic meaning that resonated with the idea of national identity: the city was named after Sejong the Great, the fifteenth century king of Korea who is also credited for the first native phonetic alphabet system for the Korean language.

There was another important reason. Sejong is situated in the swing province of Chungcheong on the border between two provinces in the center of the country. Historically the competition of the two major parties was grounded in the geography of South Korea: the conservative GNP party had more support in the southeast, while the liberal New Politics Alliance for Democracy (UDP) that Roh Moo Hyun represented had more support in the southwest. The metropolitan region of Seoul was split between two parties. The proposal to build a new capital in Chungcheong appealed to the residents of the swing province, helping Roh Moo Hyun and his party to gain its political support. Thus, the overall arrangement can be understood as a clientalist exchange, although it obviously would be short-sighted to see the underlying proposal only as an expediency to win votes, the stance that was taken by the critics.

Some political analysts and outside observers tended to view this proposal as an expression of the hubris and eccentric whims of the autocratic Korean ruler. According to this view, many Korean politicians had a penchant for multibillion dollar megaprojects, "dreaming up the most ambitious construction projects imaginable." Their megalomaniac excesses have included the proposals and the actual construction of new cities, notably Sondo, large airports that are not even used today, and the unnecessary colossal canals. All these projects were rarely economically justifiable.[106] Domestically many politicians also have casted doubt on the feasibility of the project, criticizing it as a hasty decision characterized by the lack of knowledge about the spatial dynamics and the total costs of such projects.[107] There was also an argument that relocating private firms with high inter-industry linkages is a better policy option for attaining balanced national growth and increasing non-capital regional population, rather than moving public sector servants.[108] Another cause for concern was that downsizing will be unfavorable for Seoul in its rivalry with other global cities.

Unsurprisingly, the decision to move the capital was also faced with an opposition from the GNP party. In December 2004 the opponents of capital city shift submitted a complaint about its unconstitutionality to the Constitutional Court. It has halted the move and, as a consequence, Roh Moo Hyun was forced to scale back his project. Based on the redrafted plan the Blue House, the Congress, and the Constitutional Court were to remain in Seoul; only some government departments were to move to Sejong. Based on the modified plan, in 2005 the new law was adapted that provided for the relocation of nine ministries, four departments and about 10,000 civil servants to a new place. The law also provided for the dispersion of the administrative functions between different cities of the country. 40,000 civil servants were expected to move out of Seoul.

Lee Myung-bak, the next president of the country (since 2008), GNP member and notably the ex-mayor of Seoul, has opposed even the smaller scale plans to relocate civil servants to Sejong, considering it a waste of resources. He was concerned that the transfer of even some government departments to Sejong will lead to failures in the coordination and execution of the administrative regulations and will make the government operations less efficient. However, the coalition of liberal UDP along with some members of the ruling GNP party still insisted on the relocation consistent with the revised plan. The government finally has followed this plan: Sejong is currently functioning as a mini-capital of the country.

The future of the Korean capital city is still debated. Some politicians insist that Sejong should be transformed into a regular capital city that houses executive, legislative, and judicial powers. Other politicians and scholars anticipate that the capital city might become again a contentious issue in the course of the expected unification of the two Koreas.

Harry Richardson and Chang-Hee Bae, the experts in urban studies and territorial development, have tackled this problem in their intriguing article on the choice of the future capital of unified Korea. They believe that part of the reason that the original plans were scaled back in 2004 were the prospects of such unity.[109] Although there is still no evidence that the reunification of South Korea and PRK is imminent, many politicians are confident that such unification can become more or less viable in the next 10 years. In this context the question about the new capital will inevitably become not only an economic and geographic problem but will acquire more fundamental political significance. Certainly, the choice of the capital city will play a momentous and fundamental role in the nation-building efforts and in the integration of the two Koreas long separated by their social and political systems.

Four possible candidates for the role of the new capital of unified Korea, their merits and drawbacks from the standpoint of the unified country, are discussed in the article. Each part of Korea has two likely candidates for this role: Pyongyang and Kaeson in North Korea, and Seoul and Sejong in South Korea.[110] The benefit of Pyongyang, Kaeson, and Seoul is that they are located on the north-south axis that coincides with the trade route to China. Sejong is not located on this route and does not have an international airport. The benefit of Pyongyang is that it is not as overpopulated as Seoul, but it has a poor infrastructure and is dominated by communist imagery. Additionally, it is unlikely that its candidacy will be accepted by South Korea. By the same token, it is unlikely that the candidacy of Seoul will be accepted by North Korea. Hence the most likely candidate, according to Bae and Richardson, is Kaeson. Kaeson is a symbolic capital as it served as the ancient capital of the country in the Koryo dynasty era from the tenth to the fourteenth century. It is also centrally located relative to the combined territory of North and South Korea. The land and labor in this city are also inexpensive relative to other contenders, and this will allow to reduce spending on new capital city construction.[111]

The context of nation-building and the prospect of future unification will likely provide stimulus for the new cycle of capital city relocation debates. The defenders of this decision are hopeful that it will help to overcome the current impasse in the relations between the two countries. Meanwhile, Sejong is growing and is gradually becoming a more attractive place to live.

Mongolia

In 2004 Tsakhiagiin Elbegdorj, the prime-minister of Mongolia, initiated the establishment of a special commission tasked to provide a New Development Plan for Karakorum, the ancient capital of Mongolia that was founded by Genghis Khan in 1229. The new cult of Genghis Khan has fueled the wide public interest in this project. The prime-minister has proposed that the city should resume its capital city status by the time of its 800 years anniversary.[112]

The prospects of moving the capital were initiated not only because of the nostalgia for the old imperial past but were also fueled by the specific issues that the current capital Ulaanbaatar is facing. More than 40 percent of the citizens of Mongolia reside in Ulaanbaatar. In recent years the population of the city increased by 70 percent. Some other serious problems include the scarcity of water, pollution, smog, shortage of housing, and the high concentration of industrial activities in the city. The concentration of resources in Ulaanbaatar also contributes to the misbalanced development of country.

There was a break in the discussion of this topic after Elbegdorj's term as prime-minister ended. However, when Elbegdorj was elected the president of Mongolia in 2009, the discussions of the new capital resumed. He has established a special analytical group to research the distribution of the population and industry in the country and the feasibility of a new capital city project. The group was tasked to explore different options beyond the original Karakorum plan. In 2012 a prominent member of the opposition Mongolian People's Party proposed Zuunmod to be its candidate for the role of the new capital of the country.

In 2015 the Cologne-based practice RSAA and some other German firms have come up with a plan of a new administrative capital of Mongolia in Maidar, 20 km from Ulaanbaatar. Originally Maidar was conceived as an eco-city, built around a 54m-high statue of the Buddha. As the plans grew more ambitious, the Mongolian government took over administration of the project. Chinese and other international investors are willing to finance this project as the Mongolian economy is growing fast. The large-scale construction is expected to start in 2017.[113]

The Middle East

Turkey

At the period of the rise of the Ottoman Empire, Istanbul was located in the center of the country between Anadolu in Asia and Rumeli in Europe. However, with the course of time, the empire lost the Balkans and almost all of its territories in Europe, and its capital had become the most vulnerable city on the very border of the country. As a result, whenever the country was losing the war, the armies of the enemy were right at the gate, as it happened in 1878 and in 1918. In March 1920 the Triple Entente armies occupied Istanbul. Under the circumstances the Turkish administration started to look for a more suitable place for its capital city in the Asian part of the country. It was finally found deep in Anatolia in the heartland of the Turkish nation. Kemal Ataturk, the charismatic president of the country was the initiator and the organizer of this project.

The main goal for Ataturk was the building of the nation and its reconstruction on the ruins of the Ottoman Empire. Initially, Ankara served as a temporary capital, the headquarters of the national resistance movement. The new Turkish parliament was convened in Ankara in 1920, and in his address to the parliament Ataturk pledged that from this moment on, it will be Istanbul to take orders from Anatolia and not the other way around. Nevertheless the official designation of Ankara as the capital city of the country was delayed until 1923, as the earlier recognition could have been interpreted as a renouncement of territorial claims to Istanbul and would weaken the drive of the Turkish army to liberate it.[114]

In October 1923 thirteen members of parliament led by the first prime-minister presented a bill to designate Ankara a seat of government. In response to the claims of the detractors about the historical significance of Istanbul and continuity of Turkish history, the new leaders emphasized the geopolitical advantages of Ankara in terms of security and communications, insisting that Istanbul can still serve as the economic and cultural capital. As a result Ankara was pronounced the new political center of the state almost unanimously.

Meanwhile the opponents continued to promote their position in the public debates. For instance, one of the prominent opponents claimed that self-isolation in Anatolia, like the Chinese Great Wall, will separate the Turkish people from the trends and processes of modern civilization. Fending off this argument, a journalist from Ankara compared Istanbul and its rulers to the

Chinese Great Wall that kept separating the Turkish nation from the civilized world, which they can now join.[115]

The most important considerations that have determined the choice of Ankara were related to nation-building and to the liberation from the legacy of empire. For Turks the fall of the empire and the defeat in the war meant also the birth of the nation. The text of Istanbul was already covered with the multilayered and long history of the Ottoman Empire and other civilizations. Turkey needed a *tabula rasa* to start producing its own text of the nation and to create new forms that would epitomize the new aspirations of the Turkish people.[116]

The new capital city has catalyzed the establishment of the nation and the formation of its new identity and facilitated the de-imperialization of its political thinking. Although Mustafa Kemal initially appealed to military-strategic arguments, the scope of his reforms of different spheres of state, religious, and cultural life of the country reveals that nation-building and the establishment of the new identity in a new geographic area of the country was no less important for him. It also must be noted that the first capital cities of the Ottoman state – Yenişehir and Bursa – were founded in the interior of Anatolia in close proximity to Ankara.

The symbolism and architectural plans of Ankara were opposed to the imperial ideology, on the one hand, and to Islamism, on the other.[117] The imperial legacy of the Ottomans was proclaimed obsolete and even dangerous for the new nation. The reformers have made efforts to "nativize" Turkish traditions and to embrace the elements of pre-Islamic and pre-imperial cultures. The iconography and the monuments in Ankara reveal the interest of the new government in the Anatolian symbols and imagery. These symbols are absorbed into the iconography, and their revival is celebrated in the emblems and the plan of the city. Notably, the Hittite Sun has embellished the coat of arms of the new Turkish capital.[118] Later on, the form of the mausoleum (Anytkabir), another artifact of pre-Islamic cultures of the Middle East, was adopted as the central architectural form in the city that was used to commemorate Ataturk and to visually represent the national Turkish history.

The national traditions of new Turkey were presented as an antipode to orientalism, ornamentation, and ornateness that the reformers attributed to the Orient. The capital city relocation also aimed to move Turkey closer to the ideals of modernism and simplicity which were attributed to the very ethnic substance of a nation liberated from the imperial and oriental sentiments.[119] It is noteworthy that after the revolution the new Turkey also abandoned the Arabic script and adopted the Latin alphabet. This new modern and functional attitude was articulated in the phrase by Falih Rıfkı Atay, the writer and journalist close to Kemal and the honorary member of the Ankara City Planning Committee: "The Ottomans were building monuments, while the Turks build cities."[120]

Iran

In 2003 the government of Iran pledged to move its capital city from Tehran. The specially appointed Expediency Discernment Council was tasked to develop the strategy and the details of this project. Since 2009 the discussion of this project has intensified not least because of special interests in this concept from the spiritual leader of Iran, Ayatollah Ali Khamenei.

Iran presents an intriguing case where the change of capital is expected to help accomplish many different goals not all of which are mentioned in the official documents.

One of the main official rationales to shift the seat of government was to release the 14 million Tehran from traffic jams and overpopulation and to mitigate the consequences of a large earthquake which the seismologists consider almost inevitable in the region of Tehran. According to Bahram Akasheh, the professor of geophysics at the University of Tehran, there is a 90 percent chance of a 6.0-magnitude quake hitting the capital. Being located on the convergence of multiple fault lines, Tehran in its present architectural form would not be able to withstand even a moderate earthquake, and a 6.0-magnitude quake will kill 6 percent of its population and will destroy 80 percent of its buildings. It was also forecasted that in case of such a quake, all the roads leading to Tehran will be destroyed, and it will make the rescue operations extremely difficult to carry out. Requesting a move of the capital to Isfahan, Akasheh claimed that "either we have to put up with millions of dead, millions of injured, or we need to move the capital somewhere else and take steps to decrease the population here and make Tehran more resistant to earthquakes."

The concerns about the infrastructure of the city and the trends of its fast demographic growth are no less important. In the last 100 years Tehran's population increased from 250,000 to 14 million. This growth was accompanied by uncontrolled construction, which transformed the city into a jungle of concrete.

Many observers also believe that the proposed capital city shift is also politically motivated, as Tehran is often rightfully considered to be a large liberal-minded enclave in the traditionally religious and conservative country. The frequent anti-government protests in Tehran is a matter of concern for the Iranian leadership. Students, which constitute a large portion of the population of Tehran, were the main propulsive force of the opposition rallies and manifestations. In a new place the government authorities will be freed from their current dangerous neighbors, namely the liberal minded Tehran public and turbulent pro-Western students. Hence the security of the government offices is a large concern behind the debate.

There are several contenders for the role of a new capital city.

The city of Qom or its vicinity is a popular candidate as its immediate surroundings have never experienced any earthquakes in the last two thousand years. The religious and conservative population of the city is considered an additional advantage. Notably, Qom was a place where Ayatollah Ruhollah Khomeini was studying and teaching. It is expected that the city with such a glorious past can become a reliable stronghold of the current political regime. It is interesting to note that the candidacy of Qom for the role of a capital was already considered by the National Defense Committee in 1915 when the Russian troops came close and were at the gates of Tehran.

Parand, 35 km to the southwest of Tehran, is also considered for this role. It has the necessary infrastructure for its new functions such as a large airport, subway, and highways. The candidacy of Parand is implied by the construction of the administrative capital and the transfer there of several ministries and government agencies.

The candidacies of Isfahan, which served as the capital city of Iran in the sixteenth century, and Shahrud in the north of Iran are also considered.

The recent promotion of the candidacy of Tabriz for the role of a capital city is propelled by a very different reason, the necessity to strengthen the control over the potentially separatist territory of Eastern Azerbaijan. The proponents of this plan believe that moving the seat of government to Tabriz will prevent the escalation of the separatist sentiments in the region, provoked and putatively supported by Azerbaijan. The proposals in Azerbaijan to rename the country Northern Azerbaijan were perceived by Iran as a preparation for the unification of two parts of the split nation. Some Iranian politicians also see in Tabriz important strategic merits, that is the proximity of friendly Russian and Armenian territories and the remoteness from the countries of the Persian Gulf where the US aircraft carriers are being deployed. It was proposed that several government departments, including the Ministry of Foreign Affairs, the Ministry of Industry, and National Security Service should be moved to Tabriz immediately.

The Eastern Azerbaijan where Tabriz is located is also promoted as a place associated with ancient Persian identity. The defenders of relocation to Tabriz claim that these lands where one of the three great fire temples was sited are closely connected with the emergence of Zoroastrianism and the very origins of the spiritual life of the first Iranian tribes. Accordingly, they believe that the movement of the capital to these lands of fire-worship will help to preserve original Persian identity and to strengthen Iranian ties to the territory where the Turkic-speaking population became prevalent only in the sixteenth through eighteenth centuries. The protagonists of the move also assert that the local Azeri population preserves the old Iranian ethnic substrate in spite of the Turkic language that they use in everyday life. The advocates of this plan consider Tabriz not just as a city that needs to be Iranized and brought back to the titular nation but as a forgotten center of the original Persian culture that can be revived through the transfer of the capital city. This romanticized version of history and the vision of a problem has transformed Tabriz into one of the most popular candidates for the role of a new capital.[121]

It must be noted that the capital city shift was included in the comprehensive 20-Year National Vision Plan (2005–2025) and was approved by Ayatollah Ali Khamenei.

Afghanistan

In 2008 the decision was made about the construction of a new capital of the country New Kabul City, 20 km from the old Kabul. The Master Plan for this New Kabul City was endorsed by the Afghan Cabinet in 2009. It was planned as a modern and well technologically equipped satellite city with 3 million of population. Japan and several international donor organizations have dedicated $500 million for the construction of the new city. It was estimated that the full-scale realization of the project will take 15–30 years and $34 billion. One of the senior advisors of the president Hamid Karzai is managing the project.[122]

At the moment Kabul serves as the main economic and cultural center of the country. The reasons to build a new city include the overpopulation of Kabul, caused by the high level of migrations into the city and large number of refugees residing there, and its poor infrastructure that was damaged by the swarm of wars and civil conflicts in the country. The city was designed to house 750,000 people and now has five to six million residents. The new city was conceived as an international center providing new external linkages with the largest regional economic centers in Central Asia, South Asia, and the Persian Gulf states. It is also expected that New Kabul will revive the role of old Kabul as the major city on the Silk Road, connecting Europe with India and China. It also should provide jobs to 300 thousand of Afghanis, which is important considering the very high unemployment rates in the country. The new city is envisioned as "the greenest city in the world" because of the ecologically clean renewable energy resources deployed for the city; the name of the valley Deh Sabz where the construction is currently going on translates as "the Green Village."[123]

The opponents of the plan dub the construction of the city a "neo-colonialist project," designed to build a city for the moneyed elite of the country and for the global corporations and not meant for its regular citizens. The project is also faced with an opposition from the nomadic tribes of Kuchi and some of the residents of the Valley. They demand high compensation for taking their land. The nomadic tribes have traditionally used Deh Sabz as a camp on their way from the foothills of Hindu Kush to the grasslands used as their pastures and also for the seasonal trade in the markets of Kabul.

Egypt

The congestion in Cairo along with its poor urban infrastructure is the main driver of the capital city relocation debate in Egypt that has a long history.

In the 1970s Anwar Sadat, the president of the country, envisioned a new capital and started to build it in 1979 in the city that was called after him, El-Sadat. He was hoping that by 2000 Egypt would have a new seat of government. However, his plans never came to fruition and the Complex of Ministries built there currently is housing a university.

In 2005 a group of experts proposed to move the capital to El-Minya al-Gadida, 250 km to the south of Cairo. A less radical decision to move the seat of government to one of the suburbs of Cairo was approved during the session of the government chaired by Ahmed Nazif. The government announcement has explained that this arrangement should alleviate the pressure on the infrastructure of the gigantic city. The population of Cairo was estimated then at 18–20 million people, that is 20 percent of the total population of the country and the city was growing at 2 percent annually. Three candidates for the role of a new capital have been proposed at the session: October 6 City is 35 km from Cairo, New Heliopolis situated at a place of an ancient sacred capital, and one of the regions on the way from Cairo to Suez. In 2007 the government prepared the plan of the new city. However, Hosni Mubarak, the president of Egypt, rejected the project as too expensive. After the Egyptian revolution the new government resumed the debate and pledged to get started on the construction of the new city on the Cairo-Suez highway. The cost of the project was estimated then at $200 million. The new capital city construction was incorporated into the *Roadmap of the Future*, a comprehensive strategy of the country development that implied the technological modernization of the Egyptian economy.[124]

Finally in 2015 Abdel el-Sisi, the new president, has unveiled plans to construct a huge capital city, 50 km from Cairo, receiving pledges of financial support from the Emirates (UAE's Capital City Partners) and the leading architectural and urban planning firms. The announcement was made at an investment conference that aimed to revive the Egyptian economy. The new capital city will cost the country $45 billion, and it will bring the new seat of government closer to the Suez Canal. Initially, it was estimated that it would take 12 years to build the new capital. Later on it was announced that Egypt signed an agreement with a Chinese company, "China Construction," on building and financing part of a planned new administrative capital.

Jordan

Hashemite Kingdom was founded as an independent state in the wake of anti-Ottoman revolt. The seat of government was transferred from Salt to Amman shortly after in 1921. Amir Abdullah I, King of Jordan and the founder of the state, aimed to marginalize the old elites and family clans that served as mediators between the Ottoman Empire and the Arab provinces. The nation-building plans were faced with several challenges. Abdullah I was born in Hejaz, half of the population of the country was Bedouins, and the country experienced the influx of the migrants from Syria and Palestine. This was a background against which Abdullah sought to find a reliable social and ethnic base for his political regime. Under the circumstances the most urgent task was the integration of the Bedouins and the reliance upon the new settlers, the tribal leaders, and ethnic minorities that were expected to provide loyal support in the governance of the country. As a consequence, the old ruling elites residing in Salt were excluded from the power structures, and Amman, a small settlement that did not have any strong political identity, was selected as a place for a new capital city. The Circassian population of Amman was an important factor in its choice; among other minorities, they were the most loyal to Abdullah and served as his royal bodyguards. Subsequently, the Circassians were recruited to occupy important positions in the national Jordanian army. The location of Amman on the newly constructed railway linking Damascus and Mecca turned out to be an additional benefit as it strengthened the nodality and the international role of a new capital city.

Bahrain

In Bahrain the capital city transfer from Muharraq to Manama took place in 1923. Muharraq was an enclosed capital city sited on a well-fortified island. It epitomized the tribal rule of the Al Khalifa ruling clan. The good fortification system that defended the city from the pirates and from the invasion of the neighbors constituted the main advantages of this city. However, Muharraq was a Sunni stronghold, while the majority of Bahrain's population was Shia Muslims. The capital in Manama better reflected the identity and interests of the Shia majority of the population.

The movement of the seat of government to the more cosmopolitan and commercial Manama also marked the transition to a more open and modern type of state. Muharraq was the center of the provincial pearl economy, while Manama has ushered in the epoch of oil economy that contributed to a higher international standing of the country.[125]

United Arab Emirates

In 2009 the president, Sheikh Khalifa bin Zayed bin Sultan Al Nahyan, and the prince of Abu Dhabi and general, Sheikh Mohammad, initiated the transfer of the capital city from Abu Dhabi to Khalifa City, 20 km from the current capital. According to the plans, the city will be built in 20 years and will be able to accommodate 3 million residents in the course of 25 years.

The new capital will house offices of all the ministries and departments of the government, the federal government, the university, along with the embassies and the consulates of the foreign countries. The construction commenced in 2010 and is being successfully carried out.[126] The government will be situated in the center of the new city. Seven large boulevards, each representing one of the seven constituent emirates, will link the center of the city with the surrounding regions. The proponents of the project stress that the new capital is designed to reinforce and strengthen the federalist identity of the United Arab Emirates.

Yemen

In contrast to Vietnam, Korea, and Germany the division of Yemen into the Northern and Southern parts was caused not by the ideological cleavages but by the vicissitudes of colonial history. Northern Yemen was a part of the Ottoman Empire, while the South of Yemen was ruled as a part of British India until 1937. In 1937 Aden, the port and the preeminent city of the south, was made a crown colony with the remaining land designated as east Aden and west Aden protectorates.

After gaining independence from the Ottoman Empire, Sana'a was declared to be the capital of Northern Yemen. In 1948 the unpopular king of Yemen, Ahmed ibn Yahya Humidaddin, moved the capital city to Ta'izz, which used to be the royal seat of power until 1962. In 1962 the capital city was moved back to Sana'a in the course of an antimonarchic revolution that overthrew the imamate and the royal dynasty. The critical factor that determined the choice of Sana'a was the fact that it was the longest serving seat of power of the state before the country has lost its independence in the sixteenth century.

The unification of the two countries, Yemen Arab Republic in the north and People's Democratic Republic of Yemen in the south, in 1990 invited the question about a common capital city. Northern Yemen was a larger and wealthier state, and it played a more important role in the unification process. Besides that Aden, the capital of South Yemen, was a classical colonial port, and the movement of the capital city inland from the more commercial and cosmopolitan port cities followed the classical pattern of most post-colonial countries.

However, the unification of the state under the leadership of Northern Yemen propelled civil conflicts and confrontations. At least in part they can be explained as a result of underrepresentation of South Yemen in the governing bodies and political life of the unified state. In 2013 due to the civil war and military confrontations in the north of the country, the National Dialogue conference proposed federalization of Yemen. Some delegates, notably the president of the country, have proposed to move the capital city to Aden and to consolidate political power there. There were also proposals to move the capital city to Ta'izz, which is in between Sana'a and Aden. Interestingly, the concept of dual capitals was also introduced as a long-term solution: the winter capital in Aden and the summer capital in Sana'a. This dual capital arrangement, the defenders of this solution have argued, will facilitate the national unity and will help to balance the representation of the six federated entities.[127]

Oman

In 1932 Said bin Taimur has moved the seat of his power from the coastal and commercial Muscat to Salalah in the Dhofar Province closer to the interior of the country. On the one hand, he was aiming to isolate the country from the outside influences and prevent the modernization of Oman. On the other hand, he sought to integrate the tribes in the desert hinterland and Dhofar Province in particular, as it was recently unified with Muscat. There was a powerful breakaway movement seeking independence from the Muscat Sultanate. The acquiescence of the interior tribes was also indispensable for oil exploration activities, and oil export revenues were necessary to secure the financial independence of the country. In 1970 the coup led by his son ousted Said bin Taimur, exiled him, and the seat of power moved back to Muscat.

Post-colonial nation-building in Latin America

The high level of centralization with a high concentration of resources in the capital city is typical for the countries of Latin America. This political centralization finds its expression also in the high level of primacy of its capital cities and the spread of monocephalic urban structures on the continent. For example, a third of Chile and Argentina's populations resides in Santiago and Buenos Aires. Similar proportions are characteristic for Mexico and the countries of Central America; this pattern of population distribution reflects the peculiarities of Latin American colonial history.

In their comprehensive and informative survey of the primate cities in the 18 countries of Latin America, Sebastian Galiani and Sukko Kim come to the conclusion that the status of the capital city in these countries has a much stronger impact on the level of population concentration compared to the countries of North America. According to their calculations, while the status of the capital city in Latin America increases its size by 232 percent, in the US and Canada their impact factors are 154 and 175 percent respectively. In Argentina, Colombia, and Peru their impact factors are even higher at 300 percent, and it is 495 percent in Mexico.[128] The researchers trace the origins of such differences to the Spanish traditions of highly centralized states that are contrasted with the Anglo-Saxon political conventions. This tendency manifests itself in the size of both national and subnational capital cities in the New World.[129] In their opinion the Portuguese political traditions were not as rigid and centralized as the Spanish, and therefore the Brazilian political system was also less centralized. The high level of corruption and the economies based on the export of resources also contributed to a high level of urban concentration. The headquarters of extracting companies and licensing for exporting operations being controlled by the officials from the capital cities also contributed to their hegemonic character, primacy, and large size.

Notably, the Spanish colonial administration was guided not so much by economic but by administrative considerations in its choice of colonial capital cities. Hence only in a few cases the capital cities were based in ports of Latin America.[130] Arnold Toynbee explained this difference by reference to the presence of natural resources. Mexico and the Atlantic Ocean in general were resource poor, and therefore the capital city was preserved in Mexico City at the site of the ancient pre-Colombian capital city. On the other hand, the Pacific coast of Peru was resource rich and therefore the Spaniards did not adapt the ancient Inca capital in Cusco and established a capital city in Lima instead.[131]

Most of the capital cities of the Spanish colonies in the western hemisphere were established in the historical heartlands of these territories: Bogota in Colombia, Sucre in Bolivia, and Quito in Ecuador. The coastal city of Trujillo served as a capital of Honduras for a short period of time but it was moved inland soon because of the threat of the Caribbean pirates and possibility of the attacks of other colonial countries active in the Caribbean Sea.

The capital city transfers or intense discussions thereof occurred mostly in the Spanish colonies of the New World in the same countries where the capital was established in the coastal areas: in Peru, in Venezuela, and in Brazil. These debates were often propelled by the intentions to establish larger federalist entities such as the Federation of the West Indies, the Central American Federation, and the Federation of Rio de la Plata encompassing Uruguay, Paraguay, and Argentina. In Nicaragua the capital city transfer was motivated by the necessity of reaching a compromise between two premier cities of the country that represented the two most conspicuous poles of its political orientation.

Besides the rareness of coastal capitals there was another factor that made capital city relocations in Latin America less popular than in the countries of Africa and Asia. The closer and tighter linguistic, religious, and ethnic integration of Latin American countries with their Spanish and Portuguese metropoles has made the necessity to break with the colonial legacy less critical and arguably their need to establish separate identity was less acute. The confrontation with their metropoles did not acquire the form of identity politics that many African and Asian countries have adopted accompanied by the need to confront the symbolic and cultural representations of colonizers' architecture and culture was much less relevant for Latin American countries.

Brazil

The decision to move the capital city of Brazil was made in 1956 under the newly elected president Juscelino Kubitschek, and the designed capital Brasília was built in record time in only 41 months. The urban planner Lucio Costa developed the urban plan of the city, and the acclaimed architect Oscar Niemeyer developed the architectural blueprint and constructed the key buildings of the new city.[132] In 1953, a special federal commission was charged to identify a good site for the new capital and to study the technical aspects of the project.

There were several important reasons to start this project, all of which were ultimately related to the needs to integrate the country economically, politically, and socially.

The concept of the new capital city in the hinterland of Brazil was envisaged already at the end of the eighteenth century by the fighters for the independence of the country.[133] The previous capital cities of Brazil were situated on the Atlantic coast at the place of concentration of the export-oriented economic activities and were marked by the symbols of Portuguese colonial domination.[134] The inauguration date for Brasília, April 21, 1960, was symbolically significant. It was the date of public hanging of Tiradentes (1746–1792), the Brazilian national hero and independence fighter. The date of inauguration was also timed to the discovery of Brazil by Pedro Álvares Cabral on April 22, 1500, and the founding of the ancient Rome. Remarkably, the inauguration of Brasília was introduced as the second founding of the country.

More importantly, the construction of the new capital city was a part of the plan to develop the interior regions of the country known as the *cerrado*, a vast tropical savannah with extremely acidic soil. It was recognized as the top national priority due to the unique challenges of Brazilian geography. The arable lands in the south forming the core territories of Brazil that were originally settled in the early colonial period form only a small fraction of its territories. Most Brazilian cities in this core were located on small, isolated pockets of relatively flat land due to the fact that the coast of Brazil is inhospitable to ports development and appears as a wall dropping steeply to the Atlantic ("Grand Escarpment"). This enclave topography and lack of a coastal plain made it difficult for the Brazilian cities to integrate, expand, and to achieve economies of scale. The standard development pattern around transport corridors, the formation of smaller cities between mega-cities and hinterland around them was precluded. All these circumstances contributed to weak intra-Brazilian relationship both in terms of economy and politics. To exacerbate the problem the regional rivalry between the Minas Gerais area, where Rio de Janeiro is sited, and Sao Paulo, sharing control over the central government left remaining states isolated and underdeveloped. As a result Brazil was more geographical concept rather than a national concept.[135] The construction of a new capital promised both to provide better interconnectivity between different regions of the country and to move the economic and political center of gravity from the coastal areas to the *cerrado*. The conversion of these lands into an agriculturally viable place required tremendous efforts, and the movement of the capital city there aimed to concentrate the national energy and resources in this region. Ultimately, the goal was to integrate the country both economically and politically, creating a growth pole in *cerrado*.

Another critical aspect of the relocation was the social transformation of the country. The capital city in Rio de Janeiro was marked by class conflict and sharp polarization between the rich and poor areas, the *favelas*. The new capital city was to be designed as a city without poverty, free of social and racial discrimination. The modernist apartment housing blocks were envisioned to provide housing for all, regardless of the class and rank, forming the foundation for the egalitarian state. The concept of Brasília was based on the modernist ideas of Le Corbusier about the potential of social transformation contained in the very concept of the city. While it was commonly assumed that the city is a product of historical development, the modernist architects believed that the purpose-built cities should serve as blueprints for the social transformation and catalyze the development of the nation. The morphology and symbolism of old cities, they believed, not only epitomize the obsolete architectural and artistic styles but also reinforce and perpetuate ossified political institutions, social injustice, and the patterns of inequality. Architecture was conceived as a tool of social engineering and the revolutionary transformation of society and the world as a whole.[136] Not surprisingly, the authors of this project saw themselves not only as the followers of Le Corbusier but also as Marxists. It is in this context that Umberto Eco has dubbed Brasília "the city of hope" and "the ultimate utopia of the 20th century."

Last but not least, Brasília was also conceived as a declaration of cultural independence of Brazil, emphasizing the distinctively Brazilian elements in its architectural style. Niemeyer placed a great emphasis on curves and free, open spaces. He had a distaste for straight angles and hard and inflexible straight lines, preferring free-flowing and sensual curves. These are the curves, he wrote, "found in the mountains of Brazil, in the sinuousness of its rivers, in the waves of the ocean, and on the body of the beloved woman. Curves make up the entire Universe, the curved Universe of Einstein."[137] In effect these curved architecture and open spaces of Brasília produce the feeling of freedom, flight, and suppleness. The overall surreal impression of the city resulting from these curves and open spaces is well summarized by a critic:

> Taking the horizon and dynamic sky as their backdrop, Niemeyer's buildings "approximate dream-scapes in which discrete elements are distributed in space in a fashion similar to the disposition of objects in surrealist painting".[138]

The iconography of the city and its topography served to emphasize the topics of de-colonization and modernity. The metaphor of flight is ingrained in the very Master Plan of the city where the crossing of two highways and two terraced embankments represent the flying airplane. According to Styliane Philippou, the architectural historian, this airplane has several important meanings. The supply of materials by air transport was a part of Brasília construction. The new airport built in Brasília provided air linkages with all major cities of the country and with the main global cities. At a deeper level Brasília represented the capital of the airplane era. "Brasília was the first place built to be approached by jet," and only the aerial view revealed the key elements of its Master Plan, in contrast to colonial coastal capital cities that were built to be approached by ship. The airplane was also a symbol of emancipation from the water element associated with the era of colonial dominance. Simultaneously the speed of the airplane epitomized the era of economic dynamism that have allowed the construction of Brasília in record time.[139] The new capital city projects on the entire country its enlightenment mission of organization and stimulation of technology and innovations.[140]

The evaluations of Brasília as a capital city and the attitudes towards this project in the rich and diverse literature dedicated to this topic are very ambivalent and the city still evokes antagonistic opinions.

In his book *Global Super-projects that Form our Future*, the futurist writer McKinley Conway has recognized it as the best government project in the recent human history. UNESCO has included the city in the list of the World Heritage sites. The enthusiastic and raving reviews of both the concept and architectural style of the city can be found in Brazilian media. For instance, Claudio Queiroz, professor at the School of Architecture and Urbanism at the University of Brasília, has dubbed it "the moment of truth in human history":

> The construction of Brasília was a basic moment of mankind. It was as though Michelangelo and Leonardo da Vinci were working together, invoking Wittgenstein's maxim that aesthetics and ethics are one. Brasília is the synthesis of all human knowledge.[141]

On the other hand, many other experts have lambasted the city as a failure of modernist central planning. They have excoriated Brasilia for its insipid streets, the lack of human warmth, the formalism and the alienating effects of its grandiose buildings, the morbidity and monotony of its uniform and bland superblocks. The critics also lamented the lack of amenities and the standardization and unification of the living spaces. The authoritarian urban planning, these critics claimed, has led to the emergence of expensive and unpractical buildings insensitive to time and social changes. The reliance on highways and the lack of streets for pedestrians was another common criticism. Holston's seminal book, *The Anthropological Critique of Brasília*, is one of the works that takes such a stance.[142]

Another common criticism was applied to the monumental public spaces, uninhabited by people and showcasing the iconic buildings. They were criticized again for their alienating effects and for the lack of conventional urban environment experience. They were also often portrayed as the monument to the architectural style that outlived its time, the "yesterday's science fiction," and as a mausoleum to the architectural ideology of modernism.[143]

Many critics also have stressed the obvious gap between the declared egalitarian goals of the new capital and the realities of Brasília that have reproduced the social inequality and spatial segregation typical for the rest of the country. Furthermore, some critics claimed that Brasília turned into one of the most socially segregated places in the country. The poor people could afford to settle only in the satellite cities located 8–45 km away from the new capital. It is noteworthy though that both Niemeyer and Costa later denied that their social transformation plans were as ambitious as many of their critics claimed.

The economic strand of criticism also attributed the high inflation and later economic turmoil in Brazil to the large public expenditures associated with this project. The expenses that have burdened the country's budget, the critics argue, could have been spent more productively elsewhere. Some critics even opined that Kubitschek was motivated not as much by the idea of the new growth pole but by the idea of isolation of the political elite of the country from the social protests in Rio. This opinion, curious but lacking any serious grounds, was expressed by Claudio de Magalhaes, professor of Regeneration and Management at UCL. Three years after the transfer, Magalhaes argued, the military came to power in Brazil; thus the founding of the new capital city, isolated from the demographic center of the population, has contributed to the success of the military regime.[144]

In spite of all these putative failures it is hardly appropriate to describe the project of Brasília as a fiasco and an "unparalleled urban catastrophe" as it was commonly done in the 1970s and in the 1980s. Presently, many of the urban scholars and political scientists see it as a measured success and apply more realistic standards to assess the performance of this new capital city and its implementation. Recently some urban scholars and architects have questioned the persistently negative images of Brasília that dominated western scholarship and particularly British media since the inception of the city, explaining them by various biases and preconceptions.[145] Today many critics agree that cities cannot be all things for all people and that the inability to achieve social harmony through its construction do not necessarily represent the failure of Brasília as a city and the failure of the relocation project as a whole.

The observers have noted that many of the urban issues that plagued Brasília at the beginning have been resolved or largely ameliorated. The super blocks have acquired a soul and necessary amenities. Many neighborhoods have been developed, and social life started to flourish in many public places. "Brasilienses have created a very new type of a Brazilian city, one that starts with a modernist plan and ends with the desires of its inhabitants."[146] Remarkably, by 2010 Brasília has grown to 2.5 million people. The job creation in Brasília and in its region has attracted significant migrations from different parts of the country that otherwise would probably flow to overcrowded Rio.

Most importantly, whereas Brasília might not be recognized as a paragon of a successful city, it is definitely a success as a capital that aided in the rebalancing of the economic and political life of the country. Brasília has helped to accomplish the mission of developing the interior of the country. In 1998 the Lucio Costa obituary in *Economist* known for its very skeptical and cautious attitude towards government mega-projects has observed:

> Brasília is in many ways a success. Forty years on, it is not too far from Mr Costa's vision of a city "monumental but comfortable." Not only have Mr. Niemeyer's concrete and glass palaces worn surprisingly well; the economy has flourished (less surprisingly, maybe, given that almost the sole industry is government). At 9,600 reais ($8,350), the federal district's income per head exceeds that of any Brazilian state. To the middle classes it offers unpolluted air and green space . . . And, very important for all, despite a recent rise in crime, Brasília remains safer than Rio or Sao Paulo. Above all, Brasília has succeeded in what it was meant to do: shifting the country's centre of gravity towards its vast interior, after 450 years in which settlers had clung to the seaboard. What Brazil's statistics call "the centre-west", a great swathe of plateau and savannah (yes, and cleared forest) is its fastest-growing region, producing large harvests of soya: by 1995 it accounted for 7.3% of GDP, up from 2.4% in 1959.[147]

This praise is as remarkable as it is unexpected from *Economist*. The relocation contributed to the transformation of Brazil's backlands and the revolutionary changes in agriculture of this region. Due to the development of *cerrado*, Brazil has turned itself from a food importer into one of the world's great breadbaskets. The construction of Brasília also improved transportation connections and spurred the emergence of secondary economic centers in the less developed North. The national road construction program that was initiated shortly after the construction of Brasília in 1960 was successful in connecting the new capital to state capitals and other main population and economic centers. The resulting radial highway system connected different inland municipalities, integrated the country, and had significance far beyond the economics and challenges of countries geography.[148]

Finally, it must be added that the project has been universally recognized as remarkably well-organized. The construction of the city involved the spirit of experimentation, the spontaneity and even improvisation. Hanford Eldredge, the geographer who has produced one of the first reviews of capital city relocation in Brazil has aptly observed:

> Had Kubitschek sought to begin with a series of lengthy and very likely social and economic studies, it is more than likely that the city would never have come into existence.[149]

The project has evoked the enthusiasm of the people whose hearts were touched by the concept of the capital city in the heartland. The capital city transfer has facilitated the formation of the new identity of the Brazilian people and turned into an important milestone in the process of nation-building. Its example still inspires many other projects in dozens of other countries far beyond Latin America.

Chile

In Chile in 1990 the aging general Augusto Pinochet moved the parliament from Santiago to Valparaiso, 116 km from the capital, to disperse political power. De-centralization was recognized as a step necessary for modernization of Chile's economy. Guided by neoliberal principles Pinochet and his technocrat military government believed that de-centralization would improve the macroeconomic climate, enhance efficiency, and would eventually attract more investment to Chile from multinational banks. Moving the Congress along with several key ministries and other institutions of national importance to Valparaiso was a component of this strategy. It is interesting to note that Valparaiso was also a native city of Pinochet.

Another reason was probably related to the economic situation of Valparaiso, since the city's economy and the port activities declined in the wake of the opening of the Panama Canal in 1914. The transfer of legislature was an attempt to provide the economic stimulus to Valparaiso. The movement of the legislature to Valparaiso has boosted the economy of the city and its political importance. Pinochet also sought to balance the pattern of settlement in the country. Being the second largest city Valparaiso had only a small fraction of Santiago's population: more than 5 million in Santiago vs. less than 300,000 in Valparaiso.

More cynical critics have argued that the move was also designed to limit the political power of the legislature. Indeed, the dispersal of political power had only limited effect under the military regime. However, the transfer of the seat of power definitely laid the foundations for further administrative de-centralization that was accomplished by more democratic Chilean governments later.[150]

Argentina

Like in Brazil the relocation of the capital city in Argentina had a long and intriguing historical background.

In the second half of the nineteenth century the intense constitutional debates about the establishment of a new capital city took place and lasted for over three decades. Many participants in these debates have argued that the federalist system of government based on the model of the US was the call of the day and the most suitable solution for the country.[151] Domingo Faustino Sarmiento, an Argentinian writer and the president of the country (1868–1874), was the most vocal contributor to this debate. He has put forth the concept of Argirópolis, the imaginary new capital of the country situated in the Island of Martín García on the Río de la Plata river.[152] Being an insular

Capital relocations in world regions 135

and neutral place, *Argirópolis* should have become a symbol of independence and lay the foundations for the unification of Argentina, Uruguay, and Paraguay. This neutral capital city was intended to remove the disproportional influence of Buenos Aires on the political life of the country. The interior provinces also demanded a federalist form of government, the autonomy and a national capital outside of Buenos Aires. Rosario and Córdoba were among the candidates. The new designed capital La Plata for the wealthy residents of the Province of Buenos Aires was created in 1882 in the wake of the debates but not the federalist new capital that was envisaged. While the unification with Uruguay and Paraguay was dropped from the agenda, the dispute about the new federal capital resumed only one century later.

In 1987 the National Congress of Argentina approved the law that was proposed by Ricardo Alfonsín, the president of the country, about the relocation of capital city functions from Buenos Aires to the northeastern Patagonia. The consolidation of two smaller settlements – Viedma and Carmen de Patagones – should have formed a new federalist capital.[153] The proposed names for the new city were "Patagonopolis" and "Patagolandia." There were also suggestions to commemorate some Catholic saints in the name of the new city.[154]

Official rationale for the construction of new capital was to ease the congestion of Buenos Aires, where a third of the population of the country resided. Similar to Brazil, the government also sought to achieve more ambitious goals of social transformation of the Argentinian society through the new city. The following three goals were most important: reducing the high concentration of resources and functions in Buenos Aires; stimulation of development in the hinterlands of Argentina, especially in the northeast and in the south of the country, and establishment of the new growth pole in Patagonia. The new city was also taken to task to transform and modify the inefficient state bureaucracy.[155]

But aside from all these considerations the new capital city was also a part of a broader geopolitical agenda. "Patagonopolis" was intended to strengthen the Argentinian presence in the south of the country. The construction of a new capital was to reposition Argentina as a Pacific power ruling from the southernmost capital of the world and to solidify its claims to several southern islands that belonged to Chile. Tellingly, the border conflicts with Chile and the territorial claims of Argentina to these islands in the 1970s foreshadowed the new cycle of capital city debate. Throughout the colonial period these islands and the straits were not very significant. However, since the end of the nineteenth century, they acquired importance due both to the increasing role of the Pacific in the world trade and to Antarctica development. The capital city in Carmen de Patagones was intended to play a role in the "Southern project" of Argentina and to buttress the Argentinian claims to precedence in the South American continent. The underpopulated "empty spaces" of the south were to be developed and populated to ward off Chilean incursions. The idea of the capital in the south also contributed to the concept of tri-continental Argentina (mainland, insular, and polar) that was actively promoted since the 1940s.[156] These geopolitical considerations were probably only secondary, but they should not be underrated.

Initially, the plans to transfer the seat of government included relocation of 15,000 civil servants. It was also planned that the new capital city will have 315,000 residents by 1995 and 554,000 by 2025.[157] Originally the project budget was $2 billion but gradually it was increased to $5 billion. Half of these funds were to come from government budget and half from private investments. It was expected that this amount will be spent in the course of 12 years.[158] Nevertheless, the project was never implemented due both to its high cost and the change of cabinet.

The project to move the capital from Buenos Aires was resuscitated in the recent years as it became increasingly clear that the problems of excessive concentration in the capital persisted. In 2014 Christina Kirchner, the president of Argentina, urged to move the seat of government to Santiago del Estero in the north. It is the oldest city of the country, situated between Atlantic and Pacific oceans, 1,042 km from Buenos Aires. The candidacy of this city was originally proposed by Julián Domínguez, the speaker of the Lower House of the parliament. He explained that this move would re-conceptualize Argentina and improve its international standing, opening it up to the Pacific and to the members of the Mercosur and Unasur. Unlike Buenos Aires, which limits the overall vision of the world for Argentinians, Domínguez argued, the capital in the north will make it easier to have links with the great Pacific basin. He further contended that port-capitals are more suitable for the colonized states, and those countries with greater ambitions should avoid them.

Venezuela

In Venezuela the debate surrounding capital city relocation centered around the problems of Caracas. Overpopulation, poor infrastructure, and the gridlocks on its main motorways were recognized as the most pressing issues of the current capital city. The special commission of the Venezuelan parliament formed in 2004 was tasked to develop the concept of a new city. The project was supported by Hugo Chávez, the president of the country. The commission proposed to name the new city Ciudad Libertad, or the City of Liberty.[159]

The site on the right bank of the Orinoco River in Bolivar state, 700 km to the south from Caracas, was selected as the most suitable place for the new capital city. It was planned that the extraction industry in Bolivar state, including iron and gold mining and rich oil resources, will be the economic base for the development of a new city.

The city was also expected to acquire the transnational significance as a center of the continent at the crossroads of South American integration.[160] The new communication systems were envisaged to underpin these plans and to provide access to the city from other countries. In pursuit of this goal, it was necessary to construct railways in the underground tunnels under

Orinoco River connecting Ciudad Libertad with Brazil and the hinterlands of Venezuela. Additionally, the construction of the river port was planned to serve as a gateway to the Caribbean Sea. This multi-billion dollar project was to be funded both from the oil revenues of Venezuela and from the international investments.[161]

Several other candidacies besides Ciudad Libertad have been proposed, including Carbuta in the center of the country, Caicara del Orinoco, Maracaibo, and Valencia, among others. The debates on this topic continue, but the difficult economic situation of Venezuela make the realization of this project less feasible and less topical.

Peru

The debates about the possible capital city shift in Peru are motivated mainly by three reasons: the overpopulation of Lima and the lack of space for expansion, its seismic vulnerability, and by some geopolitical reasons. In only ten years from 1965 to 1975 the territorial expansion of the city caused the absorption of 14 thousand hectares of the most valuable arable irrigated lands in the Rímac River valley. Lima was also included in the list of the most earthquake vulnerable cities compiled by an American seismologist Roger Bilham.[162]

Initially, the concept of a new capital city outside of Lima was introduced by Fernando Belaúnde Terry (1912–2002), the president of the country, who was also a prominent architect. He was teaching architecture at National Engineering School in Lima and at Harvard for some period of time. During his second presidential term in 1980–1985 he has flashed out his vision of the new capital city that was clearly inspired by the example of Brasília.

Already in 1956, in the course of his election campaign, Terry has published a book *Peruanicemos Peru* (Let's make Peru Peruvian), where he has laid out and expounded his vision of the future development of the country. His vision provided for the colonization and development of the hard-to-reach interior of the country and its central jungles. He also envisioned the road that would connect the country with Ecuador and Bolivia, on the one hand, and establish linkages between the Andes and Amazon River for the integration of the citizens of the country. The construction of the new capital was also a fundamental part of his plan. Julio Ernesto Gianella, the 1982 competition-winning architect of the new city, amplified and elaborated Terry's vision in his booklet *The City of Constitution: the new urban nucleus in the central jungles of Peru* ("Ciudad Constitucion : nuevo nucleo urbano en la selva central del Peru").

Laid in 1984, the new city was named Ciudad Constitucion, or the City of Constitution. The roads were built through the previously impassable mountains and jungles, and the construction of a highway linking the city with the Pacific coast was launched. However, the construction of the city was soon stopped, as the funds reserved for this project mysteriously disappeared.

138 *Capital relocations in world regions*

In the late 1980s Alan García Pérez, the young president of the country, proposed to relocate the capital city from Lima to Huancaya in the Andes. It was situated in the Mantara Valley between Lima and Cusco, the ancient Inca capital. One of the goals of the young president was to organize a large state-funded project that would provide employment opportunities for the underemployed population. However, this idea was later discarded and discredited as his comprehensive program of economic reforms did not appeal to the public, causing high inflation and the pauperization of large segments of Peruvian population.[163]

Presently the proponents of capital city transfer bring this topic again to the political agenda and revive some elements of Pérez's proposal. They stress the potential benefits of siting the capital city in the Andes region in terms of national security of the country. They also highlight the importance of the Mantara Valley for the national identity, emphasizing its significant role in Peruvian history. Relatedly, this region was the center of the native Indian Huanca culture that was controlled and subjugated by the Incas. The name of the proposed capital, Huancaya, is derived from the name of this culture. The backers of these plans contend that the geographic position of Mantara Valley, in the middle between the Spanish colonial capital Lima and the Inca capital Cusco, promises to establish a more lasting, neutral, and universal historical identity to the citizens of the country.[164]

Bolivia

In Bolivia the capital city debate turned into a capital city war in 2007 when Evo Morales, the president of the country and the head of his ruling party, redrafted the Constitution aiming to strengthen the rights of indigenous groups and the central government in La Paz at the expense of other provinces of the country. Remarkably, the New Constitution was approved only by four out of nine provinces of Bolivia. It has provoked the opposition to protest the changes of the constitution and to demand the return of the seat of government to Sucre. Sucre was Bolivia's capital until 1899 and currently is housing only the Supreme Court. Overall, more than a million people participated in rallies to support keeping the capital in La Paz, with a population of 1.7 million, and thousands of people in Sucre, population 250,000, to support moving the capital city.

The confrontation between La Paz and Sucre proponents reflects the division of the country between the wealthy lowland east of the country rich in natural resources, petroleum, gas, and arable land, and the poor western highlands where La Paz is located and home to Aymara and Quechua Indians. The capital city issue has deepened regional and ethnic divisions in the country.

The issue of more autonomy from the central government also lies at the heart of the debate. The Sucre backers, representing the more conservative and wealthier provinces, insist on more autonomy and federalist governance of the country, while the supporters of Morales, the first indigenous president, describe the autonomy moves as racist and view their proponents as "oligarchic remnants of the white and mixed-race elite who long dominated, and plundered, Bolivia."[165]

Thus the conflict over the geography of the seat of government camouflages deeper tensions and social and ethnic problems of the Bolivian society and is likely to remain on the political agenda of the country until the mutually agreeable solution will be found.

Nicaragua

In the last 130 years Managua, the current capital city of the country, was ruined three times by earthquakes. The most recent earthquake in 2014 has ruined the capital again, propelling the politicians and scientists of Nicaragua to discuss various capital city reconstruction options, including the idea to relocate the government to a new capital. In 1972 the candidacies of Masaya and Carazo have been discussed. Today the most popular contender is the city Estelí, the third largest city of the country.[166]

Honduras

The port city of Trujillo was the original capital of the country. However, the vulnerability of the city to pirates has forced Honduras to move its capital inland to Comayagua before the country was granted independence in 1838. After independence the capital city oscillated between Comayagua and Tegucigalpa. In 1880 Marco Soto, the president of the country, declared Tegucigalpa a permanent capital city.

The rise of both of the contenders was related to gold and silver extraction. While Comayagua was the stronghold of the conservative party, Tegucigalpa was associated with the liberal party. Soto was a member of the liberal party and the liberal-mindedness of Tegucigalpa determined its choice as a capital city. It must be noted that detractors related Soto's choice to the city's proximity to the US silver mining company where the president had a large share. The choice of Tegucigalpa has reinforced the victory of the liberals in the debates about the future development of the country.

It is remarkable that in 1921 Tegucigalpa was selected as a possible capital city of the federation of Central American Republic that encompassed Salvador, Guatemala, and Honduras, evidence of the high level of recognition of this city as a transnational political and economic center with high integrative potential.

Belize and Haiti

The complete destruction of Belize City, the old capital, due to the large hurricane in 1961 prompted the construction of the new capital city of

Belize in Belmopan. The decision was made in 1962 to build the new city away from the sea closer to the center of the country, 87 km to the south of the old capital. The construction was carried out in the period from 1967 to 1970.[167]

After the earthquake in Haiti in 2010 that destroyed 75 percent of Port-au-Prince, the capital of the country, the same idea was floated in Haiti. According to the seismologists, an even stronger earthquake is awaiting Port-au-Prince in the next 20 years. The concept of the new capital city away from the ocean was proposed by a number of scientists and politicians, including Bernhardt Etheart, the head of the government's institute for land reforms.

The Libertarian economist Tyler Cowen has suggested relocating the capital to Cap Haitien. The goals of the new capital city are similar to those of Brasília – new jobs generation and economic revival of the country. There were also some proposals to found a new "charter city" similar to Hong Kong to be administered by the third parties.

Post-Soviet countries

The motifs of de-colonization and de-communization did play some role in capital relocation debates in post-Soviet countries. Much more common and important considerations were the assertion of greater control over the contested territories and the needs of de-centralization. The borders drawn by Stalin that divided nationalities were largely administrative and did not reflect ethnic divisions. The internal migrations were often intended to alter the balance between different ethnic groups. Therefore, the collapse of the USSR has posed some questions about proper ethnic attributions of the territories.

The proposals to move capital cities have emerged in several Central Asian countries and in the Caucases. Notably, in Georgia, Armenia, and Uzbekistan, some proposals to move the seat of government were prompted by ethnic considerations. In Armenia there were proposals to move the capital to Stepanokert on the territory of Nagorny Karabakh that is claimed by Azerbaijan; in Georgia to Sukhumi on the territory of Abkhazia, the breakaway autonomy; and in Uzbekistan to Samarkand, dominated by Tajiks. In Moldova the transfer of the seat of government to Bender (Bendery) in the Trans-Dnestr region populated mostly by ethnic Russians was proposed to ward off the demands for larger autonomy and potential Russian claims to these lands. The proposal was also underpinned by the need to federalize the country due to separatism in breakaway "Trans-Dniester Republic" and in Gagauzia. There were also proposals to merge Tiraspol, on the Russian controlled territory, and Bander in Moldova.[168] In Ukraine the country was also split between Eastern and Western Ukraine, and the proposals to move the capital were motivated by the need to integrate the two parts of the state. However, overall the movement of the capitals of all these countries was expected to weaken the actual and potential claims of the neighboring states to these territories. It must be noted that in most of these cases such proposals were very marginal in the political life of these countries.

The contested territories problem was also important in Central Asia. However, there were some additional reasons that motivated the debate. After the collapse of the Soviet Union, five Central Asian republics were granted independence. Prior to Soviet period these countries did not have their statehood and, therefore, were the least prepared for independence compared to other former republics of the USSR. To exacerbate the problem, tribal and clan loyalties have persisted in these republics over Soviet-constructed identities. The capital city relocations have been proposed in these countries both to balance the subnational identities and to "nationalize" the contested territories.

Kazakhstan

Shortly after the demise of the USSR, Nursultan Nazarbayev, the president of the country, made a decision to shift the seat of government from Almaty, the capital city of Soviet Kazakhstan, to a new city and embarked on its construction. His selected city was Tselinograd (City of Virgin Land) in the north of the country that was to be renamed Astana (meaning The Capital in Kazakh). The new capital was built in the desert steppes on the other side of the river from Tselinograd, and its architectural plan was based on the sketches of Norman Foster, the renowned British architect. In 1997 civil servants and diplomats started to move to the new capital, while the construction was still in process.

Several official reasons for relocation were cited in the media and government documents. Most of them were related to the drawbacks of Almaty, including its proximity to the Chinese border, its vulnerability to earthquakes, the lack of space in Almaty Valley for expansion, the unfavorable climate, and pollution.[169] However, most of the international and domestic observers were puzzled by the undertaking of this project, as the country obviously had many more pressing issues to take care of, and its financial situation was not good enough to embark on such an expensive project. Most of the international media have attributed the zeal of Nazarbayev to his personal self-aggrandizement efforts not uncommon for the Oriental authoritarian rulers both in the present and in the past. Some of them referred to the servilist suggestions from some members of the Kazakh parliament (*Majilis*) to name the city "Nursultan" to honor the president. Many scholars and journalists perceived the official reasons bogus or at least questioned their validity and weight considering them only an excuse in the presence of many other urgent needs and acute problems.

Indeed, in the aftermath of independence Kazakhstan was facing many serious issues. Similar to other Central Asian republics of the USSR, Kazakhstan did not have its own statehood prior to the establishment of the Soviet Union. Hence the country was not as well-prepared for independence as many other republics of the former USSR, and the issues of state- and nation-building were much more critical.

Several challenges were specific and quite unique for Kazakhstan. At the time of the collapse of the USSR, Kazakhs, the titular nation of Kazakhstan, was not the majority in their own country.[170] In the north of Kazakhstan, the proportion of Kazakh population relative to Russian population was even lower compared to the south of the country, and the irredentist sentiments in Russia were running high. Because of the nomadic background of Kazakh people the territorial identities in Kazakhstan were much weaker than clan and family identities. The sub-national identities based on clan membership created obstacles for the formation of the national consciousness and identities. They did overlap with regional identities. There were also tensions between the resource-rich west of the country and the rest of Kazakhstan. These divisions and cleavages could become an obstacle for nation- and state-building efforts that were the order of the day.

To respond to these challenges Nazarbayev had to consolidate his power base and to develop a new system of loyalties: to find a new balance between the interests of the sub-ethnic groups, to identify an ideology that would integrate the ethnic Russians and other ethnic minorities such as Germans and Cossacks prevalent in the north, simultaneously building the viable economy of the country. This historical background gives some cues as to why the capital city project was undertaken.

The Russian majority in the north of the country constituted a serious challenge for Kazakhstan state-building efforts, especially against the background of the success of Russia-supported separatist movement in Transistria, the Russian-dominated region in Moldova, in the early 1990s, and other violent ethnic conflicts on the territory of the former USSR in the Nagorny Karabakh, Abkhazia, and South Ossetia. Under the circumstances Nazarbayev tried to solidify the presence of ethnic Kazakhs in the north of the country, balancing the Russian majority there. Among other things, the transfer of the capital has helped to accomplish this goal. Considering the future separatist crisis in eastern Ukraine and annexation of Crimea, the measures taken by Nazarbayev look sensible and farsighted.

Apparently, these efforts of Nazarbayev to change the demographic balance in the north were intended not only to achieve numerical superiority over Russians as a tactical maneuver but also to rectify a historical injustice. Many Russian nationalist parties have portrayed North Kazakhstan as essentially Russian territory given to Kazakhstan as a "gift" when the borders between Soviet republics were mere bureaucratic boundaries. The Russian majority in the north have justified this view in their eyes. However, historically the ethnic Kazakhs formed the majority of population in the north, and the demographic balance there has changed only as a result of the *Holodomor*, the artificial famine in 1932–1933 that took the lives of almost 1.5 million Kazakhs. As a consequence, thousands have also migrated to neighboring countries after these events. Given the scarcity of the Kazakh people at the time, this amounted to approximately one-third of their population. The famine contributed to the fact that up to the 1980s the ethnic Kazakhs remained an ethnic minority in their own country. Notably, *Holodomor* struck down the north of the country more than the south, taking the lives of almost 900,000 Kazakhs, about 75 percent of the population there. The movement of the capital to the north has helped to repopulate the north and the center of the country with ethnic Kazakhs, rectifying the historical injustice and moving the demographic center of gravity to these lands.

However, it would be an oversimplification to view capital city relocation only as an effort of Kazakhification of the north of the country. In his penetrating analysis of the transfer of the capital in Kazakhstan, Edward Schatz has emphasized several other important aspects and motivations of this project. Highlighting its state- and nation-building aspects, he developed a comparative framework to analyze and compare Kazakhstan's case to other capital city relocation projects in other parts of the globe.[171] In his article Edward Schatz has stressed the importance of clan politics in Kazakhstan and the traditional reliance on the kin-based clans that survived under the Soviet regime. The plan to move the capital of Kazakhstan to the north was motivated in part by the necessity to find a new balance between the interests of the clans, to prevent separatism and civic discord, and to develop a new system of loyalties and patronage.

The ethnic system of Kazakhstan was defined by the relationship between three major sub-ethnic groups (*zhuz*) or kin-based clans: the Greater Horde (*Uly Zhuz*), the Middle Horde (*Orta Zhuz*), and the Smaller Horde (*Kishi Zhuz*). Each group had its own geographic power base: south for the Greater Horde, north and center for the Middle Horde, and west for the Smaller Horde. Contrary to intuitive interpretation the Hordes received their names not based on their size and total population but based on seniority of their families within the ethnic group. Numerically the Smaller Horde is the largest, while the Greater Horde is the smallest. Since the Soviet times the members of the Greater Horde were dominant in the political leadership of the country; Nazarbayev himself belongs to the Greater Horde. In the post-Soviet period this clan preserved its political leadership and also received high-ranking positions in the management of the largest state oil monopolies.

Moving the capital to the north Nazarbayev was making a concession to and benefited the Middle Horde whose position as a result has strengthened. The Middle Horde suffered the most from *Holodomor* – notably, it was the largest clan before 1917 – and the movement of the capital to their tribal lands provided some compensation for their losses. As a result the territory of the Middle Horde received the most development, and its members also benefited from better economic and commercial opportunities. Proximity to the seat of government also meant access to national political officials and offices and hence an opportunity to influence and achieve higher social mobility.

It is important to note that most of the oil resources of the country are located on the territory of the Smaller Horde, which is also the largest of the three. As a consequence, the Smaller Horde constituted a larger potential challenge for Nazarbayev's leadership, and the alliance with Middle Horde helped him to solidify his political support. Through the movement of the capital to Astana, Nazarbayev also muted the potential separatist tendencies and marginalized the elites of the Smaller Horde. Capital city transfer also brought the capital city closer to the Smaller Horde, giving its members better access to the public goods available in the capital city but also making it easier to monitor the political sentiments in this resources-rich area.

Hence, the movement of the capital can be interpreted in terms of clientelist politics that implies the exchange of goods for political benefits. Nazarbayev has treated capital city status as a public good that was traded for formal and informal political support from the Middle Horde. However, under the circumstances and the presence of the existing loyalty system, it was a sensible option for Nazarbayev to make these choices, consolidating his political power and making it more stable.

Being the most politically underprivileged compared to other two, the Smaller Horde had most of the natural resources of the country on its territory, and it provided a sort of compensation for underrepresentation in the central government. The new system of loyalty established by Nazarbayev was thus based on the regrouping and rebalancing of the interests of three hordes and revision of the system of patrimonial relations. The construction of a new capital has fostered the consolidation of political power in the country and reorganization of the ruling elite without violent conflicts.[172]

The described rebalancing also involved the attempt to integrate the Russian population of Kazakhstan. Nazarbayev has utilized the ideology of Eurasianism, stressing the unity of the Russian and Turkic people, to solidify the stability of Nazarbayev's political power. The Astana project was one of the tools to flash out this new ideology. The architecture of Astana was designed to emphasize not only the Kazakh identity of the new nation but also its Eurasian roots and concomitant imagery. One of the best universities of the country established in the new capital was named after Lev Gumilev, the Russian historian credited with the original development of Eurasian ideas.

The Eurasian rhetoric and symbolism was intended primarily for the domestic consumption, while the project had also an important international component. The new geography and the architecture of the new capital projected an image of a futuristic forward-looking city. The capital city shift has brought Kazakhstan closer to Russia and Europe and distanced it from other Central Asian republics that at that time were associated with backwardness. In this context relocation has highlighted the new aspirations of Kazakhstan to become a major regional economic and political player and made a statement about the emergence of a new modernizing power open to the world outside. In this sense it was Kazakh's "window to Europe."

The recognition of these different layers and aspects of the capital city relocation in Kazakhstan and their analysis provided by Edward Schatz dispel the simplistic ideas, according to which the Astana project was intended only for self-aggrandizement efforts of the Oriental ruler as it was often portrayed by the media.[173] This analysis demonstrates that Nazarbayev was aiming to identify a lasting strategy of long-term national development.

If the specter of separatism was indeed the main reason for the relocation, the project turned out to be quite successful. In 2010 the population of the new capital reached 700,000 people with 65 percent Kazakh population. In 1989 Kazakhs were only 18 percent of the population. It is also remarkable that while in the 1990s the project was not popular in Kazakhstan, presently the sociological surveys show that most people find this project very helpful and believe that Nazarbayev was extremely prescient in his decision.[174]

To be sure Astana remains in some ways a very problematic choice and still faces many issues. Many civil servants still need to commute to Astana from Almaty. In summer the temperature here reaches 40 C and drops minus 40 C in winter. It is the second coldest capital in the world after Ulaanbaatar in Mongolia. It is very expensive to heat and air-condition the government offices. Some detractors lament the low quality of housing constructed under the emergency conditions.

Overall, however, many international and domestic observers consider the new capital of Kazakhstan a success story. Similar to Brasília, which has become a model for many countries in Latin America and beyond, the Astana project has inspired many post-communist political leaders. Many of these countries were facing similar problems such as contested territories, the need to replace the old Soviet elites and to regroup the regional interests, and to resolve ethnic and sub-ethnic tensions and conflicts. Two other Muslim republics of the former USSR were particularly sensitive to the experience of Kazakhstan and especially to the idea of reconstitution of their capital cities—Kyrgyzstan and Azerbaijan.

Kyrgyzstan

Similar to Kazakhstan the main reasons for the emergence of capital city relocation debates in Kyrgyzstan reflected the ethnic and sub-ethnic tensions in the country. First and foremost, this debate has its roots in the old subnational rivalry between the tribes of the South and the tribes of the North. Historically within the Kokand Khanate in the nineteenth century the North of the country was populated by the nomads, while the South was populated mainly by the farmers and artisans. Relatedly, the South is more Islamic, while religion does not play a large role in the North of the country. It also must be noted that the South of the country has a substantial Uzbek population. Before the collapse of the Soviet Union, the Kyrgyz were a minority in Osh, the main urban center in the south.

In the Soviet period the representatives of the South and the North have alternated in the power positions promoting the members of their own clans. More recently, the migration of ethnic Uzbeks from Uzbekistan to the South and the migrations of the ethnic Kyrgyz population to the North, especially since the 2000s, tipped the ethnic balance in the South in favor of the Uzbek population and became a cause for concern among the Kyrgyz political elite.

The political leaders of Kyrgyzstan, including the presidents Askar Akaev and Kurmanbek Bakiev, have proposed to move the capital from Bishkek in the North to Osh in the South. The proposal aimed to halt or abate the separatist tendencies in the South, on the one hand, and to augment and strengthen the Kyrgyz identity of this region, on the other. The conversion of Osh into a capital also will have helped to consolidate control over this troublesome region known for its ethnic tensions and violent confrontations and to prevent potential Islamization of this region.

The proponents of capital city relocation also have argued that the economic development of the South associated with capital city transfer will decrease the migration of ethnic Kyrgyz to the North, particularly to Bishkek. It will balance the economic development of the country and will ease the congestion and overpopulation of Bishkek. It is noteworthy that compared to the capitals of other former republics of the USSR, Bishkek, excluding the suburbs, has one of the highest levels of population concentrations at 27 percent of the total population of the country. The backers of Osh argue that currently the South does not attract sufficient investments. Switching the capital to the Fergana Valley in the South and the development of adequate road systems and communication infrastructure linking Bishkek with the Fergana Valley where Osh is located will further facilitate the economic and cultural integration of this region and the territory of the country as a whole.[175]

It is also remarkable that the concept of the capital city in Osh was promoted by the political leaders both from the north and from the south. Understandably, the political leaders with their roots in the south, notably Asimbek Beknazarov, the leader of the Asaba party and once the vice-chair of the Provisional government, were more vocal.[176] There were also some alternative candidates for the role of a new capital city. Issyk-Kul Lake region was proposed due to its central location; Cholpon-Ata in the north and Toktogul in Jalal-Abad Province in the south were also proposed.

The critics of the proposal point out the risks of the southern capital in case of confrontations with Uzbekistan and the possibility of exacerbation of ethnic conflicts. Other critics point to the shortage of funds for such a mega-project.

Tajikistan

Tajik republic was carved off from the Uzbek SSR in 1929, but the two largest cities, Samarkand and Bukhara, having a majority Tajik population, remained in Uzbekistan. The city of Dushanbe – its population remained mostly Russian until 1970s – was made the capital of the country. Since 1992 the question about the capital city transfer was raised more than once. The main stated purposes in the proposals are to free Tajikistan from the Soviet legacy and to create a new capital city with more adequate infrastructure. The backers of the proposals, including Suhrob Sharipov, the Director of the Center for Strategic Research attached to the president of Tajikistan, referred to the capital city model of Kazakhstan and Pakistan to justify their proposals.[177]

The proposals and debates also reflect the sub-ethnic clan divisions in Tajikistan. The cities Khoujand in the north and Kulyab in the south represent two dominant clans in the country. Khoujand was dominant most of the Soviet era, while in the post-Soviet years the members of the Kulyab clan have acquired the dominant positions in the government. The current president of the country, Emomali Rahmon, is its member. The third clan of the country in the Pamir region has largely lost its influence on the government of the country.

During the civil war from 1992–1997 there were some proposals to move the capital to Khoujand in the north at least as a provisional measure. The candidacy of this city is still discussed. Presently another candidate from the north is the ancient city of Panjakent, the closest to Samarkand on the territory of the country.

However, today the cities in the south are considered stronger candidates due to the support of the Kouliab clan that is in power. One of the contenders is Kulyab itself, which, is considered the oldest Tajik city. The proponents of Kouliab argue that one of its merits is the closer proximity to international centers such as Karachi, Kabul, Delhi, and Beijing. However, the most likely candidate is Danghara, 100 km to the southeast of Dushanbe, due to the fact that it is the birthplace of the current president Emomali Rahmon. Another cited advantage of this area is that it is thinly populated and can be easily expanded.[178] There were some indications that the preparations for this project have already started. The roads in the Danghara area are being renovated, and the government embarked on the construction of a large international airport in the neighborhood of Danghara. In the last 10 years the government also promoted the migration of families from rural areas to Danghara.

Azerbaijan

The overconcentration of population and economic resources in Baku has triggered the debate in the 2000s. Currently Baku absorbs close to 90 percent of all investments in the country. The development of urban infrastructure did not match the pace of demographic growth of Baku that drew migrants from the rural areas and the refugees from Nagorny Karabakh and elsewhere. Consequently the population density has increased 3–4 times, exacerbating the gridlock and the environmental problems in the city. The precarious tectonic situation of Baku is another important reason. The idea was supported by Geidar Aliev, the president of the country. Oil rich Azerbaijan also has the financial resources to finance this government mega-project.

So far three options have been considered: the construction of the satellite administrative capital, switching the capital to an existing city, and the construction of a new capital.

Alyat, 75 km from Baku, is one of the candidates. Another strong candidate for this role is Ganja, the second largest city. Being equidistant from Georgia and Armenia, it is considered by many to be the geographic center of the South Caucasus, having a potential to become an important transnational hub of the region. Ganja is also sited in between mountains and the valleys, making it a critical connecting point within the territory of Azerbaijan. Additionally, it has a merit of being centrally located relative to the regional capitals of the country that makes it indispensable for the development of the hinterlands of the country. Its long and glorious history is considered another benefit. It also must be noted that during the Safavid period, Ganja served as the capital of the Karabakh Beylerbeydom, one of the Safavid provinces. Historically the disputed region of Nagorny Karabakh was a part of the Karabakh Beylerbeydom. Under the circumstances of ongoing confrontation with Armenia over this territory, the capital in Ganja might strengthen Azeri's claims on it and reinforce the position of Azerbaijan *vis-à-vis* the Armenian-Azeri conflict.

The opponents of the project charge that the country cannot afford such large public expenditure having many other priorities, especially "the restoration of territorial integrity of the country." The members of the urban planning expert community in Baku have suggested several other options as alternatives to capital city transfer: the development of the regional blueprint of Larger Baku that would provide a different type of solution to the urban infrastructure issues in the current capital city.[179]

Georgia

The government of Saakashvili has launched the rearrangement of the capital city function in the framework of the program of de-centralization of the country, balanced development of the regions, and de-communization. The parliament of Georgia was moved to Kutaisi in 2012, while the Constitutional Court was relocated to Batumi. The more central location of Kutaisi was recognized as a benefit for the legislative function. This strategy also helped to diversify the Georgian cities and to develop a better urban system.

Alberto Domingo Kabo, the Spanish architect, has developed the concept of a new parliament building. The glass dome that covers the building epitomizes the transparency of the new parliament and the integration of different regions of the country. Remarkably, this new building was often contrasted with the old Soviet-style building in Tbilisi, constructed by Lavrentiy Beria.

Earlier in his career Saakashvili alluded to the possibility of moving the capital city from Tbilisi to Sukhumi, the capital of Abkhazia. In his opinion in the case of peaceful development, the transfer of the capital of Georgia to Sukhumi could facilitate the reintegration of the breakaway republic and would help to reach a peaceful resolution of ethnic conflict.

Russia

In Russia the debates of this topic started in the 1990s. Remarkably the proposals to move the capital city out of Moscow have been made by the members of practically all major political parties. The intensification of the debate in recent years can be attributed, on the one hand, to the dissatisfaction of many Moscovites with the congestion, infrastructure, and municipal services in Moscow and, on the other, to the grievances of the population in the rest of the country about overconcentration of political power and economic resources in the center. It must be noted that the post-Soviet decades have witnessed the unprecedented growth of the city of Moscow due to migration inflows from Russia and many post-Soviet states and the declining population in the rest of the country. The move of the capital, the proponents have argued, will abate the prevalent collusion between business and government that hampers the economic and political development.

Another fundamental rational of the debate is the fear of disintegration of the country. In many cases the proposals to move the seat of government were intended as a tool for reintegration.

In the 1990s some liberal-minded politicians proposed to transfer the capital to the west; St. Petersburg, Novgorod, and Pskov were the main contenders. These choices stressed the European identity of Russian culture and nationhood and were meant to highlight the continuity between the ancient democracies in Novgorod and Pskov. These candidacies epitomized the aspirations of the country to integrate into Europe and promote the program of liberal reforms. The proponents of the Western capital have stressed the negative role of Moscow in Russian history, accusing it in the suppression of the ancient Russian princedom, servile attitudes, introduction of extreme authoritarian rule, and reinforcement of the Mongolian traditions of statecraft. The current levels of hyper-centralization exhibit continuity with these centuries-old traditions.

The other group of the participants in the debate developed more sophisticated geopolitical arguments and even put forward the anti-westernist agenda, emphasizing the geopolitical reasons to move the capital city. In this context the relocation aims to physically separate Russia from the West and its deleterious influence. Most of their proposals suggest shifting the seat of government to the east of the country. Some of their arguments have stressed the strategic importance of southern Siberia for the Eurasian integration of the country and proposed to move the capital to the Asian part of Russia. The eastern capital city, they argue, will also help to strengthen the unity of the Slavs and the Turks. What is more, they believe that the new capital will weaken the secessionist sentiments in Siberia and in the Far East. According to Tsymburskii, the geopolitician, Russia needs to establish its capital in southern Siberia; the importance of this region is underscored by the fact that it is centrally located relative to the three distinct geographical zones of the country, the European part of Russia, the Far East, and the Ural-Siberian region, and can secure the country's economic base. Others have emphasized the importance of control over particular territories or ethnic groups.[180]

Other groups see relocation more in economic terms as a vehicle of economic development. Their proposals aim to enhance the regional development, to alleviate the disparities between the prosperous Moscow and the distressed regions, and to prevent the depopulation of the eastern territories of Russia. Their most popular candidates were Novosibirsk, Krasnoyarsk, and Yekaterinburg. The most radical of these proposals suggest the capital city in the Far East to re-orientate Russia towards the countries of Asia and the Far East specifically. The capital city in Vladivostok, they argue, will help Russia to make a better use of its far-eastern territories, to integrate with the dynamic economies of Japan, China, South Korea, and other countries of the region and to position itself as an important player in the Asia-Pacific region.[181]

Ukraine

The ideas to transfer the capital also had some circulation in Ukraine. Baturin, the Hetman capital of Ukraine; Donetsk; Kharkov; and Sevastopol were suggested as candidates. There were also ideas to build a new administrative capital in close proximity to Kiev.

Dmitry Vydrin, the advisor to Kuchma, the president of Ukraine, has proposed Baturin, the residence of Ukrainian hetmans, as the new capital. He referred to the overconcentration of all resources in Kiev and anti-Kiev sentiments in the regions. He also argued that Baturin, which served as the Cossack capital of Ukraine in the seventeenth and eighteenth centuries and was sacked by Russian troops in 1708, can restore the historical continuity between hetmanhood and current Ukrainian history. The other reasons cited by Vydrin included the separation between business and political power, anti-corruption measures, among others.

In 2006 there was also an idea to create special Government Quarters or satellite city that would house different government departments that are spread out throughout Kiev. To de-centralize the administration there were also proposals to move the administration of Kiev region to Bila Tsrekva and to move the Constitutional Court to Kharkov.

In 2012 Yuri Boldirev, the MP from the Party of Regions, proposed Sevastopol in Crimea as a new capital city to make the country closer to Russia and Moscow.

However, the civil conflict in Ukraine and annexation of Crimea has changed the geography of the proposals. In 2013 Dobkin, the governor of the Kharkov region, has suggested to transfer the capital of the country to Kharkov to marginalize the Right sector and radical Ukrainian ultra-nationalists in Kiev. The candidacy of Dnepropetrovsk was also proposed as a neutral city in the center of the country that can balance the interests of the west and the east of the country. The candidacy of Odessa was also suggested. One recent proposal called to build a new city between Odessa and Crimea to assert control over the contested territory.[182]

Curiously, the transfer of the capital from Kharkov to Kiev in 1934 can explain the background of the current debate. Kharkov was made a capital of Soviet Ukraine as an industrial city with a higher proportion of industrial proletariat deemed to be more congenial to the Bolshevik regime. The likely reason to move the capital to Kiev, the initiative that was taken by Stalin personally, was to de-Ukrainize Ukraine and to weaken its ruling nationalist elite, which was not showing sufficient commitment to the Soviet leadership at the time of *Holodomor*. In the early 1930s Stalin halved the membership of the Ukrainian communist party, aiming to decrease the role that Ukraine played in the leadership of the USSR. Kiev appeared to be much more loyal compared to Kharkov. Historically Kiev had a much higher share of ethnic Russians in its population. Remarkably, before the revolution it was one of the centers of Russian nationalism. In contrast, in the 1920s and 1930s Kharkov looked more like a stronghold of Ukrainian nationalism both demographically and ideologically. According to the official declaration at the time of the transfer, the relocation to Kiev has "brought the capital city closer to the most important agricultural regions in the Right-Bank Ukraine." The Right-Bank Ukraine was even less loyal to the Soviet regime, and the transfer was intended to put it under closer Bolshevik control. The Soviet leadership believed that Kiev would be a better place to spearhead the patriotism campaign of Josef Stalin in the rural areas of Ukraine that largely remained aloof to the Soviet regime.

Europe

The capital city relocation debates are least prevalent in Europe. The operation of the laws of differential urbanization that describe the asynchronous patterns of growth of different groups of cities, the moderate pace of growth of most capital cities, along with the relative ethnic homogeneity of these countries and lack of serious sub-ethnic tensions have helped most of these countries to avoid the sharp political and economic misbalances that has motivated the discussion of this topic in other continents. The morphology and good urban infrastructure of these cities also make them comfortable places to live. Due to a high density of cities in Europe and other reasons, the phenomenon of monocephality is not characteristic for most of the countries of the continent. Although the UK and France have exceptionally large primate cities, some seven times the size of the second city in both cases, in virtually all other European countries, the second city is about half the size of the primary city. The relatively large size of capital cities where it is present can be explainable by a small size of the country and typically does not cause the acute problems that trigger the debates in other regions of the world.

In those few countries where the debate took place, it was motivated primarily by the eccentric position of the capital city, the breakdown of federations, and by separatist movements. Hence in Slovakia some proposals to move the capital were spawned by the extremely eccentric position of Bratislava relative to the rest of the country.[183] The leaders of some separatist movements in Western Europe also raise the questions about the new capitals of their countries. For instance, the Flemish and Walloon nationalists insist on the establishment of two separate states on the territory of Belgium with capital cities in Antwerp and Namur. Lega Nord in Northern Italy has established the Padanian parliament near Mantua chosen as a capital in self-organized elections.

Nevertheless the general trend of insensitivity of European countries to capital city change ideas has several notable exceptions that we will discuss.

Germany

After the fall of the Berlin wall in 1991, in the course of long debates the Bundestag made a decision to transfer the capital city from Bonn to Berlin for the unification of East and West Germany. In the voting Berlin won by a narrow margin: 338 for and 320 against. It is noteworthy that in 1949 Bonn was designated as a temporary capital city; the constitution provided that the free elections in the unified Germany will open the possibility of moving the capital city back to Berlin.

Konrad Adenauer, the first Chancellor of West Germany and the founder of the Christian Democratic Union (CDU), believed that Berlin should be a capital of German democracy.

In the course of the long debate of these issues, two main topics have crystallized that determined the attitude towards capital city problem regardless of political party affiliation: the concept of the federalist capital city and the attitude towards the historical memories of Berlin. And the predicaments associated with each decision. . .

The opponents of the capital city transfer argued that the concept of the federalist capital in Bonn better reflects the spirit of the liberal-democratic state capable of balancing the interests of different lands compared to such a large city as Berlin. They also believed that the historic background of Berlin epitomizes those political traditions – imperialistic, communist, and Nazi – that modern Germany tries to disengage itself from and which it does not plan to reassume.

In the minds of modern Germans, Berlin also was closely tied with the traditions of Prussian militarism and Prussian domination that were inappropriate for the newly reunified state. They felt that the character and the size of a German capital city should satisfy the requirements of federalism and the principles of a pluralistic and polycentric urban system. The position was upheld by the leader of the CDU, Norbert Blüm.

The proponents of Berlin, on the other hand, argued that the establishment of the capital city on the border of two Germanies will facilitate more effective political and economic integration of the Eastern Germans into a new country and that the goals of federalism under such a capital city will be fostered and not diminished. The peripheral location of Bonn was recognized as its significant disadvantage in the cause of unification. The return of the capital to Berlin was also presented as a restoration of the constrained sovereignty of Germany as a nation.

The proponents of Berlin reinstatement also believed that it would be a mistake to be oblivious and simply turn away from those negative political traditions that were epitomized by Berlin. These traditions should become a subject for moral reflection. Only in the course of such reflection the new nation can be formed. They were hopeful that Berlin will be much more suitable for such national self-reflection as a larger center of social life of Germany compared to the administrative small town on the western edges of the country.[184]

The candidacy of Berlin was also associated with some benefits that went beyond the German case. The location of Berlin in the east transformed Germany into the leader of Central and Eastern Europe and provided it with a unique role in the context of not only pan-German but also pan-European integration.

The proponents of Berlin also saw thinly settled and empty spaces of the city as its additional advantages that permitted the development of the new city in conditions somewhat close to Canberra or Brasília. In the absence of the compromising buildings from the communist and Nazi era, Berlin had enough empty spaces to build new buildings and form a new narrative of national identity reflecting upon the vicissitudes of national political history.

Several important individuals including Helmut Kohl, the leader of CDU and the first chancellor of reunified Germany, were among the advocates of the move. Koll believed that the transfer was necessary as a gesture of solidarity with the east and new federal lands.

The reinstatement of Berlin as a capital did not deprive Bonn of all its capital city functions. Six out of 10 ministries stayed in Bonn to preserve the continuity of the foreign politics of the country. The government officials continue to travel between Bonn and Berlin, although the main elements of the capital transfer were finished in 1999 and most of the officials were relocated to Berlin long time ago. According to some estimates these business trips are costing 5 million euro a year.

It is important to emphasize that in the contest of the two capital cities, both sides of the arguments had in mind the same standards and normative principles. The choice of Berlin was determined by the fact that most voters have recognized Berlin as a more suitable place for the maintenance of federalist agenda and Germany's sovereignty. The return of the capital to Berlin stressed the importance of the reconstruction of the nation.

Albania

The ports, Vlorë and Durrës, were the first capital cities of Albania. In 1913 the independence of Albania from the Ottoman Empire was declared in Vlorë. In 1914 the capital moved to Durrës, which became a residence of Wilhelm Wied, the new king who was assigned by Austria. However, due to the Islamic riots, the king escaped from the capital. At that time the government in Durrës contemplated the adoption of the Italian protectorate under the threat of the division of the country between different states.

Ismail Qemali, the founder of modern Albania, insisted from the very beginning on the transfer of the capital inland to Elbasan located closer to the center of the country. The central location was important for his plans to federalize the country; Qemali also disliked Durrës as a stronghold of Islamists. In 1920 the decision was made to move the capital to Tirana, and the pro-Italian government in Durrës was declared illegitimate.

Hence, the new capital in Tirana confirmed the independence of the country that was declared seven years earlier and prepared the transition from monarchy to national republic that went official in 1925. The capital was also located in a more secure location and removed from a port city that was vulnerable to foreign influences and invasions.

Romania

The concept of a new capital city is floating today in Romania. This concept had a long intellectual history and acquired special interest between the two world wars. Initially, this idea was advocated by Queen Maria and Nicolae Titulescu (1882–1941), the important Romanian statesman, diplomat, and the Minister of Foreign Affairs. In 1924 the Romanian engineer Nicolae Theodorescu has penned a book, *The Establishment of New capital of Romania*, where he insisted that the capital should be moved to the center of the country estimating the cost of this project at $30 billion in contemporary dollars.[185]

Mircea Vulcănescu (1904–1952), renowned Romanian writer and sociologist, put forward the concept of a peculiar Carpathian essence and unique *existentia* of Romanian people that should be crystallized in a new capital in the mountainous part of the country. He also has argued that modern warfare and the possibility of airstrikes make Bucharest vulnerable and a risky choice for a capital city. The new capital city in Brasov protected by the Carpathian Mountains would be a better option in terms of security, and it would also help to prevent the Balkanization of Romania (the term is used to describe the fragmentation of the states) and bring Romanians closer to their historical roots.

In the 1940s the renowned nationalist intellectuals and leaders of the far right ultra-nationalist parties, Constantin Noica and Corneliu Codreanu, also have entertained this idea. In the period of the National Legionary State, they insisted that the transfer of the capital from Bucharest, plagued by the spirit of corruption and moral decay, will invigorate the spirit of the nation.[186]

Nicolae Ceaușescu in his later years also supported the idea of moving the capital to Târgoviște, the old capital of Wallachia and the city of Dracula, where Ceaușescu felt more support and, oddly, where he was persecuted.

After the collapse of communism the concept of a new capital city, more centrally located, was supported by several prominent politicians and leaders of nationalist parties. Mihail Hardau, the Minister of Education, proposed the transfer of the capital to Brasov. The concept of a new capital in Brasov was also advocated by Partidul Poporului (People's Party). Some other politicians and intellectuals proposed to build a new capital *de novo* in close proximity to Brasov. The other contenders in Transylvania are Sibiu, Cluj, and Timisoara.[187] Clement Negruț, the MP from the Liberal-Democratic party, advocated the candidacy of Alba-Iulia sited in close proximity to the ancient capital of Dacia. He submitted it as a bill for approval to the Commission on the revision of the constitution.

Alba-Iulia occupies a special place in the imagination of Romanian nationalists, and its history serves to justify the current political agenda and the dream of a unified and united pan-Romanian state. In 1600 Michael the Brave, the ruler of Wallachia, united the principalities of Wallachia, Moldavia, and Transylvania under his rule, which lasted for a year and a half until he was murdered in 1601. After the First World War in 1918 Transylvania was declared to be a part of Romania, and four years later Ferdinand I and Queen Maria were crowned in the local cathedral as rulers of the united country. Hence the candidacy of Alba-Iulia not only lays claims on the Dacia legacy and reinforces Romanian identity but also implied a much broader geopolitical integration of the region that is the goal of some Romanian politicians.

According to their plans, the capital in Transylvania will solidify Romanian identity there and establish a counter-balance to the separatist trends. The main threats are the movement for autonomy of the ethnic Hungarians, the largest ethnic minority residing there, and the irredentist sentiments and ultra-nationalist parties in Hungary.[188]

Additionally, such a capital city, the backers of the plan believe, can facilitate the establishment of the strong and unified Romanian state, the Greater Romania (*România Mare*). The more central position of Alba-Iulia in the region can facilitate the reunification of Romania and Moldova. That is what Traian Băsescu, close to the Liberal-Democratic Party, had in mind when he declared in 2006 that "after the unification of Germany Romanians are the last people in Europe that remains divided." The EU does not support these plans or at least makes them contingent on the membership of Moldova in EU.[189]

There are some other valid reasons to move the capital. Bucharest is considered the most vulnerable city in Europe in terms of earthquakes that have devastated the city more than once in recent history. Moreover, Bucharest is four times larger than any other city in Romania and attracts 60 percent of all investments. This monocephality does not help the development of the country.[190]

The urban transformation and brutal reconstruction of Bucharest in the communist period is another important consideration. The government aims to distance itself from the communist past. However, the colossal People's Palace erected by Nicolae Ceauşescu in the center of the city and its major landmark, is dominating the landscape of the city emphasizing the country's communist identity. The construction of the Palace in 1984–1989 required the demolition of a fifth of the buildings in the historical center and other monuments and churches important for national memory. The removal of the Palace and the reconstruction of the city would be as expensive as the construction of the new capital.

Poland

During the Second World War, Warsaw was singled out by Nazi leadership for destruction. Kraków was spared of such destruction, as the Nazis perceived the Germanic characteristics in its medieval monuments. Due to the devastation in Warsaw in the course of the war after the liberation in 1945, there were some proposals to move the capital city to Kraków.

However, from the standpoint of Polish communists, Kraków had important drawbacks: it was too intellectual and too Catholic for their taste. Kraków also appeared to be hostile to communist ideology, and its population had wrong class sympathies. Due to these circumstances Lodz, the largest industrial center and the second largest city in the country, was proposed as the most likely candidate. The industrial character of the city made it look like a place with required class orientation, and the proximity to Warsaw gave it additional benefits. Boleslaw Bierut, the Chair of the State National Council and the first president of the country, supported the candidacy of Lodz. However, the Polish leadership could not reach a consensus on this issue, providing cons and pros for each solution. Upon the return from his trip to Moscow in 1945, Boleslaw Bierut informed his comrades that Stalin supported the idea of reconstruction of Warsaw and offered his support. Thus the question of capital city transfer was solved and removed from the political agenda.

After the collapse of communism in the 1990s, the capital transfer to Kraków was proposed again. Some leaders of new Poland saw Warsaw as a conduit of Russian domination and communist influence. However, this idea never took root and was later abandoned.

Lithuania

At independence in 1920 Lithuania was facing a difficult situation. Poland and Germany laid claims on the two largest cities of the country, Vilnius and Memel (Klaipeda). In Vilnius the majority population was Jewish and in Memel, German. The history of the Polish-Lithuanian Union and the demography of the Vilnius region gave Poland some grounds to consider Vilnius to be a part of its territory. The League of Nations resolved the issue in Poland's favor due to the fact that the nobility in Vilnius was pollonized, and many members of Polish governments were originally from Vilnius. Poland also had a higher international standing, and it was supported by France. As a result Vilnius was recognized as a territory of Poland, and Kaunas (Kovno) became the temporary capital of Lithuania until 1944.

Memel (Klaipeda) was the only port and the second largest city of the country. It was founded as Memelburg by the Teutonic knights as a German castle. After the defeat of Germany in the First World War, the Versailles Treaty granted the city and its region to Lithuania. In 1923 Memel and its region, populated mostly by Lithuanians, was annexed by the Lithuanian Army. However, ethnic Germans were still the majority in the city.[191]

This situation explains the emergence of the proposal in the 1920s to transfer the capital to Memel. Kazys Pakštas (1893–1960), an important Lithuanian intellectual, geographer, and geopolitician, urged to move the seat of government to Memel. His idea of a new capital was closely connected with his geopolitical vision of Baltoscandia or the Baltoscandian Confederation. Pakštas insisted that Lithuania needs to reinforce its presence in the Baltic Sea, stressing the fact that Lithuania is the only Baltic republic that does not have its capital city in the port. In his opinion, the port-capital was an essential component for the membership in the Baltoscandian Confederation. Indeed, at this time the Klaipeda port has acquired a more important strategic role. Additionally, Pakštas believed that the transfer of the capital will reinvigorate the nation and will facilitate the development of its creative potential. This proposal was meant to alter the demographic balance in Memel, tipping the demographic balance in favor of the titular nation, strengthening the attachment and the allegiance of this region to Lithuania.

The plan to transfer the capital to Memel was never implemented. The Ribbentrop-Molotov Pact has contributed to a different solution of the problem. In 1939 Lithuania was forced to surrender Memel without any fighting after the ultimatum from Adolf Hitler. After the annexation of Poland and Lithuania by the USSR Vilnius was given to Lithuania and, subsequently, was transformed into the capital city.[192] The question about the capital city status of Memel was never raised again. The choice of Memel would probably weaken Lithuania's claims to Vilnius that was also contested by the Poles, as we have already noted.

United Kingdom

The North-South divide of the country that has economic, political and social ramifications is the main rationale for the discussion of the seat of government transfer in the UK. In spite of the promises and commitments of several government cabinets, the gap between the north and the south was deepening over the years, encompassing such spheres as the income, wealth, real estate prices, level of education, and the job creation dynamics. Due to this growing divide one observer has facetiously labeled London "a first-rate city with a second-rate country attached."[193]

The dispute in the UK has centered on the estrangement of London from the rest of the country. The resentment of London has a long history in the UK. It was frequently excoriated as "the Great Wen," a consuming cancer on the face of rural England. Presently many people in the UK feel that London is losing its connection with the country that it runs. The capital becomes a world of its own, with distinct interests and demands. Macroeconomic policies of the UK are often governed by the interests of Londoners rather than all British citizens, who have different priorities.[194] Danny Dorling has argued that the economic dominance of London in the UK is much more pronounced compared to other capitals located in global cities if the size of the population is taken into account.[195] Some critics also have claimed that London's ties to the club of the global cities are much stronger than its attachment to the UK proper. Niel O'Brian, the advisor of George Osborn, aptly labeled the main problem of the UK "Londonitis," that is the dominance of London in all critical spheres of the country's life.

The danger of such a development is associated with separatist tendencies in the rest of the UK, social problems, and the political disruptions. Many believe that the secessionist trends unfolding in the recent Scotland referendum, and in Brexit, are the results of this development.[196]

It is also a matter for concern that London is getting less and less affordable for the middle class and this leads to a dramatic change in the demographic profile of the city. Another negative trend associated with such a development is the growing social polarization within the city and urban issues.[197] In recent years the population of London was increasing by 100,000 annually, and there is not much space for expansion due to the greenbelt limitations. Hence the commute time in London is the longest compared to the metropolises in Europe and America.

The proposals to move the capital from London started to float around in the early 2000s. In 2003 Adam Price, MP from Plaid Cymru, the Welsh nationalist social-democratic party, urged to move the capital to Anglo-Celtic Liverpool. Subsequently, high-profile members of mainstream political parties, mostly Laborists, have voiced their support for the change of capital. Lord Adonis, a member of Labor Party, proposed to move the House of Lords to the north. Graham Stringer proposed Manchester to be a new capital city. In 2012 John Mann from the same party suggested to disperse the headquarters of most government departments to different cities outside of London. Notably, many of the proposed candidates are located in the geographic and demographic center of the country. Among the contenders there are also Birmingham, Middleborough, Litchfield, Newcastle, and Nottingham. In response to the Scottish referendum, there were also more radical proposals to move the capital to Glasgow.[198] The unionists believe that the capital city in Scotland will help to reintegrate the country and will placate Scottish nationalists.

The motives of all these initiatives are not limited to the regional balancing, and they cannot be explained only by the political maneuvers of the Labor Party, whose base of support lies in the north of the UK. Some politicians and intellectuals argue that the UK needs a "professional" capital city of the union, and that such a capital will ease the federalization of the UK which is the order of the day. Notably the concept of such a capital was proposed by Danny Dorling, Oxford geography professor. Through the establishment of a new federal capital city the UK will follow suit of other Anglo-Saxon countries such as the US, Canada, and Australia.[199] The transition from unitary to federalist state, they believe, will also facilitate other beneficial social changes.[200]

Curiously, some proponents of a new capital consider it necessary to strengthen the English identity of the capital city that was historically diluted in London and to establish an English capital in one of the central counties of England. This capital will balance the Scottish capital in Edinburgh, Welsh capital in Cardiff, and Irish capital in Dublin. This argument was advanced by David Davis in his article "Nottingham: New capital of England."[201]

Recently the need to renovate the Palace of Westminster also served as an excuse to discuss permanent relocation of the seat of government. It is estimated that the renovation will cost £3 billion and will take about five years. Several politicians have suggested the redevelopment of Westminster into a cultural centre, museum, or a hotel and moving the capital to the north instead of a temporary solution.[202]

It is noteworthy that in contrast to many other countries that we have discussed, the protagonists of the debate in the UK most often suggest the relocation to one of the existing industrial centers and rarely discuss the construction of a capital *de novo*. They emphasize the need to develop the decaying former industrial areas. But the chief dispute revolves around the need to liberate the country from London's hegemony and to free London from the results of its own hegemonic status to preserve the national unity.

France

The concept of capital city relocation was floating in France since the 1960s. The emergence of this idea was related to the historical trends of hypercentralization of the country and to the sharp divide between the capital and *la province* that is causing resentment in the rest of the country.[203]

In the early nineteenth century the hyper-centralization was already so pronounced in France that Napoleon Bonaparte toyed with the idea of moving the capital to Lyon, perhaps trying to appeal to his soldiers' resentment of Paris.[204] Later on he gave up this idea in favor of ambitious military campaigns and his grand reconstruction of Paris plans.[205]

Intellectually the concept of a new capital was prepared by the publication of some seminal works that emphasized the overconcentration of the national resources in Paris. The book by Jean-François Gravier, the right-wing scholar and pro-Fascist intellectual, *Paris and the French Desert* that came out in 1947, turned into a milestone in this development.[206] The book became very influential and was reprinted several times. The main theme of this book was the uncontested and total domination of Paris in the economic, political, and social life in France. Gravier described the situation in the following way: "The Paris and its suburbs behaved, not like a metropolis vivifying its back-country, but like a monopolist group devouring his national substance."[207] He claimed that the excessive growth of Paris has spawned the stagnation in the French provinces and led to the decay of the whole country, marshaling shocking quantitative evidence to support his thesis. Between 1880 and 1936, 3.3 million people from the provinces had come to Paris. As a result the population of French capital tripled while the population of the rest of the country squeezed. While the employment in the industrial sector of Paris has increased by 45 percent, it has dropped 3 percent in the rest of France.[208] The conclusion that Gravier drew was that Paris is growing dangerously and irresponsibly at the expense of the provinces.

Notably, Gravier never proposed to move the capital city elsewhere; his suggested remedy was to downsize Paris. Generally, he felt a distaste for all large metropolises and mega-cities regardless of their character and saw the future of France in ruralism. Unsurprisingly, some of his thoughts have echoed the ideas of Jean-Jacques Rousseau that we have described earlier. However, his vibrant images of the decay of the provinces and overpopulation of Paris fuelled a debate on the possibility of transference of the French capital city. It also must be added that the trends that he chronicled in his book have continued throughout the 1970s. While in 1881 only 5% percent of French population resided in Paris region, by 1975 19 percent of the total were residing there.[209]

The French technocrats proposed to move the seat of government to the designed city *La Roche-Guyon*. Undoubtedly, their ideas were very much influenced by the recent construction of Brasília. Tellingly, the new capital of France was labeled "French Brasília." The city was also branded as Monaco on the Seine. A competition for the best architectural plan of the new city was won by the acclaimed architects Albert Laprade and Jean Brasilier. The idea, however, never took off.

Ostensibly, the debate has swayed the agenda and the domestic politics of France and the activities of the later presidents. In the post-war years such presidents as Valéry Giscard d'Estaing and François Mitterrand have focused on the different aspects of regional planning and on the devolution of the political power to the provinces and regions, aiming to de-centralize the country.[210] By the end of the 1970s the population of Paris stopped growing, arguably at least in some measure due to the partial success of these policies. The efforts to stimulate economic growth of the regions, however, were less successful. Overall, the de-centralization efforts of the French government, especially of the territorial development department (*Aménagement du Territoire*) attached to the Ministry of Reconstruction and Urban Development were recognized as a measured success. The urban and morphological solutions to many infrastructure problems in Paris, including the Métropole du Grand Paris project undertaken by French government under Nicolas Sarkozy, have ameliorated many of the problems of congestion and gridlocks that Paris was facing and ushered France on a path of more balanced regional development. Perhaps, as a result of these policies the issue of capital city change never again emerged on the political agenda as a serious issue.

Anglo-Saxon countries besides the United Kingdom

In spite of some differences, the countries of the Anglosphere with their peculiar pattern of settlements share many common elements in the organization of their capital city function and have developed very similar capital city models. The capital cities of the US, Canada, Australia, New Zealand and South Africa are smaller than the largest cities of these countries. All of them besides Pretoria are located between their most powerful cities or on the border between two of its greater communities.

Capital city relocations in South Africa and Australia apparently drew their inspiration from the US, Canada, and New Zealand. Washington DC was a compromise between the North and the South of the country. Ottawa was a compromise between Upper and Lower Canada, and it was chosen as a capital in 1855 because it was equidistant from Quebec City and Toronto. Historically Ottawa was chosen because it was situated in a safe distance from the American-Canadian border in a well-fortified place in the close proximity to military garrison. Wellington became a capital of New Zealand in 1865, situated on the border of the South and North Islands; it was chosen as an alternative to Auckland, the largest city in the country.[211]

It is noteworthy that the capital cities of both Canada and Australia were tasked not only to offer a compromise solution for the two largest and most powerful communities but also to integrate and recognize the aboriginal communities of these countries at least in a symbolic fashion. The evidence for this is found in the very names chosen for their respective capital cities. These names and these countries' toponymic policy in general were meant to root a nation in a territory, embracing the aboriginal population and their culture, and to establish a stronger bond between the land, its native population, and the political administration. Ottawa was named after an Indian tribe Odawa that inhabited this site. The names of these capital cities valorized the experience of the native population, creating a sort of a linguistic hinge between the aboriginal communities and the colonists.

However, there were some notable differences in their historical backgrounds. While in the US, Australia, and South Africa, dedicated professional capital cities were established, in Canada and New Zealand, smaller cities were converted into administrative capital cities.

Australia

In the nineteenth century Australia consisted of six provinces that did not form a unified country. The establishment of a federation from these six provinces quickly raised the question about their common capital city. Melbourne was selected as a temporary capital city that served as a seat of government between 1901 and 1927, although the decision to build a new capital city was made already in 1908. The challenge was to find such a place that would not give special privileges to any province at the expense of others. It was decided that the new city would be situated equal distance from the two largest cities of the country that represented its largest provinces. The South Wales province was expected to provide the site vested with special status for the construction of a new capital city.[212]

Establishing the new capital, the government was also seeking to "nativize" the population of British origin in the new geography and to adopt and integrate the aboriginal population. After an international competition for the best design, the blueprint of the city by the Chicago architects, Walter Berly Griffin and his wife, Merion Mahonny Griffin, both the students of van den Rohe, was adopted for the development of a new city. The construction of the new capital started in 1913, but because of the First World War and the concomitant financial problems, the construction was postponed and delayed. There were also some controversy and disagreements about the original plan submitted by Griffins.

Because the concept of the garden-city was chosen to be implemented in Canberra, the Australians have called their new city "the bush capital." The wilderness itself in the blueprint of the city, providing the unique sense of Australian identity, has played a critical role in its visual plan. The Griffins sought to blur the distinction between nature and culture and to encapsulate nature into their plan of Canberra that was featuring this emblematic wilderness as an integral part of Australian identity.[213]

It is also remarkable that both the name of the city and its location were endowed with some special meaning. The word Canberra is derived from the word "Kambera" that means "the meeting place" in the dialect of the local Ngunnawal tribe. In the past, Aboriginal people from many different tribes gathered in the area for the ceremonial meeting (*corrobori*) at the time of the seasonal migration of the moth (*Agrotis infusa*), to eat them and to hold ceremonies. Accordingly, many streets of the city use the names derived from the languages of Australian Aborigines. Perhaps not surprisingly, one of the main museums of the city is a National Museum of Australia exhibiting many artifacts of Aboriginal cultures.

Echoing Washington, D.C., Canberra uses the triangular figure as a key structure of the urban design of the city. This Parliamentary Triangle is formed by three axes: the first one extends to Capitol Hill where the Parliament building is sited, the second one is along the Constitution Avenue to Defence on Russell Hill, and the third along Kings to Capitol Hill. The city is built on three hills which form the key part of its architectural plan.

South Africa

Pretoria was sited practically in a new place, and it was not built in the existing city. The city was created in 1855 for the integration of Transvaal, which consisted of diverse immigrant groups from the Netherlands. After the Anglo-Boer War in 1909 the country incorporated four distinct territories – Transvaal, Cape Province, Orange Republic, and Natal – in need of further integration. The reorganization of capital city function was a part of this process.

Pretoria turned into the seat of presidential power; Cape Town, the legislative; Bloemfontein, the judicial. Pietermaritzburg, the capital of Natal, was excluded from the list of capital cities but was receiving financial compensation for 25 years after the event. Some compensation was also given to the Free State province. Although today such a multi-capital system might look a bit unwieldy and extravagant, it has much in common in its intentions with the logic of spatial compromise that we have described earlier. In South Africa the division of capital cities was used to ensure equal participation of the four provinces in the governance of the country, serving as a compromise solution echoing the location in the middle of other countries.

The triple capital arrangement was not the only instrument to promote the goals of polycentricism and de-centralization. Bantustans had their own capitals with strong regional identities. Moreover, the most prominent political parties of South Africa typically had their headquarters outside of the three capitals in different other cities of the country.

Remarkably, after the fall of the apartheid regime, the question about the change of capital city appeared again on the country's agenda. There were proposals to move the capital city from Pretoria, as its history and iconography was associated with apartheid and Boer dominance, and there were other proposals to consolidate all capitals in Pretoria. The Constitutional Court was moved to Johannesburg from Bloemfontein but no other radical changes to the capital city structure have been made so far.

Notes

1 Therborn, G. "Identity and Capital Cities: European Nation and European Union." In: Cerutti, F. & Lucarelli, S. (eds.), *The Search for a European Identity:*

Values, Policies and Legitimacy of the European Union (New York: Routledge, 2008), 65–70.
2 The scenario where the opposition to the king/religion forged the nation did not preclude the possibility of capital city change. Such options have been considered in France where the seat of power was moved from Versailles to Paris. In Turkey where the nation asserted itself against the Sultan and Islam, the capital was moved from Istanbul, the seat of the empire, to Ankara.
3 Jahn, F.-L. "An Essay on Capital Cities," *Essai sur les Moeurs, la Littérature, et la Nationalité des peuples de l'Allemagne* (Paris: J.B. Nichols & Son, 1832). The Gentleman's Magazine, vol. 103, (Jul–Dec, 1833), part 2, 229.
4 Kolbe, L. "Helsinki: From Provincial to National Centre." In: Gordon, David (ed.), *Planning Twentieth-Century Capital Cities* (London: Routledge, 2006), 74–77.
5 Makas, G.E. & Conley, D.T., eds. *Capital Cities in the Aftermath of Empires: Planning in Central and Southeastern Europe* (London: Routledge, 2010).
6 Murphey, R. "New Capitals of Asia," *Economic Development and Cultural Change*, vol. 5, no. 3 (April 1957), 218–219.
7 Ibid., 219–221.
8 Tarling, N., ed. *Cambridge History of South-East Asia* (Cambridge: Cambridge University Press, 1999), 4–5.
9 Rigg, J. "Exclusion and Embeddedness: The Chinese in Thailand and Vietnam." In: Ma, Laurence J.C. & Cartier, Carolyn L. (eds.), *The Chinese Diaspora: Space, Place, Mobility, and Identity* (Lanham, NY: Rowman & Littlefield, 2003), 106.
10 Ibid., 100.
11 From the beginning of the eighteenth century, the Phanariote Greeks exercised great influence in the administration in the Ottoman Empire's Balkan domains. Right up until the 1820s, the Greek language remained the predominant language in Bucharest. The Greeks also dominated the commercial life of the city right up until the twentieth century.
12 Therborn, G. Capitals and National Identity. European Variants, 2006, 231.
13 Gerasimov, I. *Novaia imperskaia istoria postsovetskogo prostranstva* (Kazan: New Imperial History, 2004), 322.
14 Encyclopedia Iranica. "Erevan" www.iranicaonline.org/articles/erevan-1
15 Ovsená, B. "Na obranu Svätopluka a o potrebe tieňového hlavného mesta Slovenska," *Sclabonia*, August 8, 2010.
16 Therborn, G. Capitals and National Identity. European Variants, 2006.
17 Ibid., 223–224.
18 Three comparative articles on the subject can be mentioned here. Vernon, C. "Capital Connections: Australia, Brazil and Landscapes of National Identity," *15th International Planning History Society Conference* (Sao Paulo, 2012); Stephenson, G. "Two Newly-Created Capitals: Islamabad and Brasilia," *The Town Planning Review*, vol. 41, no. 4 (October 1970), 317–332; Koch, N. "Why Not a World City? Astana, Ankara, and Geopolitical Scripts in Urban Networks," *Urban Geography*, vol. 34, no. 1 (2013), 109–130.
19 Hamdan, G. "Capitals in the New Africa," *Economic Geography*, vol. 40 (1964), 245.
20 Ibid., 239.
21 The said renaming of cities was not unique for African countries; they were also common in India and other post-colonial countries. Such European capital cities as Oslo (Christiania), Petrograd (Saint-Petersburg), and Bratislava (formerly Pressburg) were also renamed to emphasize their own national identity.
22 Clarke, J. "The Growth of Capital Cities in Africa," *Africa Spectrum*, vol. 61, no. 2 (1971), 34–35.

23 Schatz, E. "What Capital Cities Say about State and Nation Building," *Nationalism and Ethnic Politics*, vol. 9, no. 4 (2003), 21. Edward Schatz is using the Ethno-linguistic Fractionalization Index to measure cultural heterogeneity.
24 Best, A.C. "Gaberone: Problems and Prospects of a New Capital," *Geographic Review*, vol. 60 (1970), 1–14; Clarke, J. "The Growth of Capital Cities in Africa," *Africa Spectrum*, vol. 61, no. 2 (1971), 34–35.
25 Garnett, A. "The Capitals of Morocco," *Scottish Geographical Magazine*, vol. 44, no. 1 (1928), 31–41.
26 Naipaul, V.S. "The Crocodiles of Yamoussoukro." In: *Finding the Center: Two Narratives by V.S. Naipaul* (New York: Alfred A. Knopf, 1984), 149–150.
27 Mabogunje, A. *Urbanization in Nigeria* (London: University of London Press, 1968).
28 Falola, T. *Power of African Culture* (Rochester, NY: University of Rochester Press, 2003).
29 Eyinla, B.M. "From Lagos to Abuja: The Domestic Politics and International Implications of Relocating Nigeria's Capital City." In: Sohn, A. & Weber, H. (eds.), *Hauptstädte und Global Cities and der Schwelle zum 21. Jahrhundert* (Bochum: Winkler Verlage, 2000), 239–266; Adebanwi, W. "Abuja." In: Therborn, G. & Bekker, S. (eds.), *Capital Cities in Africa: Power and Powerlessness* (Pretoria & Dakar: HSRC & CODESRIA, 2011), 84–102.
30 Moore, J. "The Political History of Nigeria's New Capital," *The Journal of Modern African Studies*, vol. 22, no. 1 (March 1984), 174–175.
31 Adebanwi, W. "Abuja." In: Therborn, G. & Bekker, S. (eds.), *Capital Cities in Africa: Power and Powerlessness* (Pretoria & Dakar: HSRC & CODESRIA, 2011), 97–99.
32 Nwafor, J.C. "The Relocation of Nigeria's Federal Capital: A Device for Greater Territorial Integration and National Unity," *Geographical Journal*, vol. 4, no. 4 (1980), 320.
33 Moser, G., Rogers, S., & Van Til, R. "Nigeria: Experience with Structural Adjustment," *IMF Occasional Papers* (Washington D.C.), (March 1997), 37.
34 Adama, O. "State, Space and Power in Postcolonial Africa: Capital Relocation as a State Building Project in Nigeria," *Hemispheres: Studies on Cultures and Societies*, no. 27 (2012), 35–39.
35 Adebanwi, W. "Abuja." In: Therborn, G. & Bekker, S. (eds.), *Capital Cities in Africa: Power and Powerlessness* (Pretoria & Dakar: HSRC & CODESRIA, 2011), 99–100.
36 Ibid., 96–97.
37 Ikoku, G. "The City as Public Space: Abuja—The Capital City of Nigeria," *Forum*, vol. 6, no. 1 (2004), 41–43.
38 Kironde, J.M.L. "Will Dodoma Ever Be the New Capital of Tanzania?," *Geoforum*, vol. 24, no. 4 (November 1993), 437.
39 Mosha, A. "The Planning of the New Capital of Tanzania: Dodoma, an Unfulfilled Dream," (2004), www.etsav.upc.es/personals/iphs2004/pdf/148_p.pdf
40 Callaci, E. "'Chief Village in a Nation of Villages': History, Race and Authority in Tanzania's Dodoma Plan," *Urban History*, vol. 43, no. 1 (2015) 96–116.
41 Ginneken, S. van. "The Burden of being Planned: How African Cities Can Learn from Experiments of the Past: New Town Dodoma, Tanzania." In: *New Towns on the Cold War Frontier* (Crimson Architectural Historians, 2015) www.newtowninstitute.org/spip.php?article1050; Yoon, D. "The Rationalization of Space and Time: Dodoma and Socialist Modernity," *Ufahamu: A Journal of African Studies*, vol. 36, no. 2 (2011), 7–12.
42 Kironde, J.M.L. "Will Dodoma Ever Be the New Capital of Tanzania?," *Geoforum*, vol. 24, no. 4 (November 1993), 450.

43 Mosha, A. "The Planning of the New Capital of Tanzania: Dodoma, an Unfulfilled Dream," (2004), www.etsav.upc.es/personals/iphs2004/pdf/148_p.pdf, 9.
44 Kironde, J.M.L. "Will Dodoma Ever Be the New Capital of Tanzania?," *Geoforum*, vol. 24, no. 4 (November 1993), 451–452.
45 Mosha, A. "The Planning of the New Capital of Tanzania: Dodoma, an Unfulfilled Dream," (2004), www.etsav.upc.es/personals/iphs2004/pdf/148_p.pdf, 12.
46 Potts, D. "Capital Relocation in Africa: The Case of Lilongwe in Malawi," *Geographical Journal*, vol. 151, no. 2 (1985), 182–196.
47 Dieye, Y. "Faut-il déplacer la capitale sénégalaise?," *Assirou.Net*, mai 22, 2013. www.seneweb.com/news/Economie/faut-il-deplacer-la-capitale-senegalaise_n_96236.html
48 Rabinovich, I. & Shaked, H., eds. *Middle East Contemporary Survey*, vol. XI (Boulder, San Francisco & London: Westview Press, 1987), 546–547.
49 Sakyi, K. A. "Does Ghana Need a New Capital city?," *GhanaWeb*, October 21, 2011.
50 "Liberia: President Sirleaf Unveils Plan for a New Capital City." In *African Press International* on January 25, 2011. https://africanpress.wordpress.com/2011/01/25/liberia-president-sirleaf-unveils-plan-for-a-new-capital-city/
51 Yahye, M. "Move the Capital from Mogadishu?," *wardheernews.com*, May 30, 2005.
52 This apparently eccentric idea of the construction of the capital city in the shape of an animal or a bird was not singular and unique. Some of the ancient capital cities on different continents are constructed in such a way. The ancient Cusco, the capital of the Incas, was built in the shape of puma, and Brasília in Brazil had a shape of an ibis in the blueprint of the city.
53 Carlstrom, G. "Juba: East Africa's Economic Boom Town," *Al Jazera*, July 7, 2011.
54 Marlow, J. "Relocation: The Pros and Cons of Plans in South Sudan," *Geographical Magazine*, December 2011.
55 Ibid.
56 Magutt, J. "Need to Relocate the Capital City," November 10, 2009. www.josephmagutt.com/social-development/need-to-relocate-the-city/
57 Lungu, J. "What about moving the capital city?" *Zambia Daily Mail*, March 11, 2015.
58 Murphey, R. "New Capitals of Asia," *Economic Development and Cultural Change*, vol. 5, no. 3 (April 1957), 218–219.
59 Palatino, M. "Will ASEAN Countries Move Their Capitals?," *The Diplomat*, July 18, 2013.
60 King, R. "Re-Writing the City: Putrajaya as Representation," *Journal of Urban Design*, vol. 12, no. 1 (2007), 118.
61 Ibid., 136.
62 Ibid. 135–137
63 Ibid., 117.
64 Kotarumalos, A. "Indonesia Mulls Plans to Relocate Capital City," *Huffington Post*, September 30, 2010.
65 Ibid.; Prakoso, H. "Moving Capital City to Improve Transport Conditions? The Case of Jakarta," *Colloque international La fabrique du movement*, Paris, Mars 26–27, 2012.
66 Kotarumalos, A. "Indonesia Mulls Plans to Relocate Capital City," *Huffington Post*, September 30, 2010.
67 Prakoso, H. "Moving Capital City to Improve Transport Conditions? The Case of Jakarta," *Colloque international La fabrique du movement*, Paris, Mars 26–27, 2012.

68 In Indonesia the roads occupy only 6 percent of the general square of the city, while 20 percent is an average for the developed countries.
69 Ibid.
70 Zenn, J. "New Capital Ambitions in Indonesia," *Asia Times*, August 4, 2011.
71 Bangkok Post. "PT MPs Propose New Capital City," November 15, 2011.
72 Osathanon, P. "Action Required to Stop Sinking of the Capital," *Nation*, July 23, 2015.
73 London, B. "Is the Primate City Parasitic? The Regional Implications of National Decision Making in Thailand," *The Journal of Developing Areas*, vol. 12, no. 1 (October 1977), 49–68.
74 Pitithawatchai, W. *Eke Kasat Tai Ratthathamanoon* (Royal Power under the Constitution) (Bangkok, 1985).
75 Chanco, B. "Decongest Metro Manila," *Philippine Star*, August 12, 2015.
76 In reality there were probably more than seven capitals (Qutab Minar is also sometimes included). But the accepted number is seven (excluding New Delhi), and these are cities whose remains are extant.
77 Kumar, N. "Decapitate *Capital* Tag from *Delhi*- Commemorating a Century of Coronation," *Perspectives on Pan-Asianism*, August 29, 2009.
78 Cited in Metcalf, T. *An imperial Vision: Indian Architecture and Britain's Raj* (London: Faber and Faber, 1989), 222.
79 Gupta, H. "Pataliputra: The New Capital?," *Swarajya*, June 1, 2015. http://swarajyamag.com/ideas/pataliputra-the-new-capital/
80 Ambedkar, B.R. "India and the Necessity of a Second Capital: A Way to Remove Tension between the North and the South." In: *Thoughts of Linguistic States* (Bombay: Ramkrishna Printing Press, 1955); Kumar, N. "Decapitate *Capital* Tag from *Delhi*- Commemorating a Century of Coronation," *Perspectives on Pan-Asianism*, August 29, 2009; Anandan, S. "Make Mumbai Second Capital of India, City Forum Petitions PM," *Hindustan Times*, June 26, 2012; Gupta, H. "Pataliputra: The New Capital?," *Swarajya*, June 1, 2015.
81 Rehmat, A. "50 Years of Islamabad 1960–2010: Capital Crown," *Pak Tea House*, January 11, 2010.
82 Ibid.
83 Boukoeu, A. & Boukeau, L. "Paranoia, repressii I narkobiznes v Birme," *Svobodnaia mysl*, vol. 9–10 (2006).
84 Rogachev, S. "Naypyidaw—novaia stolitsa Myanmy," *Geografia*, no. 19 (2008).
85 Ibid.
86 Ibid.
87 More recent accounts provided by Burma experts debunk both the astrological and the simplistic political treatment of the capital city relocation in Myanmar, showing important geopolitical considerations behind this decision. See Goma, D. "'Naypyidaw vs. Yangon': The Reasons behind the Junta's Decision to Move the Burmese Capital." In: Dittmer, Lowell (ed.), *Burma or Myanmar?: The Struggle for National Identity*, Ch. 7. (Singapore: World Scientific Publishing, 2010), 185–204. Egreteau, R. & Jagan, L. *Soldiers and Diplomacy in Burma: Understanding the Foreign Relations of the Burmese Praetorian State* (Singapore: NUS Press, 2013), 227–232.
88 Preecharush, D. *Naypyidaw: The New Capital of Burma* (Bangkok: White Lotus, 2009).
89 Goma, D. Op.cit.: 199–200.
90 Morshed, A. "A Post-Dhaka Bangladesh," June 16, 2011. http://opinion.bdnews24.com/2011/06/16/a-post-dhaka-bangladesh/
91 Gurund, A. "Maoists to Propose Chitwan as Federal Capital of Nepal," *Nepal News*, April 25, 2012.

92 Corey, K. "Relocation of National Capitals," *International Symposium on the Capital Relocation* (September 22, Seoul, 2004), 58–59.
93 Takamura, Y. & Tone, K. "A Comparative Site Evaluation Study for Relocating Japanese Government Agencies Out of Tokyo," *Socio-Economic Planning Sciences*, vol. 37 (2003), 86.
94 Ibid.
95 Vogel, R.K. "Decentralization and Urban Governance: Reforming Tokyo Metropolitan Government." In: Ruble, Blair A., Stren, Richard E., & Tulchin, Joseph S. (eds.), *Urban Governance Around the World* (Washington D.C.: Woodrow Wilson International Center for Scholars, 2001), 116–117.
96 Ibid., 137–138.
97 The Economist. "The Capital: Removal Time," December 15, 2012.
98 Gao, J. "Discussion on Relocating China's Capital Resumes after Beijing Is Deemed Unlivable," *China News*, December 18, 2010. www.ministryoftofu.com/2010/12/discussion-on-relocating-chinas-capital-resumes-after-beijing-is-deemed-unlivable/
99 Ibid.
100 The Economist. "The Capital: Removal Time," December 15, 2012.
101 Gao, J. "Discussion on Relocating China's Capital Resumes after Beijing Is Deemed Unlivable," *China News*, December 18, 2010. www.ministryoftofu.com/2010/12/discussion-on-relocating-chinas-capital-resumes-after-beijing-is-deemed-unlivable/
102 Wang, J.-H. & Huang, S. "Contesting Taibei as the World City," *City*, vol. 13, no. 1 (2009), 103–109.
103 Lin, P. "Options Are Plentiful for the Capital's Relocation," *Taipei Times*, October 26, 2006.
104 Ibid.
105 Lee, R. & Pelizzon, S. "Hegemonic Cities in the Modern World-System." In: Kasaba, Reşat & Wallerstein, Immanuel (eds.), *Cities in the World-System: Studies in the Political Economy of the World-System* (New York: Greenwood Press, 1991), 82.
106 The Economist. "Sing a song of $40 Billion," July 22, 2010.
107 Richardson, H.W. & Bae, C.-H.C. "Options for the Capital of a Reunified Korea," *SAIS Review of International Affairs*, vol. 29, no. 1 (2009), 71.
108 Jun, M.-J. "Korea's Public Sector Relocation: Is It a Viable Option for Balanced National Development?" *Regional Studies*, vol.41, no. 1. (2007).
109 Ibid., 67.
110 Ibid., 73–76.
111 Ibid.
112 Stratfor. "A Shift in Asia as Mongolia Stirs," *Global Intelligence Update*, May 19, 2000.
113 Rogers, David. 2015. "Why Mongolia is Considering a German Plan for New Eco-Capital," *Global Construction Review*, April 21.
114 Bilâl, Ş. "Ankara: The Republic's Capital—To Be or Not to Be!," *The Guide Ankara Magazine*, 192078, 2007.
115 Ibid.
116 Evered, Kyle. 2008. "Symbolizing a Modern Anatolia: Ankara as Capital in Turkey's Early Republican Landscape," *Comparative Studies in South Asia, Africa, and the Middle East*, vol. 28, no. 2 (2008), 326–341; Kacar, D. "Ankara, a Small Town Transformed to a Nation's Capital," *Journal of Planning History*, vol. 9 (2010), 43–65.
117 Kezer, Z. "The Making of a National Capital: Ideology and Socio-Spatial Practices in Early Republican Ankara," Ph.D. diss., University of California at Berkeley, 1992.

118 Çinar, A. "The Imagined Community as Urban Reality: The Making of Ankara." In: Çinar, Alev & Bender, Thomas (eds.), *Urban Imaginaries: Locating the Modern City* (Minneapolis: The University of Minnesota Press, 2007), 161.
119 Bozdoğan, S. *Modernism and Nation Building: Turkish Architectural Culture in the Early Republic* (Seattle & London: University of Washington, 2001).
120 Cited in Çinar, A. "The Imagined Community as Urban Reality: The Making of Ankara." In: Çinar, Alev & Bender, Thomas (eds.), *Urban Imaginaries: Locating the Modern City*, (Minneapolis: The University of Minnesota Press, 2007), 153.
121 Borisov, G. "Perenos stolitsy Irana—tekhnicheskie, ekonomicheskie i politicheskie aspekty," *Regnum*, December 17, 2012. www.regnum.ru/news/polit/1723028.html; Mammadova, S. "Iran's Capital Relocation Threatens Azerbaijani Minorities," *Harvard Business Review*, January 8, 2014.
122 Johnson, G. "The Drivers of Dehsabz: Who Is Building New Kabul City?," *Family Security Matters*, July 14, 2011 www.familysecuritymatters.org/publications/id.9940/pub_detail.asp
123 Ibid.
124 Egyptian Street, "Egypt to Build a 'New Administrative Capital City'," July 18, 2014.
125 Al Sultani, A. "Muharraq City: A GIS-Planning Strategy for Its Ancient Heritage," Ph.D. Dissertation, University of Portsmouth, 2009, 38.
126 Raafat, H. "UAE to Get New Capital," *The National*, April 17, 2008. www.thenationalae/article/20090311/NATIONAL/786098729/1010
127 Rodrigues, C. "Yemenis Divided Over Capital: Can Aden Replace Sanaa?," *Middle East Eye*, March 19, 2015. www.middleeasteye.net/news/yemenis-divided-over-capital-can-aden-replace-sanaa-1498766749#sthash.ZUxeNDLx.dpuf
128 Galiani, S. & Kim, S. "The Law of the Primate City in the Americas," *Proceedings of a Conference Honoring the Contributions of Kenneth Sokoloff at UCLA* (2008), Los Angeles, 5–6, 14.
129 Ibid., 15–17.
130 Eisenstadt, S.N. & Shachar, A. *Society, Culture, and Urbanization* (Newbury Park: Sage, 1987), 89–90, 319.
131 Toynbee, A. *A Study of History: Abridgement of Vol. VII–X by D.C. Somervell* (New York & Oxford: Oxford University Press, 1987), 41.
132 Epstein, D. *Brasilia from the Plan to Reality: A Study of Planned and Spontaneous Urban Development* (Berkley: University of California Press, 1973).
133 There was a persistent interest in the topic of a new Brazilian capital city throughout nineteenth century history that transpired in political constitutions, various proposals of political transformation, and even religious visions. The legend has it that the Italian priest (and later Catholic saint) Giovanni Bosco prophesied in 1883 that the new promised land of milk and honey will emerge in the southern hemisphere between the parallels 15 and 20 where the golden treasures are hidden in the bowels of the earth.
134 Salvador was the capital of the country since 1763, and it served as the center of administration of the plantation economy cultivating sugarcane and coffee. The capital was later moved to Rio de Janeiro because the center of gravity of the colonial economy moved to the Minas Gerais area in the vicinity of Rio that also had a convenient bay.
135 Stratfor. *The Geopolitics of Brazil: An Emergent Power's Struggle with Geography*, May 13, 2012.
136 Holston, J. *The Modernist City: An Anthropological Critique of Brasilia* (Chicago: University of Chicago Press, 1989); Evanson, N. *Two Brazilian Capitals: Architecture and Urbanism in Rio de Janeiro and Brasilia* (New Heaven: Yale University Press, 1973).

170 *Capital relocations in world regions*

137 Philippou, S. *Oscar Niemeyer: Curves of Irreverence* (New Haven & London: Yale University Press, 2008), 62.
138 Read, J. "Alternative Functions: Oscar Niemeyer and the Poetics of Modernity," *Modernism/modernity*, vol. 12, no. 2 (April 2005), 263.
139 Philippou, S. *Oscar Niemeyer: Curves of Irreverence* (New Haven & London: Yale University Press, 2008).
140 Evanson, N. *Two Brazilian Capitals: Architecture and Urbanism in Rio de Janeiro and Brasilia* (New Heaven: Yale University Press, 1973).
141 Donahue, B. "The Believers," *Washington Post*, September 18, 2005.
142 Holston, J. *The Modernist City: An Anthropological Critique of Brasilia* (Chicago: University of Chicago Press, 1989).
143 Williams, R. "Modernist Civic Space and the Case of Brasília," *Journal of Urban History*, vol. 32, no. 1 (2005), 120–137.
144 BBC News. "Taking the Capital Out of a City," November 3, 2009.
145 Lara, F. & Nair, S. "The Brazilianization of Brasilia," *The Journal of the International Institute*, vol. 14, no. 2 (2007) http://quod.lib.umich.edu/j/jii/4750978.0014.214/--brazilianization-of-brasilia?rgn=main;view=fulltext; Mangabeira da Vinha, D. "Brasília through British Media," *Vitruvius*, ano. 14, 2014.
146 Lara, F. & Nair, S. "The Brazilianization of Brasilia," *The Journal of the International Institute*, vol. 14, no. 2 (2007). http://quod.lib.umich.edu/j/jii/4750978.0014.214/--brazilianization-of-brasilia?rgn=main;view=fulltext
147 The Economist. "Who Says Brasilia Does Not Work?," June 20, 1998.
148 Bird, J. & Staub, S. "The Brasília Experiment: Road Access and the Spatial Pattern of Long-Term Local Development in Brazil," *World Bank Research Working Paper*, Report Number WPS6964, July 2014, 2.
149 Eldredge, H. *World Capitals: Toward Guided Urbanization* (New York: Anchor Press, Garden City, 1975), 477.
150 Myers, D. "The Dynamics of Local Empowerment: An Overview," *Capital City Politics in Latin America: Democratization and Empowerment* (Boulder, CO: Lynne Riener, 2002), 279–280.
151 Shmidt, C. "Argentina's Cuestión Capital," In: del Real, Patricio & Gyger, Helen (eds.), *Latin American Modern Architectures: Ambiguous Territories* (Routledge: London, 2013), 175–180.
152 Sarmiento, D. *Argiropolis: O la Capital de los Estados Confederadus del Rio del Plata* (Buenos Aires: Biblioteca Quiroga Sarmiento, 2007).
153 Gilbert, A. "Moving the Capital of Argentina: A Further Example of Utopian Planning?," *Cities*, vol. 6 (1989), 235.
154 Rowley, S. "Argentina Wants to Grow a New Capital," *Chicago Tribune*, February 8, 1987.
155 Gilbert, A. "Moving the Capital of Argentina: A Further Example of Utopian Planning?," *Cities*, vol. 6 (1989), 237.
156 Atkinson, D. & Dodds, K., eds. *Geopolitical Traditions: Critical Histories of a Century of Geopolitical Thought* (London: Routledge, 2004), 179–180, 164.
157 Rowley, S. "Argentina Wants to Grow a New Capital," *Chicago Tribune*, February 8, 1987.
158 Gilbert, A. "Moving the Capital of Argentina: A Further Example of Utopian Planning?," *Cities*, vol. 6, (1989), 236.
159 Poliszuk, J. "Ciudad Libertad," *El Nacional*, de Julio 29, 2004.
160 Zurga, G. "Cambio de Capital: Una solución estratosférica," *Analitica.com*, de agosto 1, 2011. www.lahistoriaparalela.com.ar/2011/08/03/cambio-de-capital-una-solucion-estratosferica/; Poliszuk, J. "Ciudad Libertad, *El Nacional*, de Julio 29, 2004.

161 Ibid.
162 Bilham, R. "Millions at Risk as Big Cities Grow Apace in Earthquake Zones," *Nature*, vol. 401 (1999), 739–740.
163 Richardson, H.W. "National Urban Development Strategies in Developing Countries," *Urban Studies*, vol. 18 (1981), 267–283.
164 Callegari, L. "La Geopolítica Aconseja Trasladar la Capital de la República a la Sierra Central," *Eco Andino. Revista de Cultura*, de octubre 17, 2009.
165 McDonnell, P. & Ordonez, O. "Plan to Move Capital Seen as Step to Divide Bolivia," *Los Angeles Times*, August 12, 2007.
166 La Prensa. "¿La capital a otra parte?," April 27, 2014. www.laprensa.com.ni/2014/04/27/reportajes-especiales/192104-la-capital-a-otra-parte
167 Kearns, K.C. "Belmopan: Perspective on a New Capital," *Geographic Review*, vol. 63 (1973), 147–169.
168 Chubashenko, D. "Chetvertaia Moldavskaia respublika," *Regnum*, April 9, 2012.
169 Smirnyagin, L. Puteshestviya stolits. Istoriko-geograficheskiy ocherk (1998) http://neweurasia.info/archive/98/book.html
170 Wolfel, R.L. "North to Astana: Nationalistic Motives for the Movement of the Kazakh Capital," *Nationalities Papers*, vol. 30, no. 3 (2002), 485–506.
171 Schatz, E. "What Capital Cities Say about State and Nation Building," *Nationalism and Ethnic Politics*, vol. 9, no. 4 (2003), 111–140.
172 Ibid.
173 Ibid.
174 Alimbekova, G. *Otnoshenie astanchan i almaatintsev k perenosu stolitsy: resultaty sotsiologicheskogo issledovania*, 20^{yi} vek: perenosy stolits (Astana: Elorda, 2008).
175 Luneva, G. "Stolitsa pereedet v Chayok?," *Slovo Kyrgyzstana*, July 3, 2013.
176 Ata-Meken. "Perenos stolitsy Kyrgyzstana v Osh nevozmozhen i neeffektiven—eksperty," July 9, 2010.
177 Averchenko, T. "Tadzhikistan pomeniaet stolitsu?," *Pravda*, July 22–25, 2011.
178 Salimpur, M. "Dushanbe—stolitsa tadzhikov Movarounnakhra," *Radio Odzi*, April 21, 2012.
179 Musavat, "Novyi grandioznii proekt Alieva," October 10, 2014
180 Rossman, V. "In Search of the Fourth Rome: Visions of a New Russian Capital City," *Slavic Review*, vol. 72, no. 3 (2013), 512–513.
181 Ibid., 515.
182 Voloshin, D. "Zachem Ukraine nuzhen perenos stolitsy," *Khvilia*, December 28, 2014.
183 Ovsená, B. "Na obranu Svätopluka a o potrebe tieňového hlavného mesta Slovenska," *Sclabonia*, August 8, 2010.
184 Chocrane, A. & Jonas, A. "Reimaging Berlin: World City, Capital City or Ordinary Place," *European Urban and Regional Studies*, vol. 6, no. 2 (1999), 145–164; Daum, A. & Mauch, C., eds. *Berlin-Washington 1800–2000: Capital Cities, Cultural Representations, and National Identities* (New York: Cambridge University Press, 2009).
185 Țene, I. "C. Noica și mutarea Capitalei României," *Frontpress*, December 14, 2009.
186 Ibid.
187 Toma, A. "Ce-ar fi daca am muta Capitala Romaniei in Ardeal?," *Ziare*, May 25, 2008. www.ziare.com/politica/stiri-politice/ce-ar-fi-daca-am-muta-capitala-romaniei-in-ardeal-317255
188 Țene, I. "C. Noica și mutarea Capitalei României," *Frontpress*, December 14, 2009.

172 Capital relocations in world regions

189 Tache, C. "Klaus Iohannis, impins de la spate sa mute Capitala la Alba Iulia," *National*, October 2, 2015.
190 Toma, A. "Ce-ar fi daca am muta Capitala Romaniei in Ardeal?," *Ziare*, May 25, 2008. www.ziare.com/politica/stiri-politice/ce-ar-fi-daca-am-muta-capitala-romaniei-in-ardeal-317255
191 Manning, C. *The Forgotten Republics* (New York: Philosophical Library, 1952), 150–157.
192 Nyrko, V. "Gorod razdora," *Sovershenno sekretno*, January 15, 2003.
193 Flanders, S. "Should Britain Let Go of London?," *BBC News*, March 25, 2013. www.bbc.com/news/business-21934564
194 Ibid.
195 Dorling, D. "The London Problem: Has the Capital become Too Dominant?," *New Statesman*, September 4, 2014.
196 Ibid.; Dorling, D. "Should Parliament Move Out of London?," *The Guardian*, March 7, 2015.
197 Dorling, D. "The London Problem: Has the Capital become Too Dominant?," *New Statesman*, September 4, 2014.
198 Butler, C. "Want to Save the United Kingdom? Move the Capital to Glasgow," *Independent*, June 19, 2014.
199 Dorling, D. "Should Parliament Move Out of London?," *The Guardian*, March 7, 2015.
200 Dunnet, J. "Great Britain—The Case for a New Capital City," *The Architectural Review*, November 26, 2011.
201 Davies, D. "Nottingham: The New Capital of England?," *Britology Watch: Deconstructing 'British Values'*, November 6, 2007.
202 Dunnet, J. "This House Moves to Move: The Case for Relocating Parliament," *The Architectural Review*, May 7, 2015.
203 Marchand, B. *Les ennemis de Paris* (Rennes: Presses Universitaires de Rennes, 2009); Marchand, B. *The Image of Paris in France since Two Centuries: From Good to Bad to Worst*, 2010.
204 McLynn, F. *Napoleon: Biography* (New York: Arcade Publishing, 1997), 406.
205 Napoleon envisaged Paris as the center of the imperial universe. "It came into my perpetual dreams, to make of Paris the veritable capital of Europe. I wanted it to become . . . something fabulous, colossal, something unknown before our own time." (Quoted in Berger, S. & Miller, A., eds. *Nationalizing Empires* (Budapest: Central European University Press, 2014), 115.)
206 Gravier, J.-F. *Paris and the French Desert* (Paris: Portulan, 1947).
207 Ibid.
208 Hansen, N., Higgins, B., & Savoie, D. *Regional Policy in a Changing World* (New York: Plenum Press, 1990), 47.
209 Marchand, B. *The Image of Paris in France since Two Centuries: From Good to Bad to Worst*, 2010.
210 Keating, M. "Decentralization in Mitterrand's France," *Public Administration*, vol. 61 (1983), 237–252.
211 Levine S. *What if Nelson Had Been Made the Capital of New Zealand?* (Wellington: Victoria University Press, 2006), 60.
212 Pegrum, R. *Bush Capital: How Australia Chose Canberra as Its Federal City* (Sydney: Hale & Iremonger, 1983).
213 Ibid.; Statham, P., ed. *The Origins of Australia's Capital Cities* (Cambridge: Cambridge University Press, 1989).

4 Strategies of capital city relocations and their critics

The common themes in capital city relocations

The above analysis in Chapter 3 of capital city transfers in different regions of the globe and the debates thereof enables us to develop a taxonomy of the most common reasons for capital city relocations and to pinpoint the patterns, strategies, principles, and locational logic of new capital city transfers prevalent in particular mega-regions and specific political regimes. However before we turn to the analysis of these reasons and mega-regions, it behooves us to make some preliminary observations and to introduce several distinctions and categories to make our further analysis sharper and more fruitful.

Negative and positive reasons

Migration theory applies the terms "push" and "pull" factors to differentiate between the reasons that explain migration patterns for people. By the same token, the same push and pull factors also operate in capital city migrations. The push factors can be labeled negative reasons and pull factors represent positive reasons.

The negative reasons represent the drawbacks and undesirable qualities of the old capital city. They include such factors as the deficiency of its current location, its vulnerability in terms of natural disasters and calamities, external threats, excessive concentration of people and resources, along with negative historical and symbolic connotations. On the other hand, positive reasons represent the advantages of a new place.

The most common negative reasons in the cases discussed above are earthquake vulnerability, exposure to flooding, sand storms, hurricanes, typhoons, tornadoes, and the like natural calamities. Seismic hazards represent the most common threat that is referenced by the proponents of capital city shifts in cases discussed. Kathmandu, Dhaka, and Delhi in South Asia; Managua, Caracas, and Lima in the Americas; Tehran, Baku and Dushanbe in Central Asia; Tokyo and Taipei in the Far East; Accra and Nairobi in Africa; and Jakarta and Manila in Southeast Asia face significant seismic hazards and belong to the group of the most tectonically precarious capital cities.[1]

174 Strategies of relocations

Wellington is another example of an earthquake-prone city and despite its politically convenient location between the South and North islands, the topic of moving the seat of government elsewhere has stirred the debate also in New Zealand. Another threat is the shortage of water or difficulties and expense of its supply to the city that are especially troublesome and critical when the capital city is undergoing a process of explosive growth. Sana'a and Beijing are the prime examples of cities facing serious water shortages. In Southeast Asia flooding vulnerability constitutes a more imminent threat for such capital cities as Jakarta and Bangkok.

The congestion, gridlocks, and insufficient absorption capacity of the capital city along with attendant environmental issues are the most common social reasons cited by the proponents of capital city shifts. The powerful protest movements in the existing capitals, the needs of de-colonization and de-centralization also represent negative reasons.

The fundamental advantages or opportunities associated with particular new locations represent positive reasons. These new places, cities or regions, are deemed to enable countries to resolve new tasks, develop new territory, to facilitate the integration of the country into a new cultural or social-economic zone or to build new geoeconomic or political alliances. The consolidation of the nation, the establishment of new symbols and reaching of domestic peace, federalization, and new geopolitical positioning that promises to give a country specific economic and political benefits also belong to positive reasons. The more successful capital city transfers tend to be motivated by the new opportunities provided by a new geographic region.

Hidden and open political agendas

The declared goals of some capital city transfers do not always match the real and more important goals that the initiators of these projects have in mind. The governments are often pursuing goals that diverge from the acceptable norms of international law and generally accepted principles and need to appeal to reasons that do not reflect their real objectives and political agendas. In reality their motives are often very different from the officially cited.

As we have seen, the isolation and marginalization of the protest movements concentrated in the capital city is an important goal of the government moving its capital city. Such agenda is suspected in the case of Tehran and several other countries, including Brasília. We have also seen that specific ethnic politics in Malaysia and Kazakhstan also stimulated the capital relocations in many other countries although it was not cited among the official reasons.

We have also seen several cases where the capital cities were moved to the birthplaces of the rulers or to places where their ethnic or tribal group were dominant. In these cases the ruler or the governments were relying on the pre-modern tribal and clan loyalties to strengthen their support base and to maintain its political power. This type of motivation was more prevalent for

African countries. We have observed these type of motives in Malawi, Côte d'Ivoire, Zimbabwe and Nigeria.

Some governments were also using more sophisticated schemes and calculations in their capital city relocation plans, establishing or substantially revising clientalist networks or relying upon the existing clan systems to solidify their control over regional elites and to maintain political control in general. Through capital city transfers they were seeking to ensure the loyalty and support of certain regional elites.[2] Another type of clientalist arrangement was taking place in South Korea where the votes of the crucial swing province of Chungcheong were secured by the president Roh Moo-hyun in exchange for the promise to relocate the capital city there.

All the above mentioned motives are downplayed and are rarely referenced in the official capital city relocation plans and declarations.

The reasons that are not emphasized or downplayed by politicians also include self-aggrandizement and megalomaniac excesses of the rulers, the elements of patronage, the solidification of control over contested regions, isolation of the government from the metropolitan residents, opposition and liberal political fractions, and from the international community, the marginalization of the old and rival elites. The attempts of self-aggrandizement, self-glorification, and immortalization through architectural monuments are also not uncommon motives of such arrangements that are especially characteristic for autocratic regimes. All the above mentioned covert reasons and ulterior motives are either extremely unpopular within the countries or do not square well with internationally accepted norms of politics, international law, and political correctness.

Most of the capital city relocation projects have both open and hidden agendas. Albeit the fact that all these reasons, hidden agendas, and ulterior motives are very real and do not represent only a conjecture of the political analysts who unravel them, it would be short-sighted to discount more substantive reasons. The presence of the hidden agenda by itself does not necessarily disqualify the officially cited motives as bogus and artificial. However, it is important to recognize these additional reasons.

Nature and culture

The construction of a new capital city often involves not only the reconstruction of society but also the transformation of nature and these two elements are often intertwined. One of the most pervasive themes in new capital city constructions is the theme of conquering nature. The new capital cities were often built in the swamps, in tropical *selva*, in the virgin lands, in the sand dunes, in the wilderness, and in the uncultivated lands. The reporting on the new capital cities often highlighted the pathos of transformation of the emptiness and disorder of the surrounding landscapes. The examples of such problematic landscapes include the swampy banks of the

Neva River in Saint-Petersburg and Ishim river in Astana, the tidal marches of Washington D.C. and Manama, the marches of New Belgrade, the rugged and empty mountain site of Ankara, and the malaria-infected swamps of New Delhi. These landscapes also include the jungles of Central Myanmar, Peru, and Equatorial Guinea along with the tropical swamps of Yamoussoukro in Côte d'Ivoire. The more recent precedent in Egypt involved the virgin sands of the Egyptian desert adjacent to Suez that were chosen as a site to build a new capital. Curiously, the name of Brussels (*Broeksele*) translates from Old Dutch as "settlement in the swamps."

Ironically, the marshiness and the poor quality of the land where a new capital city is being built can be putative or largely exaggerated. Today many critics rightfully claim that in reality the territory of Washington D.C. was not too much swampier than that of many neighboring counties and territories.[3] The desolation and marshiness of the site where Saint-Petersburg was later built ("a wave-swept shore, remote, forlorn," to use the words of Alexander Pushkin) was also probably a bit overstated as the city was built in close proximity and almost on the same site as a Swedish city Nyenschatz that existed there until it was destroyed by Russian troops in the early seventeenth century. The canonical representations of modern Turkey's capital obscure the image of the old city around the citadel that existed at least since the Roman period.

However, the notions of the emptiness and disorder of the landscapes where new capitals have been constructed were deemed important both for the mythography of a new city and for the mythology of national history. The disorderly nature of these landscapes has emphasized the cultural world-building mission of the state and the nation that is building a new city under most unfavorable conditions. The nations were building themselves in confrontation not only with the invaders and foreign rule but also in confrontation with the wild nature. Such confrontations were deemed to be important for Washington D.C., Brasília, Canberra, Astana and Naypyidaw. The purpose-built cities evince the pathos of a civilizing mission and transformation of useless and inhospitable landscapes. One can easily see an important symbolic and emotional sense in this triumph over nature. The inhospitable environment of the new site where the new capital is built shows the commitment of the people to the national project and to the idea of nation-building. Following this logic, some proponents of the new Russian capital in Siberia have stressed the importance of the unfavorable natural conditions that will discourage the career-seekers from participation in this nation-building project.[4]

Such urban mythology is characteristic not only for modern capital city builders but probably represents a momentous mythopoeic concept. The legend has it that the territory of today's Mexico City was situated on the swamps not suitable for agricultural activities and was given to the nomadic Aztecs by local agricultural tribes as the least useful for their lifestyle.

Six integrative strategies for capital city relocations

Based on our analysis we can distinguish six distinct rationales and attendant strategies for capital city relocations: (1) strategy of spatial compromise, (2) strategy of historical integration, (3) geopolitical repositioning strategy, (4) strategy of economic integration and rebalancing, (5) de-centralization strategy, and (6) strategy of territorial integration.

Although it is not always easy to draw a line between these strategies, and they are not mutually exclusive, the distinction is still important and valuable for analytic purposes.

In the case of all these strategies, the new capital city serves as an instrument of integration and as a tool to establish a balance between existing social, economic, and political forces or parts of the country. In contrast to three other strategies that we will discuss later, these six strategies are intended to maximize the inclusivity of the country that might have ethnic, religious, political, or economic aspects and manifestations.

1 *Strategy of spatial compromise*

As a general rule, the strategy of spatial compromise is employed when two distinct and relatively equipotent sides are seeking integration. The ideal place for a capital city under such conditions is a neutral point in between these two sides. It can be a border point between two ethno-linguistic, ethno-religious or religious communities. This type of capital city epitomizes a sort of a new testament that lays the foundation of a new community. This type of strategy existed already in the ancient times although it has become more popular and gained more traction in the modern period.

Below we will provide many illustrations of this type of strategy that involved equanimous logic of locating the capital at a relatively central position.

In Ancient Egypt the capital city Memphis served as a compromise between the Lower and Upper Egypt, between Thebes and Tanis. For that reason this city was labeled "The Balance of Two Lands" in ancient Egyptian texts.

King David transferred his capital city from Hebron to Jerusalem because the latter was situated on the border between the two ancient kingdoms of Judea and Israel, between Hebron, the capital of Judea, and Samaria (*Shomron*), the capital of Israel. Such a capital facilitated the more effective unification of the two kingdoms.[5]

In 1561 the capital of Spain was moved to Madrid, which is located in the middle of the country. Its central location played the decisive role in its selection. Madrid was situated between the old royal residences of the Spanish kings, between Valladolid and Segovia in the north and Toledo in the south. Moreover, Madrid was equidistant from Burgos, the capital of Castalia, and Saragossa, the capital of Aragon, the two kingdoms the union of which formed the basis for the unified state. The new capital was also founded between the northern kingdoms that served as a springboard of Reconquista and Andalucía in the south that was conquered from the Moors.

In 1598 the capital city of Poland moved from Kraków to Warsaw due to the emergence of *Rzeczpospolita*, a bi-confederation of Poland and the Grand Duchy of Lithuania. Stephen Báthory, the king of Poland first moved the capital city to Hrodna (Grodno) on the territory of Lithuania already in 1576. He later moved it to Warsaw. Warsaw was situated in an equal distance from Hrodna and Kraków and therefore epitomized the unity of two parts of the republic. The new capital not only facilitated the union between Poland and Lithuania but also marked a vivid and dramatic transformation of the nature of the state. Warsaw has epitomized the Jagiellonian concept of Poland as a federal and multi-confessional state in contrast to the Piast idea of Poland as a national Polish state that was emphasized in Kraków. In addition the Polish king, Sigismund III, who was the first to move to Warsaw, never left hopes to regain the Swedish throne. The new capital city in the north made the city closer to Sweden and to the Baltic Sea.

The transfer of the capital of the Arab Caliphate from Damascus to Baghdad in 762 AD was also meant to better integrate the Persians and to transform the state into a more inclusive empire. The capital city shift reflected the rise of *Shu'ubiyyah*, the social and political movement that called to recognize a special role of Persian culture and alternative Muslim sects in the Caliphate. Under the Abbasids who moved the capital to Baghdad, the post of vizier, the high-ranking advisor to the ruler, was typically occupied by the members of Persian nobility such as Barmakids who also contributed to the founding of Baghdad. Similar to the Jagiellonian concept of Poland, the new concept of the Caliphate as a dual union of Arab military aristocracy and Persian culture formed the ideological basis for the transfer of the capital to Baghdad. Notably, it was founded in close proximity to Ctesiphon, the old capital of Persia.

When one part of the state is stronger and it integrates a smaller and weaker part, it can afford itself an asymmetrical compromise locating the capital on the territory of the weaker participant of the alliance or unity. Curiously, the option to transfer the royal capital from Madrid to Lisbon was seriously contemplated at the time of the establishment of the Iberian Union (1580–1640). For several years King Philipp II governed the united country of Spain and Portugal from Lisbon.

In 1830 Brussels, situated between Wallonia and Flanders, was declared the capital of the country. The location of this city on the border between the Romance and Germanic Europe has determined its choice as a capital of the EU. Perhaps this choice was also prompted by the proximity of Brussels to Aachen, the capital established by Charlemagne, the first emperor of the Holy Roman Empire and "the father of Europe."

In 1848 Berne, situated in close proximity to the French-speaking part of the country, was selected to be the capital city of Switzerland. It was a compromise between the German- and French-speaking parts of the country. It was also a compromise between conservative Catholic Lucerne that was not sufficiently committed to the concept of federation and the liberal and Protestant Zurich the wealth and power of which prompted the misgivings of the other cantons. Berne was selected as a result of the election where 79 votes were cast for Berne, 48 for Zurich, and 9 for Lucerne.[6]

In 1858 the capital of Nicaragua was moved from Leon to Managua. It was a compromise between two major cities of the country, liberal Leon and conservative Granada.

Many federalist countries provide examples of the compromises reached by relatively equal parties. The location of capital cities of the Anglo-Saxon federations exemplify this principle.

Washington D.C. is situated on the border between historical North and South and represents a compromise of the independence era. Ottawa in Canada was a compromise between English-speaking Toronto and Francophone Quebec City, between the Ontario and Quebec provinces. Canberra is a spatial compromise between Melbourne and Sydney. In 1865 the capital city of New Zealand was transferred from Auckland, which remains the economic capital of the country, to Wellington, located between the North and South islands, the main territories of the country.

In the aftermath of the Second World War, the Yugoslav federation was formed, and since 1948 the New Belgrade was built as a federal capital on the border between the Orient and the Occident, between Old Belgrade, the border town of Ottoman Empire, and Zemun, the border town of the Austro-Hungarian Empire. New Belgrade was also close to the border between Serbia and Croatia, the two largest constituent entities of the federation.

In Nigeria the relocation of the capital to Abuja was an attempt to find a politically neutral ground that would serve as a compromise between the Muslim north and Christian south of the country.

The model of the distributed capital city represents substantially identical but technically different mechanism of compromise-building between two or more most powerful constituent units of the state. It also represents a trade-off. This strategy helps to avoid large public expenditures associated with the construction of a neutral new capital city to integrate the two sides. However, it is associated with the inconveniences of communication between two or more co-capitals. This strategy is exemplified by the Netherlands and South Africa.

Initially, the Netherlands was comprised of 12 provinces. Two of the states of the United Kingdom of Netherlands, North and South Holland, were the most powerful and economically developed. They were also more densely populated. Accordingly, the candidacies of Amsterdam and The Hague as the cities representing these provinces turned out to be the most sensible and realistic. They represented not only the two geographic regions but also the two *ethoi* and moral principles of the state: the Protestant restraint of The Hague was opposed to the liberal mores of the larger metropolis. North Holland was dissatisfied with the transfer of the Supreme Court to The Hague and insisted on the separation of the two parts of the country. South Holland won, as other Dutch provinces resented and resisted the domination of the larger city. As a consequence, the queen, the Parliament, and the Supreme Court all have settled in The Hague. North Holland has received a consolation prize in the form of the formal status of a capital city where the coronation ceremonies of the kings of Netherlands take place.

In 1910 the Union of the four ex-colonies – Transvaal, Cape Province, Orange Republic, and Natal – was formed in South Africa. Each one of them aspired to make its own territory or its own capital city a capital city of the unified state. At the end, capital city functions were split and distributed between three provinces of the country. Executive power was housed in Pretoria, legislative in Cape Town, and judicial in Bloemfontein. The fourth ex-colony has received some financial compensation for political underrepresentation.

The two models of the capital of compromise described above are not always suitable for countries that have more than two state-forming sides. The geometry does not give any cues as to where the site in between three and more sides representing different constituent entities of the country should be located. Obviously, this arrangement is tenable only for the countries of relatively small size where the co-capitals are not separated by large distances; otherwise the distributed capital system will create problems and inefficiencies in terms of intra-government communications. Another difficulty with the distributed capital arrangement is that it is predicated on the idea that some parts of the state are more important and powerful than others. Needless to say that such ranking of the constituent entities of the state is not always possible or politically desirable. It must be added that multiple capital city solution also might be less efficient in terms of administration even in the smaller countries, albeit arguably being fairer. The inconveniences of administration from multiple capitals gave rise to proposals to consolidate the three capitals after the demise of the apartheid regime in South Africa.[7]

Due to all these reasons in cases when more than two communities form a new state, the capital in the middle might be a more effective and suitable model to organize a capital city function. Such capital in the middle of the country provides better opportunities for the multipolar integration taking into account the factors of distance and centrality. Some of the reconciliations and balances, as we have seen, are much more complex, as many countries are fractured along a number of fault-lines, notably north-south and east-west axis, urban-rural tensions, and ethnic fissures. The case in point is Kazakhstan where several balances, regional, ethnic, sub-ethnic, and historical, had to be reached. The choice of a more central location is a better solution since it gives equal access to the capital to different parts of the country and does not need to involve ranking of the constituent entities of the state.

It is interesting to note that compromise strategies in different parts of the world often acquired some features of *quid pro quo* exchange. Capital city status brings significant economic benefits in addition to symbolic capital that it confers upon a city. Therefore, the selection of capital city inevitably becomes a matter of negotiations and exchange between the participants of the national pact. As a prestige item and as a sign of rank and glory, capital city status is often exchanged for more tangible and immediate economic benefits.

Not infrequently, a stronger but less wealthy side can relinquish the capital city status and give it to a weaker side in exchange for acceptance of some financial liabilities or for funding of certain projects or taking other commitments. The capital city selection process in the US can serve as a good illustration of that point. The North of the US was in bad need of financial funds after the end of the independence war and paid with the currency of capital city prestige to the South, which assumed some debts for the war. The clientelist exchange between the incumbent president and the swing province or disadvantaged ethnic or sub-ethnic group of the country is another example. Under these conditions, the capital city status is traded for political support. As we have seen earlier these types of implicit exchange took place in South Korea and in Kazakhstan. As a result the compromise is transformed into the particularistic exchange, compromising the goals of national unity. The schemes and methods of such exchanges and compromises are quite interesting and can become a subject of more specialized study.

Overall, the concepts of the distributed capital and capital in between are two ways to reach a compromise, although they are not the only options available.

2 Strategy of historical integration

Not infrequently, the nations that have recently gained independence from colonial dominance bring their capital city to the old sanctified historical centers where their national essence was crystallized. This path was often chosen by nations that have been divided or detached from their native soil for extended periods of time, experiencing a break in the continuity of their historical memory. Through the return to their old historical centers and to their real or putative roots, these nations are hoping to reconnect with their past and to restore the continuity of their historical experience. After many years of dislocation, dependency, and conflicts they cling to the old historical centers that mark more glorious moments of their history. If under the compromise strategy the center in between integrates the points in space, under historical integration strategy the new capital links together the two moments in time. In these cases the capital of the past becomes a historical hinge, and it helps to rekindle the connection between the present and the past. It is also an opportunity to revive the old symbols and in some cases to assert ownership of the contested past.

The new capital city established in the old historical core of a particular culture aids in the merger of space and time. The lost time is now found or rediscovered in the built environment of the old capital. Such capital city

182 Strategies of relocations

transfers are often presented by nation's leaders initiating these decisions not as capital city changes but as restoration of the real capital cities in their full glory.

Greece, Italy, and Israel can serve as prime and vivid examples of the countries where this strategy was implemented. Notably, in all three cases, Athens, Rome, and Jerusalem did not become capital cities immediately after independence. The seats of government were moved to these ancient citadels shortly after independence, as these cities represented essential and unique national centers, the cradles of the great nations. In all three cases the new capitals were conceived antithetically and were often contrasted with the larger commercial and industrial centers, Thessaloniki, Milan, and Tel Aviv.

In spite of the anti-Jerusalem positions of many early Zionists, since the 1930s Jerusalem was embraced by all nationalist groups, including secular Zionists, as the only possible site to place the capital as it reconnected the Jews and the Jewish history in exile to their past, the time before the Roman destruction of Herod's city in 70 AD. In December 1949, shortly after the War of Independence ended, the Knesset and the Cabinet were moved to Jerusalem from Tel Aviv. "A nation that, for two thousand and five hundred years, has faithfully adhered to the vow made by the first exiles by the waters of Babylon not to forget Jerusalem," Ben-Gurion told members of the Knesset, "will never agree to be separated from Jerusalem."[8] Although moving Israel's capital to Jerusalem has been contended by the UN and other countries ever since, it was and remains one of the cornerstones of the State of Israel's Jewish identity. Jerusalem was chosen as the place emphasizing the historical continuity of Jewish community.

Berlin can also illustrate this strategy, as the choice of Berlin aided in the reconstruction of the nation, restoring the connection between the post-war Germany and historical Germany, becoming an instrument of the historical integration. The proposals to move the capital city to Karakorum in contemporary Mongolia are inspired by the same considerations and can be viewed as an example of the same strategy.

The idea of returning to the sanctified and primordial territories had an appeal for many other nations. All such proposals have been presented as prerequisite for the revival of the ancient cores of these nations.

In Romania some proposals to move the capital city were justified based on the idea of historical roots. The authors of these proposals have argued that Romanians need to reclaim their past by moving the capital to Alba Iulia, closer to the Dacians' homeland in Transylvania and to Sarmizegetusa Regia, the ancient capital of Dacians. In Iran the concept of a new capital city in Tabriz was presented as a bid to revive the ancient centers of Persian fire-worshippers in Eastern Azerbaijan. Earlier in Persian history, attempts have been made by Reza Shah, who had emulated Ataturk, to revive the ancient capital city of Persepolis.[9]

In South Asia, Kotte and New Delhi, the new capital cities of Sri Lanka and India respectively, also reveal the adherence to this strategy. The new administrative capital cities were placed in the immediate proximity to the old pre-colonial capital cities of these two nations. Kotte was the last capital city of the centralized Singhalese state. New Delhi was placed close to the constellation of the Seven Cities of Delhi, the historical core of the nation.

The strategy of historical integration does not necessarily imply the restoration of the old capital in an effort to consolidate the historical meanings and symbols deemed important for present-day needs of nation-building. Not all nations had such old capital cities in their disposal. In most postcolonial contexts, the territories in the center or in the interior of the country, which represented the real or putative ancestral homeland of the titular nation, have played such a role. These interior regions were often associated with the revival of the nation and the movement of the capital there was meant to reestablish its ties with the ancestral homelands. Ankara in Anatolia, where the capital city of Turkey was moved, was presented as such a primordial territory from where the Turks have settled the whole country. The Nok culture archeological sites have played such a role in Nigeria. By the same token, in Myanmar Naypyidaw was sited in the Dry Zone, in the cradle of Burmese civilization.

It must be noted that the principle of moving the capital city to the old historical capitals was by no means trivial or self-evident. In Africa the seats of traditional kings and hereditary rulers like Nyanza in Rwanda or Lobamba in Swaziland or Abomey (capital of legendary kingdom of Dagomey) in Benin have not been chosen to become new capital cities.[10] After independence Bulgaria and Senegal have chosen to site their capitals in the former administrative centers of the larger colonial regions that have never been the historical capitals of these nations in pre-colonial times. For four hundred years Sofia was the residence of the beylerbey (governor) of Rumelia, the European part of the Ottoman Empire. It was chosen in spite of the fact that prior to subjugation by the Ottoman Empire, Bulgaria had many historically important and revered capitals like Veliko Tarnovo, Pliska, and Ohrid. Similarly, Dakar served in the colonial times as an administrative capital of the French Western Africa. The choice of these capital cities have aided these countries to establish themselves as leaders in the larger mega-regions and to project their power beyond their own borders, but it did not help them to restore and reinforce their old identities.

The tendency of the newly-formed nations to create linear histories is often supplemented by the tendency to create singular geographies centered on their old capitals and historical cores. These singular geographies aid in establishing a sense of continuity and permanence against the backdrop of the torn histories, exile and dispersal. Through its capital the nation is seeking to reestablish the torn connection of times and to reconnect its present with its past. Such capitals merge together the sentimental and political reasons, and symbolisms that result from such projects facilitate the consolidation of national memory.

3 Geopolitical repositioning strategy

While the strategies of historical integration are intended to reactivate the role of the capital of the days of yore and to reestablish the connection of the people with its past, the geopolitical repositioning strategy aims to reposition the country on the global arena relative to its neighbors and macro-regions. So if the previous strategy was focused on the past, geopolitical strategy is more focused on the future. Geopolitical strategy highlights the importance of a specific group of countries belonging to the same macro-region or civilization for the development of the nation. Moving the capital closer to this group of countries helps to insert the country into these mega-regions and to receive some momentous development impulses from them. It also helps to forge a new identity for the nation. The membership in international organizations in these mega-regions and development of transnational communication infrastructure are important strategic steps in the pursuit of such strategic goals. Understood in such a way, the new capital cities are strategic places for the insertion of the state to the mega-region. In the framework of such a strategy the capital city of a country is, figuratively speaking, like a head of the sunflower attracted to a strategic place where the sun of the most dynamic political and economic development is rising. The British geographer Oskar Spate has coined the term "head-link capital" to describe the seats of government that play such a role.[11] In contrast to strategies described above, the capital cities in geopolitical strategy are outward-oriented.

Saint-Petersburg and Tokyo are prime examples of these capitals. The transfer of the seat of government from Moscow to Saint-Petersburg has underscored the new orientation of the Russian politics, economics, and culture to the European countries. "The window to Europe" to use the famous expression of Count Francesco Algarotti positioned Russia more forcefully as a European power. The sea entry also facilitated the intensification of the communications between the Russian Empire and Europe. Although the Japanese Shogunate moved its center of gravity to Edo already in 1603, only the Meiji reforms permitted Japan to overcome its centuries-old isolation. Capital city relocation to Tokyo from inland Kyoto facilitated the more effective modernization of the country and opened Japan up to the European influences.

The project to move the seat of government of Lithuania to Memel (Klaipeda) that we have discussed earlier also aimed to integrate the country with the other states of Baltoscandia. It was intended to make the capital city of Lithuania more congruent and congenial to the pattern of port capital cities that was common for the Baltic-Scandinavian mega-region in which the country aspired for a membership.

It might be noted that inserting the country to the region might be as important as distancing it from those regions that are perceived as backward. These motivations are found in the concept of a new Kazakh capital and in some proposals to move the capital city of Romania. The movement of the seat of government to Astana underscored the European orientation of Kazakhstan and its interest in distancing itself in a social-economic sense from the other states that emerged from the former Central Asian republics of the USSR. By the same token, the new capital in Transylvania should bring Romania closer to the more developed countries of Central Europe and distance it from the Balkan countries and their political climate characterized by the vicious cycle of political fragmentation. Of course, these reasons are not necessarily explicitly stated in the plans.

Some proposals to move the capital city of Russia to the Far East found their justification in the fact that the world economic development centers have shifted from the Atlantic to the Pacific, and the new capital should track and reflect such a power shift. They imply that relocation of the center of gravity of Russian economic and political activity to the Far East will facilitate the more dynamic development of the country. By the same token, the defenders of the movement of Australian capital from Canberra to Perth have argued that the center of global economic development has shifted from the Pacific to the Indian Ocean, and with a new capital in Perth the country will be better positioned to participate in the economic cycle of the new millennium.[12]

Geopolitically motivated capital transfers view new capitals as places that will receive impulses for national development from abroad or as channels of influence of the country in the mega-region or both. There is a considerable variation between nations in the emphasis they place on these two aspects. The head-link capitals mentioned above have been presented as only or mostly the receptors of cultural influences. Another type of head-link capitals aspires to establish geopolitical dominance for a country or some sort of leadership in the mega-region. The goals of these new capital cities go beyond nation-building. They not only boost the global standing of the nation and make a statement about their leading role in the mega-region but also provide advanced linkages between the key cities and countries of particular mega-region. Pursuing this goal, they become instruments of nation-building and tools for broader region-building.[13] The new capital cities or their plans in Southeast Asia and in Latin America are often focused on the development of such new linkages and transportation networks, and they underscore the aspirations of these countries to become transnational centers in their respective mega-regions, amplifying their global visibility and exposure.

The geostrategic calculus probably determined the choice of Belgrade as the capital of Serbia and later Yugoslavia. Belgrade yielded in its geographic centrality, economic significance, and demographic size to several other cities in Serbia. Kragujevac, the first capital of independent Serbia, was more centrally located. However, Belgrade was sitting on the Danube in closer proximity to Central Europe, and its position in between Vienna and Istanbul gave it additional advantages for region-building.[14]

186 *Strategies of relocations*

The choice of Berlin as a capital city of Germany after unification also betrays some elements of region-building agenda. Berlin is sited much closer to the countries of Central and Eastern Europe compared to Bonn, and this proximity and position fosters the leadership and influence of Germany in this mega-region. The proximity of the German capital to Central-Eastern European countries was more important because arguably Germany can play a more important role in their integration into the EU with a capital in the east.

The geopolitical motivations of capital city transfers also played a role in several Latin American countries. In Argentina the capital in the south was intended to project power and control in the southern edge of the continent (e.g., South Pole project) and to provide better integrative potential to a country in the economies of the Pacific. The proponents of a capital city shift in Peru also referenced the consideration of better integration of the country with the economies and cultures of the neighboring Latin American countries, describing the siting of the capital city in Lima as a "geopolitical blunder of Francisco Pizarro and conquistadors."[15] Some Brazilian politicians have stressed geopolitical advantages in the centrality of Brasília on the Latin American continent.[16] Geostrategic calculus that emphasized the importance of the Indo-Pacific region motivated the proposal to move the capital of Australia.

4 *Strategy of economic integration and rebalancing*

The choice of the strategy of economic integration is most typical for the countries trying to overcome the problem of the socio-economic divide. The divergence in economic development and in the pace of economic growth often produces inefficiencies in the use of resources. It is also giving rise to problems of national unity, sometimes threatening the very existence of a country as a unified state. Not infrequently, the unequal distribution of wealth and opportunities on the territory of the country induce political polarization and secessionist sentiments. To reintegrate the country some politicians have proposed to move the seat of government to the desolated and underdeveloped parts of the country.

The elements of such a strategy are found in Kazakhstan and Brazil, where the capital cities were moved to the hinterlands hundreds of kilometers away from the economic and demographic cores of these nations. The new capitals were tasked to develop the hinterlands also in many African countries such as Tanzania, Malawi, and Côte d'Ivoire. The same framework of analysis in the debates is present also in such dissimilar countries as China, Taiwan, Russia, and the UK. The divide between the wealthy south and desolated and economically declining north has stimulated the debate in the UK. The contrast between the prosperous coastal line and the underdeveloped interiors of the country in the west has fuelled the debate about a new capital city of China. The gap between the developed north and underdeveloped south animate the capital city transfer debate in Taiwan. The resentment of wealthy Moscow by the residents of the abandoned and poorly developed territories in the rest of the country, especially to the east of the Ural mountains, have played a prominent role in the debates on this topic in Russia. In all of these countries, proposals have been made to transfer the seats of government to the lagging regions to bridge the gap between the core and peripheral regions and to accelerate the growth of the latter.

The capitals tasked to provide the stimulus to the far-flung regions of the country remote from the historical cores of the nations have been dubbed *forward-thrust capitals*. They were often understood as new growth poles intended to integrate the lagging regions and to make them economically efficient territories of these countries. The new capitals were to become cornerstones in the development plans for neglected territories. In some countries, notably in Brazil, the governments have targeted specific regions that were considered strategically important for the economic development of the country as a whole. Géraldine Djament has labeled such capitals, *mission capitals*.[17] The development purposes have also animated the proposals of capital city shifts in Argentina, Venezuela, and Peru.

In other cases these proposals have been prompted by the need to provide stimulus and to attract investments for the economic development of those regions that lacked natural resources and other means for normal economic development. In all these cases provisions have been made in the plans for the development of both the territories and the people living there. In the UK some proposals to move the capital are inspired by the development agenda.

In some cases conquest over nature becomes an essential part of nation-building plans, and the site of the new capital city located in the interior is turning into a "frontier of conquest," critical for the national identity formation of the nation. The construction of a new capital in the unfavorable natural conditions, the backers of these plans argue, will infuse and enrich the sense of national identity. In these countries capital-building is envisaged as a fundamental part of nation-building.

5 De-centralization strategy

The term "de-centralization" connotes mostly negative reasons for capital city transfers. However, the agenda of de-centralization often goes beyond measures against overconcentration of resources in the preeminent city of the country and its dominance in the life of the nation. It is aiming to remove the undue influence of the primary city. But in most cases, the policies of de-centralization also promote or at least imply the comprehensive positive program and institutional reforms that might involve devolution, separation of the economic and political centers of the country, and possibly federalization. De-centralization can complement or be a part of the strategy of economic integration. However, in contrast to the strategies of economic integration, it is most often invoked in the situations when there is no clear and pronounced polarization between the two parts of the country. Typically, de-centralization does not promote the development of a specific region of the country and its scope is not defined only by the economic policy objectives.

The application of this strategy is often justified by reference to the overpopulation, congestion, or inadequate infrastructure of the existing capital city under the conditions of a high pace of demographic growth. The need to move the capital stems mainly from the conditions of monocephality and the hypertrophied role of the capital city in the life of the nation. The concentration of most functions in one place makes the system vulnerable and unstable and dramatically heightens the risks for the whole country in case of turmoil or natural disasters. This strategy is applied when the problem of development of the hinterland is not recognized as a fundamental national priority and the countries are not split along regional lines, notably the north-south or west-east axis. Accordingly, this strategy does not require the transfer of the capital city over a long distance. Hence, the construction of the administrative capital in close proximity to the existing capital city is often considered sufficient to solve the problem of excessive concentration of resources in the primary city.

The proposal to move the capital city of France to La Roche-Guyon, "the French Brasília," debated in the 1960s in France is one example of this de-centralization strategy. Pinochet was guided by the de-centralization strategy when he moved the capital to Valparaiso. In Egypt, Japan, Afghanistan, Georgia, and the countries of Southeast Asia, notably in Indonesia, Thailand, and the Philippines the question is coached in such terms. With some reservations the South Korean case will also qualify as an example. Not surprisingly, in all these countries the debates centered on the concept of an administrative capital city located in close proximity to the existing capital. The supporters of capital city change often use Putrajaya in Malaysia as their model.

Similar to the strategy of compromise, the de-centralization strategy aims to resolve conflicts between the two parts of the country. However, while in the case of compromise strategies the parties are typically represented by two sides having different political, religious, or ethnic identities, in the case of the de-centralization strategy the parties involved are the dominating center and the rest of the country. Whereas compromise capitals offer a neutral geographical point between the two geographically distinct regions, administrative capitals are chosen to reconcile tensions between the generic periphery and the center – the large metropolitan area where the former capital was sited. The administrative capital is the only tenable solution to the predicament as there is no clear point where the generic periphery can meet the center. There could be some other reasons for administrative capital arrangements as capitals often are sited in the historic core of the nation. Thus, the administrative capitals imply a special type of spatial compromise between the country as a whole and its old capital. The establishment of such capitals can help to de-centralize the country, although such de-centralization will be very limited if it is not augmented by other important institutional changes.

6   Strategy of territorial integration

This strategy is geared to integrate the territories of the country, especially in those cases when these territories are contested or were recently absorbed and when the population of these territories exhibits separatist tendencies. The irredentist sentiments in the neighboring countries and the strong secessionist trends among the ethnic minorities living in these territories provide additional incentives to governments to apply such strategies. The transfer of the capital to the contested or contestable territory highlights its attachment to the country and reinforces the identity of these countries in *terra irredenta*. Such transfers aim to "nationalize" this territory and are often accompanied by demographic policies and encouraged migrations that are intended to establish numeric superiority of the titular nation or its more conspicuous presence on this territory. The capital cities formed as a result of this strategy can be labeled *incorporated capital cities*.

Kazakhstan can serve as a good example of this strategy. As we have seen earlier, Nazarbayev launched his project at least in part to increase the ethnic Kazakh population in the north of the country to prevent and discourage the escalation of Russian separatist tendencies there. The same rationale is found in the proposals to change the capital cities in some post-Soviet countries (Kyrgyzstan, Armenia, and Moldova). The same motive is found in the initiatives in Romania to establish a stronger presence of the ethnic Romanians in Transylvania through the movement of the capital to prevent separatist tendencies there. In Lithuania the proposals to move the capital to Memel (Klaipeda) between the world wars were also geared to change the demographic balance in this region. In some African countries, notably in Botswana, the same strategy was used.

In Iran the proposals to move the capital to Tabriz were also justified by the growth of separatist sentiments among the local Azeri population. In the wake of the Scotland independence referendum, the candidacies of such cities as Scottish Glasgow and "Anglo-Celtic" Liverpool for the role of a new capital of the UK were motivated by the consideration of better integration of Scotland and Wales within the United Kingdom.[18] The choice of these candidates, the proposers believe, would stimulate federalist development and will weaken secessionist sentiments.

In some cases the transfer of the capital to the territory of a weaker partner can also be construed as a type of compensation for its lack or loss of independent statehood. The status of a capital and the signs of prestige that it endows can help to integrate a new region. We have witnessed the elements of such strategy in the capital city transfer in Germany. The assignment of capital city status to Berlin in the territory of East Germany was welcomed by 90 percent of Eastern Germans, and this gesture facilitated the faster and smoother integration of Eastern Germans into a unified country.

Competition of strategies

It must be noted that the analyzed integrative strategies in different ways and measures accentuate the normative criteria of security, efficiency, identity, and fairness that we have distinguished earlier in our book. Accordingly, all six strategies have their unique focus. The compromise strategies accentuate the importance of fairness. The strategies of historical integration highlight the importance of identity. The strategies of territorial integration have their focus in security; the strategies of economic integration emphasize the economic and administrative effectiveness. The strategy of geopolitical repositioning focuses simultaneously on security and identity. In contrast to the historical integration strategy, it emphasizes the importance of fundamental reconstruction of the old identity and in some cases enables the country to project its power and control beyond the borders of the state. The de-centralization strategy in turn is guided by both the principle of fairness and economic efficiency. Under this strategy the new seat of government – typically an administrative city – serves as a compromise between the old dominant capital located in the primary city and the rest of the country. Additionally, the separation of the political capital and the main economic hub represents a more economically and politically efficient model of distribution of resources of the country. Table 5 visually represents the relationship between the six strategies and the normative criteria.

It is not always easy to separate the economic and political considerations within the framework of such analysis. As noted earlier, in the case of de-centralization the economic inequity that is caused by the misbalanced distribution of resources throughout the country tends to create political problems that can potentially lead to disintegration. The economic efficiency parameters also can be important for the strategy of geopolitical repositioning as such a repositioning can be associated with additional economic advantages that are accrued to the country that enters a more dynamic transnational economic zone. The considerations of fairness are not always central to compromise strategies as they aim to achieve balance not only for the sake of fairness but also to secure a more politically stable and expedient system. So the difference here is of a degree, accents, and priorities, not necessarily of a kind.

Many of the strategies expounded above are very much compatible with other strategies. Accordingly, most relocation projects involve the amalgamation of different strategies. In their official declarations, the governments of many countries simultaneously alluded to several reasons and motives. Kazakhstan engages at once five strategies that we have described: the territorial integration, economic integration, de-centralization, geopolitical repositioning, along with the strategy of spatial compromise that establishes a new domestic balance of power between the three sub-ethnic groups of the country. Germany has relied in its decision upon the strategies of historical integration, territorial integration, economic integration and, ostensibly, geopolitical repositioning. The Brazilian authorities appealed to the strategy of economic integration of the territories, de-centralization, and the compromise strategy (the rivalry between the cities Rio and São Paulo and between the states of Minas Gerais and São Paulo have defined the political life of the country). In Pakistan the goal of economic integration was complemented by the strategy of territorial integration. In the case of Italy we have seen the combination of the compromise strategy (between the north and south of the country) and the strategy of historical integration connecting the ancient Roman history and modern Italy.[19]

This compatibility of motivations does not contradict the fact that in most cases one can identify the main reasons that prompted the decision about capital city change. However, it does not mean that other strategies are used only as an excuse, pretext, or a rhetorical instrument to justify the decision. They often complement or serve as significant aspects of the main strategy that has been used.

However, it would be a mistake to overlook the antagonistic elements in the described strategies. Some of these strategies clearly are aiming to obliterate, weaken, or downplay elements that other strategies are aiming to emphasize. The compromise strategy is seeking to weaken and find a replacement to the ancient sacred and particularistic identities that are deeply ingrained in national histories, the same identities that the strategies of historical integration bring in a sharper focus. The strategies of geopolitical repositioning are also often adversarial to strategies designed to revive and perpetuate the old identities. While the first ones bring the capital city to the crossroads of intensive contacts with the outside world, the second ones move them to the interior to emphasize its ties to the past. The underdeveloped or desolated territories in the interior where the proponents of historical integration are seeking to place the seats of government typically are located far away from the areas of favorable international contacts where the proponents of new geopolitical positioning propose to site them. Table 6 schematically represents the pairs of the opposing types of capital cities.

The choice of the capital city tends to be less controversial in those cases when there is a consensus on the strategy of national development and a country is facing particular challenges. In the context of post-colonial development, the movement of the capital into the interior reflects the needs for a new identity formation. It also promises a fair resolution of ethnic rivalries, the development of the territories, and better economic and administrative efficiency. These goals do not contradict each other. However, the lack of consensus stirs heated debates about both the national priorities and the site of the national capital. The situations when the strategies of national development compete with each other are much more common.

Different candidates typically epitomize different national priorities and are associated with different policies and programs of state- and nation-building. Some contenders can be more or less suitable for different strategies and in various degrees can promote specific public policy objectives. The debates on this topic reflect not only different interpretations of the most pressing and urgent tasks of nation- and state-building but also articulate different visions of development and different futures of the nation in a long-term perspective. Not infrequently, the chosen strategies can favor particular geographies for the role of a capital but they do not necessarily promote a particular candidate for this role.

The strategies of geopolitical repositioning, economic integration, and territorial integration often imply the peripheral location of the capital city on the edge of the country that is deemed to be strategically critical. The compromise capitals are often founded in the middle of the country in a neutral place on the border between two most powerful communities. The strategies of de-centralization most often prompt countries to choose administrative capitals in close proximity to existing capitals. The capitals within the strategy of historic integration can be located anywhere but they tend to be sited in more central geographic regions. In short, the principle of betweenness is favored by the compromise strategies, the principle of proximity to the old capital is favored by de-centralization strategy, the proximity to the external border with the most influential mega-region by geopolitical repositioning strategies, the proximity to the historical core or heartland of the nation by the strategies of historical integration. The economic integration strategies favor the underdeveloped regions wherever they are located.

Remarkably, all strategies are sensitive to considerations of centrality. But their centralities are not uniform. Most often centrality is defined relative to the border of the state. However, it also might be a centrality relative to the historical centers of the two most powerful constituent entities of the state. In some cases it is a centrality relative to the *oecumene* of the country located in the demographic centroid in the most densely populated part of the state. In spite of the fact that geopolitical repositioning strategies typically favor very peripheral locations for this role, they also can be concerned about the centrality of capital cities within a mega-region or relative to other capital cities of the continent/mega-region.

The cross-region comparison is also showing considerable variation in the motives and prevailing strategies between world regions. Particular motives prevail in some world regions, mega-regions, and continents and find very little appeal in others. Our analysis has shown that in African countries, identity politics played a larger role, and capital city transfers were more often motivated by new identity establishment considerations. The clan politics and the reasons of territorial integration play a more prominent role in the debates in several post-Soviet countries. The countries of the Far East are more concerned about balanced economic development and their proposals are geared to rectify the economic misbalances. The countries in Southeast

Asia laid considerable emphasis on the place and role of their capital cities in the mega-regions, the roles that influence the international standing of these countries. The region-building considerations also play a larger role in their debates. Likewise, in Latin America we have also seen stronger emphasis on the creation of intra-continent linkages as well as on the hinterland development. The capital city transfers plans aim to promote a country as continental/mega-regional economic hubs and establish them as more important players in the international and intra-continent affairs. Needless to say that these variations highlight only the tendencies of development in the world regions as the same motives can be found in varying degrees in other mega-regions and continents.

Three strategies of an exclusive capital city

The capital city relocation projects can also emerge for the purposes that are the exact opposite of integration. We have already briefly mentioned some of these reasons in our analysis of the hidden agendas of capital city shifts. These projects are intended to maintain regime stability and to reinforce the political power that they hold.

The initiators of such projects focus on the tactical tasks seeking to maintain political power and to isolate the political leadership of the country from the real or putative centers of protest. They often tend to have a narrow concept of a nation, its tasks and available integration options. While most of the integrative strategies are aiming to foster the inclusive capital cities, the three strategies that we will describe below are aiming to exclude or limit the participation of certain groups in political power – the ethnic minorities, the members of alien social classes or even the majority population of the larger cities – and deny them adequate representation in the political center.

The strategies of exclusive capital include (1) strategy of marginalization of the protest movements, (2) strategy of ethnic homogenization of the capital city population, creating special privileges for the titular nation, and (3) strategy of particularistic capitals that sometimes implies the reliance on the subnational forms of solidarity and moving the capital to the native territory of the ruler.

1   Strategies of marginalization of the protest movements

The British historian Arnold Toynbee aptly labeled the capital cities "the powder kegs of protest," alluding to the fact that capital cities and primary cities oftentimes become the breeding soil for turmoil and protest movements.[20] The level of social inequality is typically dramatically higher in these cities compared to the country average. The larger cities also tend to absorb more people from the rural areas and provinces who are employed in lower income occupations and experience difficulties adapting to new conditions. Students and intellectuals also tend to concentrate in capital cities and, merged with the crowds, can become the detonators of formidable social protests transforming private dissatisfactions into political causes. The string of color revolutions in different parts of the globe and the recent events of the Arab Spring reconfirmed the rebellious and inflammable nature of the capital.[21]

The concentration of protest in the capital cities also maximizes the impact of these movements on the political climate of a country and can lead to regime changes. The larger capital cities are especially vulnerable. According to recent analysis by Jeremy Wallace, a political scientist, urban concentration increases the risk of regime-threatening unrest. He argues that the larger capital cities increase the vulnerability of the states and political regimes by amplifying the risks of turmoil. Based on his analysis, for the 237 regimes with urban concentration levels above the mean level in the data, the mean duration is 8.6 years and the annual regime death rate is 9.2 percent. Regimes with capital cities that dominate the urban landscape fail nearly four years sooner and face 60 percent greater death rates.[22] Many governments have taken steps to prevent such developments.

In some cases the autocratic regimes have resorted to the tactics of segregation and localization of the protest movements in certain parts of the city. The convergence between capital cities and revolutions became most apparent in Paris where the revolutions on several occasions resulted in regime changes.[23] It was argued that the morphology of Paris and its crooked streets were to blame for these intense revolutionary activities. To address this problem Baron Haussman flattened much of the medieval and revolutionary Paris, annihilated the crooked streets and built noble boulevards that, to use the words of Mark Twain, "a cannon ball could traverse from end to end without meeting an obstruction" and that "will never afford refuges and plotting places for starving, discontented revolution breeders."[24] Thus, apart from better sanitation and beautification, the reconstruction of Paris was politically motivated and was aiming to achieve better control over the social space of the capital and to weaken the revolutionary activity entrenched in the city. As a consequence, the revolutionary masses and the protests were segregated in the working class areas of the city.

More radical strategy was pursued by some other governments that have decided or mulled the idea of a capital city change to prevent the development of protest movements close to the seat of government. They sought to isolate themselves in smaller and more distant cities from the larger metropolises with their high social temperature.

Examples of the importance of these motives abound in history.

During the insurrection of the Paris Commune in France in 1871 which Haussmann's urban planning did not stop, there were calls to transfer the capital from Paris to Bordeaux. Galembert, a prominent conservative member of the National Assembly based in Bordeaux, penned a pamphlet, arguing that the distance between Paris and Versailles, where the temporary capital was placed, was not sufficient to secure the new capital from the Paris revolutionary crowds.[25]

Some military and dictatorial regimes were more successful in isolating their seats of government from the protest movements and revolutionary masses. As we have seen, this motivation has played an important role in capital city transfers in Myanmar, Nigeria, and Pakistan. In the course of Burmese political history, Rangoon, the previous capital of Burma, was often the focal point of protests with wide participation of Buddhist monks. Reportedly, the transfer of the capital helped to minimize the impact of the "Saffron Revolution" in Burma in 2007. The Nigerian historian Toyin Falola also attributes a significant role to the transfer of the capital city to Abuja in the prevention of the "color revolution" in Nigeria.[26] Prior to the transfer of the capital city to Islamabad, Karachi was also the driving force and the main springboard of the wide protest movements in Pakistan. In many ways this tactic was much more efficient compared to the reconstruction of Paris undertaken by Haussmann. The rulers of these countries managed to establish the seats of government where the ruling bureaucracy composed practically the whole population of the city creating the buffer and protective shield for the government.

The abortive plans of Suharto to move the capital city of Indonesia, the proposals in Iran to move the capital city functions to Qom against the backdrop of the protests in Tehran, and the concept of the new capital city advanced by Robert Mugabe in Zimbabwe also probably have followed the same logic of separation of the seat of government from the actual and potential centers of protest. They were aiming to establish docile capitals isolated from the main demographic centers of the country. Certainly, it would be short-sighted to ignore the other rationales that these government had and that we had discussed earlier. But the fear of disloyalty often tipped the balance in favor of the decision to relocate capitals.

The same held true even more for the colonial rulers. The British and French colonial administrations were keen to consider loyalty as an important consideration in their choice of a capital for their colonial domains in India and Morocco. The old colonial capitals in Calcutta and Fez became focal points of protest in these two countries. They were particularly prone to uprisings not only by virtue of their metropolitan status but also because of their role of regional centers of the Bengalis and Berbers. In the eyes of colonial administration, the concentration of anti-colonial protest activities in Calcutta and Fez made both of these cities unsuitable for execution of their administrative functions. The disloyalty of these cities served as a reason for British and French administrations to move the capitals of India and Morocco to less rebellious cities. Thus Calcutta and Fez yielded their place to Delhi (1911) and Rabat (1925) as more convenient and docile places for colonial management and administration.

In the wake of revolutions and regime changes, the capital cities also often become the sites of potential resistance and protest. Fearing disloyalty, the new political regimes seek to move the seats of government to potentially more loyal places. This pattern repeats itself throughout history.

The transfer of the capital city from Saint-Petersburg to Moscow in 1918 was originally triggered by the proximity to the battlefront, and this decision was considered a provisional solution at the time. However, the government never moved back to Saint-Petersburg. The old imperial capital was considered a stronghold of the social classes hostile to the Bolshevik regime and a potential breeding ground for the counter-revolutionary protest activities. The Bolsheviks felt that the impoverished peasants in the central Non-Black Earth region of Russia centered around Moscow would be more loyal to Bolshevism. Even the working class in Saint-Petersburg employed mostly in heavy industry enjoyed higher standards of living under the old regime compared to the majority of workers in the Moscow region employed mostly in the light industry that did not require such skills. So the Bolshevik regime would be more stable with a capital in Moscow.

Similarly, Polish communists suggesting the movement of the seat of government to Lodz in the aftermath of the Second World War felt that the proletariat of Lodz would be more pliable and receptive to the communist cause compared to the residents of Kraków.

In earlier periods the fear of disloyalty also prompted many rulers acquiring the new kingdoms to move their seats of power from the old capitals. Predictably, the capitals inherited from the prior dynasties were often rife with opposition and dissent. In the thirteenth century after the conquest of the Sicilian Kingdom, Charles of Anjou relocated his capital from Palermo in Sicily to Naples. He perceptively understood that Palermo would not be a loyal place for him to recruit new power elite because many of the members of local aristocracy remained faithful to the Hohenstaufen dynasty. Through the capital city shift, he also sought to bring the center of gravity of his domains closer to the sphere of influence of Guelfs and to Northern Italy, where he felt more solid political support. His misgivings about Palermo were later confirmed when the rebellion in 1282 known as Sicilian Vespers transferred the power over Sicily to the Aragon dynasty.

2 *The strategy of ethnic homogenization of the ruling elite*

The attempt to displace or marginalize specific ethnic minorities and to tilt the balance of ethnic power in favor of the titular nation is another example of the strategy to develop exclusive capital city.

The construction of the purpose-built capital where the demographic balance is tipped in favor of the titular nation is one of such options. The recruitment of the civil servants for such capital cities is often based on their ethnic origins. The fundamental element of such a strategy is the isolation of the ethnic majorities of the capital cities or minorities that are different from the titular nation. These political regimes aim to create and nurture the new political elite in a purpose-built capital city that it would be able to control more fully and will replace the ethnic minorities in the managing and executive roles. The elements of such motivations are found in the concept of the new capital of Malaysia.

Another manifestation of exclusivity of the capital is its symbolic exclusivity manifested in the iconography. To exemplify, the boundaries of the Outer City of Kotte in Sri Lanka are marked by Buddhist stupas and the capitol environment of Kotte is clearly and inexorably Buddhist. Hence it excludes Hindus and other religious minorities, Muslims and Christians, from the system of symbolic representation.[27] We have seen a similar type of symbolic exclusivity in Abuja, where the capital is dominated by Muslim symbols.

Within the framework of this strategy the national identities are often defined in ethnic or religious terms, favoring the titular nation. Unsurprisingly, the capital city of such states reflects such priorities and identities couched in exclusivist terms.

3 Strategy of particularistic capitals

The political weakness of some political regimes often makes them seek the sources of their stability in the reliance upon the principles of tribal solidarity and ethnic favoritism. The ruling elites of such countries transferred their seats of governments to the territory of their own tribes or clans to recruit the loyal elites. This strategy was prevalent mostly in the countries of Africa, where the national forms of solidarity never took root and where the premodern forms of solidarity based on family and clan networks prevailed. Instead of promoting nation-building goals, the rulers of these newly independent countries have attempted to rely on their native towns or ancestral homes. We have seen that this strategy was deployed in a host of African countries, including Côte d'Ivoire, Malawi and, Libya, where Muammar Gaddafi established an informal capital in his native Sirte. The plans of Robert Mugabe, the president of Zimbabwe, to transform his native town into a political capital of the country also well illustrate this strategy. The plans of Ayub Khan in Pakistan to place the capital in his native Abbotabad and the plans of the president of Tajikistan to place it in Danghara also show that such strategies are not unique for the African continent and were tempting for rulers beyond Africa.

Central to the idea of a capital city in all three cases described above is the concept of loyalty that was already discussed in chapter 2 of this book. The new capital city creates this loyalty in a new place that is separate from the existing centers of power. In all three cases the capital is isolated from the alien ethnic groups, dominant in primary cities, the sub-ethnic groups that do not belong to the ruling clan, and from disloyal social classes. The establishment of the new capital is taking place not through the embracement and integration of the representatives of all communities that compose the state. In this sense the strategies of loyalty-building are radically opposite to the compromise strategies that we have described earlier. While the first group of strategies aims to reach a consensus and provide at least some form of inclusivity, the second group of strategies aims to consolidate political power through the exclusion of certain ethnic and social groups. Hence, the described loyalties are fostered at the expense of other groups as the access of the latter to the public goods concentrated in capital city becomes limited or constrained.

The strategies of exclusive capitals tend to substitute legitimate security and identity concerns that define integrative strategies with the regime survival/security and the identity of the group in power. However, this preoccupation with loyalty and stability often inadvertently weakens the stability of these political regimes. Remarkably, the described three strategies represent consecutively shrinking powerbases that they offer to the ruler. In the case of tribal loyalties, this power-base is the narrowest as it includes only the representatives of one tribe. The state built on such a foundation is the most fragile. The titular nation is a broader power base, although it limits the ethnic minorities in government. Finally the strategy that removes the capital from the center of protest movement is less restrictive, as it is willing to consider the participation in the government of any groups loyal to the ruling class. However, the power elite in such countries aim to distance itself from the alien and potentially hostile social classes, the students, the intellectuals, and the members of the opposition parties entrenched in the large metropolises. Not infrequently, these elites also tend to provide better conditions for capital city residents to prevent the development of protest movements and to ensure their loyalty.

The exclusive capital city in all its versions has much in common with the "disembedded capitals" of the despotic states that we have described earlier. The political leaders building such capitals miss the opportunity to establish more durable capital cities on a firmer foundation of a more inclusive type of identity. By doing this they neglect the strategic goals of building lasting national identities in favor of tactical power- and hegemony-maintenance considerations.

The fact that the seat of government is moved away from the former capital because of the opposition to the reforms there does not necessarily mean that it was done specifically for the exclusion. Many political regimes pursue their own goals, and they need to marginalize the resistance. The goals of such projects can still be predominantly integrative. So the critical factor is the balance between disintegrative and integrative elements of the project.

Capital cities in the dominant regions

The exclusive capitals have much in common with the capital cities sited in the dominant regions. They do not formally limit the participation of specific groups in the government, but practically they constrain the access to power of other regions. Typically these cities are chosen to be capitals because of their decisive role in the national independence movement and national unification. Not infrequently, these capitals are located in the periphery of the unified country and have a distinct regional particularity. Berlin in Germany and Turin in Italy can serve as the examples of such cities. Their choice as capitals of the newly unified states has often led to unfavorable consequences for the political stability of the new nation.

The choice of Turin as the first capital of independent Italy was determined by the decisive role that the Kingdom of Piedmont-Sardinia played in the unification of the country. The selection of Rome as the capital of Italy in the 1860s was by no means a foregone conclusion. The Italian politicians quickly realized the merits of a more neutral place for siting the country's capital. Hence the capital city was first moved to Florence, probably due to its special role in the integration of Italy. Notably, the Florentine dialect was later recognized as the official language of all the Italian states. However, both Piedmont and Toscana had stronger regional identities than it was considered desirable to house the capital city of the country. Rome, located almost in the middle of Italy and historically much more cosmopolitan due to its role as pan-European religious center, was perceived as a better place to house the government having the advantages of neutrality.[28]

Unlike Italy, Germany did not change its capital city location in the aftermath of unification. Being a city that represented the Prussian monarchy, Berlin never had the advantages of neutrality, and its candidacy was challenged and contested by other German principalities. These states and statelets have proposed the candidacies of such German cities as Frankfurt am Mein, Leipzig, and Erfurt for this role.[29] Arguably, the choice of Berlin has played a negative role in the consequent German history. The centralistic paradigm in German internal affairs, pervasive conservatism, and the "Prussianization" of Germany were the consequences of political domination of Prussia and siting of the political capital in Berlin. Berlin did not promote unity in the same way as Rome did in Italy.

There is a stark difference between the political implications of Bismarck's choice of Berlin in 1871 and the choice of Berlin after the fall of the Berlin Wall. Whereas in 1871 Berlin was chosen because of its dominant position, in 1989 Berlin became a capital of compromise between Eastern and Western Germany. It was chosen to ensure the national unity and to integrate the two German states.

In many other countries the excessively strong cultural identity of the region where the capital city was sited was also regarded as a drawback. In the colonized countries, the siting of the capital in one of its regions having strong cultural identity provided special benefits to its residents. These privileges for specific regions and ethno-religious groups, dominant there, caused the resentment of other communities and often provoked ethnic conflicts and strife after independence. The strong regional identity of Bengal was considered a disadvantage even under the colonial administration of India. It was one of the reasons to transfer the capital to Delhi.

200 Strategies of relocations

It is interesting to note that the residents of such culturally distinct regions did not always welcome the opportunity to house the capital city on its territory in spite of the economic advantages that it could bring. They often had legitimate concerns about the possibility that such a capital might have a potential to erode or weaken their unique sub-national cultural identity. These types of sensibilities were not alien even to the Piedmonts' residents and the Prussians. Bismarck himself had serious misgivings about the placement of the capital of the German Empire in Berlin.[30] The prospect of placing the capital of a larger country on their territories is a cause for concern among the Azeri minority in Iran and among the Bari tribe members in South Sudan.

The examples above highlight the advantages of placing national capital cities in more neutral places and the problematic situations arising from siting of national capitals in places with stronger cultural identities.

The budgets and the appraisals of the relocation total costs

The budget for the transfers of the capital cities is one of the most critical issues in capital city relocation debates. The public expenditures necessary to carry out capital relocations are extremely high, and the final decision to transfer the capital is often contingent on the availability of funds for these projects. Considering the specialized nature of this subject, we will be able only to make several observations about this topic and mention some of the financing schemes that have been employed in different countries.

There is a considerable variation in the financing arrangements that have been used or suggested by different governments. In most cases they involved the reliance on both public and private funds with predominant use of public funds dedicated to such projects by the national government. Not infrequently, the regional government and administrations also contributed financial and management resources. Kazakhstan, Malaysia, and Germany have relied mostly on the public funds. In the case of Malaysia and Kazakhstan, the state oil and gas monopolies have also heavily contributed to the development and implementation of these projects.

In a number of cases the countries borrowed funds from foreign governments and investors (e.g., in Tanzania and Malawi). In Afghanistan the project is financed by the state, foreign governments (most of the funds come from Japan), and the Asian Development Bank. The construction of the new capital city of South Sudan relies primarily on the foreign aid: the budget of the country is significantly lower than the estimated cost of the project. Notably, the governments of some African countries (Malawi) have borrowed funds from the apartheid regime in South Africa, compromising its political integrity. The real estate investment funds of UAE and Chinese construction companies have committed significant funds to finance the projects in Egypt and Zimbabwe. German firms have offered financing for the construction of the new capital of Mongolia. The issue of special long-term government bonds, the sale of land to larger developers, and rent of buildings in the former capital cities have been suggested as other opportunities to raise funds for these projects.[31]

The information about the costs of capital city transfers is not always available, and when it is available from the government sources it is rarely reliable. The official amounts spent by the governments are especially hard to verify, and total cost is often a subject to debates. Generally, there is a tendency on the side of the government to significantly understate the total of costs of the project.

The inconsistent and divergent estimates of the costs result not only from purposeful manipulations and misrepresentations. They often stem from the objective difficulties associated with an understanding of the structural components of the budget, their breakdowns and cost allocation to specific components. To make the issue more complicated, there are also some contestable and controversial expense items. For instance, in Tanzania the cost of the construction of the airport and of the transportation infrastructure servicing the capital city was excluded from the calculation of the total costs dedicated to capital city construction.[32] In all such cases it might be perplexing to decide whether or not a certain expense was spent on the tasks related to capital city construction or if it should be treated as a national development expense. It is also hard in most cases to estimate the full and final cost of the project, as buildings and infrastructure were often put into operation before the construction works were completed. It is also difficult to ascertain total costs because many Master Plans are open-ended. Unsurprisingly, many numbers and quantitative data for various expense categories are based on the estimates of the experts and are very imprecise.

Table 7 compares several project budgets by country collected from various sources. The data consolidated in Table 7 also presents the expenditures as percentages of GDP of the respective countries at the time when project was launched. To compare the numbers properly all expenditures are converted into US dollars. According to the cross-country comparison, the project expenditures often represented a large share of GDP of the countries ranging from 3 to 12 percent. The projects in Germany and Kazakhstan seem to be the most cost-efficient partly due to the fact that the seats of governments were moved to already existing cities having prerequisite infrastructure in place.

However, even the most detailed and comprehensive cost calculations probably miss some cost components. It is probably not feasible to quantify such expense categories as the disruptions in the functionality of the system caused by the introduction of a new capital city. However, they also should be taken into consideration. In a way capital city transfers can be compared to the introduction of technological innovations. New capital cities produce some additional costs that are related to the breakdown of the old routines and patterns of communications embedded in the old system. The economists use the term lock in effect to describe the situations involving the implementation of new technological innovations.[33] The lock in effect represents the hidden cost that explains the reluctance of many companies to adopt more effective technologies. The same holds for the new capitals because even when the benefits of the new site are quite obvious, the lock in effect still discourages its adoption. The governments are reluctant to adopt a more rational solution because the old capital city is deeply entrenched in the social fabric of the state and the symbolic capital of the capital city sanctifies its role in the life of the nation. The path of development of a country is often determined by the capital city. Therefore, the decision to move the capital is difficult both financially and psychologically. Obviously, the adaptation of a new capital city is more complex and challenging compared with new technology adaptation.

Administration and timetables of capital city shifts

The comparison of the terms and timetables of capital city shifts in a cross-country perspective can give some cues about the most efficient ways to organize these projects. In many countries this process extended for dozens of years due to adverse political and economic factors: wars, financial problems, the issues of political continuity, and various controversies. In India and Australia the projects were lagging behind the schedules for many years: 12 years in the case of New Delhi and 20 years in the case of Canberra. In the case of Canada even the large-scale reconstruction was going on for 22 years, from 1947 to 1970. On the other hand, in such countries as Brazil, Turkey, and Kazakhstan, the projects have been completed in record short time.[34] The wealth of the respective nation and the availability of funds is not the only relevant factor. The comparison of Malawi and Tanzania comparable in terms of GDP per capita well illustrates this point. While in Malawi the capital city transfer took 10 years to compete (1968–1978), in Tanzania Dar es Salaam remains the *de facto* capital. This stark difference can be explained by the efficacy of the organization and administration of this project.[35]

There was a considerable variation in the administrative arrangements and organization of the transfer of capitals in different countries. Some countries have established special agencies to plan and develop their new capital cities. These agencies and consultative bodies might have had different scopes of authority ranging from some aspects of capital city development to more comprehensive responsibilities. In some cases, notably in Brazil, they were responsible for all problems involved in the development, planning, and marketing of the new capital city.

In Australia, India, and Brazil these agencies were developing the plans of the whole city. In Australia it was a Federal Capital Advisory Committee that was later renamed to a Commission for the National Capital Development that was working under the auspices of the prime-minister and the Cabinet. In India it was the Delhi Development Trust, and in Brazil, the federally owned corporation Urbanization Company of the New Capital.

In Brazil this corporation had special authorities and was accountable only to the president, allowing it to bypass many regulations and red tape and to work extremely fast. In Argentina in 1987 the government established the special state company ENTECAP for the construction of a new capital. In the US and Canada their counterparts were focused only on the urban planning issues.

In those countries that continue to discuss and develop capital city relocation plans, the new consultative and executive authorities to develop the construction plans have been also established. In South Korea the Presidential Committee for the Construction of the New Capital has been formed. After the adoption of the law in Argentina, a special agency to deal with new capital city issues such as financing and design was set up. In Japan the bill to transfer the Diet adopted in 1992 enabled the central government to establish a Special Council (Wise Men Committee) attached to the prime-minister office focusing on new capital city plans and site evaluation studies. The Committee was chaired by the ex-president of the University of Tokyo Wataru Mori. The same type of commission was set up in Iran comprising the Minister of the Internal Affairs and the Minister of Urban Planning, two representatives of *Mejlis*, two representatives of Ali Khamenei, the representatives from the Expediency Discernment Council, the Council of National Security, among others. Similar commissions attached to the office of the president have been set up also in Malaysia and Indonesia. The governments also hired some international agencies, architectural bureaus, and urban planning consultants.

Several countries such as Argentina, South Korea, Kazakhstan, and Japan have held special international conferences on this topic where different aspects and scenarios of capital city transfers have been discussed. These conferences drew not only government representatives but also many internationally renowned specialists in different fields ranging from geography to transportation experts. In 1988 Buenos Aires hosted a conference "Capital City Transfers: World Experience." In 2003 the international symposium was held in South Korea dedicated to the topic of new administrative capitals, organized by the Korean Geographic Society together with different other public organizations. In Kazakhstan two conferences were held at the 10th anniversary of Astana dedicated to the subject of capital city transfers and the outcomes of the capital city relocation in Kazakhstan.

"The brilliant mistakes" at best: the critique of capital city transfers

The capital city relocation projects attracted a lot of criticism both domestically and globally.

Domestically, these projects have been often criticized by the conservatives and by those interest groups that have been deeply entrenched in the capital cities. Some of them have dismissed them on religious or other conservative grounds. There were concerns that the movement of the capital elsewhere will undermine the sanctified symbols of the country and will even disrupt the course of national history. Not surprisingly, the most vocal opponents of these plans were the mayors of the existing capitals. The mayors of Tokyo, Seoul, Moscow, and Tehran have invariably found many faults with these projects. Remarkably, the mayor of Tokyo described the new capital proposal as an attempt "to contaminate Japanese history." The mayor of Seoul raged against the plan, pledging to resist pork-barrel politics epitomized by the proposal to "wastefully split the capital between Seoul and Sejong." The same script has repeated itself in Tehran and Moscow, where the mayors have provided extremely high estimates of the costs of these projects to discourage the debate. These criticisms reflected the deeply ingrained conservative sentiments and a sense of entitlement typical for the attitudes of capital city mayors. It also reflected their structural positions of power and parochial interests as the status quo situation benefits the holders of such views. It must be noted that existing capital city residents also often opposed such proposals.

Much more relevant and intellectually interesting arguments have been advanced by the libertarian critics of capital relocation projects. Unsurprisingly, the sustained critique of these projects can be found in such media as *The Economist* and *Independent*.[36] Overall, most economists and political analysts contributing there have expressed their skepticism concerning the prospects of capital city transfers to resolve any serious economic and urban development problems of different countries or to solve the problems of existing capital cities. Some articles have indiscriminately painted the history of capital city shifts as a grim chain of urban catastrophes, arbitrary decisions, or extremely expensive mistakes.[37] Their authors do not see in the proposals to move capitals any potential to fix the anomalies of the country's urban systems and to rectify the problems of its political development. Rather they tend to stigmatize them as forms of state interventionism into the existing natural logic of urban network development and into historically entrenched political and economic structures, distorting the market economic forces. Some of the libertarian critics have also drawn on the trickle-down arguments, claiming that in spite of the appearance the larger and wealthier cities benefit the population of the far-flung regions and the country as a whole through the trickle-down effects of their wealth.

Quite often the proposals to move the capital have been described by these critics as populist and demagogical slogans appealing to the provincial and regional voters not having sufficient access to capital city goods. The inspiration of these projects, according to these critics, lies in the follies and megalomaniac excesses of the autocratic rulers who use them to maintain their power and to marginalize the disagreeable elites. The support for these mega-projects, they charge, comes from the state bureaucracy that sees them as an opportunity to profit from them through various corruption schemas.

Some libertarian critics also have maintained the idea that the transfers of the seats of power tend to isolate the governments in distant capitals from their constituents, accusing the resultant isolated capitals of inefficiency and lower democratic quality. In a recent article public policy experts Filipe Campante (Colombia University), Quoc-Anh Do (Sciences Po, Paris) and Bernardo Guimaraes (São Paulo School of Economics) have analyzed major capital city shifts in the last 100 years, coming to the conclusion that most of these transfers were overwhelmingly in the direction of greater isolation and that the governments in the isolated capitals were less effective, less accountable, more corrupt, and less able or willing to sustain rule of law. These countries also had less power sharing and more capital city premiums. The isolated capitals typical for autocratic states also contributed to the persistence of inefficient institutions.[38] The researchers have labeled them both the "symptoms and the enablers" of corruption and misgovernment.

Many academic studies also point to the availability of other alternatives that are more likely to bring the socio-economic and political outcomes that are stated as major goals of capital city shifts and can do it at a lesser price. Among the proposed measures are the devolution, de-bureaucratization, delegation of authority to the regions, the creation of counter-magnet towns, the development of regional metropolises, and the large-scale reconstructions of the existing capital cities.[39] The pursuit of such measures complemented by such economic instruments as subsidies and tax breaks provided to the territories targeted for economic development can make the capital city transfers suboptimal or redundant.[40] Some economists also have suggested that liberalization of macro-economic policies, including the removal of the protectionist measures and the monopolies of international trade, can facilitate economic integration of the far-flung regions into the world economy and can help to achieve de-centralization. These measures can help to overcome hypercephalism and to reduce the level of primacy of the capital cities.[41] The removal of the capital city biases in the investment politics and financing business projects in general is suggested as another important measure.[42]

The libertarian critics also stress the high economic costs of these projects. The large public expenditures that they require often burden the budget of the country for many years to come. The funds dedicated to these projects, they argue, could have been used more productively for more urgent needs of these countries. They also point out the tendency for these projects to become a long-term liability and work-in-progress that creates an atmosphere of uncertainty and even chaos.[43] The new capitals also have been excoriated for their grandiose and colossal scales that have alienated the people from the government.

In short, libertarian critics invariably perceived capital city relocations as extremely inefficient projects engendered by the interests and ambitions of the corrupt power elites. Many of them consider even those cases of capital city transfers that have been acknowledged as measured success as nothing more than "spectacular failures" or at best as "brilliant mistakes" to use the expression of the famous Russian historian Nikolai Karamzin that he used to describe the transfer of the capital from Moscow to Saint-Petersburg carried out by Peter the Great.[44]

Another strand of criticism, articulated by the urban scholars, focuses on the deficiencies of the purpose-built capitals. These cities are often being described as sterile and artificial cities produced in the retort by urban alchemists. The relationship between the designed and evolved cities has been compared to the relationship between a human being and a homunculus. Some have even drawn parallels between them and the medical transplants. These critics feel that such "engineered cities" are tainted by the very artificial history of their creation and their estrangement from the evolved urban system of the country. They also believe that the sterile climate of the new administrative capitals often isolates the governments from the atmosphere of regular cities where the spirit of democracy is produced by the very streets where people walk. Whereas democracy naturally emanates from the public spaces of large metropolises with their predicaments and protests, the isolated capitals are alien to democracy and detach the civil servants from the needs of the people.[45] They see the built environment of the purpose-built cities to be only clones of the natural and authentic urban environments that are much more dynamic. They sometimes appeal to the very human anthropology that is alien to these types of cities and denounce them.[46]

Indeed there are some stark gaps between the declared goals and the real outcomes of capital city transfers. Moreover, some of these projects not only failed to deliver the promised outcomes but often compromised at least some of their original goals and intentions. Not infrequently, they also led to the results that were directly opposite of their objectives and expectations.

One of the declared goals of the project in Pakistan was the political stability of the country. However, the construction of Islamabad in the close proximity to the military garrison created the breeding soil for the military coups d'états overthrowing the government. In addition to two successful coups in 1977 and 1999, an abortive coup attempt took place in 1995. Some political analysts also see the relocation of the Brazilian capital as a background and prerequisite for the military coup in Brazil in 1964.[47]

In Nigeria the relocation was supposed to balance the Muslim and Christian populations of the country. However, according to some assessments, the capital city shift has exacerbated the strife, and ethnic fissures tipped the balance in favor of the Muslim part of the country.

De-centralization of political power was declared a prominent part of the political agenda in many countries undertaking this type of projects. However, in reality the new capital cities have often amplified the role of central government and strengthened the level of centralization of these states.

In Brazil the capital city shift was intended as a blueprint of social reforms facilitating social and political equality in human relations. But Brasília, it was argued, has reproduced the worst forms of social segregation and social inequality in the country.

Many capital city transfers promised to deliver tangible economic benefits through the development of hinterlands remote from the demographic cores of the country. However, the projects often failed to expedite the development of these territories and did not create any clusters of economic growth around them. Moreover, the large public expenditures even deprived the struggling regions of the resources vital for their welfare.[48]

In many African countries and elsewhere, capital city shifts were intended to stress their independence and unique cultural traits and identity, while the realization of these projects and the actual cities built only exposed again their dependence on the European countries in terms of expertise, financing, architectural styles, and imagery.

Some counter-arguments in defense of capital city shifts

Most of the arguments against capital city relocations referenced above have been successful in highlighting their failures and negative outcomes and deserve most careful consideration. Indeed, most capital city relocations have failed to deliver the promised results. Many of them went over budget, took longer than planned, and produced fewer positive results, under-delivering on their original scope. The governments often committed enormous funds relative to their GDPs to build flashy and majestic capital cities poorly integrated with the country and dwarfing in their opulent design the impoverished cities in the periphery. Not infrequently, these projects have involved corruption schemes, and many rulers undertaking these projects had in mind motives other than public interest. Nevertheless, the arguments against capital city relocations as a means of resolving social and political problems and the marshaled evidence fall short of being conclusive and convincing. Many criticisms contain overstatements and sweeping generalizations, and their conclusions require serious qualifications.

Many of the mentioned critics appeal to the criteria that were not central to the new capital's original stated purpose. Quite often they have overemphasized the economic criteria or used the standards of the comfortable and livable city in their judgments about the success or failure of the new capital cities. Additionally, many of these critics ignored the development strategies that were central to many capital city relocation plans. Few of them were interested in how these plans fit into the envisioned larger strategies of country development. In some cases the critics also provided simplistic explanations of the rationales for capital city shifts. In our view, such narrow assessments, along with the appeal to external criteria are not able to provide a relevant framework for the analysis of these projects.

Generally there are three components in the capital relocation projects: public policy objectives, the mechanism through which these objectives are satisfied, and the implementation. The critics rarely questioned the merits of public policy objectives that motivated capital city relocation plans. They also have seldom analyzed the specific implementation blunders. The critique was often focused on castigating the very idea that capital city change can serve as a vehicle of social change and as the efficient mechanism that can solve or mitigate the economic, social, and political problems. The most unproductive part of this critique was the indiscriminate treatment of capital city shifts globally as misguided attempts to fulfill the public policy objectives and to solve these problems.[49] There was a clear tendency in many of their arguments to denounce capital city shifts on principle as instruments of social and political reconstruction of the country. Regrettably, many of these critics were not paying enough attention to the overarching national-building needs and the national development agendas that animated these projects. Being centered on the deficiencies and failures of the new capitals, they also have neglected more successful elements in their plans and did not go at a more granular level in their appraisals of their different aspects. By doing so, they have often missed the most important strategic considerations that bolstered the original plans and failed to identify the real reasons and specific mistakes behind the disasters that they have witnessed.

Below I will distinguish, analyze, and expose some flaws in several arguments that have been most central in the critique of the seat of government transfers: the state intervention argument, the ghost city argument, the authoritarian ruler argument, the isolated capital argument, alternative options argument, and arithmetic argument.

State intervention argument

The libertarian critics tend to exaggerate the power of market mechanisms to resolve hyper-centralization and underestimate how the path-dependence, political pull, and gravitational force of primary cities and current capitals distorts the market mechanisms that are expected to resolve these problems. However, under conditions of extreme overcentralization, these market forces are most often disabled or incapable of performing their regulatory functions. The economic benefits produced by the capital city's status and conferred upon its citizens are significant even in not so corrupt countries. The blind trust in the ability of the market to naturally rebalance the overconcentration of resources – the idea found in the proposals of some economists – appears to be naïve given the current level of corruption and entrenched traditions in many of these countries. The tendency to view the dominant capital city as an element in the "natural" urban hierarchy is misleading as this dominance is itself a result of the state intervention and of the special treatment of capital cities in this system and seldom a result of only their competitiveness. Arguing against state intervention manifested in capital city changes, the libertarian critics often fail to see that the existing system is not a "natural" phenomenon. The corruption effects and rent seeking behaviors tend to perpetuate the cycle that reinforces the capital city dominance.

Strategies of relocations 209

The state intervention argument is often complimented and buttressed by the implicit assumption about the isomorphic relationship between causes and effects. Since the capital city dominance was engendered by particular misguided policies of the government that permitted or encouraged hyper-centralization, the government can backtrack through the reversal of these policies. According to this assumption, the capital city transfer is a radical step vastly disproportional to the character of government involvement that engendered the situation of hyper-centralization. Thus, under this assumption capital city transfer is regarded as higher order government intervention. In practice, however, it might not be sufficient to stop the policies and other trends that reinforce centralization – corruption, the political culture of rent seeking, capital city bias and the like – to solve the problem; it might be also necessary to take more forceful steps creating structural conditions that will forestall such developments in the future and will facilitate the reversal of these trends. Indeed capital city shift might be viewed as a radical step aiming to change the deeply entrenched tendencies of hyper-centralization.

The ghost city argument

By design many capital city transfer projects imply a long-term strategic perspective to achieve the benefits for the nation or for the region that they declare to be their goals. Horizons of these projects tend to be long, and their realistic full assessments, including the appraisal of their economic outcomes, can be given perhaps only several decades after the project was completed. It is important to emphasize that many proponents of capital city shifts were well aware that the construction of the new capitals and its insertion into the fabric of national life is a long-term process. Based on the estimates of some urban scholars, it might take anywhere from 100 to 150 years to see the city fully integrate into the urban system.[50] The ghost city narrative fails to see that the alienation effects produced by the newly built cities are temporary, and that the failures of capitals as cities are partially compensated by their new role in national politics and in nation-building.

The critics of purpose-built cities also tend to overstate the distinction between purpose-built and evolved capital cities when they accuse the purpose-built capitals in the paucity of urbanity. However, this contrast is not as stark as it appears to many of these critics. As we have observed earlier, the radical reconstruction of many evolved capital cities made them much more similar to purpose-built capitals in terms of their urban layouts and morphology. It also should be reminded that many very successful capital cities initially emerged as purpose-built capitals. The revered Constantinople, Baghdad, Cairo, Madrid, and Valetta, the capital of Malta, emerged as designed capitals. The trajectory of transformation and the speed of integration of the new capital is far more important than the origin of the city.

The argument that new capitals are not "successful cities" is less poignant and less relevant for another reason. The "citiness" (urbanity) is not the essential characteristic of capitals. Some new capital cities do not even have a title of a city, and their designation as cities is only provisional. This is evident from the labels some of them have. The founding fathers have described Washington D.C. as a "Village on the Capitol Hill." In the Fifth Article of the Constitution of Spain, the Spanish capital is called "The Village of Madrid" (Villa) since the king never granted the status of a city to the capital. The Hague even today has not received the charter of a city and is called "the largest village in Europe." Pretoria was also described as an "administrative village." In some countries, notably in the US and Tanzania, capitals were envisaged as a compromise between the city and the village, representing the interests of both types of human settlements. Such nominations are probably not an accident and point to the unavoidable anomalies of the urban development in the capitals of modern states and to their ambivalent roles. Not infrequently, capitals are not self-governed entities, and in this critical sphere they violate the most important imperative and defining characteristic of a city. Understandably, the execution of national and federal functions interferes with the *ethos* of a proper functioning city.

Authoritarian ruler argument

It is also remarkable that many critical assessments of capital city relocations tend to interpret all decisions of the authoritarian rulers in the Machiavellian fashion as self-serving. Such assessments often disregard the pluralistic motives that have triggered the decisions to transfer seats of government. We have seen in our cross-country analysis many cases where several rationales were equally important. The authoritarian ruler argument is often based on the generic fallacy neglecting the fact that autocratic governments can pursue different goals. For example the capital city shift in Myanmar often derided as irrational by many international observers have delivered some positive outcomes within the framework of tasks set forth by the Myanmar administration. Russian geographer Sergey Rogachev has persuasively demonstrated that there were some compelling reasons for the government of Myanmar to move the capital stemming from the challenges of the country's geography and its ethnic make-up and that the outcome of this relocation can be conducive to more healthy reforms and for better integration of the country in the future.[51] Generally, the presence of self-serving motives in the decisions does not disqualify other valid reasons motivating these projects.

Isolated capital argument

The concept of an isolated capital city also rests on the notion that most of the capital city shifts are motivated by the intentions of the rulers to isolate their seats of governments from the main centers of population to prevent rebellions. Notably, the link between isolated governments and misgovernance is found only in non-democratic countries.[52] Indeed history and case studies from this book are replete with examples where the capitals were moved at least in part because of the fear of insurrections. Obviously the isolated capital argument is complex and requires a more serious and detailed critique of the research design and assumptions made than can be given here. But several brief critical observations about this concept will suffice for our purposes without going into the technicalities of the research design.

There are at least two contradictions that the "isolated capital city" argument entails. Most of the capital cities of the world are located in the largest cities of their countries, and most of the political regimes in the world are non-democratic or have low quality democracies. Intuitively, one would expect to see that most of the countries in the world will have isolated capitals, which is not the case. More to the point, according to the rich body of literature in spatial economics – we will discuss it in more detail in a separate chapter – dictatorships and corrupt regimes have capital cities that are, on average, 45 percent larger than their democratic counterparts.[53] Accordingly, the countries that have oversize capitals tend to be less democratic and more corrupt and have lower quality of government compared to countries with smaller and more isolated capital cities which directly contradict the "isolated capital" argument.

The isolated capital argument is also premised on the assumption that most capital city relocations are narrowly motivated by the interest of the rulers. The fear of insurrection and protection against perceived instability threat, they argue, is a pervasive concern behind capital relocations, either planned or actually implemented.[54] Hence they tend to discount most other rationales and considerations and describe capital city shifts as the ultimate "insurance against regime change" and as "extreme policy levers."[55] However, this description fits only the minority of cases, and it is debatable to what extent this motive influence the decision in each particular case. It also must be noted that isolation represents only one parameter in the debate among many others: there are far more important parameters that are being discussed. Apart from the pursued strategy, the political dynamics of the country and the available transportation options to reach the capital, "isolation" has very limited value for the understanding of the performance of a capital city. What matters the most for the performance of the government/capital is not so much physical but its figurative isolation from the bulk of the country's population. It is also remarkable that a relatively isolated capital is a fundamental feature of democratic federations.

The characterization of isolated capitals as the "enablers" of the autocratic systems seems particularly misleading. This argument could be more persuasive if it can be shown that after the establishment of an "isolated capital" the quality of democracy substantially deteriorated and that comparable countries with dominant capitals from the same world region have significantly better quality of governance. However, it is not the case. As of 2015 the Index of Economic Freedom score in Turkey (63.2) with isolated Ankara was better than that of Iran (41.8), in Kazakhstan (63.3) was significantly better than in Uzbekistan (47) and all other countries of Central Asia, in Brazil (56.6) was better than in Argentina (44.1), in Nigeria (55.6) was better than in Angola (47.9), in Tanzania (57.5) was better than in Mozambique (54.8), in Malaysia (70.8) better than in Indonesia (58.1), in Pakistan (55.6) and India (54.6) better than in Bangladesh (53.9). The only case where the economic freedom of a country that relocated its capital is worse than in a comparable country is Myanmar (46.9) vs. Thailand (62.4). These numbers are consistent with the corruption perception indexes for these countries.[56] So the conclusions of the research directly contradict the political situation in the countries with relatively isolated capitals.

Additionally, the new capitals were rapidly growing and did not remain ghost towns, isolated from the bulk of the population of the relevant countries, for long. In fact many of the new capitals were the fastest growing in the world. The population of Ankara grew from 20,000 (1920) to 75,000 in 1927. By the mid-1960s it grew to 750,000 and to 3.6 million by 1990.[57] The population in Brasília grew from 140,000 (1960) to 537,000 in 1970 and to more than 2 million by 2000. Islamabad's population grew from 100,000 in 1951 to 1.3 million in 2012. Since it became the country's capital, Astana's population more than doubled to 750,000 in 2012 and it became the second largest city. The population of Naypyidaw in Myanmar grew from a few thousand people in 2005 to close to 1 million, although it is only an official figure. By 2006 Abuja was a city of almost 800,000 people and is expected to grow to 10 million by 2018.

Curiously, the moves to "isolated capitals" in some cases were suboptimal solutions at least for some rulers who were trying to protect their seat of power from uprisings and coups, as the experience of Pakistan has testified. Such capital cities were also able to foster social upheavals and turmoil and were no less dangerous to the rulers compared to the larger cities.

Alternative options argument

The most persuasive argument against capital city relocations is the availability of alternative solutions that can bring similar outcomes and can restrain the growth of the capital city and improve its infrastructure. Indeed some of the problems that capital transfer projects aimed to address could be solved or mitigated with these alternative strategies that are much easier, cheaper, and without the shock therapy involved in capital city moves for the population. However, these alternative measures have two important limitations.

First, these alternative strategies could be very comparable to capital city shifts both in terms of their potential costs and the realistic amount of time necessary to reach the promised outcomes as a result of their implementation. The cost of radical reconstruction of a large capital city runs in the tens of billions of dollars as the recent "Le Grand Paris" project testifies.[58]

Second, while the mentioned alternative strategies can aid in solving some problems related to overpopulation and traffic gridlocks, they cannot help countries to assert their identity, to reposition themselves geopolitically, to lay the groundwork for future federalization, or to find a neutral place to reconcile several ethnic groups. The appeal to such alternative strategies makes sense only in cases when strategies of de-centralization are proposed.

The arithmetic argument

According to the arithmetic argument, the change of capital cannot produce any qualitative incremental changes in society as they only rearrange the terms of the equation. The proponents of this argument fail to see capital city shift as an element of the strategy that creates structural conditions fraught with serious implications for social and political change. They castigate the supporters of capital transfers for their naïve belief that the transfers can help to mitigate social inequality and to overcome corruption and over-centralization through the separation of business and government. The social maladies pertaining to the whole of society – inequality, corruption, and over-centralization – cannot be alleviated and removed locally, and they will inexorably reproduce and manifest themselves in the new capital. This argument fails to see, first, that capital transfer is only one element of the strategy and that relocation can contribute to the change of the quality of governance. The location of the capital city, its size relative to other cities, and the relationship between the capital and the regions is one of the structural conditions that have a potential to impact the political and social relations in the society-at-large. The reconstruction of the relations between the capital and the regions might pave the way for the satisfaction of important public policy objectives. The transfer involves not simply the replacement of one element of the equation with the other. Being embedded into a strategy, it creates a structural change that has a potential to resolve hyper-centralization and to produce incremental qualitative change if other congenial policies are also deployed.

The more granular analysis of the outcomes of the projects reveals that the reasons of their failure often lied in their organization and administration. The public policy objectives that they have pursued were often consonant with the nation's development strategies and reflected, at least in some respects, the needs of the country. However, the projects have been botched by poor and hasty implementation strategies and poor planning. In short, they were often planning disasters rather than flawed visions, immanently futile, or the fallacies of choosing the wrong vehicle of change.[59] Better strategic planning could have helped these projects to become more successful. The measured success of these projects in some countries is the best argument against the attempts to denounce all of them as the malign fantasies of the autocratic rulers.

Fortunately, the totalizing critiques do not represent the consensus of analysts, and many geographers, political scientists, and economists have offered more sanguine approaches to the subject, suggesting more comprehensive and nuanced views of capital city transfers.

214 *Strategies of relocations*

Their works provided more constructive analysis in the richer contexts and broader frameworks encompassing nation- and state-building and conflict resolution.[60] Not showing any excessive enthusiasm about the newly built cities and not making recommendations to embark on these projects, these scholars and analysts have cautiously researched the circumstances, motives, and outcomes aiming first to understand the logic, context, and the multifaceted motives of the governments undertaking them before making judgments about their merits and rationality. Drawing upon different theoretical and methodological approaches, their research has helped to overcome the economistic biases and to present a much more balanced view of the topic. It also has helped to identify positive lessons and some acceptable results – in view of the given circumstances and available alternatives – even in such obviously problematic case as Abuja in Nigeria and Naypyidaw in Myanmar.[61]

Success factors: the good, the bad, and the ugly

The analysis and the critique of the arguments against capital transfers can help us to formulate the principles and conditions that determine the success of these projects. But before doing this, it behooves us to redefine success.

It is generally agreed that some capital city transfers have been more successful than others, and we have seen in Chapter 3 of this book the outline of the good cases, the bad cases, and the ugly cases. There is a stark difference between quite successful cases of Germany, Malaysia, and Kazakhstan, on the one hand, and more problematic cases of Nigeria and Tanzania, on the other. The relocation to Astana from Almaty permitted Kazakhstan to assert its control over Northern Kazakhstan, which could become a source of conflict, and to balance the interests of the three sub-ethnic units (hordes) of the country. The transfer of the capital to Berlin has facilitated the integration of Eastern Germany and slowed down the mass migration from there. The capital city transfer to Brasília has succeeded in the establishment of the new growth pole helping to develop the interior of the country and to link different parts of Brazil. Ankara has facilitated the transition from empire to the republic.

The more granular view of the project's outcomes enables us to see the successful and less successful components of these projects. By the same token, the more inclusive concept of success can also enable us to recognize some signs of success even in less successful projects. Avoiding the appraisal of these projects wholesale, one can find the modicum of success in many obviously bad and even in some ugly capital city transfers. Despite the fact that these projects obviously failed, there were at least some redeeming qualities in them.

In Myanmar the capital was moved closer to the interior of the country helping to focus the national consolidation efforts there and bringing it closer to many ethnic minorities and mountain tribes, integrating them better into the country. Some other projects have provided the roadmap for better integration of the country, drew attention to the misbalances, envisioned the opportunities in the far-flung regions, and offered new options and devices for reconciliation for ethnic and sub-ethnic groups. By doing so, they have laid the foundation for more successful developments in the future. Many capital city transfers also served as a gesture of government commitment to the fairer distribution of resources and to the development of the backward regions, the issue that was brought into sharper focus. Some of the new exclusive capitals built by the authoritarian rulers can be reembedded into the fabric of national life and resignified to better reflect the respective national identities in the future. Although the success of these projects was limited to only some aspects and was achieved at a very high price, their failure was often attributable more to the poor planning and less to the flawed visions that animated them. They have set the noble goals, in many cases quite consonant with the needs of the country – development of the hinterland, integration of the diverse ethnic groups of the countries, and the like – but these goals have been tarnished by the self-serving agendas of the governments, corruption, and poor implementation strategies.

It is difficult to compile a comprehensive list of the factors that determined the success of the project. Although some of the factors will sound a bit trivial, they need to be spelled out. Most importantly, the plan should be a part of a strategic vision of the national development. Early on the government needs to set up its strategic priorities and the possible trade-offs between different public policy objectives. Generally the organization of these megaprojects should be based on the best project management practices. Project management involves defining the scope of the project, setting the milestones and the timelines for different phases of the project, developing the budget, and the like. Success of different phases and components of the project determines its success. The creation of a special agency with defined competencies and responsibilities is most helpful in this process.

The reconstruction of the transportation system and the creation of the infrastructure necessary to house the government functions should accompany the construction of the new capital and should be considered a top priority.

To be successful a capital city relocation plan should take into account the interests of the diverse regions and different ethnic and religious groups. The location of the capital should reflect these interests, maximizing the access to the capital city for all communities and constituent entities. Ideally, all stakeholders should take a part in the decision-making process; the decision-making procedures should provide for their active participation in the decision. The claimant for the title of a new capital city that epitomizes the vision of the future of the country should reflect both the objective and subjective interests of these groups. The presence of several rationales, economic, political, and cultural, to move the capital, especially the integrative goals and the goals of reconciliation of different groups of the country,

216 *Strategies of relocations*

and the support of ethnic minorities also tend to warrant the success. The articulation of only negative reasons such as overpopulation and congestion, on the other hand, tends to hamper their success. The more rationales the project has and the stronger the support for a single site is the more chances the project has to succeed. The consensus of the power elites and the major political parties can ensure that the administration of the project will be well organized and cohesive.

It is also critically important to develop a plan for the former capital city and to develop strategies to transition it to a new status. The future of the former capital city should be a critical component of the capital city relocation plan. These strategies have to take into account the employment situation in the former capital, the use of the government buildings and the metropolitan infrastructure. The transportation routes and communication system between the new and the former capitals are also critically important.

Obviously, the financial support also plays a critical role. The important success factor is the availability of the budget funds to finance these projects, the interest of the private businesses to invest into it, and the ability to form the public-private alliance in the construction process between the government and private businesses. The plan of the new capital should be commensurate with the GDP of the relevant country.

The project also needs to have utopian impulse and to have popular support to be successful. The character of the popular support and the role of utopian impulses in the success of these projects have been debated. Many critics have lambasted the project in Brazil, Turkey, and elsewhere for their strong reliance on the "utopian impulses."[62]

On the other hand, there was a tendency to overemphasize them at the expense of rational considerations and planning. Some romantic nationalist ideologists have laid emphasis on the spontaneity and popular appeal of these projects. Not infrequently, such leaders have considered the planning procedures and the rational calculation of the costs and benefits of such plans as counter-productive and contradicting the spontaneous and romantic spirit of these decisions. The sentiments and the spirit of such idealistic politicians were well captured by Count Camillo Benso di Cavour (1810–1861), one of the inspired visionaries and ideologists of the unified Italy. In the course of debates about the choice of the new capital of Italy, Cavour argued:

> The question of the capital is not determined by climate, or topography, nor even by strategical considerations. If these things affected the selection, I think I might safely say that London would not be the capital of England, nor, perhaps, Paris of France. The selection of the capital is determined by great moral reasons. It is the Will of the people that decides a question touching them so closely.[63]

Cavour's attitude is echoed also in the works of some contemporary geographers studying the capital city relocations in different parts of the globe.

The British geographer David Lowenthal has remarked: "Capital sites are generally chosen in spite of, rather than because of, expert advice; and emotional judgments may succeed better rather than rational ones."[64] The congenial remark was made by Hanford Eldredge regarding the construction of Brasília: "Had Kubitschek sought to begin with a series of lengthy, and very likely *social* and *economic studies*, it is more than likely that the city would never have come into existence."[65]

However, the presented cases of capital city relocations point to a rather different conclusion. The disregard for rational urban planning and the reliance only on the temperature, pulse, and the intuition of the *Volksgeist* tend to provide not only unreliable guidance but can be extremely dangerous. As we have witnessed, the recent history is replete with examples of less successful, problematic, and unintelligible experiences of this sort even when there was no shortage of "great moral reasons" and high grounds for such decisions. It must be added that since the times of Cavour, the social theory has learned to be much more cautious and apprehensive about the sentiments of the people, People's Will, and intuitions of the national spirit.

Ideally, the procedures of rational planning should not contradict the intuitions of the "national spirit." The more suitable and sensible approach should combine the elements of strategic planning and the "truth" of national Romanticism. To paraphrase the words of Alexander Pushkin, they should verify the harmony of national sentiments with the algebra of precise accounting of the costs and consequences of the adopted decisions. The Cavour's imperative – let us call it the availability of high moral temperature – should not be treated as an antithesis but rather as an ingredient in the accounting for the strategic parameters. Generally the presence of these utopian impulses does not necessarily imply the total reconstruction of the world and of the state based on utopian grounds. Rather it involves the system of idealistic motifs that move the nation and that find their manifestation in the process of social and political transformation.

The availability of the charismatic and popular national leaders capable of consolidation of the political parties and national movements in the cause of new capital city construction is definitely one of the hallmarks of success. The presence of such leaders facilitates not only the mobilization of different strata of population but helps in the administrative arrangements involved in the implementation of this project.

Last but not least is the factor of political regime that contributes to the success or failure of the project. The successful political regime sets the appropriate goals and uses the legitimate procedures to reach a consensus on this topic. Successful political regimes also develop more realistic budgets and timetables for the capital city relocation project. It also has better control mechanisms to monitor spending and audit the public expenditures dedicated to it. Conversely, the overambitious plans, unrealistic targets, and heavy budgets more characteristic for authoritarian regimes is a liability for these projects.[66] In the next subchapter we will elaborate on the topic of the relationship between the political regimes and the character of the capital city transfers characteristic for them.

Capital city transfers within different political regimes

Different political regimes use different strategies and set different goals for capital city relocation projects. They also tend to have different rationales and use different methods to make a decision about the move.

The totalitarian regimes rarely favor capital city transfers as a way to solve political and socio-economic issues and more often embark on the total reconstruction of the existing capital cities. They seek to subvert and undermine the chances for any alternative visions of the national identity. They also tend to see in the iconography and identity of the old capital a threat to their own vision of the political identity. Following these totalizing visions, Stalin, Hitler, and Mussolini have offered and in various measures have managed to realize their plans of total ideological reconstruction of the nations in Moscow, Berlin, and Rome respectively. The grandiose socialist reconstruction of Moscow undertaken by Josef Stalin sought to lay the groundwork for the transformation of the capital of the USSR into a showcase of global communist utopia. It was accompanied by the radical transformation of urban morphology and the key elements of its architectural plan that included both a large-scale and massive destruction of the churches, the legacy of the old Russia, and their replacement with the universal symbols of communist utopia.[67] The government of Mussolini embarked upon lesser scale but not less ambitious ideological project of a totalizing transformation of Rome aiming to introduce the fascist symbols in its plan and architecture.[68]

On several occasions Hitler expressed his admiration for Ataturk, who managed to transfer the capital to Ankara, and found in Berlin that he disliked the same spirit of decay and decadence that Ataturk felt in Istanbul. He also toyed with the idea of moving the capital of Germany to Munich or to one of the smaller towns in Germany. The capital city on Lake Müritz in Mecklenburg in the north of the country was considered as one of the options.[69] However, Albert Speer, Hitler's chief architect, persuaded Hitler to abandon this idea, and they concentrated on the radical plans to transform Berlin instead, just like Stalin and Mussolini did in Moscow and Rome. According to Hitler's plans, Berlin was to be renamed into Germania and made a capital of all territories subjugated to the Third Reich.[70] Hitler believed that Germany needed a majestic capital with colossal monuments exuding power unrivaled by any other city in the world.[71]

The concept of radical reconstruction of the state through the establishment of a new capital city was much more typical for the autocratic leaders of the modernizing states of semi-periphery. They were trying to make a statement about the new international standing of their respective countries and to promote themselves as leaders not only in the regional politics but also on the broader international scene. Ataturk in Turkey, Kubitschek in Brazil, Muhammad in Malaysia, and Nazarbayev in Kazakhstan clearly belong to this generation of autocratic rulers. It was critically important for all of them to create a new narrative of the modernizing nation. The new capital cities were supposed not only to balance the existing political forces in their countries and to mitigate domestic problems but also to declare themselves important players in the global politics and economy. Depending on the circumstances and the area where the most acute problems of the country laid, their new capital city plans took into consideration the specific ethnic make-up of these countries, the location of the contested territories, or the needs for the development of peripheral lands.

With some reservations the leaders of Pakistan, Argentina, and South Korea and the current leadership of Indonesia also belong to this type of autocratic leaders. Aiming to replicate the perceived success of the precedents in Turkey, Brazil, and Malaysia, they sought to emulate and create their own versions of these projects. The autocratic regimes were typically more efficient in securing public finances for infrastructure development, in expediting the decision-making process, and in mobilizing administrative resources necessary to carry out these projects. They did not have the political continuity problem, and it was easier for them to commit financial resources for these projects long-term.

The transfers of the capital cities in Turkey, Pakistan, Chile, Nigeria, and Myanmar were carried out not just by autocratic regimes but by authoritarian military regimes. At the time when the decision was made, these countries were headed by the generals. Notably, all presidents of Indonesia who have proposed capital city shift, including Sukarno, Suharto, and Yudhoyono, had a military background.

The most successful capital city transfers were carried out by liberal-federalist regimes in Anglo-Saxon countries. We have already distinguished two different rationales for these projects. On the one hand, they sought to separate the economic and political centers of the country for de-centralization. The second and more important goal was to seek a compromise and to reconcile different groups and to lay the structural conditions for successful social and political development. Although most of these capital city shifts occurred before the twentieth century, their experience is still topical and a subject of emulation in other countries. The capital city shift in Germany also belongs to liberal and federalist capital city shift projects. Similar to Anglo-Saxon models it was intended to integrate the country and to showcase the new priorities of unified Germany. Understandably, the former British colonies, India, Nigeria, and Malaysia, were especially receptive to the experience of Anglo-Saxon countries and have consciously borrowed some elements of capital city arrangement in Anglosphere. The concept of a capital city that is much smaller than its major economic hub became an imperative not only for federal politics but also for the politics of individual states of India.

There was a considerable variation in political agendas of different dictatorships in African countries. Apart from the reasons that they most often articulated in their official pledges and declarations – the independence and emancipation from the colonial legacy – many of them were also motivated by the need to preserve power in the hands of their own clans and power groups. This political power consolidation was achieved through the movement of the capital to the most loyal parts of the country and through granting special privileges to existing power coalitions. In contrast to the modernist projects mentioned above they were more often motivated by the problems of overpopulation of their colonial capital cities.

Notes

1 Bilham, R. "Millions at Risk as Big Cities Grow Apace in Earthquake Zones," *Nature*, vol. 401 (1999).
2 The suspicion that the choice of the capital city reflected the personal interests of the ruling elite or at least tipped the balance is not unique for authoritarian regimes. In case of such democracies as the US and Germany, there were some rumors and suggestions that the choice of Washington D.C. and Bonn reflected the personal interests of George Washington and Chancellor Konrad Adenauer. Bonn was close to Adenauer's house in Rhöndorf, just a few miles across the Rhine river from Bonn, while the mansion and property of George Washington at Mt. Vernon was a short distance away from the new American capital (Nagel, K.-J., ed. *The Problem of the Capital City: New Research on Federal Capitals and Their Territory* (Barcelona: Collecció Institut d'Estudis Autònomics, 2013), 104). The presence and weight of such motives and the explanations based on self-interest is often exaggerated although their role cannot be ruled out. They might have played their role but they hardly can qualify as the propulsive force for the decisions made.
3 Hawkins, D. "No, D.C. Isn't Really Built on a Swamp," *Washington Post*, August 29, 2014.
4 Rossman, V. "In Search of the Fourth Rome: Visions of a New Russian Capital City," *Slavic Review*, vol. 72, no. 3 (2013), 505–527.
5 Flanagan, J. "The Relocation of the Davidic Capital," *Journal of the American Academy of Religion*, vol. 47, no. 2 (1979), 223–244.
6 Slack, E. & Chattopadhyay, R. *Finance and Governance of Capital Cities in Federal Systems* (Montreal: McGill-Queen's University Press, 2009), 240–241.
7 Du Preez, P. *One Nation: One Capital, the Case of Pretoria* (Pretoria: Adams & Adams, 1995).
8 Omer-Man, M. "The Knesset Moves to Jerusalem," *Jerusalem Post*, December 11, 2011.
9 Parker, G. *Power in Stone: Cities as Symbols of Empires* (London: Reaktion, 2014), 200–203.
10 Kuper, H. "The Language of Sites in the Politics of Space," *American Anthropologist*, vol. 3, no. 74 (1972), 416–417.
11 Spate, O.H.K. "Factors in the Development of Capital Cities," *Geographical Review*, vol. 32, no. 4 (1942), 622–631.
12 Orr, A. "Move Over Eastern States—Perth Could Be Moving on Up," *WAToday*, October 26, 2012.
13 On region-building concepts, see Kühnhardt, L. *Region Building* (Oxford, NY: Berghahn Books, 2010).

14 Lohausen, H.J. von. "Wien und Belgrad als geopolitische Antipoden," *Staatsbriefe*, Heft 12, 1992.
15 Callegari, L. "La Geopolítica Aconseja Trasladar la Capital de la República a la Sierra Central," *Eco Andino. Revista de Cultura*, de octubre 17, 2009.
16 Denicke, Lars. "Fifty Years' Progress in Five: Brasilia—Modernization, Globalism, and the Geopolitics of Flight." In: Hecht, Gabrielle (ed.), *Entangled Geographies: Empire and Technopolitics in the Global Cold War*(Boston: MIT Press, 2011), 185–208.
17 Djament-Tran, G. "Les scénarios de localisation des capitales, révélateurs des conceptions de l'unité nationale," *Confins. Revue franco-brésilienne de géographie*, no. 9 (2010). http://confins.revues.org/6414
18 Administratively and geographically Liverpool is located in England, on the Welsh border. However, unofficially it is known as the "capital of North Wales."
19 Djament, G. "Le débat sur Rome capitale," *L'Espace Géographique*, Tome 34, no. 3 (2005), 369–380; Djament, G. "Le débat sur Rome capitale (1861–1871): choix de localisation et achèvement de la construction nationale italienne," *Revue historique*, no. 1 (2009), 99–118
20 Toynbee, A. "Capital Cities: Their Distinctive Features" and "Capital Cities: Melting-Pots and Powder-Kegs." In: *Cities on the Move* (New York & London: Oxford University Press, 1970), 67–78, 143–152.
21 Harvey, D. *Rebel Cities: From the Right to the City to the Urban Revolution* (London: Verso, 2012).
22 Wallace, J. "Cities, Redistribution, and Authoritarian Regime Survival," *Journal of Politics*, vol. 75, no. 3 (2013), 639.
23 Traugott, M. "Capital Cities and Revolution," *Social Science History*, vol. 19 (1995), 147–169.
24 Twain, M. *The Innocents Abroad* (Hartford: American Publishing Co., 1869), 157.
25 Marchand, B. *The Image of Paris in France since Two Centuries: From Good to Bad to Worst*, 2010,; Comte de Galembert (mars 1871) De la décentralisation et du transfert en province de la capitale politique de la France, Mame, Tours, 68 p, (Lettre à nos représentants à l'Assemblée Nationale).
26 Akam, S. "Not Such a Capital Idea after All," *Independent*, February 24, 2011; Falola, T. *Power of African Culture* (Rochester, NY: University of Rochester Press, 2003), 135–136.
27 Vale, L. *Architecture, Power, and National Identity* (Yale: Yale University Press, 1992), 243–244.
28 Djament, G. "Le débat sur Rome capitale," *L'Espace Géographique*, Tome 34, no. 3 (2005), 369–380; Djament, G. "Le débat sur Rome capitale (1861–1871): choix de localisation et achèvement de la construction nationale italienne," *Revue historique*, no. 1 (2009), 99–118.
29 Large, D. *Berlin* (New York: Basic Books, 2000), 5–6.
30 Ibid., 6.
31 Gordon, D.L.A., & Seasons, M.L. "Administrative and Financial Strategies for Implementing Plans in Political Capitals," *Canadian Journal of Urban Research*, June 2009.
32 Kironde, J.M.L. "Will Dodoma Ever Be the New Capital of Tanzania?," *Geoforum*, vol. 24, no. 4 (November 1993), 435–453.
33 The classical example of lock in effect is the situation with the placement of the buttons on the typewriter. The first key placement system was invented in the 1860s and, although since then several new and more optimal solutions that expedited the typing process have been proposed, they were not adopted and we are still using the old keyboard system. There are many other examples of the lock in effect of the dominant technology. The unlocking of the system requires

so much time investments and habits changing that new technologies are often not embraced for many years. Another good example of the sort is the transition from VCR to DVD technologies that took 30 years despite the fact that DVD technology was available many years earlier.
34 Gordon, D.L.A. & Seasons, M.L. "Administrative and Financial Strategies for Implementing Plans in Political Capitals," *Canadian Journal of Urban Research*, June 2009.
35 Kironde, J.M.L. "Will Dodoma Ever Be the New Capital of Tanzania?," *Geoforum*, vol. 24, no. 4 (November 1993), 448.
36 The Economist. "The Pros and Cons of Capital Flight," August 13, 2004; The Economist. "Sing a Song of $40 Billion," July 22, 2010; Akam, S. "Not Such a Capital Idea after All," *Independent*, February 24, 2011.
37 Akam, S. "Not Such a Capital Idea after All," *Independent*, February 24, 2011.
38 Campante, F., Do, Q.-A., & Guimaraes, B. "Isolated Capital Cities and Misgovernance," *Harvard Kennedy School of Government, Working Papers Series*, RW12–058, 2012; Campante, F. & Do, Q.-A. "Isolated Capital Cities, Accountability and Corruption: Evidence from US States," *NBER Working Paper No. 19027* (May, 2013), 10.
39 Keating, M. "Decentralization in Mitterrand's France," *Public Administration*, vol. 61 (1983), 237–25; Richardson, H.W. "National Urban Development Strategies in Developing Countries," *Urban Studies*, vol. 18 (1981), 267–283.
40 Richardson, H.W. "National Urban Development Strategies in Developing Countries," *Urban Studies*, vol. 18 (1981), 267–283.
41 Krugman, P. "Urban Concentration: The Role of Increasing Returns and Transport Costs," *Proceedings of the World Bank Annual Conference on Development Economics*, Washington, D.C. (1995), 241–243.
42 Dijkstra, L. "Why Investing more in the Capital Can Lead to Less Growth," *Cambridge Journal Regions, Economy and Society*, vol. 6, no. 2 (2013), 251–268.
43 Akam, S. "Not Such a Capital Idea after All," *Independent*, February 24, 2011; BBC News. "Taking the Capital Out of a City." November 3, 2009.
44 Karamzin, N. *Zapiska o drevnei i novoi Rossii v eyo politicheskom i grazhdanskom otnosheniakh* (Moscow: Nauka, 1991), 26.
45 King, R, "Re-Writing the City: Putrajaya as Representation," *Journal of Urban Design*, vol. 12, no. 1 (2007), 135–136.
46 Holston, J. *The Modernist City: An Anthropological Critique of Brasilia* (Chicago: University of Chicago Press, 1989).
47 BBC News. "Taking the Capital Out of a City," November 3, 2009.
48 Potts, D. "Capital Relocation in Africa: The Case of Lilongwe in Malawi," *Geographical Journal*, vol. 151, no. 2 (1985), 186.
49 Akam, S. "Not Such a Capital Idea after All," *Independent*, February 24, 2011.
50 BBC News. "Taking the Capital Out of a City," November 3, 2009; Ruble, B. *Leningrad. Shaping a Soviet City* (Berkeley: University of California Press, 1990).
51 Rogachev, S. "Naypyidaw—novaia stolitsa Myanmy," *Geografia*, no. 19 (2008).
52 Campante, F. & Do, Q.-A. "Isolated Capital Cities, Accountability and Corruption: Evidence from US States," *NBER Working Paper No. 19027* (May, 2013).
53 Ades, A.F. & Glaeser, E.L. "Trade and Circuses: Explaining Urban Giants," *Quarterly Journal of Economics*, vol. 110 (1995), 195–227.
54 Ibid., 4.
55 Ibid., 9–10.
56 According to the Corruption Perception Index (2014), the score for Kazakhstan (29) is better than for Uzbekistan (18), for Brazil (43) better than for Argentina (34), for Nigeria (27) better than for Angola (19), for Turkey (45) better than for Iran (27), and for Georgia (52) better than for Azerbaijan (29).

57 Evered, K. "Symbolizing a Modern Anatolia: Ankara as Capital in Turkey's Early Republican Landscape," *Comparative Studies in South Asia, Africa, and the Middle East*, vol. 28, no. 2 (2008), 339.
58 La Grand Paris project was initiated by former French President Nicolas Sarkozy to develop the capital and region around the French capital.
59 Hall, P. *Great Planning Disasters* (Berkeley: University of California Press, 1980).
60 Richardson, H.W. & Bae, C.-H.C. "Options for the Capital of a Reunified Korea," *SAIS Review of International Affairs*, vol. 29, no. 1 (2009), 67–77; Corey, K. "Relocation of National Capitals," *International Symposium on the Capital Relocation* (September 22, Seoul, 2004), 43–107; Schatz, E. "What Capital Cities Say about State and Nation Building," *Nationalism and Ethnic Politics*, vol. 9, no. 4 (2003), 111–140.
61 Marlow, J. "Relocation: The Pros and Cons of Plans in South Sudan," *Geographical Magazine*, December 2011.
62 See, for instance, Mangabeira da Vinha, D. "Brasília through British Media," *Vitruvius*, ano. 14 (2003).
63 Cavour (Benso), C. "Rome as the Capital of United Italy," In: Bryan, Willim (ed.), *The World's Famous Orations: Continental Europe (380–1906)*, vol. VII (New York & London: Funk and Wagnalls Co., 1906); Djament, G. "Le débat sur Rome capitale," *L'Espace Géographique*, Tome 34, no. 3 (2005), 372.
64 Lowenthal, D. "The West Indies Chooses the Capital City," *Geographical Review*, vol. 48, no. 3 (1958), 363.
65 Eldredge, H. *World Capitals: Toward Guided Urbanization* (Garden City, NY: Anchor Press, 1975), 477.
66 Corey, K. "Relocation of National Capitals," *International Symposium on the Capital Relocation* (September 22, Seoul, 2004), 83–92.
67 Wusten, H. van der "Dictators and Their Capital Cities: Moscow and Berlin in the 1930s," *GeoJournal*, vol. 52, no. 4 (2001), 331–352.
68 Kallis, A. *The Third Rome, 1922–43: The Making of the Fascist Capital* (New York: Palgrave-Macmillan, 2014).
69 Hitler, A. *Hitler's Table Talk, 1941–1944*. Introduction H. Trevor Roper (Oxford: Oxford University Press, 1988), 45.
70 Ibid. Hitler's Germania echoes Teutona, the new capital city of the united Germany that was advocated by a radical German nationalist writer Friedrich Ludwig Jahn (1778–1852) more than a century earlier (Jahn, F.-L. "An Essay on Capital Cities," *Essai sur les Moeurs, la Littérature, et la Nationalité des peuples de l'Allemagne* (Paris: J.B. Nichols & Son, 1832). The Gentleman's Magazine, vol. 103, (Jul–Dec, 1833), part 2, 229). Jahn believed that it should be situated near the Elbe, in a district equally distant from Geneva and Memel and from Trieste and Copenhagen. Jahn claimed that it was Frederick the Great who promulgated this concept (Ibid., 229).
71 "Once a year we shall lead a troop of Kirghizes through the capital of the Reich, in order to strike their imaginations with the size of our monuments." Hitler, A. *Hitler's Table Talks* (Oxford: Oxford University Press, 1988), 24.

5 Three standards to assess the effectiveness of a capital city

As we have seen in many instances, by transferring their capital cities, governments and rulers seek to increase the effectiveness of these cities in resolving various developmental problems of their countries. It is as if such transfers increase the lever arm or degree of efficiency required for the successful implementation of reforms, strengthening of state authority, or other tasks. What are the criteria for the effectiveness of a capital city as a social institute, and what evaluation criteria should be used to determine if the new capital exceeded the previous one in performance? Worded differently, what are the normative criteria of capital city effectiveness, and what parameters should be taken into account to assess this effectiveness?

To answer these questions, we will first describe several methodologies and theoretical models that inform decision-making related to capital city siting and capital city performance assessment. Then, in the second part of this chapter, we will discuss three evaluation criteria of capital city performance and provide a few examples showing how scholars use some of these methodologies and assessment tools and what conclusions they can make using them.

Methodologies to assess the role and location of a capital city

Parascientific approaches: geomancy

In the ancient times and the Middle Ages, the archaic perception of capitals as the ritual centers embedded into the system of cosmic harmony dictated the need for special methods of their siting and legitimation. This factor underlined the particular importance that two disciplines – astrology and geomancy – had as the auxiliary tools used for the search of a proper capital city location and subsequently for the legitimation of the capital. While astrology examined celestial bodies to determine the proper timing for the foundation of a new capital, geomancy examined features of the earth to determine a prospective location of a capital. Astrological recommendations were especially prevalent in the Byzantine Empire, Persia, and Arabia.[1]

Furthermore, astrological considerations played a major role in urban planning in some medieval European countries.[2] Distinct astrological methods have been traditionally applied to the capital siting process in Burma (currently Myanmar); in fact, as it has been shown above, Myanmar's most recent capital relocation was conducted in conformity with the most strict astrological rules and reglamentation.[3] By contrast, most of the East Asian countries, especially in the Far East, tended to build and relocate capital cities relying mostly on geomantic factors.

While no systematically developed and consistent procedures and methods of capital relocation could be found in the West, in the countries of the Sinosphere, the regions that have historically been culturally influenced by China, notably Korea, Japan, and Vietnam, they became most important and, in fact, mandatory instruments used in making decisions on capital relocation. Thus, China's oldest written sources – *Classic of Poetry* or *Shijing*, and *Book of Documents* or *Shujing* (both dated approximately eleventh through seventh centuries BC) – reveal that the principles of geomancy or *feng shui* (Chinese for "wind and water") were relied on in the process of founding a capital. Masters of geomancy initiated capital transfers or strongly influenced decisions to make these transfers, taking an active part in the process of capital city siting.[4] It was them who chose locations for such famous cities as Chang'an (now Xi'an), which served as the capital of China during the Western Han (third century BC–first century AD) and then Tang (seventh through tenth centuries AD) Dynasties; Luoyang, capital of the legendary Xia Dynasty (twenty-first through sixteenth centuries BC) and subsequently Western Zhou (eleventh through seventh centuries BC) and Eastern Han (first through third centuries AD) Dynasties; Kaesong, an ancient capital of Korea, and Seoul; Hue, a royal capital of Vietnam; and Nara and Kyoto, ancient Japanese capitals.

These countries gave rise not only to special decision-making procedures but also to a whole elite class, scholars who had expertise in these procedures. These scholars or experts were believed to have specialized knowledge about how the world was structured and what place and time were the most suitable for founding a new capital.

Selecting a location for a new capital was a state matter of the highest importance. According to the common belief, the country's destiny was largely dependent on the geographical location of its capital. Using area maps, site plans, and a special geomantic compass, preceded by a turtle shell in the more ancient times, geomancers thoroughly examined the source and direction of *geomantic arteries* and sought to gain favor of the local spirits; they were also responsible for properly siting palaces, other important constructions, and graves of ancestors.[5]

At the heart of geomancy was the concept of the corporeality of space. The main principle was to harmonize the environment with the Five Elements, *wu xing* – Earth, Wood, Metal, Fire, and Water. Special significance was given to Earth as the symbol of motherhood underlying the origin of life.

Earth, which gives birth to everything in the world, and Earth's energy present in each given piece of land have a decisive influence on those who exploit this land. The ideal location is where the earth is in harmony with the sky while the female principle, *yin*, is in harmony with the male principle, *yang*. The mountain (hill) and the water (river) were considered key components of the landscape: the former contained the life force while the latter prevented this force from being exhausted.

The popular sixteenth century Chinese treatise *Everything Geomancers Should Know About Geography* or *Dili Renzi Xuzhi*, authored by the Xu brothers, discusses capital siting principles from the perspective of distribution and conservation of energy. It is noteworthy that China's major historical capitals were believed to be located near the mountain ranges stemming from the legendary Kunlun Mountain, perceived as the backbone of the world and a powerful source of energy pulses. In accordance with this belief and in relation to the Kunlun Mountain, Beijing, Luoyang, and Nanjing were viewed as the Northern, Central, and Southern Dragons, respectively.[6]

Although the capital relocation solutions offered by geomancy were mystical in nature, they had an important grain of truth and were based on good intuition. Given its main principle that the balance of energies must be maintained in a human settlement, geomancy, in a sense, was energetic ecology. One of its main achievements was that it introduced the first-ever systematic procedure for a settlement site assessment using multiple parameters. Some modern geographers and architects have abandoned an unreservedly negative appraisal of geomancy as a collection of superstitions and presently view it as a special branch of urban ecology. Furthermore, some modern geopoliticians tend to rely on the categories and concepts that despite their purported scholarly origin, approximate those employed by ancient masters of geomancy.[7]

Centrography

Economic geographers use the methods of centrography to identify the "center of gravity" and track the dynamics of its movement by applying demographic indicators and weighing the population distribution in different countries. Exploiting special mathematical and graphical techniques, centrography focuses on the issues of productive force distribution. Measuring various parameters, centrographers locate industry sector centers and other centers within a given country.

One of the pioneers of centrography as a branch of economic geography was the Russian Dmitri Mendeleev.[8] It was further developed by a number of his disciples and followers, notably the economy geographers Vladimir Svyatlovsky (1869–1927), Vladimir Dehn (1867–1933), and Veniamin Semenov-Tyan-Shansky (1870–1942).[9] In 1934 the Soviet authorities declared centrography "fascist bourgeois pseudoscience" along with cybernetics and genetics.[10]

Centrographic theories point to several important facts: First, space by its nature is extremely multicentered; second, it would be unavailing to search for one definitive center, whether geometrical, dynamic, or military; third, even in highly centralized countries there exist multiple centers; and last, at least several options that are most relevant for a particular task may be identified in each given case.

System dynamics theories

Commonly used in management practice, system dynamics theories are invoked by the experts not for the purpose of determining strategic priorities of states, but rather, as a tool for modeling the capital relocation process and its key components. These theories focus on the system of casual connections and interdependencies in the systems. In the context of capital relocation, this methodology is quite relevant as it allows to track down consequences of the various phases of this phenomenon. Instrumental in forecasting various scenarios of potential disruptions and changes in the subsystems, it optimizes the sequence of transferring capital city functions to the new location.[11]

Furthermore, the system dynamics approach also allows the foresight of a variety of long-term consequences of economic and political decision-making, as well as to identify critical links and elements in the chain of events. It facilitates both the development of capital relocation projects and the implementation of various secondary processes such as growth dynamics of the new capital, attainment of economic maturity or self-sufficiency by the new capital, and demographic changes in the old capital. Last, it enables the identification of feedback loops, which is crucial for the analysis and modeling of nonlinear processes. This approach is premised on the assumption that the elements of the system are interrelated and reproduce the system's negative features such as overcentralization, for example.

The system dynamics approach is exemplified by the analysis of the capital transfer from Seoul proposed, among others, by a multidisciplinary group of Korean scholars. Pointing both to the isolation and the tendency to self-perpetuation as characteristics of an overcentralized system, these scholars have concluded that capital relocation may not be successful unless auxiliary deconcentration strategies are employed.[12]

Geopolitical analysis

Geopoliticians maintain that spatial orientation of a state is dependent on the state's geographical location and strategies of political development. River civilizations, sea civilizations, and ocean civilizations as described by Léon Metchnikoff, naturally choose different centers for their development.[13]

The most common type of geopolitical analysis focuses on strategic military issues and is intended to identify areas of political influence based on the geographical location or landscape features of a given territory. For this purpose, geopoliticians locate the key spatial points and natural seats of power, which, in their opinion, ensure state's dominance or prevalence in the region.

Although none of the classics of geopolitics have ever specifically addressed the issue of capital city siting, many of them believed that capital transfers in major states are driven by cycles of change from continental dominance to ocean dominance. Thus, according to Karl E. Haushofer, the transfer of the capital from Calcutta to Delhi reflected the triumph of the continental system of rule, marking the demise of the specifically British idea of India as the Empire of the Indian Ocean.[14] Furthermore, some geopoliticians have pointed out that it is particularly important that a capital occupy a central or intermediate position with respect to the region as a whole, not necessarily in relation to the country's internal borders. Such a capital would mark the state's sphere of influence stemming from the concept of imminent living space. It is in these terms that the rightist Austrian geopolitician Heinrich J. Lohausen describes the position of both Vienna and Belgrade.[15]

Another distinguishable type of geopolitical analysis may be termed the "macrospatial analysis"; it purports to provide a natural scientific explanation to social processes but often does so in a speculative and parascientific way. This approach is illustrated by an essay authored by Olga Tynyanova, editor-in-chief of the Russian scholarly journal *Space and Time (Prostranstvo i Vremya)*. Discussing favorable and unfavorable "directions of social energy transfers," she claims that the success of either a military expansion or a cultural interaction is dependent on whether or not their direction is aligned with the "fundamental lines of force, which are the electromagnetic and gravitational fields of the Earth, transfer of solar energy, and course of world time."

According to her, the "energetically favorable directions" are the movements from east to west, as well as those from north to south. Although Tynyanova does not raise the problems of capital relocation, her conclusions imply that capital transfers or people's migrations from west to east, i.e., reversely to the direction of the world time course, can hardly be successful.[16]

Growth poles theory

Proposed by the French geographer François Perroux (1903–1987), the growth poles theory explains the uneven economic development of different territories and distinguishes the *propulsive* economic sectors that are capable of simulating the development of adjacent areas. This theory has become one of the most prominent and important strategies of the territorial structure development both in the developed and the developing countries.

Although the growth pole theory was originally developed as a purely economic theory focusing on the search for industries and economic sectors that could serve as a motor driving the development of a specific region, it is also closely related to capital cities and opportunities to create countermagnets for the development of a given territory.

Many of the projects discussed above did view capitals and governments as the main industries of their kind, the motors of growth for the underdeveloped parts of the country. Thus, *forward-thrust capitals* were intended to become magnets for migrants from the central parts of the country, serving as the motors of economic growth for the surrounding territories. It was believed that these capitals would lessen the burden on the center and attract resources to the remote parts of the state, making them more economically efficient.

A classic example of growth poles are some new African capitals, which have been set to attract investments and to boost the economy of the poorly developed inner areas.[17] The governments moving to these capitals were expected to become nuclei of growth, producing public benefits, functioning as propulsive industries of their kind, and implementing innovations in the inner territories. In many African nations, notably Nigeria, capital relocation was specifically described as an application of the growth poles theory, whereby the new capital often served as the growth pole of the first order, and its erection was part of the regional development planning.

It is interesting to note that in a sense, the growth pole theory was a result of the impression made by the British capital on Perroux's predecessor William Petty (1623–1687), who had laid the foundations of this theory. Petty saw the seventeenth century London as both the urban motor of economic growth and the basis of England's wealth.[18]

The theory of Perroux may be also viewed as a response to the seminal book *Paris and the French Desert* authored by the French geographer Jean-François Gravier, which was released two years prior to the publication of the theory and which has been already mentioned above in connection with the proposals on capital relocation in France. Perroux believed that the interrelation between Paris and the rest of the country was a negative example of polarization, where the attractiveness of Paris was as strong as to prevent any development beyond it. However, Perroux maintained that polarization did not always have a negative effect as in the case of Paris. Gravier's book reasonably called for some counter-magnets and some alternative to the monocentric dominance of the French capital.

The growth poles theory has been rightfully criticized for being insufficiently realistic and not bringing the desired results. In practice, particularly in the context of building a new capital, the growth was often confined to the boundaries of the city that was considered the actual point of force application. The new city expected to become a growth pole (to do so, it did not necessarily have to be the capital) rarely developed into an epicenter of economic development, remaining poorly integrated with both the countryside and other cities.[19]

World-system analysis

The world-system school proposes to approach the study of capital city functions from the global perspective of power relations.

Contrary to spatial economists and economic geographers, adherents of this approach believe that neither the location nor the transfer of capitals can be fully understood solely on the basis of the country's internal economic and political problems. The logic of capital city siting, growth, and relocation can be grasped only in the context of the international division of labor. Accordingly, they proffer a new typology of capitals that is based on *the nature of relations between the core and the periphery* in the international division of labor.

The founding fathers of the world-system analyses – Immanuel M. Wallerstein and Andre G. Frank, among others – did not specifically address the problems related to capital cities, and it was eventually applied to capitals by their disciples.

Thus, R. Scott Frey and Thomas Dietz have correctly pointed out that the growth rate of capital cities is inversely proportional to their countries' place in the core-periphery system. In the countries of the periphery, capitals grow at a much faster pace than in the countries of the core. This growth rate has little to do with the degree of state intervention in the economy of these countries and is driven by the nature of the international investments in these countries.[20]

Peter Taylor emphasizes that the dominance of any city can be understood only from the outside, in the context of international relations, not from the inside as economists propose to do. With this in mind, he extrapolates the conclusions made by the fathers of the world-system analysis to the global urban hierarchy, distinguishing three types of capitals: *core, peripheral, and semiperipheral capitals*. Peripheral capitals are those of the colonized countries – e.g., African countries – and they were usually sited in the seaports, from which goods were exported to the metropole. Peripheral capitals are monocephalic and, being heavily overpopulated, are characterized by a strong dominance over the rest of the country. As to semiperipheral countries, it is typical for many of them to divide their capital functions between two cities, one of which is usually located on the seacoast – e.g., Saint-Petersburg's "window to Europe" in Russia – and the other one inland – e.g., Moscow in Russia. Examples of semiperipheral countries include Russia, Turkey, Brazil, Pakistan, Nigeria, China, and the United States (as of the end of the eighteenth through the beginning of the nineteenth century).

Followers of the world-system analysis interpret capital relocations in semiperipheral states as attempts to avert the process of peripheralization, attributing capital transfers in the former colonies to the quest for overcoming their subordinate subaltern position in the global capitalist system.[21] Unlike these two groups of countries, states of the core are characterized by a well-balanced urban system; their capitals are monolithic, self-sufficient, and not overpopulated.

Closely related to the world-system theories are the economic theories that view primate cities as parasitic, contrasting them with generative cities. The categories of productive and generative cities were introduced by the

American economist Bert Hoselitz.[22] According to Andre G. Frank, primate cities, as well as many capitals, are nothing but links in the global parasitic system of capitalism.[23]

Contrary to the above theorists, numerous neoliberal economists and political analytics insist on the productivity of the major European capitals, arguing that these capitals subsidize the economies of their respective countries. By the way of example, the financial data these scholars present leads to the conclusion that both London and Paris, often seen as parasitic, in actuality support the economies of multiple regions in the UK and France, respectively, providing subsidies that compose a substantial part of the regional budgets.[24]

Relational theory and network theory

The relational theory may serve as effective methodological guidelines for capital city relocations. This theory holds that cities always exist within a particular system of relations and within a particular urban hierarchy. Therefore, the most significant aspect of capital relocation is not the physical transfer, but rather, the change in the totality of relations within the state and the international system. States emerge as a result of the interaction between the market networks and political networks, and these networks form a determinative influence both on the nature of the emerged states and on their choice of a capital.[25] From this perspective any capital transfer reformats the whole system of network interaction among the cities.

The urban network can be shaped by political factors or by economic factors. The networks shaped by economic hierarchies tend to be more horizontal. Some relational theorists have pointed out that in the larger centralized states having a sufficient number of cities, the urban hierarchy was commonly shaped by political rather than economic factors. The states with a strong national economy saw both the "nationalization" of the largest, cosmopolitan cities and the emergence of the national urban hierarchy, relatively autonomous in relation to the global economy. In this national hierarchy, the capital tended to capture the "gateway" function between the "national" economy and the global economy. London, Paris, and Tokyo are more than four times more connected with the world city network compared to the second cities of these countries. Therefore, the second city of these states – Osaka, Lyon, Manchester, Saint-Petersburg, Melbourne, Rio de Janeiro, etc. – was often put in the position of a loser.[26]

The interdisciplinary social network analysis, as well as the mathematical, graph-theoretic analysis, may also facilitate understanding of the concept of centrality.[27] These analyses distinguish four types of centrality, none of which coincides with the geometric center, and view centrality in terms of (1) closeness, (2) betweenness, (3) number of interactions or volume of interaction, and (4) structural importance.

This classification is indicative of how ambiguous and polysemic the notion of centrality may be. Centrality of a city or region may be determined by its position between the major cities, regions, or ethnic groups, as well as its significance in the system of economic and political interactions. Although the graph-theoretic approach is usually applied to the analysis of technical and social networks, it also has some implications both for the analysis of urban hierarchies in various countries and for the examination of capital siting criteria on the basis of different types of centrality.

Capital city relocation may cause a redistribution of authoritative power or rebuild the urban hierarchy in accordance with the size of the cities, creating a new balance of functional connections among the cities.

* * *

The above theories and analytical methods of evaluating urban hierarchies do not necessarily serve as the ultimate tools for choosing the ideal candidate city to become the capital. They do, however, provide valuable considerations for the analysis of siting options for a capital city, as well as for the relevant strategic planning. Those who propose a new geopolitical positioning for the country or emphasize the need to retain certain strategically important territories often rely on geopolitical theories. The methods of centrography may be used when accessibility of the capital and its administrative efficiency are the top priorities or when it is necessary to delineate the most active economic zone of the country. Where the priority is to ensure development of the hinterlands, the growth pole theory is often resorted to. To identify optimal sites for a new capital within de-centralization and compromise strategies, centrography and network theory can be used.

In addition to the above, there are other interesting approaches to the subject of capital city relocation that stem from the fields of economics and public administration. Thus, Sidney and Richard Turner view the relations between the capital and the periphery in the context of the *principal-agent problem model*. In this model, a capital city is conceived as an agent of the state that can exceed its legitimate power and start acting as a principal.[28] The spatial economic perspective, which may also influence the ideas of capital relocation, will be examined in one of the following subsections.

Last, we should mention a methodological approach that places the emphasis on the consensus building opportunities. Yoshihara Takamura and Kaoru Tone have described the consensus-making method for reaching a group decision and systematically developed the criteria necessary for evaluating different sites. They have proposed to use a combination of the analytic hierarchy process (AHP) and the assurance region model of data envelopment analysis (DEA) to decide the best sites among the contenders. This approach was developed and used for the selection of the site for a new Japanese capital and presented to the "Wise Men" committee.[29]

In the opinion of the author of this book, the theories of nation-building and state-building allow to integrate all of the above analyses and methods so that they can be employed within the framework of these theories.

Three standards to assess the effectiveness of a capital city

The most important measures of performance of national capitals in the modern world are their economic, political, and symbolical efficiency. Each one of these measures or criteria associates with a separate set of questions.

The first set of questions is concerned with the nexus between the size of the capital city and the performance of national economy. Does the co-location of the main economic hub and political capital city facilitate the development of national economy? What reasons would justify such a combination of functions in one city? What are the social and political implications of such a combination? Are there any optimal capital city sizes for any given societies from the point of view of national economy and its dynamics?

The second set of questions explores the nexus between the political constitution of a state (unitary and federalist states) and the character of its capital city. In what ways can the character of a capital city hinder or foster implementation of particular political principles? Do the particular challenges of different political constitutions and different political regimes encounter different governance problems and require specific types of capital cities?

Finally, the third set of questions is concerned with the adequacy of symbols and iconography of the capital city for nature of the state and for realization of its goals and political programs.

These three sets of questions will be discussed in the next three paragraphs.

1 Capital cities as primate cities from the standpoint of spatial economics

By definition, capital cities do not have any specific economic function. However, the *size of a capital city* and its *role and place* in the country greatly influence the development of the national economy. The excessive economic dominance and large size of capital cities relative to the total population of the country is considered by many economists as a serious disadvantage for the national economy. Bruce Herrick has coined the term "hypercephalism" to describe the economic predicament that such countries are facing.[30] As we have seen in our analysis, in some countries hypercephalism and excessive economic dominance of the capital city are used to justify the transfer of the capital city. Table 8 presents a sample of larger countries from different world regions ranked by the level of economic dominance of their capital cities.

As stated before, a primate city is defined as a city that is twice as big as the next city in the urban hierarchy and that plays a disproportional role in the life of the country.[31] Thus, the primacy of a city is determined not by its absolute size but by its role in the urban system. Table 9 shows the Zipf plots representing the urban systems of several countries that highlight the place of their primate cities. The works on primate cities are especially valuable for our study because most capital cities are also primate cities. The majority of political capitals (83 percent) are located in the biggest cities of their respective countries: only in 25 out of 146 relatively big countries the capital is not sited in its largest city.[32]

The existence of a nexus between the size of the primary city and their economic effectiveness was tackled in many works in the field of spatial economics. The authors of these works have tried to bring into a sharper focus the political factors that facilitate the formation of such oversize capital cities, to pinpoint the indicators of their excessive size, and to identify the anomalies and problems that such dominant capital cities can entail. Some of them also have tried to assess and quantify the costs of oversize capital cities for the national economy. Although the said works rarely address the questions about the desirability of capital city transfer, these works have important implications for the subject of our study and offer helpful insights about possible economic and social outcomes of the choice of such cities and their fast pace of growth. They can also help to formulate the standards necessary to evaluate capital city performance.

Corrupt states and their oversize capitals

The primacy is often the effect of capital city status. Capitals as urban giants most often emerge due to a high degree of political centralization and due to the corrupt nature of political regimes. In such countries the capital cities extract rents from their status, and it gives them unfair advantages in the structure of national economy. For that reason these cities often cause resentment and are perceived as parasitic.

In their seminal and widely quoted study Alberto Ades and Edward Glaeser have explored the mechanism explaining the reasons for a high level of concentration of nation's urban population in a single city. In this study they have found robust causality between misgovernance and urban concentration and claimed that capital cities tend to be located in the primate cities of their respective nations. As a consequence, the *non-democratic, unstable, or corrupt states* tend to have larger capitals.[33] In dictatorships and in *unstable states* it might be beneficial for the governments to provide privileged access to material goods for the residents of capital cities in the form of subsidies, higher incomes, lower taxes, and the like to forestall potential political unrest in close proximity to its residence. Moreover, the proximity to the decision-making center increases the chances of unpunished involvement in illegal forms of economic activity such as bribery. The less democratic the country is, the easier it is to put these practice in place.[34] Ades and Glaeser have calculated that in countries where the human rights are not respected, the capital cities are on average 45 percent larger than in more democratic countries.[35] They have argued that unstable dictatorships, fearing overthrow, provide "bread and circuses" for the first city, typically a capital city, to prevent unrest. The most primate-city dominated nations are typically the most corrupt. This capital city bias also provides incentives for migrants to move to such a favored city, contributing to its fast pace of growth.[36]

Thomas Reichart has identified another aspect of this situation, the proximity to legislation, law-making, and attendant informational benefits.[37] Since laws are adopted in the capital city, proximity to the political center provides special informational benefits that are critically important for business activities under the condition of uncertainty in unstable political regimes. Such proximity permits businesses to quickly respond to the changes in legislation and sometimes to influence the decisions.[38]

The corrupt states provide rent-sharing benefits associated with capital city status and better opportunities to the residents of capital cities such as better wages, jobs, better infrastructure, and higher standards of living to buy off the population of these largest cities and to prevent popular uprisings. They concentrate national resources in the national capital, creating the enclaves of metropolitan wealth. In many cases the bureaucracies in such corrupt states control the whole of the economic life of the country. The more important the role of government and bureaucracy, the more crucial it is for businesses and lobbyists to reside in the capital and the faster the city grows. This tendency can be illustrated with the example of such countries as Russia, Argentina, and Zimbabwe, all ranked very high on the corruption perception index. Although crude-oil and gas recovery is centered in the eastern part of Russia, most of the headquarters of the largest gas and oil corporations are located in Moscow. The headquarters of major Argentinian companies and licensing of foreign trade activities are concentrated in Buenos Aires, providing benefits for the capital city's elite, while most of the country's agricultural and mineral wealth is generated in the provinces. In Zimbabwe the diamonds, one of the main sources of the country's wealth, are mined in Mutare, while the head offices of Mbanda Diamonds are located in the capital Harare.

The insights of Ades and Glaeser's have been confirmed and qualified in a number of other studies extending and tailoring this analysis to different regions of the world, notably to Asia and Latin America,[39] and in cross-country comparison of capital cities in North and South America.[40] These studies also have suggested that the phenomenon of capital cities gigantism is much more pronounced in poor countries with lower GDP and is more evident in the countries of Latin America.

The statecraft technique that implied the provision of metropolitan residents with special benefits was known already to Niccolò Machiavelli. In *The Prince* the weak rulers are advised to strengthen and fortify the capital cities where they dwell, establish good relations with the subjects in this city, and take no heed to the country outside. The subjects in the capital city should feel the need for the State and for the ruler. It is difficult to attack a Prince whose town is strengthened in this manner, claims Machiavelli.[41] It must be noted though that this advice is preserved only for the weak rulers, and Machiavelli calls the state of this sort "weak," because its good governance is sufficient only for a part of its citizens.

The nexus between the large size of the capital city and the level of corruption established by Ades and Glaeser does not apply equally to all countries. Their conclusions explain well the reasons for capital city gigantism in highly centralized and territorially larger states such as Russia, Argentina, Mexico, and many African and Asian countries. Having high levels of corruption, these countries are also showing wider gaps between capital cities and the rest of the country in terms of their living conditions.

The spatial economists believe that political de-centralization, the openness of trade, and lower tariffs can help to eliminate the gaps between the primate cities and the rest of the country and integrate smaller cities into the international economic system.[42] Conversely, the world-system theorists believe that hyper-centralization, the concentration of all resources in the primate city, and the anomalies of urban development that it entails stem from the openness of the economy of these countries and their outward orientations. They believe that such imbalance in the urban system results from the investments into big cities that are coming from the world capitalist system.

Oversize capitals in developed nations

The nexus between the political regime of the state and its urban system discovered by Ades and Glaeser can explain the primate city dominance in many countries, but it is much less helpful in the explanation of capital city gigantism and their high growth rate in developed democracies. The wealth and large size of some capital cities such as London, Paris, and Tokyo compared to other cities in these countries cannot be explained only by their parasitic rent-extraction potential and by the corrupt nature of the political regimes that exist in these countries.

One of the possible explanations is that these capital cities serve as the economic capitals of the world regions that are much larger than their national economies. London and Paris are located in the core of the world economy and play the role of primary cities in their respective mega-regions. In economically developed countries the disproportional size of their capitals can be explained to some extent by their prominent transnational role in the international trade as they serve as economic centers not only of their national economy but also as the hubs of the mega-regional and global economy. If we take London and Paris as the major economic hubs of Europe and follow the logic of Zipf Law, than their population should be about 25 million citizens.[43] Hence, London and Paris are not excessively large cities relative to the cities of the whole of Europe. By the same token, Tokyo stands at the apex of the Asian urban hierarchy. This effect should be magnified for London, the most important financial center unequalled even by such transnational financial centers as New York and Frankfurt.

London and Paris are also not too large in absolute terms compared to mega-cities in other world regions. The agglomeration effects and the large labor markets are necessary for these cities to produce their wealth effects. The larger and more competitive labor markets in general are more efficient; higher labor costs and lower commodity costs result from spatial rapprochement of production and consumption, which further leads to reduction in transport charges.[44] The large size also contributes to the innovative and creative potential of these cities due to intellectual spillovers and cross-pollination between different industries.

It is a consensus of the economists that every time the size of the city doubles, productivity and innovation per resident increases by 10–15 percent due to the economies of scale effects in large labor markets.[45] Accordingly, economies of scale reduce costs and increase average income of citizens by approximately 15 percent.[46] Subject to certain constraints, cumulative results of all the agglomeration effects manifest themselves in rapid growth of the city economy.

Many economists argue that these advantages not only induce the development of these larger cities but create benefits for the national economy within which they function. Being international centers with high productivity, London and Paris act like donors for the regions. The rest of the UK and France, the argument goes, benefits from the trickle-down effect produced by their prosperous capital cities.[47] So in a way they compensate other cities for their disproportional role in the life of these countries and their economic dominance.

The applicability of Ades and Glaeser's findings to the territorially smaller states is also problematic. The area of the country has important bearing on the decisions about the optimal size and organization of the capital city. The size of the country tends to be inversely related to the size of its capital.[48] Accordingly, in most of the territorially large countries – USA, China, Australia, and Brazil – capitals are sited in relatively small cities. Conversely, many countries with smaller areas have larger capital cities with a higher proportion of their population being concentrated there. Many of them are monocephalic, that is more than 20 percent of the urban population of these countries resides in their largest cities.[49]

In sum, in smaller countries the transfer of the seat of government to smaller cities can lead to economic inefficiencies, because it would deprive larger cities of their agglomeration benefits or at least significantly reduce them. These benefits can be achieved only in one place because these countries typically have only one city that is large enough to accrue agglomeration benefits.[50] Hence the opponents of capital city transfers in relatively small countries such as South Korea and some countries in Eastern Europe have argued that a capital city shift can render their economies less efficient by reducing or taking away the agglomeration advantages from their preeminent cities. So they have at least one good reason to keep the seat of government in the main economic hub of the country.

Capital city premiums and public policy

The wealth of the capital cities under democracies does not always originate in their higher level of productivity, entrepreneurship, innovations, and agglomeration effects associated with the large size of these cities. Generally democratic regimes do not eliminate political and economic benefits for the residents of national capitals. However, the privileged status of capital city residents under democracies is rarely comparable to the capital city utility for the metropolitan residents under corrupt political regimes. To illustrate, while the incomes in Moscow on average were 3–4 times higher than the average for the rest of Russia, the incomes in London were only 40% higher than the average for the rest of the UK.[51] Still, even smaller capital city premiums can cause some social and political problems and tensions, and it would be a mistake to underestimate the range of negative social outcomes associated with the sharp divide between the capital city and the rest of the countries. At the very least they deserve acknowledgement and the most serious attention of both researchers and policy makers.

In addition to higher incomes capital city residents have other advantages. Capital cities produce public goods and peculiar capital city goods that are not easily available to people in the rest of the country. The residents of capital cities have privileged access to these goods and are their main beneficiaries. Kristof Dascher has explained this phenomenon as a distance-decay effect or higher spoilage of public goods with the distance from the capital city. The further is one's distance from the capital city, the fewer benefits one can receive from these public goods. Such situations represent deviations from the principles of fiscal equivalence since these public goods are financed by all the citizens of the country, and metropolitan residents do not pay anything extra for them.

Horst Zimmerman has identified four groups of factors that create benefits for capital cities in democratic countries and have quantified some of them.

The most obvious benefit of a capital city for its residents is the availability of a large number of jobs in the public sector, which is a direct result of the residence of the government in the city. The government also creates a high level of demand for goods and services within the capital region. Taking into account the fact that in many states the government is the major employer, the economic benefits of such a situation may be very significant. Comparing current and former regional capital cities of Germany, Kristof Dascher estimates that jobs' gains directly related to capital city status are about 7 percent of the overall employment level in the region.[52]

The second set of benefits is related to the fact that capital cities tend to attract private companies, groups, and organizations that perform services exclusively for the national government (NGOs, lobbyists, consultants, political parties, embassies, private research institutes, etc.). For example, in the case of Germany the benefit for the economy of a capital city of this type is about 4 percent GRP (Gross Regional Product).

Many private companies also set up their operations in the capital city, working as suppliers, subcontractors, and consultants of organizations from the second group. Companies providing software and information technologies may serve as an example.

There have been also some valuable estimates of the causal effects of capital city designations, including employment and spillovers in the private sector. Brian Quistorff reported that for every additional government job that was created in Brasília, an addition 1.7 non-public jobs were created.[53] Jörg Stahl also has shown that within the two days following the decision to move the capital from Bonn to Berlin, the private firms with operational headquarters in Berlin experienced mean cumulative abnormal returns of about 3 percent.[54]

Capital cities also provide a significant amount of economic benefits due to their symbolic functions. The main cultural and educational institutions are increasingly concentrated in the capital city, stimulating tourism and other related industries in these cities.[55] To exemplify, tourism brings half the revenue of some prominent capital cities such as Paris and London. Tellingly, the transfer of the capital of Germany to Berlin has made it the most important tourist destination in the country, and it remains the fastest growing tourist city in Europe.

It must be noted that differential regional growth and uneven regional development in general can hardly be regarded as an anomaly. Economic inequality may serve as an additional incentive for economic growth of a country as a whole. The libertarian economists have argued for a long time that the gain of the capital/primary city does not necessarily represent a loss for the regions, and the relationship between the two should not be judged on the basis of the zero-sum game rivalry. This is what Herst Zimmerman meant when he contrasted the allocative and redistributive principles in the socio-political sphere. While the distributive principle is aiming to achieve equality and/or justice, the allocative principle aims to achieve the economic efficiencies associated with cumulative benefits of larger capital cities at a higher level.[56] Moving a capital city to less developed regions would imply under this interpretation the use of the distributive principle, and it might be viewed as less efficient from the standpoint of total benefits.

However, economic dominance of larger capital cities may take such forms and scales that it would be difficult to justify it based on the allocative principle of development. Such dominance or hegemony can manifest itself in the elements of macroeconomic policies and in the design of the national transportation networks that create extremely unfavorable conditions for the residents of neighboring cities and regions and make their competition for resources difficult and almost impossible.[57]

The most striking example of such inefficiency would be a situation when the size of the capital city will become a reason for its own economic inefficiency and will hinder its own economic potential. This type of situation might arise in cases of low return on investments due to high costs of the factors of production (land, labor, and capital) and the high level of transportation expenses.

Several metrics have been suggested to measure the inefficiency of the metropolis. Allain Bertaud along with some other urban scholars consider the average commuting travel time to be one of the critical measurements of the efficiency of metropolises. The work place should – at least potentially – be physically accessible from the place of residence of all households within about an hour travel time. Whenever this average time exceeds one hour, the labor market of the metropolis is considered fragmented, and it becomes economically inefficient. This situation contradicts the very economic raison d'etre of larger metropolis, the increasing return to scale procured by a large integrated labor market.[58] Notably, some prominent capital cities are not doing well on this point. In London the average commute time in 2014 was 74.2 minutes.[59] In Beijing and Moscow the average commute times are in excess of 90 minutes. Traffic jams in Jakarta cost the city at least US$3 billion each year, according to the country's Transportation Ministry.

Therefore the design of the transportation system together with the morphology and size of the capital city can suggest some limits to the growth of the metropolis serving as a measure of its efficiency. The designation of capital city to such a metropolis only exacerbates its problems. The co-location of these functions might be efficient only for smaller states.

Conceptually the problem of primate city costs in terms of their diseconomies of scale was well formulated by Vernon Henderson.[60] He has distinguished two types of costs associated with the primacy and economic dominance of capital cities. He labeled the first type of expenses *internal costs* of the large city that include congestion, traffic jams, the pressures on transport infrastructure, pollution and other environmental issues, housing, long commute times, and perhaps emotional costs, among other size disamenities.

The second type of expenses are the *external expenses* that include the less obvious costs associated with public investments and spending on capital city infrastructure and its modernization necessary for maintenance of life in such large cities and the improvement of their deteriorating quality of life. These types of expenses are covered by the national government, and they tend to become a heavy burden for the whole country. It would be fair to say that these costs are incurred at the expense of other cities within a country.[61]

In economic terms the "external expenses" can be described as negative externalities for all those positive effects that accrue to larger cities.

To summarize, when the total economic and social costs of the metropolis exceed the economic benefits that result from their agglomeration benefits, their existence is losing their raisons d'être. The city is too large if it reduces the total welfare of the country. Under the circumstances the transfer of the capital city can be one of the options to make the metropolis more economically viable especially if other options – the fundamental reconstruction of the city, changing its morphology, developing a new Central Business District (CBD) and the like – are not available. The most problematic are the situations when the capital city provides excessive advantages to its residents beyond the natural advantages associated with agglomeration benefits and the expected advantages associated with the contributions of these cities to the level and character of employment. Under such circumstances the capital city distorts the natural economic laws that govern the inter-urban relationships. The rent-extraction potential conferred on these cities will be derived from purely political factors and its capital city status.

Thus, the capital city economic efficiency will be negative when it precludes or hinders the economic development of the country as a whole and when its maintenance consumes excessive resources from the national economy. In this case the co-location of the capital city and major economic hub will be inefficient. Under these circumstances the movement of the seat of government elsewhere might be able to ease pressure on a capital's infrastructure and its property prices.

Generally the political factors tend to influence the decisions and the effectiveness of capital cities more than the economic factors.

Political effectiveness of capital city: federal vs. unitary states

The political constitution of the state plays a fundamental role in the formation of the urban hierarchy and often determines the size of the largest city. Paul Krugman has aptly argued that "federalism is the single most clear-cut factor affecting the degree of urban concentration."[62]

The smaller capitals are most suitable for the federalist political arrangement. The idea that informs the federation is that the capital city should not be dominant among the federated entities such as states, provinces, *länder*, republics, prefectures, or other units. Therefore in such prominent world federations as the US, Canada, Australia, New Zealand, India, Germany, Switzerland, South Africa, Brazil, United Arab Emirates, and the Netherlands (Republic of United Provinces), the seats of government are not sited in the largest city. The capital city transfers in most of these countries have often been provoked at least in part by the federation-building considerations.

This rule is not universal and in some federations capital cities are sited in the primate cities. However, as we will see further, this type of capital city had often caused various problems for the functioning of these federations, mostly the problems of over-centralization. Oddly, in their level of centralization some of these federations surpassed their unitary counterparts. For instance, Russia, Argentina, and Mexico are much more centralized countries compared to many unitary states such as the UK and Japan. Arguably, it would be more accurate to describe them as unitary states with some federalist features. In general by and large the federalist states with smaller and neutral capitals tend to be more successful both economically and politically.

In what follows, we will first provide some historical illustrations of the critically important role that the choice of capital cities has played in the formation and functioning of the federations. First, we will provide some examples of the prospective federations that failed due to the problematic choice of their capitals. Second, we will briefly describe three models of federalist capital cities, their merits and potential drawbacks. Last, we will discuss the most important components of the American capital city model that represents some of the quintessential features of the federalist capital.

Federation formation and capitals

There were several prospective federalist states that have failed at least in part due to the capital city issues, notably the controversies surrounding the choice of their capital cities. These are the West Indies Federation, the Federation of Gulf States, the United Provinces of Central America, and Mexico. In each one of these cases capital city predicaments have contributed to some sort of failure: the emergent federal state was either never formed; was short-lived; was not implemented in its original scope; or severely limited or constrained the implementation of federalist values, interests, and agendas.

In 1947 the efforts to establish a new federation of the West-Indies States that was envisaged to encompass 10 former colonies of the British Empire in the Caribbean (Jamaica, Trinidad and Tobago, Barbados, Grenada, Montserrat, Dominica, and other islands) raised the question about a new capital city of this federation. Originally the cities on the territories of the three largest prospective members of the federation – Jamaica, Barbados, and Trinidad and Tobago – have been given most serious consideration. Later on the candidacy of a smaller island of Grenada has been proposed. The smaller size of this island and the state where it was located warranted its neutrality relative to other member states. However, after much discussion and deliberation, the Chaguaramas site in close proximity to Port-of-Spain, the capital of Trinidad and Tobago, had been selected as a final candidate. Oscar Niemeyer, the chief architect of Brasília, had been invited to prepare the Master Plan for the new city to be built there. However, in the course of the preparation process some technical difficulties had arisen as this site was located right next to the US military base and it never left this site. The main reason for the failure of this federation project, however, were the misgivings of other member states about the special privileges that Trinidad would acquire with a capital on its territory. Port-of-Spain served as a *de facto* capital city of the federation during a short-course of its existence, and the federated entities understood that the building of the new capital in its close proximity will reinforce the predominance of Trinidad and Tobago.[63]

Assessing effectiveness of a capital city 243

The same type of concerns and confrontations regarding the location of the capital city contributed to the fiasco of the Federation of the Emirates of the Persian Gulf in its originally envisioned scope. The initial vision of this federation encompassed not only the current seven emirates of the UAE but also two other former British protectorates – Qatar and Bahrain. The Constitution of 1971 provided for the construction of the new capital city Al Karama on the border between the two largest of the seven emirates, Abu Dhabi and Dubai. This city has never been built, and the reluctance of Qatar and Bahrain to accept the capital city in Abu Dhabi has led to their refusal to participate in this emerging federation. The five smaller emirates have insisted on the capital city between Dubai and Sharjah, the capital of the emirate with the same name, fearing that Abu Dhabi will be too dominant. However, at the end these seven emirates have reached a compromise and agreed to accept the capital in Abu Dhabi as a provisional solution. Currently, a new capital is being built at least in part to placate the concerns of other member-states.

Another example is taken from the history of Central America where another short-lived federated state was formed, the United Provinces of America (1823–1840) that encompassed five states (Guatemala, Nicaragua, El Salvador, Honduras, and Costa Rica). In 1832 the capital city of this federation was moved from Guatemala, the capital of the country with the same name, to San Salvador in El Salvador. San Salvador provided a more central geographical location relative to all other member states. More importantly, the member states were concerned that Guatemala, the larger and stronger country was receiving special privileges within the federation. The conflicts between the member states, the victory of conservatives over liberal federalists within member states, and the paucity of transportation networks for integration have led to the dissolution of this federation although several new attempts have been made to reach a consensus.

Finally, the case of Mexico illustrates another type of capital city predicament. Whereas in our previous examples the disagreements and contestation between member states about the capital city led to the demise of the federation, in Mexico the choice of the capital city weakened the prospects of the country's development into a federalist state. After the War of Independence (1810–1821) in 1824 the government debated the new Constitution and the choice of a capital city.[64] The capital city question emerged in the context of the debates between the federalists (liberals) and the centralists (conservatives). The federalists urged to draw on experience of the USA and to move the capital city to Querétaro (Santiago de Querétaro), located in the central northern part of the state. In contrast to other provinces of the colonial era Querétaro was not a province and had a status of a special type of administrative unit *corregimiento de letras* that was favorable for capital city function in the context of federation. After the US troops entered Mexico City in the course of the Mexican-American War, Santiago de Querétaro served for a short period of time as the seat of government. However, eventually the federalists lost to the conservatives in their political confrontations, and the capital city was moved back to Mexico City after the end of the war.[65] Today Mexican politicians are attempting to adopt a federalist model of government and seriously consider the need to federalize the country; however, the impulse of federation-building has been largely compromised at least in part due to the dominant character of Mexico City and its hegemonic status in the country.

Among other matters, the inability to identify the capital city that would be agreeable for all federal subunits and that would help to reach the parity of their interests in a new state was one of the reasons for the failure of all the above mentioned projects. The lack of consensus regarding the common capital in each one of these cases hindered plans to establish a new federation or to federalize the already existing unitary country.

The importance of the choice of capital city in federations was recently underscored and given a new actuality in the context of federation-building efforts in such countries as Bolivia, Somalia, Libya, Nepal, and Ukraine plagued by many domestic conflicts. The federalizing motives also play a significant role in the debates about the new capital city of the UK. The proponents of the new capital cities of these countries argue that they can help to ameliorate the ethnic and clan cleavages and the regional disparities that cause the instability of these countries. The new capital city topic is even more poignant in the proposed federations such as the East African Federation consisting of Burundi, Kenya, Rwanda, Tanzania, and Uganda. The Tanzanian city of Arusha close to the Kenyan border was proposed as its capital. It remains to be seen how these countries will handle this problem.

The variety of capital city models in federations

The founding of the federation involves not only the choice of the location for the city but also the choice of the federal capital model. In fact the choice of this model often influences the choice of the location for the capital. Different types of federations have chosen different ways to organize their capital city function. The research in the field of comparative federalism illuminates the differences between various capital city concepts, their advantages and shortcomings.[66] The capital cities can be treated as member-states of federations like Brussels in Belgium or Berlin in Germany; they can be a part of the member-states like Ottawa in Canada, or they can be special units directly governed by the federal government like Washington D.C. These different arrangements of the capital city function can be more or less suitable for different goals and can perform better or worse than others in promoting specific goals. Member-state model and "city-in-a-member-state" models give an unfair advantage to the city and state where the capital is situated. On the other hand, the district model is better equipped to serve against the encroachments of the particular states and to secure the neutrality of the capital. It also provides a better opportunity to reflect the diversity of the federation and to ward off excessive centralization, especially in comparison with the member-state model. However, it creates disadvantages for the residents of the district in terms of the opportunities for self-rule and representation in the government. The "city-in-a-member-state" model can be better for a federation when the capital is not sited in the largest city of the member state. For instance, Ottawa is located in the province of Ontario, the largest city of which is Toronto.

The large primate city as a capital city tends to weaken the federative principles and contributes the most to over-centralization. The over-centralized federations where the central government has almost unlimited powers often have a primary city as their capital. Austria, Belgium, and Mexico are much more centralized compared to Switzerland and Anglo-Saxon federations, where the competences for subunits and central government are more delineated. The extreme example of such an over-centralized federation that hollows out the very substance of federalism is Russia, which also has a large primate city as its capital. The federalization efforts in Mexico and Ethiopia seem to be more painful and difficult because of their dominant capitals.

The choice of the capital city model involves some important trade-offs. In some cases, notably in the US, the local and regional interests of the metropolitan residents and capital region in general are sacrificed to preserve the federative principle. The asymmetrical relationship between the capital and other member states emphasizes the intermediary function of capital cities. This arrangement is designed to prevent the transformation of the capital into a pole of particular political or economic interests and to prevent the abuse of their representational function.

Washington D.C. model

In this context it is important to discuss in a little more detail the origins and the peculiar features of the capital city model of the United States in Washington D.C. The importance of this city for our topic – its history, urban design, and its institutional organization – lies not only in its own peculiar features but also in the fact that it has served as a model and precedent to be emulated by many federalist states. Directly or indirectly it has inspired the construction of the new capital cities in such countries as Canada, Australia, New Zealand, South Africa, and Brazil.

The American federation is an example of the symmetrical federation where all member states have equal rights. The concept of the Federal District is an institute that aimed to secure the balance of power of the states. The United States has created an entirely new and unique type of city as its capital. According to the capital city model that was chosen, the Federal District is not represented in the Congress and it is not a part of the jurisdiction of any one of the member states. The US House of Representatives has only one representative in the Federal District who does not have voting privileges. The goal of the Federal District is to serve the interests of all states and hence it is governed directly by the central government.

In terms of governance the role of the local and municipal authorities in Washington D.C. is significantly limited and the governance is executed directly by the federal government. This arrangement minimizes the role of the city in the capital city to the point that the functions of self-governance essential for the city are significantly curtailed. In theory, this makes it possible for Washington D.C. to serve the purposes of all constituent units composing the state.

Early on the founding fathers have decided that the federalist capital should be smaller and neutral to host the administrative functions more effectively. Curiously, it has been described by some founding fathers as nothing more than "the Village on Capitol Hill."[67] The capital itself was a civil servant who should not be an independent and self-serving subject of decision-making.

The decision about the location of the capital city was made in the course of negotiations and compromise with the southern states (Residence Act of 1790). In 1790, Alexander Hamilton proposed a bill that the national government should assume the unpaid war debts of the states. The southern states opposed this bill claiming that it grants the national government undue power over the states. They had already paid off nearly all of their debts while the northern states lagged behind. The South also opposed the location of the national capital on the territory of northern states. The capital city location issue helped the two parties to reach a compromise. Making a concession to the South, the North agreed to site the new capital city in a southern locale near the Potomac River in Virginia. In exchange the southern representatives accepted the assumption of the northern state revolutionary war debts by the federal government.

The concept of the federal capital city of the US can be better understood as an element in the checks and balances system that was built into the political system of the US by the founding fathers. Balancing of different elements was an essential part of this system. The US Constitution provides for the balance between executive, legislative, and judicial branches of government. The Presidency and the US Congress, consisting of the two chambers, the Senate and the House of Representatives, correspond to the Aristotelian monarchical, aristocratic, and democratic principles that also balance each other. The capital city concept can also be seen as a natural complement of the checks and balances system. While the checks and balances focused on the separation of the branches of government, the establishment of the new federal capital city facilitated the balance between the federal subunits, on the one hand, and the major cities, on the other.[68] The separation of the federal capital city from the major economic hubs in NYC and Philadelphia was intended to provide balances in the urban system of the country. It also helped to neutralize the merchant classes in New York and Philadelphia, potentially loyal to the British government. Notably, the concept of checks and balances found its expression not only in the design of institutions but also in the morphology of Washington D.C. as its key architectural elements and landmarks represent the branches of government in the very triangular morphology of the capital.

Washington D.C. started its own tradition and became a unique capital having little in common with the capitals of universal empires, the disembedded capitals of despotic states, and the large monocephalic capital cities of Europe. It was tasked to represent the nation, reflecting the diverse interests of the federated entities, serving as a basis of a new covenant. Having in mind the capital city model of the United States, Daniel Elazar had provocatively argued that "true federal systems do not have capitals, they have seats of government. 'Capital' implies a place at the top of the governmental pyramid, whereas 'seat' appropriately suggests a place of assembly."[69] He has placed the American capital in the same league as Jerusalem and Rome, arguing that Washington D.C. is rather a grand idea of political organization and human association than a geographical name. Therefore, the concept of the American capital city, being based on the covenant tradition in both religious and secular sense, he has further argued, occupies a unique place in the development of human civilization.

Washington D.C. hardly can be portrayed today as a humble *Village on the Capitol Hill* as it was described by the founding fathers, and arguably it never was. It is a city region with a thriving economy and with one of the highest income levels per capita in the US.[70] However, the fundamental principles of neutrality critical for the covenant and ingrained in the concept of the Federal District remain intact.

Capitals of federated units

The capital cities of federal subunits such as states, provinces, and lands in the US, Canada, and Germany often follow the same locational logic as their federal capitals. Sacramento serves as a capital of California, Austin as a capital of Texas, Albany as a capital of New York, and Tallahassee serves as a capital of Florida. All of them are substantially smaller than the largest cities of their respective states, and many have been chosen because of their neutrality or geographic centrality in their respective states. Notably, Tallahassee, the capital of Florida, was founded in the compromise location between the two largest cities, Pensacola and St. Augustine. Legend has it that the place was chosen because it was where the two commissioners appointed by the governor met. One rode on horseback from St. Augustine and the other sailed by boat from Pensacola. The tradition of smaller capital cities was also adopted in India, whose political culture was greatly influenced by Anglo-Saxon political traditions. Accordingly, the capitals of many Indian states and union territories are located in the smaller cities of their respective federal subunits. The recent partitions of several Indian states prompted the relocation of their seats of government to relatively small cities. The current proposals to move the capitals of federated entities out of overcrowded cities like Mumbai, Kolkata, Chennai, Hyderabad, Bengaluru, Patna, and Lucknow also reflect the preference of many Indian politicians for a more polycentric urban structure consistent with their federal system.

3 Symbolic effectiveness of capital cities

Largely determining the political success or failure of any capital city, the symbolic function appears no less important than the political function. The character of the national symbols and iconography indicates both the level of representativeness of the capital and its potential for integration.

The effectiveness of the symbolic function has three aspects: (1) symbolic inclusivity or representativeness with respect to all the participants in the national project of the capital city; (2) integration of the symbolic and performative functions of the capital; and (3) integration of the national and universal symbols within the capital.

Symbolic Inclusivity assumes that the micro-narratives of various constituent groups of the nation are reflected both in the visual image of the capital city and in the metanarratives embodied in this image. Thus, the visual space of the capital city incorporates the identities of its constituent members, regions, lands, states, republics, and ethnic and social groups. The avenues in Washington D.C., bear the names of the US states, and in some instances the size and location of an avenue is indicative of the role the state played in the American Revolution or in the formation of the American nation. Massachusetts and Pennsylvania Avenues – the two most important transportation arteries of the US capital – occupy the central place in the communication system and the symbolic structure of the city. The central avenues of Canberra – Brisbane Avenue, Adelaide Avenue, Union Avenue, etc. – are laid out in such a way as if they connect the previously scattered Australian colonies.

Even the construction material may have a symbolic meaning. For example, the materials used in the erection of the Australian Parliament House were brought from different parts of the Australian federation. The Capitol building in Washington D.C., contains monuments and sculptures made of the materials specific to the various US states. The frescoes of the Canadian Parliament building depict the plants and animals from all of the provinces of Canada.[71] The interiors of the Moscow subway stations are decorated with rocks and minerals mined in different regions of the Soviet Union. Furthermore, toponymy of a capital city often includes place names of various geographical areas of the country.

Not only does a capital city represent the identities of various constituent states or lands, it also embodies the identities of the lesser ethnic groups. To illustrate, the Three Power Squares in Brasília features a sculpture dedicated to the small Indian tribe of Candangos, who live on the territory designated as the site for the capital and took an active part in the construction of Brasília. The name of Canada's and Australia's capitals were borrowed from the indigenous languages. A multiplicity of narratives – including micro-narratives – embodied in the reference points of the city, enhances the symbolic inclusivity and strengthens the integration potential of the new capital.

It is interesting to note the presence of some sort of symbolic continuity between the modern designed capitals and those of the ancient empires and despotic states. Thus, in ancient Egypt, religious centers of the capitals sought to incorporate holy shrines and pantheons of local deities. When the Chinese kingdoms were unified under the Qin Dynasty (third century BC), the capital city of Xianyang, purposefully sited near the ancient Zhou-era sacred capital of Qixia (Qishan), saw the integration of the religious cults practiced in the conquered kingdoms. In the vicinity of Xianyang, Emperor Qin Shi Huang built replicas of the palaces of the local rulers (*zhuhou*), thereby transferring, at least partly, the legacy of the local capitals, along with the sacredness of the altars of lands and grain, to the new imperial capital. He also ordered to move the ceremonial bronze bells and drums, which were part of the local religious cults and had been confiscated from the capitals of the conquered kingdoms, to his palaces. These actions strengthened the status of Xianyang as the sole sacred center of China, consolidating all political and religious authority in the country.[72] Similar processes took place in other countries. Thus, the Assyrian palace gardens became the place where plants and animals from the various parts of the country were conserved. Rulers of the Tsardom of Moscow were bringing the most venerated Russian Orthodox icons from other cities to their capital: the Christ Pantocrator from Novgorod, the Annunciation from Veliky Ustyug, the Hodegetria from Smolensk, the Virgin of Vladimir, the Image of Edessa and Saint Nicholas Velikoretsky from Khlynov, etc.[73] However, this form of symbolic integration had a different meaning in the old imperial and despotic states than in the modern states. While in the past its objective was to attain sacredness and to diminish private identities, today its emphasis is on inclusivity.

The most successful countries manage to create public spaces in their capitals, which allow to represent, localize, and integrate the social protest movements, thus promoting inclusivity.

Performativity. The effectiveness of symbols is also manifested in their performative and interactive nature, as well as in their relations with national rituals and ceremonies. As a result, symbols take on a special meaning and dictate certain standards of behavior. Performativity and symbology are best connected in designed capitals since the forms of these capitals are specifically created for the purpose of ceremonial activities, whereby the very organization of space encourages solemn national holidays and festivities, and the symbols of space correlate both with the symbols of time and with the national celebrations taking place in the capital.

According to the Canadian urban planners who participated in the development of the new image of Ottawa, a capital city is a place where "the *past* is highlighted, the *present* displayed and the *future imagined*."[74] The performative function ensures exactly this type of a relationship between space and time. The symbolism of some of the new capitals, as well as their accentuation of the connection between space and rituals, is as complex, sophisticated, and multilayered as that of the ancient sacred capitals.

Mikhail Vilkovsky, a Russian sociologist of architecture, points to Washington D.C., as an example of a successful performative and symbolic capital system.[75] In this city, the past, the present, the future, and the eternal are divided *among the four cardinal points* surrounding the unifying symbolic center of the Washington Monument with an observation deck on its top. As the seat of the government, the White House embodies the present; the Jefferson Memorial symbolizes the past glory and history of America; the Capitol represents the future since this is where the inauguration of the future President takes place and where he delivers his inaugural address; last but not least, the Lincoln Memorial embodies the eternal values of America while the Arlington cemetery immortalizes the everlasting glory of the American soldier.[76] Thus, all the major national ceremonies, including their various stages and steps, fit into this system and are in harmony with it.

This is how Vilkovsky describes the effect of the public participation in the presidential inauguration, embedded, in the performative way, in the symbolic architecture of the US capital:

> The inauguration ceremony carries a symbolic meaning in tune with the symbolic geography of Washington, DC. First, the President-Elect [Barack Hussein Obama] . . . arrives in the White House (the symbol of the present) where he is met by the incumbent President . . . . Thereafter they both leave for the Capitol (the symbol of the future). . . . At noon the Chief Justice of the United States swears in the President-Elect. Taking the oath, the former looks to the past, represented by the Jefferson Memorial, whereas the latter looks to present, represented by the White House. Afterward the President appeals to the eternal, embodied by the Arlington cemetery, and delivers his inaugural address. Then the President's motorcade triumphantly departs from the Capitol to the White House (the present). . . . And at last, the finale of the official ceremony, a parade reviewed by the new President standing on the podium in the front of the White House and, thus, juxtaposed against the present.
>
> The US law enforcement authorities estimate that as many as two million people attended the inauguration of the 44th President of the US at The National Mall park area between the Capitol and the Washington Monument. This includes the 240,000 people who had the opportunity to view it from in front of the Capitol. Events like this certainly bring the nation together.

Vilkovsky contrasts this ceremony with the Russian presidential inauguration, much less efficient in terms of its inclusivity:

> Only a handful of people viewed the Dmitry Medvedev [2008] inauguration ceremony live. These were the 2,000 officials allowed into the Georgievsky and Andreevsky Halls [of the Grand Kremlin Palace], 0.1% of the number of attendees at the Obama inauguration. Such an attendance does not . . . bring the government closer to the public. The inauguration took place in but one location, inside the Grand Kremlin Palace simultaneously symbolizing the past, the present, the future, and the eternal. This arrangement was fully compatible both with the singularity of Moscow's architecture and the concentration of its symbolic resources.[77]

Thus, both the symbology and performative potential of a capital city ensure, to a greater or lesser degree, the public participation in important national ceremonies and events. A major indicator of performative effectiveness is the access to the public space, which is especially important for a capital city. In this regard, urbanists distinguish three types of such access: visual, symbolic, and physical.[78] The more opportunities to participate in national rituals in the public space, the greater the symbolic access. A broader democratic access to the public spaces, along with their performative openness, enables a capital city to carry out its integrative function more efficiently, allowing its inhabitants to relate to their city as the national capital. Opportunities for mass participation in the major national ceremonies and events constitute a considerable benefit of the public spaces.

Relation to the metanarratives. Both the popularity of the capital's symbology and the efficiency of its symbolic resources are largely determined by how global they are. Therefore, many capital cities emphasize their universal appeal and their relation to the narratives of world history. Essentially, the capitals of modernism are nodes of the Enlightenment and Modernization: the modernist structures of Brasília, avenues of Saint-Petersburg, telecommunication and technology symbolism of Putrajaya, and administrative buildings of Delhi – all of them embody this universality and the vision of their role in the global processes. The imagination of the authors of these projects have led to incorporation of their respective countries into the framework of globality and modernization, absorbing them into the extended family of civilized nations where they have their own unique mission.

The connection with the global metanarratives does not necessarily have to be established using the symbols of technological progress or those of global economy; it may very well be built by stressing historical continuity and making architectural allusions to the major ancient centers that engendered the underlying achievements and values of the world civilization, notably Rome, Jerusalem, or Memphis. Numerous nations have sought to symbolically recreate Rome in their capitals. For example, Napoleon attempted to turn Paris into a new Rome.[79] Such efforts developed the multilayered semiotics of urban space in the cities where they were made.

It may be inferred from the above that national capitals are not only inward-oriented but also outward-oriented. Unsatisfied with the focusedness on their own symbols, they are open to the symbolic languages of the surrounding world and mindful of the chain of historical continuity. This approach explains the strong presence of Masonic symbols in the buildings and street layouts of Brasília, Canberra, Saint-Petersburg, and Washington D.C. Karl Schlögel, an eminent German historian and a pioneer of the integration of history, geography, and urban studies, calls Saint-Petersburg the Russian "laboratory of modernism," alluding to the role it played in the development of the ideas of modernism and Enlightenment.[80] However, the historical ambitions of the new Russian capital extended much further. The Russian historians Grigory Kaganov and Leonid Matsikh brilliantly demonstrate the importance of the Masonic symbology in the Saint-Petersburg development master plans endorsed by Emperors Peter the Great, Empress Elizabeth, and Paul I.[81] Matsikh, for example, shows how the plans for the construction of Saint-Petersburg as the city of St. Peter incorporated the symbols of both Rome and Jerusalem. In this perspective, Saint-Petersburg did not merely give Russia a taste for European progress; it also became an important nexus of historical continuity for the world.

Many scholars have pointed to Masonic symbolism embedded in the development master plan, urban concept, and architecture of Washington D.C.[82] According to them, this symbolism permeates the entire central part of the capital city including all of its monuments and transportation arteries. It must be said, however, that some historians hotly contest the idea that Masonic symbology influenced the layout and architectural image of the US capital.

In contrast to the above, there is no dispute among scholars that magic symbolism is a major component of Brasília's cultural landscape, alluding to the architecture of the Egyptian Memphis. In the 1930s, two decades before Juscelino Kubitschek became president of Brazil, he had traveled to Luxor and was extremely impressed with the Egyptian temple architecture. It is likely that his Egyptian inspirations were later reflected in the image of the new capital.

It has been often noted in this regard that Brasília is laid out in the form of an ibis (ibis, a symbol of wisdom, was a sacred bird in ancient Egypt)[83] and that the twin-tower National Congress Building, modeled after the two temples of the Egyptian Abu Simbel complex, is oriented towards the sun (on the Republic Day, the sun rises exactly between the two towers of the building). The two towers represent the sun and the moon. Some commentators claim that one of the administrative buildings in the capital contains architectural quotations from the Pyramid of the Pharaoh Djoser and that geometric references to the Great Pyramid of Giza are present in the exterior of the National Theatre.[84] Even the very Memorial JK, which is how the Kubitschek Memorial is commonly referred to and which is one of the main attractions in the capital, features an allusion to ancient Egypt, a black marble sarcophagus with the remains of the late president.

Whether these quotations are related to the Masonry remains unclear, but regardless of the answer, Brasília continues to captivate fans of mystery. Thus, one of the city sites attracts followers of the New Age movement, who use it to celebrate various festivals and other events. As the Catholic Church legitimized the construction of the new capital, Brasília has become the subject of numerous appealing prophecies and intriguing revelations.

Apparently, founders and planners of other capital cities were not indifferent to Masonic themes and symbols either. Thus, historian Peter Proudfoot authored a book entitled *Secret Plan of Canberra*. This small but thorough study discusses Masonic influence on the architecture of the Australian capital. Proudfoot provides a detailed examination of Walter B. Griffin's, the designer of Canberra, views and Masonic concepts, along with the historical and political environment in which Griffin's architectural ideas originated.[85]

Some other observers herald Astana, Kazakhstan, as the "Illuminati Capital of the World," pointing to the rich occult symbology that seems so deeply ingrained into the aesthetics of the city.[86]

Hermetic symbols are meant to reveal the mysteries of capital cities; thus, Masonic sacraments and beliefs, captured in the stone, serve both as the gate to a new civilization being born and as the introduction to its values. In a sense, the new capitals reproduce elements of the ancient sacred capitals, as well as their cosmic and world-creating functions. Certainly, it is not our intention to bring grist to the mill of the conspiracy theorists claiming that the world has been long secretly ruled by the Freemasons. However, for the purpose of this study, it is important to emphasize that irrespective of their authorship, Masonic symbols (or the symbols that are perceived as such) have meanings that transcend national boundaries and are universal. While most of Masonic symbolism is derived from the ancient civilizations, it had a great impact on the architecture of the Enlightenment.[87]

Whatever the source of inspiration for the capital city image may be, it creates a stream of semantic interaction between civilizations that flows through the framework of historical continuity, building a universal language of architecture, opening the spaces of national, local, and ethnic narratives to the rest of the world, and inscribing the names of the capitals in the annals of global history.

The new capitals outside the European ecumene use extranational symbols no less frequently. Thus, Putrajaya, Malaysia, makes numerous references to Delhi and Samarkand in its design, while the reconstruction blueprint for Juba, capital of the newly independent South Sudan, calls for its urban center to be built in the zoomorphic shape of a rhinoceros. Notably, a rhinoceros is not an exclusive South Sudanese symbol, but rather, is a symbol common to the entire African continent.

It is also worth mentioning that the leading architects and urban planners of the new designed capitals were mostly foreigners, a fact that must have influenced the concept and the perception of these cities. Thus, Japan's architect Kisho Kurokawa designed the master plan of Astana, while the British Norman Robert Foster and the Italian Manfredi Nicoletti built the city's main buildings; Nicoletti also actively participated in the construction of Putrajaya. The development plan of Ankara was prepared by the renowned German architects and urban planners Carl Lörcher and Hermann Jansen. The Government Complex in Ankara was commissioned to the Austrian architect Clemenz Holzmeister. The Prussian Gustav Eduard Schaubert was instrumental in the re-planning of Athens after the War of Independence. The leading architect constructing Islamabad was the Greek Konstantinos Doxiadis. American architect James Rossant and Canadian planners developed a master plan for Dodoma in Tanzania. Many of the design concepts implemented in Brasília were conceptualized and inspired by the Swiss Le Corbusier. The Japanese Kenzo Tange and his team of city planners designed the central area of Abuja, Nigeria, while the French-born Pierre Charles L'Enfant designed Washington D.C. The American Walter B. Griffin designed Australian Canberra. The construction master plan of Saint-Petersburg was developed by the Italian Domenico Trezzini, and many of the city's most famous buildings were built by his fellow countrymen Francesco Bartolomeo Rastrelli, Antonio Rinaldi, and Carlo Rossi. The major designer of some of New Delhi's and Pretoria's main buildings was the British Herbert Baker. After the Nationalist government selected Nanking as the capital of China in the late 1920s, an American architect Henry Murphy was invited to build a new capital out of the ancient city of Nanking and developed "adaptive Chinese architecture" for this city though these plans never came to fruition. The symbolic variety of the new designed capitals may be explained by their "inauthentic or inorganic nature" and the lack of historical memory. Without its own national history, these cities badly needed additional legitimation, alternative to the purely ethnic or national legitimation.

It should be noted that the appeal to supranational symbols is not an exclusively modern phenomenon. For example, while Moscow had not originally played a significant role in Russian history and was markedly inferior to the older Russian cities in terms of prestige, it emerged as a new capital largely because of the appeal to extra-national symbols and promulgation of its own specific philosophy of history. Positioning itself as either the Second Jerusalem, or the Third Rome, or both, Moscow was striving to find new ways of legitimizing its status as the new national center.[88] It is interesting to note that the reconstruction of Moscow also involved foreign architects. The Italian Aristotele Fioravanti (fifteenth century) built the Dormition Cathedral in Moscow; he also laid out the master plan for erecting new walls and towers of the Kremlin.

Thus, given their multiple layers of iconography and their semiotic redundancy, the symbolism of the new designed capitals may lead them to become the main beneficiaries of the achievements made by the ancient civilizations of the world. The new capitals have a short historical memory; accordingly, they have to borrow a "long memory" from the past to generate the mythos of the city.

The symbolic adaptation of the metanarratives, as well as the integration of regional and local identities, allows a capital city to overcome the possible conflicts among the global, national, and local elements of its space. Furthermore, the balance of these three elements allows capitals to successfully perform their functions and to avoid conflicts with the capital city residents.

One has to keep in mind, however, that an excessive accentuation of the global element – or a downplaying of the national element – in the capital city's iconography has a highly negative impact on the development of the capital city, which has been shown by many social anthropologists and urbanists. An inordinate penetration of global commercial projects into the urban space makes the city a less efficient capital and a less successful global city. Gavin Shatkin points to this flaw, using the example of Manila, the capital of the Philippines.[89]

Capitals and global cities

The two imperatives: capital vs. global city

While the primacy of the city is determined by its place in the urban hierarchy within the state, its global status is determined by its place in the system of world economy and world urban system.[90] In the last two decades economists and sociologists have produced many books and articles about the rise of the global cities that gradually overshadowed and overpowered capital cities of the nation-states. They believe that these cities are far more important for the understanding of the trends of world development and global processes compared to capital cities. It is expected that the global cities will continue to liberate themselves from their national economies, politics, and from their regional and local networks. They will also acquire more autonomy from the system of economic relationships in their own countries. It was predicted that by 2025 the world will have 600 global cities where 25 percent of the global population will reside and that will generate 60 percent of global GDP. The top 100 cities will be responsible for about 35 percent of total world wealth.[91]

Such a prominent role of the global cities is attributed to their innovation potential and their focus on the pioneering and the most competitive sectors of the economy. Those economic activities that will not be able to compete for the growing cost of the factors of production in the metropolis such as labor, land, and capital will move to more peripheral locations. In the course of structural change they will be replaced by higher-status urban activities and much more innovative sectors of the economy: financial and management services, consulting, and the like. In the five-sector model of the economy the tertiary sector gives way the quaternary (producer services) and quinary sector (consumer services) in the course of constant upgrade of the first city urban activities. As a result, in the global cities the dominant position will belong to the advanced service sectors of the economy (information technologies, planning, scientific research, and the like).

The following facts and figures can help to understand the relationship between global cities and capital cities. In 2015 according to A.T. Kearney's Global Cities Index, about a half of the top global cities are capital cities: 5 out of the top 10 and 12 out of the top 25. Intuitively, capital city status helps cities to establish their global reach and maintain their status of global command-and-control centers. However, the analysis of historical trends shows that in the past, capital city status was much more important as a factor determining their global status compared to the role that it plays today. In the nineteenth century the world city hierarchy simply reflected the state hierarchy in Europe, and the importance of a world city was measured by the power of its state.[92] The Global Cities Outlook (GCO) rankings provided by A.T. Kearney forecasts that the role of capital city status in determining the cities' global status and influence will be further diminished in the future. GCO measures the likelihood that a city will improve its global standing over the next 10 to 20 years. Based on this GCO ranking, it is forecasted that in 2024 only 7 out of 25 top global cities will be capital cities.[93] This observed historical trend of the diminishing role of capital cities in the global network is consistent with the distinction made by Saskia Sassen between the world cities and the global cities. While the hierarchy of world cities reflected the political status and historical standing of the countries, the global city concept emphasizes only the nodality and the role that a particular city plays within the global network. Hence, the structure and design of the global cities network is becoming more and more independent from the respective political hierarchy. Capital city transfers taking place mostly in larger countries of the globe also contribute to this trend.

The declining role of the capital cities in global cities hierarchy can be construed as a consequence of their apparent deficiencies as agents of the world economy and the lack of alignment between their rootedness in the nation-states and their aspirations for global city status. It also stands to reason that the capital cities might create the conditions under which their global aspirations can be severely constrained and their development as global cities can be hampered by their political status and the limitations that such status might entail. This status, some economists have argued, does not necessarily promote the spirit of economic innovations and full-fledged participation in the global economic affairs.

Arguably, the presence of many capital cities in the global cities index cannot be explained by their innovative potential. Many of them function as global cities because they serve as the gateways to the larger economic regions, where they do not have powerful rivals and where they create unfavorable conditions for other cities in the competition for resources of the country. They spread the innovations that they receive from the outside world to the hinterlands of their countries and thus serve as command-and-control centers of global capitalism, taking advantage of their monopolistic positions. However, they are much less effective in the generation of innovations of their own. For instance, Buenos Aires is number 20 in the list of the Global Cities Index; however, it is only number 245 in the list of innovative cities. Moscow is number 14 in the GCI, but it is only number 65 in the list. This type of city is not uncommon in historical terms. In 1927 the Spanish philosopher José Ortega y Gasset described the relationship between the capital and the provinces in Spain, portraying Madrid as an extractive and parasitic capital city. He observed, perhaps polemically exaggerating the matter:

> Madrid never had the creative culture of its own. It has learned a few poorly digested lessons from abroad. This culture acquired abroad . . . this cultural reservoir, comes straight to Madrid as the main city of the country to support its status and sober dignity. It is idiotic to assume that Madrid was a metropolis that benefited its hinterland. Six kilometers from Madrid the cultural influence of Madrid ends, and, without transition or enlightened hinterland, total backwardness begins abruptly.[94]

London, Paris, and Tokyo, the capital cities which also occupy the top spots in the list of the global cities, are obviously much more innovative compared to Buenos Aires and Moscow. However, in their respective countries – the UK, France, and Japan – we also observe a high level of dissatisfaction of their citizens with the preponderant role that these cities play in the national life. Perhaps, their very success as global cities, international financial and business centers, makes them less successful as capitals and less suitable for the role of the seats of government of their respective nation-states. Their geographical position within their national territory also highlights their role of the nodes in the system of international flows of trade and finance rather than their role of effective administrative units governing their respective countries. If in theory the saturation of one or more factors of production in the large metropolis should lead to the spread of the economic functions and innovations from the first city towards regional urban centers, than in reality the global cities are not always capable to transmit their economic development nationally. They also restrain the inter-urban competition in their countries.

The political symbolism and iconography rarely play the central role in the visual image of the most successful global cities that also have capital city functions. For instance, the Parliament Building on the Avenue des Champs-Élysées in Paris, the National Diet Building in Tokyo, and the Westminster

Abbey in London hardly play a much more prominent role in the overall architectural plan of these cities compared to buildings and public spaces that are designed for the execution of more commercial and cultural functions. Generally the architectural forms and imagery of the global cities tend to be much more homogeneous and even uniform compared to capital cities.

It is also clear that the requirements for and the expectations from the urban forms of the global cities are very different from those that are applied to capital cities. The capital city relocation debates often reveal the tensions or incompatibility of these two sets of requirements and expectations. Not all of the capital cities can be equally effective as global cities, and many global cities are unsuitable as capital cities of the respective countries. Hence, it would be helpful to outline in this context the essential differences of each type of the city, deriving from their distinct criteria of effectiveness in their respective roles and to distinguish those features that provoke tensions and conflict in their functionality.

The global cities are the nodes providing linkages and connecting the dynamic financial flows and energies. On the other hand, the capital cities epitomize the static balance and compromise. The more effective global cities tend to expedite the processes and render them free from excessive regulations and red tape, while the capital cities typically ground and slow down the processes of decision-making and localize the imperatives of global trade. The global cities are the nodes in the system of global affairs and networks. Capital cities are the points of dynamic balance within the country and serve as the international showcases of the nation-states. The global cities are aiming to minimize the interference on the side of the state and relax the importance of state borders. On the other hand, capital cities being the agents of the state appeal to the regulations and legal system and rely on state borders.

Global cities are invariably outward-oriented and are defined by their international connectivity. Capital cities are predominantly inward-oriented and are defined by their underlying hinge and connection role within the national borders. The global cities are the linking points between the global economic centers and other command-and-control centers of the world economy, housing headquarters of global corporations, global organizations, and trans-territorial marketplaces. The capital cities are the nodes in the international political affairs and hinges connecting their constituent units, the interiors of their countries, and their different cities and communities. Accordingly, capital cities emphasize hierarchy, while global cities emphasize networks and flow. The primary task of the capital city is to provide governance within the state borders and to balance the interests within the state. The main task and the measure of efficiency of the global cities is participation in the production of wealth and management of the global economy that functions beyond state borders.

The capital cities are also often contrasted to the global cities as conservative and bureaucratic cities hostile to innovations. Such characterization is unsurprising given the contradictory requirements that the capitalness and globality entail, but it is hardly applicable to all capital cities as a class of cities. Many of them have managed to become a source of important innovations beyond the economic sphere. While the global cities focus more on technological and managerial innovations, the effective capital cities produce more social, organizational, humanitarian, and cultural innovations. The conservatism, stagnation, and bureaucratization are not their immanent features, and depending on the character of political regime and the level of economic development, they can manifest themselves in different ways.

These contrasts between global cities and capital cities suggest that the combination of these two functions in the same city is not always desirable and might not befit the particular tasks of political and economic development of the state. The capital city status might hinder the development of the city as a global center and as an international economic hub. By the same token, the features of the global city do not necessarily facilitate the effective performance of capital city functions and can make a capital city less efficient in providing the public goods to the population of the country as a whole, the major rationale for the capital city function. However, these two functions might find some synergies in the smaller and mid-size nations, helping them to achieve or preserve the agglomeration benefits in their prime and preeminent centers.

The duality of capital cities and global commercial centers

In many countries we find a stark contrast between the political capitals, on the one hand, and the main economic hubs, on the other. Some economists have attributed the emergence of such separation and duality not to geography and factors of the natural order, but to the political factors and to the deliberate choice by the rulers of these states to place the seats of government of these countries at a distance from the main economic centers of their respective countries. Reuven Brenner notes in this regard:

> [T]here is a link between location and prosperity. . . . [I]t has to do with politics, rather than geography. Rulers tended to build their capital cities away from trade routes, far from seaports. That's why we have Moscow and Saint-Petersburg, Barcelona and Madrid, Beijing and Shanghai. We have Venice and Milan on one side and Rome on the other. However, the entrepreneurial nature of "trading" cities and the backward-looking bureaucratic nature of political capitals has nothing to do with geography. Rulers chose these locations knowing that information traveled more slowly to, and people had greater difficulty escaping from, landlocked places that were not on trade routes. This left people working there dependent on political favors. Rulers could exercise far more **power** over the immobile inhabitants of isolated political capitals.[95]

260 Assessing effectiveness of a capital city

The attempt to analyze the urban systems of different countries in terms of their predominant patterns of interaction between their main political and commercial centers and the possible ramifications of such patterns for the success of the states seems to be laudable and fruitful. Nevertheless, both the claim that such duality is always a result of a deliberate choice by the rulers and the historical illustrations that Brenner provides require some serious qualifications and corrections.

Historically, Brenner's thesis, especially his interpretation of the relationship between mentioned capitals and their commercial counterparts, is highly problematic. Notably, today Rome in Italy outstrips Milan economically, and Madrid is getting very close to Barcelona (see Table 10). The transfer of the capital city from Saint-Petersburg to Moscow and the movement of the capital back to Moscow in 1918 have not created the division of labor between the political and economic functions that is implied by Brenner's distinction. Saint-Petersburg was never conceived by Peter the Great as the new commercial pole of Russian statehood but rather as a political alternative to Moscow. The construction of Saint-Petersburg was intended to reproduce the functions of Moscow in a new place, creating a multi-functional capital. In the imperial Russia the main commercial functions analogous to that of Barcelona in Spain were performed by Arkhangelsk and Odessa and not by Saint-Petersburg.[96]

Such description of the relationship between the two capitals is even less accurate in view of the Soviet and post-Soviet periods. In the USSR, Leningrad (the new name of Saint-Petersburg in the Soviet period) played the role of a cultural capital but not a role of the main commercial center. Furthermore, in the post-Soviet period, Moscow in many ways replaced Saint-Petersburg as a cultural capital.

In more substantive terms, Brenner's idea about the immanent conservativeness of the capital cities is also problematic. The co-location of the political capital with their main commercial centers – most often they were also the most populous cities – has occurred in various countries for several different reasons. Although the pattern described by Brenner can be found in many countries, it is not universal. The separation of the political capital from the main commercial hub of the country does not always stem from the intentions of the political elites to dodge themselves from the participation in the dynamic economic activities and the atmosphere of entrepreneurship in the global economic centers, and the co-location of the capitals with the economic hubs can lead to much more negative political outcomes. Many totalitarian and autocratic regimes concentrate in their preeminent cities the totality of their power to provide more effective control of both political and economic life and the international affairs of their countries.

Accordingly, the separation of the seats of government and the commercial hubs did not always establish dependency on the economic favors. These separations have in many cases created more favorable conditions for both political and economic development of the state. The difference between the *modus operandi* of the global cities and capital cities that we have presented above also suggests that this kind of separation could have had some practical purposes beyond loyalty building.

Instead of ineffectual Russian illustration, the concept of duality of the political and economic capitals can be complemented by the examples taken from many other countries. The urban systems of these countries, located in many different parts of the globe, are characterized by the division of labor between politics and economics. The following pairs of cities are showing the prevalence of this pattern in various urban systems: Switzerland (Berne–Zurich), Israel (Jerusalem–Tel-Aviv), Turkey (Ankara–Istanbul), Vietnam (Hanoi–Ho Chi Minh City), Brazil (Brasília –San-Paulo), Australia (Canberra–Sydney), New Zealand (Wellington–Oakland), Morocco (Rabat–Casablanca), Ecuador (Quito–Guayaquil), Greece (Athens–Salonika), Syria (Damascus–Aleppo), Yemen (Sana–Aden), Cameroon (Yaoundé–Duala), UAE (Abu-Dhabi–Dubai), South-African Republic (Pretoria–Johannesburg), and Malta (Valetta–San Julian). This list can be complemented also by the pairs of Berlin and Frankfurt-am-Main in Germany and New Delhi and Mumbai in India. At the subnational level Edinburgh and Glasgow in Scotland can also be an illustration. In Bahrain before 1923 Muharraq served as a capital city, while Manama was the major commercial hub and economic capital of the country. Overall, about 17 percent of all sovereign states in the world have capitals that are not their largest city.

Remarkably, the separation of economic and political capitals cannot be considered a unique feature specific to present-day urban systems. This type of separation was typical for many countries located in different parts of the globe in different periods of their history. The less centralized political regimes have allowed the goods exchange to take place outside the direct control of the empires. Not infrequently, the core regions of the empires also interacted with each other indirectly through intervening peripheral zones. Despite the fact that the main economic centers did not always eclipse the political capitals in all economic indicators, they often surpassed capital cities in the total volume of economic trade, had higher global network connectivity and were comparable to them on most other economic scores. Table 10 shows the relative economic dominance of capital cities relative to "second cities" of the respective countries.

In the Almohad Caliphate in present-day Morocco, Rabat was a capital city, while Fez, possibly the largest city of the world at the time, served as the main commercial hub. In Japan in the Edo period (seventeenth through nineteenth century), Kyoto served as the capital city, while the merchant city of Osaka certainly dominated in all economic affairs of the state. The leading commercial role in the countries located on the Silk Road was often played not by their capital cities but by their main commercial hubs. In the Karakhanid Khanate it was Osh and not Balasaghun, the capital city. In Khazaria it was Khazaran and not Itil. At the time of the most intense trade on the Silk Road, non-capitals Tabriz and Merv served as the main commercial cities of the Arab Caliphate and Persia respectively. The urban polycentrism and the polycephalous urban systems emerged in many de-centralized empires that allowed the relatively independent development of the commercial functions. Notably in the Samanid empire, Herat and Samarkand developed into relatively independent commercial centers, while Bukhara served as a seat of power.

This dual structure is also found in many European countries. One can see this relationship between Rome and Alexandria in the Roman Empire, Turin and Genoa in the kingdom of Sardinia, Brussels and Antwerp in Flanders. Such separation was also characteristic for England where Westminster, the capital of the country, and the City of London, the mercantile center of the country, were for centuries geographically distinct. It was not until the sixteenth century that the two cities started to merge into one city, the greater London.

The anthropologist Clifford Geertz has described the natural, geographically determined, juxtaposition between the inland castle towns located in the river valleys and the coastal economic hubs in the structure of the settlement systems of the Java archipelago and other pre-modern archaic societies on the territory of present-day Indonesia. The first ones often served as the natural capitals of the local princedoms and important religious and administrative centers, while the second ones have specialized in trade and commerce.[97]

As can be seen from the examples above, the division of labor between political and economic centers was not always engendered by the political tricks of the rulers. It is true that many rulers have tried to distance their capitals from the commercial hubs. But it was not the only reason. In some cases it was a result of natural geographical factors. Not infrequently, the commercial centers have emerged in the peripheral areas, making possible the exchange of goods between empires. In other cases the dual structure emerged as a result of the territorial changes, the unification of areas that used to belong to different empires. But many rulers aimed to control their largest cities and established their capitals there to exercise more control over these commercial centers.

Presently the separation of mercantile cities and political capitals is considered by many proponents of capital city transfers as a favorable element of the urban system. They believe that the reproduction of this duality in the urban systems of their countries will be rewarding for both their political and economic development. Some of them believe that this type of arrangement can unleash the commercial potential of the larger cities of these countries, the potential that is presently constrained by their capital city status.

Economic explanation of capital city status and its flaws

While Reuven Brenner has tried to explain the capital city status by the deliberate politics of the rulers, some other urban scholars have suggested a nexus between the wealth of the city and its capital city status. In their view, the capital city status is an outcome of the economic success of the city. According to this view, the affluent and economically dominant cities acquire the capital city status as a prestige items, the sign of rank and glory. Jane Jacobs portrays the capital city status as an additional bonus that only successful and affluent economic centers can afford. To this effect she has made the following statement in her acclaimed book:

> The great capitals of modern Europe did not become great cities because they were capitals. Cause and effect ran the other way. . . . Paris was at first no more the seat of the French kings than were the sites of half a dozen other royal residences. Indeed, until the twelfth century, Orleans, another center of trade, was more imposing than Paris as a seat of king and as a cultural and educational center. Paris became the genuine capital only after it had already become the largest (and economically the most diversified) commercial and industrial city of the kingdom. Berlin was not even the capital of its province – Brandenburg was – until after it had become economically the most diversified, commercial and industrial city in Prussian territory.[98]

In contrast to Brenner, Jacobs does not address the question about the origins of the duality of the commercial and political centers in some countries. But she claims that economic factors contribute more to its prominence that translates into capital city status. It can be further inferred from her argument that the commercial capitals have a higher potential to be converted to the political capital in the course of the economic rivalry between cities and that the duality would represent an anomaly in urban development. However, the history shows that it was rarely the case and that political capitals have been often chosen despite all economic considerations.

Jane Jacobs is right in pointing out that the wealth of Paris or London cannot be explained only by its capital city status. As we have seen in our historical overview, London, Paris, and many other European capitals have originally amassed their wealth due to a large extent to their capital city status and the exploitation of the provinces. It is also notable that London was not always the major economic player even in the later years, and in the course of Industrial Revolution the economic dominance of London did not remain unchallenged. In the first half of the nineteenth century Manchester surpassed London as a manufacturing powerhouse, and it was widely considered to be "the city of the future." According to Fernand Braudel, capital cities have played a role of the spectators rather than the main contributors to the industrial revolution. "The capital cities would be present in the forthcoming Industrial Revolution, but in the role of the spectators," he famously claimed, perhaps exaggerating the matter for polemical purposes. "Not London, but Manchester, Birmingham, Leeds, Glasgow and innumerable small proletarian towns launched the new era."[99] However in spite of all this, the capital city status of London remained intact. The same holds true for many other capital cities.

More to the point, historically, capital cities were rarely established in the most affluent and prosperous parts of the state. In many countries the political capitals maintained their control over commercial hubs and the larger and more economically developed parts of the country. In China the Mandarin capital in the North traditionally controlled the affluent commercial regions of the South that played a conspicuous role in overseas trade from which it derived its wealth. The ascension of Moscow to political dominance took place against the backdrop of much more commercially developed cities like Novgorod that Moscovite rulers have later suppressed.

In the historical section of this book, we also have seen that many capital cities emerged in places that were much smaller and much less cosmopolitan than the larger and more established urban centers. Many of them did not have natural resources and any other obvious indications of their potential for successful independent economic development. In general, it was not uncommon for poor and underdeveloped parts of the country to take control over the more affluent regions. We have seen such tendencies in several Latin American countries where more affluent cities exhibiting strong separatist tendencies were subservient to the political domination of capital cities that were established in much poorer and often peripheral regions.

Many capital cities of the newly independent states were also established in poorer parts of the country. To exemplify, Athens did not even have its own economy to speak of. At the time of independence in 1833, Athens was only a village, while Thessalonica was a big and affluent economic hub. In Bulgaria at least three cities could be listed, such as Varna, Shumen, and Ruse, which were bigger than Sofia; Varna, a seaport on the Black Sea, and Ruse, a Danubian port city, were more promising commercially. In the area of modern-day Serbia, Subotica remained the most populous city and economically more promising to the very end of the nineteenth century, while smaller Belgrad and earlier Kragujevac were selected to become the capitals of the country.[100]

To summarize, the capital city status is rarely simply a result of economic preeminence and the prosperity of the city. Neither is it simply a result of manipulation of the political elite that aims to isolate the capital from the dynamic development of the global cities. In many countries the presence of such a dual structure is a result of the historically entrenched division of labor between the political and economic function. Many contributors to the debate about the change of the seat of government believe that such a division of labor is beneficial for both economic and political development of the country and see the establishment of designed new capital as an opportunity for the former capital city to develop into a commercial capital to realize more fully its economic potential.

Notes

1 It is known that for the purpose of building new capitals, these countries attached great importance to astrological forecasts, and the foundation of a new city was usually timed with certain astrological dates. For example, the most

influential astrologers of the time participated in the foundation of Constantinople and Baghdad. The case of Baghdad, founded on July 30, 762, involved the use of astrological techniques and concepts stemming from the Persian Sassanid era. Thus, in 762 AD, the Persian astrologer Abu Sahl al-Fadl ibn Nawbakht and the Jewish astrologer Masha'allah ibn Athari created a special astrological map of the city and directed measurement operations when the foundation of the city was laid. (Masha'allah, *Book of Nativities*. Translated by Robert Hand (Berkeley Springs: Golden Hind Press, 1994) It is also known that when Emperor Constantine decided to found Constantinople, he consulted with an astrologer who advised him to lay the foundation stone in the wall of the future city during the hour of the crab on November 4, 328 AD. Al-Biruni wrote about the connection between specific places and planet signs, pointing out that there was the "ruler of the hour" for each particular place. The great conjunction of Jupiter and Saturn was considered the most favorable time for building a new capital (Pingree, D. "Classical and Byzantine Astrology in Sassanian Persia," *Dumbarton Oaks Papers*, vol. 43 (1989), 227–239).

2 In the fourteenth century, when reconstructing Prague, the new capital of the Holy Roman Empire, Charles IV followed astrological recommendations. Accordingly, Prague was divided into 12 sectors, each one corresponding to a sign of the zodiac. The exact time for the solemn ceremony of laying the foundation stone of the Stone Bridge (now Charles Bridge) was calculated by astrologers (Spurek, M. *Praga Mysteriosa: The Secret of the Prague Solstice* (Prague: Eminent, 1996)).

3 Preecharush, D. *Naypyidaw: The New Capital of Burma* (Bangkok: White Lotus, 2009).

4 Yoon, H.-K. *The Culture of Fengshui in Korea: An Exploration of East Asian Geomancy* (Lanham: Lexington Books, 2006), 223, 231, 250.

5 Ibid., 220–235.

6 Ibid., 219.

7 Tynyanova, O. "Tekuschaya gosudarstvennaya politika i model Rossii i ekstrapolatsionniy prognoz eyo srednesrochnykh rezultatov v mirovykh koordinatakh," *Nauchnyi ekspert*, no. 4 (2011), 36–67.

8 Mendeleev, D.K. *poznaniyu Rossii* (Moskva: Iris Press, 2002).

9 Semenov-Tian-Shansky, V.P. "Tsentr Rossii, yego osobennosti i znachenie dlya strany," *Geografiya i khozyaistvo, no.3. Tsentrograficheskiy metod v ekonomicheskoy geografii* (Leningrad: Izdadelstvo Geograficheskogo obschestva SSSR, 1989).

10 Svetlyakovsky, E.E. & Ills, U.K. "Tsentrograficheskiy metod i regionalnyi analis," *Geografiya i khozyaistvo, no.3. Tsentrograficheskiy metod v ekonomicheskoy geografii* (Leningrad: Izdadelstvo Geograficheskogo obschestva SSSR, 1989).

11 Bae, S.-Y. "The Effects of Capital City Relocation in Korea Based on Total Factor Productivity Analysis," *Japan Economic Policy Association Annual Conference*, Tokyo (November 11, 2004); Lee, M.-H., Choi, N.-H., & Park, M. "A Systems Thinking Approach to the New Administrative Capital in Korea: Balanced Development or Not?," *System Dynamics Review*, vol. 21, no. 1 (2005), 69–85.

12 Lee, M.-H., Choi, N.-H., & Park, M. "A Systems Thinking Approach to the New Administrative Capital in Korea: Balanced Development or Not?," *System Dynamics Review*, vol. 21, no. 1 (2005), 69–85.

13 Mechnikov, L. *Tsvilizatsiya i velikie istoricheskie reki* (Moskva: Progress, 1995).

14 Haushofer, K. *Geopolitik des Pazifischen Ozeans: Studien über die Wechselbeziehungen zwischen Geographie und Geschichte* (Bremen: Dogma, 2013), 276.

15 Lohausen, H.J. von. "Wien und Belgrad als geopolitische Antipoden," *Staatsbriefe*. Heft 12 (1992).

16 Tynyanova, O. "Tekuschaya gosudarstvennaya politika i model Rossii i ekstrapolatsionniy prognoz eyo srednesrochnykh rezultatov v mirovykh koordinatakh," *Nauchnyi ekspert*, no. 4 (2011), 36–67.
17 Potts, D. "Capital Relocation in Africa: The Case of Lilongwe in Malawi," *Geographical Journal*, vol. 151, no. 2 (1985), 182–196.
18 Petty, W. "Sir William Petty on the Causes and Consequences of Urban Growth," *Population and Development Review*, vol. 10, no. 1 (1984), 127–133, reprint.
19 Ibid., 194.
20 Frey, R. S. & Dietz, T. "The Growth of Capital Cities in the World Economic System," *Sociological Spectrum*, vol. 10, no. 2 (1990), 271, 277.
21 Taylor, P. *Political Geography: World Economy, Nation-State and Locality* (New York: Longman, 1985), 103–104, 165–167.
22 Hoselitz, B. "Generative and Parasitic Cities," *Economic Development and Cultural Change*, vol. 3, no. 3 (April 1955), 278–294.
23 Frank, A. *Latin America: Underdevelopment or Revolution?* (New York: Monthly Review Press, 1969).
24 Marchand, B. *The Image of Paris in France since Two Centuries: From Good to Bad to Worst*, 2010,, 18; Kirkup, J. "Londoners' £2000 Tax Subsidy for Rest of UK," *The Telegraph*, September 30, 2008.
25 Taylor, P. & Derudder, B. "Tales of Two Cities: Political Capitals and Economic Centres in the World City Network," *Glocalism*, no. 3 (2014).
26 Taylor, P.J. & Derudder, B., eds. *Cities in Globalization: Practices, Policies and Theories* (London: Routledge, 2007), 294–296.
27 Borgatti, S. & Everette, M. "A Graph-Theoretic Perspective on Centrality," *Social Networks*, vol. 28, no. 4 (2006), 466–484.
28 Turner, S. & Turner, R. "Capital Cities: A Special Case in Urban Development," *Annals of Regional Science*, vol. 46 (2011), 19–35.
29 Takamura, Y. & Tone, K. "A Comparative Site Evaluation Study for Relocating Japanese Government Agencies Out of Tokyo," *Socio-Economic Planning Sciences*, vol. 37 (2003), 85–102.
30 Herrick, B. "Internal Migration, Unemployment, and Economic Growth in Post-War Chile," unpublished Ph.D. thesis (Boston: Massachusetts Institute of Technology, 1962), 57, Table 3.1.
31 The concept of a "primate city" was introduced by an American geographer, Mark Jefferson, in 1939. According to Jefferson, a primate city is a city "at least twice as large as the next largest city and more than twice as significant." Thus, it is preeminent in most spheres, like politics, economy, culture, universities, and media. A "primate city distribution" is a rank-size distribution that has one very large city with many much smaller cities and towns, and no intermediate-sized urban. Some economists and geographers use more complex technical criteria to estimate the primacy of a city in their respective urban systems, e.g., comparing the largest city to the second- and third-tier cities. See Smith, Carol. "Theories and Measures of Urban Primacy: A Critique." In: Timberlake, M. (ed.), *Urbanization in the World-Economy* (London: Academic Press, 1985), 87–116.
32 Dascher, K. "Are Politics and Geography Related? Evidence from a Cross-Section of Capital Cities," *Public Choice*, vol. 105 (2000), 373–374.
33 Ades, A.F. & Glaeser, E.L. "Trade and Circuses: Explaining Urban Giants," *Quarterly Journal of Economics*, vol. 110 (1995), 195–227.
34 Ibid.
35 Ades and Glaeser have utilized the Gastil Index, published annually by Freedom House, to measure democracy, for their calculations. They were using cross-national data for the largest cities in 88 nations, 77 of which were capital cities of these countries (Ibid., 195–196, 203–211).

36 Baron de Montesquieu already noted this relationship in the eighteenth century in his book *My Thoughts* where he discussed the correlation between the size of the capital and different political regimes. While it is quite natural for despotic states to have oversize capitals, he argued, they tend to corrupt monarchies and can destroy a republic. "In despotic States, the capital grows inexorably larger. Despotism, which presses and weighs more upon the provinces, channels everything towards the capital. In some sense, this is the only asylum that exists against the governors' tyranny. The Prince is a strange star – he warms from up close and burns from afar. . . A monarchy that has rules and laws is not ruined by the capital. It may even draw its splendor from it. The Prince has a thousand means of restoring equilibrium and bringing the people back into the provinces." He suggests the use of a taxation system, de-centralization of the legal system among others to discourage mass migrations to the capital and depopulation of the provinces. Montesquieu, C. *My Thoughts (Mes Pensées)*. Translated, edited, and with an Introduction by Henry C. Clark (Indianapolis: Liberty Fund, 2012). Fragment [1816].
37 Reichart, T. *Städte ohne Wettbewerb* (Bern: Haupt, 1993).
38 Turner, S. & Turner, R. "Capital Cities: a Special Case in Urban Development," *Annals of Regional Science*, vol. 46 (2011), 21.
39 Moomaw, R. & Alwosabi, M. "An Empirical Analysis of Competing Explanations of Urban Primacy. Evidence from Asia & the Americas," *The Annals of Regional Science*, vol. 38 (2004), 149–171.
40 Galiani, S. & Kim, S. "The Law of the Primate City in the Americas," *Proceedings of a Conference Honoring the Contributions of Kenneth Sokoloff at UCLA* (2008), Los Angeles.
41 Machiavelli, N. *The Prince*. Translated by J.G. Nichols (London: Alma Classics, 2009), ch.10.
42 Isserman, A. "Comments on 'Urban Concentration' by Krugman," *Proceedings of the World Bank Annual Conference on Development Economics*, Washington, D.C. (1995).
43 Zubarevich, N. "Agglomeratsionnii effect ili administrativnii ugar," *Rossiiskoe ekspertnoe obozrenie*, no. 4–5 (2007), 11–13.
44 Krugman, P. "Urban Concentration: The Role of Increasing Returns and Transport Costs," *Proceedings of the World Bank Annual Conference on Development Economics*, Washington, D.C. (1995); Isserman, A. "Comments on 'Urban Concentration' by Krugman," *Proceedings of the World Bank Annual Conference on Development Economics*, Washington, D.C. (1995).
45 Bettencourt, L.M.A., Lobo, J., Helbing, D., Kuhnert, C., & West, G.B. "Growth, Innovation, Scaling, and the Pace of Life in Cities," *Proceedings of the National Academy of Sciences*, vol. 104, no. 17 (2007), 7301–7306.
46 The Economist, "The city roars back," July 21, 2012.
47 According to Oxford Economics, London pays £16 billion more in taxes than the Government spends in the capital, equivalent to more than £2,000 for every person in the city (Kirkup, J. "Londoners' £2000 Tax Subsidy for Rest of UK," *The Telegraph*, September 30, 2008.) The same type of relationship holds for Paris.
48 Hardy, D. "Capital Matters: Reflecting on a Recent Meeting of the Capital Alliance Network of Capital Cities. Lessons for the UK in the Function and Organization of Capital Cities Elsewhere in the World," *Town and Country Planning*, January, 2006; Moomaw, R. & Alwosabi, M. "An Empirical Analysis of Competing Explanations of Urban Primacy. Evidence from Asia & the Americas," *The Annals of Regional Science*, vol. 38 (2004), 149–171.
49 Rigorously defined, monocephality implies that more than 20 percent of all the urban population concentrates in one city of the country. However, quite

often the countries with very large capital cities are described as monocephalic, regardless of the exact proportions.
50 Zimmerman, H. "Do Different Types of Capital Cities Make a Difference for Economic Dynamism?," *Environment and Planning C: Government and Policy*, vol. 28 (2010), 766.
51 Rossman, V. *V poiskakh Chetvertogo Rima* (Moskva: Vysshaia shkola ekonomiki, 2014), 66.
52 Dascher, K. "Are Politics and Geography Related? Evidence from a Cross-Section of Capital Cities," *Public Choice*, vol. 105 (2000), 373–392.
53 Quistorff, B. *Capitalitis? Effects of the 1960 Brazilian Capital Relocation* (March 30, 2015), 15. Available at SSRN: http://ssrn.com/abstract=2588620 or http://dx.doi.org/10.2139/ssrn.2588620
54 Stahl, J. "Capital Gain: The Returns to Locating in the Capital City," 2014. www.econ.upf.edu/gpefm/jm/pdf/paper/JMP%20Stahl.pdf
55 Hall, C.M. "Tourism in Capital Cities," *Tourism: An International Interdisciplinary Journal*, vol. 50, no. 3 (2002), 235–248; Zimmerman, H. "Do Different Types of Capital Cities Make a Difference for Economic Dynamism?," *Environment and Planning C: Government and Policy*, vol. 28 (2010), 761–767.
56 Zimmerman, H. "Do Different Types of Capital Cities Make a Difference for Economic Dynamism?," *Environment and Planning C: Government and Policy*, vol. 28 (2010), 764–765.
57 To illustrate, businesses in cities like Manchester or Leeds tend to look first to London when they need to buy in specialist help or establish a joint venture in a particular sector, even when the talent or expertise they need is also readily available, more cheaply, in a neighboring city. This is due to the fact that the train covers 120 miles between London and Birmingham in 84 minutes, while it takes the train 90 minutes to cover half of this distance between Birmingham to Manchester (Flanders, S. "Should Britain Let Go of London?" *BBC News*, March 25, 2013 www.bbc.com/news/business-21934564).
58 Bertaud, A. *The Spatial Organization of Cities: Deliberate Outcome or Unforseen Consequence?* (Berkeley: Institute of Urban and Regional Development, University of California, 2004).
59 Perception Survey on Quality of Life in European Cities. Analytical Report. Conducted by the Gallup Organization, Hungary, for European Commission, 2009.
60 Henderson, V. " The Urbanization Process and Economic Growth: The So-What Question," *Journal of Economic Growth*, vol. 8, no. 1 (Springer, March 2003), 47–71.
61 Henderson, V. "Urban Primacy, External Costs and Quality of Life," *Resource and Energy Economics*, vol. 24, no. 1–2 (2005), 95.
62 Krugman, P. "Urban Concentration: The Role of Increasing Returns and Transport Costs," *Proceedings of the World Bank Annual Conference on Development Economicism*, Washington, D.C. (1995), 275.
   Some economists believe that the formation of the federations is itself an outcome of the historical policentricity of the urban system.
63 Lowenthal, D. "The West Indies Chooses the Capital City," *Geographical Review*, vol. 48, no. 3 (1958), 336–364.
64 Anna, T. *Forging Mexico, 1821–1835* (Lincoln: Nebraska University Press, 1998), 192–194.
65 González, J. & Ríos, A. "La Ciudad de Mexico y el Districto Federal: Un Analisis Politico-Constitucional," *Estudios constitucionales*, vol. 7, no. 2 (Santiago, 2009), 230–233.
66 Nagel, K.-J., ed. *The Problem of the Capital City: New Research on Federal Capitals and Their Territory* (Barcelona: Collecció Institut d'Estudis Autonòmics,

2013), 86; Barani, L. "Fiscal Federalism and Capital Cities: A Comparative Analysis of Berlin and Brussels," *L'Europe en Formation*, vol. 1, no. 359 (2011), 21–45.
67 Henrikson, A. "A Small, Cozy Town, Global in Scope': Washington, D.C.," *Ekistics*, vol. 50, no. 299 (March/April 1983), 127. This concept of a "Village on the Capitol Hill" was also inspired by specific anti-urban ideals of Thomas Jefferson and his vision of the United States as an agrarian country. He believed that the political power should be concentrated in the governments of the states rather than in the central government. A small Village playing the role of a capital city was considered the most suitable within such a vision, reflecting the pastoral spirit of the country. Jefferson associated the cities with misery and inequality, seeing this nexus evident in the European capitals of his age.
68 The founding fathers were heavily influenced by French philosopher Charles de Montesquieu when drafting the Constitution. Besides the mentioned concept of checks and balances, it is likely that they were also receptive to his concept of provincial autonomy and the dangers of the oversize capital for the development of monarchies and especially of the republics. Montesquieu opined that oversize capitals are "extremely pernicious in a republic." See his essay "On the Size of the Capital" (fragment [1861]) in Montesquieu, C. *My Thoughts (Mes Pensées)*. Translated, edited, and with an Introduction by Henry C. Clark (Indianapolis: Liberty Fund, 2012).
69 Elazar, D.J. *Exploring Federalism* (Tuscaloosa: University of Alabama Press, 1987), 75.
70 Corey, K. "Relocation of National Capitals," *International Symposium on the Capital Relocation* (September 22, Seoul, 2004), 66–69.
71 Parkinson, J. "Symbolic Representation in Public Space: Capital Cities, Presence and Memory," *Democracy and Public Space* (Oxford: Oxford University Press, 2012), 32.
72 Gabuev, A. "Formirovanie regionalnoy identichnosti politii v Kitae III-II vv. do n. e. (po materialam " Shi Tszy")," *Put Vostoka. Kulturnaya, etnicheskaya i religioznaya identichnost*. Seria "Symposium". vol. 33 (SPb, 2004), 71–74.
73 Averianov, Y. "Moskva—natsionalniy tsentr russkogo naroda", *Rossiyskiy etnograf*, no. 3, (Moskva, 1993) (edited in 2011 for internet pages Zapadnaya Rus' 08.09.2011)
74 NCC (National Capital Commission). *Planning Canada's Capital Region* (Ottawa: National Capital Commission, 2000).
75 Vilkovsky, M. "Simvolicheskaia geografiia arkhitekturi gorodskogo prostranstva na primere Washingtona, Moskvi i Sankt-Peterburga," Materialy konferentsii *Simvolicheskoe i arkhetipicheskoe v culture i sotsialnikh otnosheniakh* (Moscow: Sotsiosfera, 2012).
76 Ibid.
77 Ibid.
78 Carr, S., Francis, M., Rivlin, L.G., & Stone, A.M. *Public Spaces* (Cambridge: Cambridge University Press, 1992).
79 Rowell, D. *Paris: The 'New Rome' of Napoleon I* (London & New York: Bloomsbury Academic, 2012).
80 Schlögel, K. *Jenseits des Grossen Oktober, Das Laboratorium der Moderne*, Petersburg 1909–1921 (Berlin: Siedler, 1988).
81 Kaganov, G. "Jerusalem on the Neva," *Rossica International Review of Russian Culture*, (Spring/Summer, 2003), 38–51; Kaganov, G. *Sankt-Peterburg. Obrazi prostranstva* (Moscow: ID Ivana Limbakha, 2004); Matsikh, L. "Metafizika Severnoy stolitsy", the lection in a series "Akademiya" in the "Kultura" TV channel. 19 Jan., 2011.

82 Ovason, D. *The Secret Architecture of Our Nation's Capital: The Masons and the Building of Washington, D.C.* (New York: Harper, 2002); Pinto, C. *Riddles in Stone: The Secret Architecture of Washington D.C.* (USA, 2007).
83 The crossing of the two highways in the Master Plan represents both the ibis and the airplane.
84 Kern, I. & Pimentel, E.F. *The Secret Brasilia: Enigmas of Ancient Egypt* (Brasilia: Porfiro, 2001).
85 Proudfoot, P. *Secret Plan of Canberra: Masonic Architecture of Australia's Capital* (Kensington, University of New South Wales Press, 1994).
86 Richter, D. "Astana: The Illuminati Capital of Kazakhstan," *Bohemianblog*, December 2012.
87 Curl, J. *Freemasonry & the Enlightenment: Architecture, Symbols, & Influences* (New York: Historical Publications, 2011).
88 Rowland, D. "Moscow – The Third Rome or New Israel," *Russian Review*, vol. 55, no. 4 (1996), 591–614; Kudriavtsev, M. *Moskva – Tretii Rim. Istoriko-gradostroitelnoe issledovanie*, Second Edition (Moscow: Troitsa, 2007).
89 Shatkin, G. "Colonial Capital, Modernist Capital, Global Capital: The Changing Political Symbolism of Urban Space in Metro Manila, The Philippines," *Pacific Affairs*, vol. 78, no. 4 (2005–2006), 577–601.
90 The primacy, globality, and capitalness are the distinct and autonomous characteristics of the city. Many of the primate cities, especially in smaller and medium size states, are not capital cities. Most of the global cities are not capital cities. Some of the global cities are not primate cities, notably Sydney, New York, and Berlin.
91 McKinsey Global Institute. "Urban World: Mapping the Economic Power City," March 2011. www.mckinsey.com/insights/urbanization/urban_world
92 Taylor, P. "World Cities and Territorial States: The Rise and Fall of Their Mutuality," In: Knox, Paul L. & Taylor, Peter J. (eds.), *World Cities in a World-System* (Cambridge: Cambridge University Press, 1995), 54–55.
93 A.T. Kearney Global Cities Index and Global Cities Outlook, Global Cities 2015 www.atkearney.com/research-studies/global-cities-index/2015#sthash.vt5INT7Y.dpuf
94 Ortega y Gasset, J. *La redención de las provincias y La decencia nacional*, Articulos de 1927 y 1930 (Madrid: Alianza, 1967), 192.
95 Brenner, R. *From the Force of Finance: Triumph of the Capital Markets* (New York: Texere, 2001). See also Brenner, R. *Labyrinths of Prosperity: Economic Follies, Democratic Remedies* (Ann Arbor: University of Michigan Press, 1994), 83.
96 Odessa was the third city of the Russian empire both in its size and significance. Most of the grain, the main article of Russian export, was exported through the port of Odessa. The port in Saint-Petersburg occupied only the third place after Liepāja in terms of volume of export of grain. Mironov, B. "Eksport russkogo khleba vo vtoroi polovine 18-nachale 19 veka," *Istoricheskie zapiski*, 1974. T. 93. c. 169. Table 9. See also *Khutor*, 1906, no. 5, c. 376–386.
97 Geertz, C. *The Interpretation of Cultures: Selected Essays* (New York: Basic Books, 1973); Eisenstadt, S.N. & Shachar, A. *Society, Culture, and Urbanization* (Newbury Park: Sage, 1987), 93.
98 Jacobs, J. *Cities and the Wealth of Nations: Principles of Economic Life* (New York: Random House, 1984), 142.
99 Braudel, F. *Capitalism and Material Life, 1400–1800* (New York: HarperCollins, 1974), 440.
100 Illés, I. "Transformation of the Territorial Structure in South-Eastern Europe," *Schriftenreihe des Europa Institutes Budapest*, Band 27 (2011), 105–119.

Conclusion

The analysis in this book shows that capital city relocation is a common phenomenon widely presented through history and in current political practice. Spatial factors and the choice of the capital city greatly influence not only the political potential of the country and its success but also the very viability of the state. Our analysis also reveals some similarities in the countries that seek to solve their political, economic, and cultural problems via relocation of their capital city. The fact that the debate on this topic takes place in dozens of countries reflects certain tendencies of global development. These tendencies might bring this topic to the agenda of many other countries.

The following factors of global development probably play the most crucial role. In developing countries these are fast growth of capital cities together with the high level of migration from regional areas due mostly to the low level of urbanization. Internally, this fast-paced growth of capital cities creates problems for the urban infrastructure. Externally, it generates patterns of misbalanced development between capital and regions. The above problems are amplified by corruption and hyper-centralization that cause political concerns and problems of integration. These matters are less pronounced in the developed countries, yet the threats of separatism and need for federalization contribute to the topicality of this issue.

The factors that stimulate relocation debates can be construed as technical problems, the problems of economic and urban development.

In the long run, the de-congestion of the old capital city, the integration of the country into the mega-regional economies and the development of the far-flung underdeveloped regions can provide certain economic benefits. The hyper-centralized system centered on a primary city that also performs the role of a capital can be economically ineffective.

The establishment of a new capital city can be viewed from the perspective of urban development. It will encourage a new type of relationship between cities and regions, create more balanced urban hierarchy, and provide better functional differentiation.

The relocation can also facilitate the introduction of innovative urban technologies and new standards in urban planning. The historical practice of capital city relocations follows the evolution of urban planning concepts, and the design of new capitals reflects attendant architectural and aesthetic principles. As we have seen, the new capital cities often implement the dominant and most fashionable urban concepts of their age: the City Beautiful (Washington D.C.), the Picturesque City (Ankara), Radiant City (Brasília), Dynapolis (Islamabad), Garden City (Canberra and Abuja), Green City (Gaborone and New Kabul), Eco-city (Sejong in South Korea), Intelligent City (Putrajaya), and Smart City (the new capital cities proposed in Egypt and India). Notably, in some cases, the new capital cities not only have embodied these principles but also laid the utopian and futuristic paradigms of national development serving as a foundation for more ambitious blueprints of social transformation.

Our analysis also demonstrates that most capital city relocations, including those that were aiming to address economic and urban problems, can be better understood in the context of nation-building. Six integrative strategies that we have outlined highlight different priorities in the choice of new capital cities. According to this classification, capital city relocations were designed to solve the problems of territorial integration, to boost economic development of the territories, to reach a reasonable compromise between major ethnic and religious communities and other constituent units of the state, to stimulate reconstruction of historical identity, to promote new geopolitical positioning, and promote de-centralization of the state.

To a large extent the acuteness of these problems depends on the phase of nation formation and particular challenges of state- and nation-building. Capital city transfers either make one of these strategic goals a priority, or reflect the optimization of two or more parameters deemed critical for the viability, stability, and overall success of the state.

Depending on specific circumstances the needs of nation-building might require the emancipation from colonial dependency and its symbols, the resolution of subnational conflicts and tensions, the preservation of territorial integrity in the face of potential disintegration, and the overcoming of geographic divides and other cleavages or misbalances in the development of the cities and regions. These particular tasks of economic, political, and cultural transformation are inscribed in the programs of nation- and state-building. New capitals help to solidify the identity of the states and preserve their unity.

Capital city relocations are most justified when they aim at the fundamental political reconstruction of the country. In such cases the choice of the new capital ensues from the search for more effective ways to integrate different parts of the state, the need of radical reconstruction of the polity, and interrelation between its constituent units. The change of geographic location of the government in the context of federalization can help to ensure optimal forms of relationship and interaction between federated entities. Through their relocation and iconography, the successful capitals of the federation are effectively binding the constituent units of the state. The topicality of capital city shift in the context of federalization is on the rise as seen in the proposals to relocate the seat of the government in such countries as the UK, Nepal, Bolivia, Somalia, Yemen, and Ukraine and the debates therein.

Finally, we have mentioned in our discussion some relatively rare, yet no less intriguing cases when the construction of new capital cities involves goals and issues beyond the national scale. Alongside the nation-building aspects these cases underscore the importance of mega-regional integration and creation of national capitals in the context of improvement of transnational and continental economic and cultural ties. These new capital cities aim both to assert the regional leadership of those countries that are building new seats of government and to provide better communication and transportation infrastructure to the whole mega-region in which they are located and potentially to host major supranational structures. These capital cities help the whole mega-region to integrate, enhancing their role in the international affairs. These motives are characteristic of some countries in Latin America and Southeast Asia where problems of region-building and mega-regional integration are most significant and acute.

Accordingly, the goals of capital city transfers can be dictated by multiple micro politics – economic politics, ethnic and cultural politics, identity and memory politics, security politics, urban and spatial planning politics, and international economy politics. The rationale behind each relocation leads to different location reasoning, as different geographies can promote different politics with different effectiveness. Whereas some of these politics can require the siting of the capital city in the demographic and economic core of the nation, others would benefit more from placing the capital in the periphery of the country, at a distance from the core areas.

It is important to emphasize that the diverse definitions and the multifaceted interpretations of capital city functions also give rise to the idea of the change of the seat of the government. Different concepts imply different and often contradictory normative requirements for the location of the seat of the government. On one hand, the concept of the capital implies that it should be a neutral center that will help to reconcile the interests of different constituent parts of the state and secure the parity of their representations. Neutrality and lack of strong local identity will be the most important features of this kind of capital.

The alternative concept envisages a capital city in its leadership role providing a sense of direction to the state and determining its major priorities being situated at the forefront of its strategic development. This concept can define capital cities as locomotives of the economic growth, the paragons of social development, or as the new geopolitical flagpoles of the country giving direction to its mega-regional development.

Not infrequently, the proposals to reposition a capital city are stimulated by the antinomies and tensions between the reality of the capital cities and their normative definitions upheld by political leadership. The resulting divergent definitions are based on quite often conflicting values of security, fairness, economic efficiency, and identity.

* * *

In the framework of our historical research we have pointed out both continuities and discontinuities in the practice of capital city transfers in modern and pre-modern periods. We have seen a wide variety of forms in the arrangement of the capital city function in pre-modern states. This arrangement is still far from being uniform across different countries, yet presently the forms of organization of capital city function appear more universal compared to the pre-modern period, as they were shaped by the concept of the nation-state.

We also have seen some important changes in the locational logic of capital cities. While in many pre-modern states the location of the seat of government was mainly determined by religious and military considerations, which could be classified as external, the modern nation-states tend to make these decisions based on internal factors. Some ancient seats of power were conceived as part of the universal cosmic order; the siting of the capital cities in despotic states reflected the disposition of the competing political fractions; colonial capital cities were sited based on the convenience of international trade and their metropolitan states. The internal parameters, the balance of power between its constituent parts, and the relationship between groups living in the country determine the selection of national capitals in most modern nation-states, especially in federations.

Along with differences, we have identified a number of similarities between capital city transfers in pre-modern and modern periods. For instance, the motive of de-colonization could be found in many ancient and medieval states – the Parthians were trying to liberate their new capital cities from the legacy of Hellenism; under the Ming dynasty and in the Kuomintang period the Chinese have tried to move their capital city from Beijing to erase the memory of foreign dynasties ruling China – Mongolian and Manchurian.

The idea of locating the capital city at the crossroads between two main entities of the state in the pre-modern period anticipated and foreshadowed the principles that governed the capital cities location rationale in modern federations. Like modern federations many pre-modern states promoted inclusivity and facilitated the change of character and nature of the state through introduction of new capital cities. Baghdad and Warsaw have solidified the union between the Arabs and the Persians and between the Poles and the Lithuanians, respectively, and created some kind of fusion strengthening the foundation of both states. The isolated capital cities that emerged in some contemporary autocratic states have much in common with the disembedded capitals in the despotic states that we have described.

Nevertheless, the reasons that often motivate the seat of government transfer debates in many countries today such as overpopulation, traffic gridlocks, misbalance in the economic development, were not familiar to pre-modern era. It should also be noted that the state apparatus of modern states, including all its departments and public servants, is much heavier today and much more expensive to support and transfer compared to pre-modern states.

Our analysis of the emergence of capital cities of nation-states in Europe also confirmed that they have played an important role of catalysts in the formation of the European nations. The transition from the rule over people based on personal ties to the rule over territorial states has significantly amplified the role of capital cities in the life of the state. The European notions of capital city and nation-state have spread around the world. The governments in non-European countries have adopted some European models defining the relationship between the nation and its capital cities. As a result, the making of the non-European nations often involved the introduction of the new capital cities, contributing to the maintenance and reinforcement of their new identity and reproduction of certain patterns in power relations from the Western world.

Our analysis has also shown the important role of nations, nationalism, and nation-building in contemporary global processes. Contrary to the thesis about the decline of the nations as the agents of world history promoted by some social theorists – they were supposedly displaced by large geopolitical complexes, civilizations, transnational corporations, and other supranational entities – our analysis ascertains that nations continue to play a conspicuous role in global political processes, and nation-building stays firm on the agenda of mature nations in the developed countries, not to mention the rest of the world. The capital city transfers are also critical in the processes of national and mega-regional integration and consolidation.

We have also found that different political regimes carry out capital city relocation projects with different success rates. The liberal-democratic political regimes appear to be more successful in that respect – with their city relocation projects relying upon the integrative strategies and democratic decision-making processes. The less successful political regimes seem to be struggling with the mission, although they can still achieve some more efficient administration of the country and establish particular loyalties and control over territories. Under these regimes the official de-centralization plans that were often declared to be one of the aims of capital city transfers in reality were translated into a more centralized state. We have also determined that many autocratic regimes fail to achieve not only major goals of better integration and inclusivity but even to reach specific targets related to their hidden political agendas such as suppression of dissent, marginalization of the protest movements and solidification of their power base.

The multiple case studies demonstrate that capital city transfer might not be the most efficient method to address the major social, economic, and political problems they aim to solve. Due to complexity and high costs of these projects, the change of the seat of the government remains a highly unpredictable social enterprise involving certain risks, which some governments

276 *Conclusion*

are hesitant to take. Therefore, it can be classified as a radical strategy of urban system transformation comparable to shock therapy in economics and surgical intervention in medicine.

Furthermore, the proposals to relocate the capital city in some cases mystify and camouflage real social and political problems and misrepresent them. Quite often the problems these projects seek to resolve, e.g., hyper-centralization, geographic inequities, corruption, the relationship between different regions, can be more effectively resolved via application of various alternative policies. Political debates on capital city relocations tend to draw public attention to the importance of these issues placed on the agenda and help to bring them into sharper focus. There are also issues like the political constitution of the state, strategies of national development, and the geographic identity of the state often added to the list. Ultimately these debates prove to be constructive and fruitful regardless of the relocation related outcome.

In spite of all potential concerns, the reasons to move the capital city might be very compelling, and capital city transfers can in principle contribute to positive social and political change. They are especially relevant for territorially large countries with oversize primary cities serving as their capitals. Capital city relocation projects often fail not because of their principal inability to solve particular social and political problems but because of their poor organization and administration indicating lack of strategic planning. Therefore, new approach and analytical methods, new decision-making models and planning procedures are necessary to better understand the problematic matter and improve the success rate.

In this context, politicians, policy-makers, and researchers are facing multiple challenges that need to be addressed in a more systematic fashion. These are issues associated with the administration of the transformational projects, institutional arrangements necessary to carry them out, and corruption prevention arrangements, as corruption often plague all large government mega-projects. There are also issues of urban technologies, their development and implementation linked to the infrastructure of the new capital cities. It is also extremely important to identify and develop appropriate decision-making processes related both to the principal decisions regarding capital city transfers and the choice of appropriate site for them. These processes need to reflect the right balance between expert views and opinions raised via democratic procedures.

Last but not least is the identification of the innovative financing models and options with the optimal combination of private and public funds. Some of these financing arrangements might involve external loans and land sales by developers. The most recent precedents of funding these projects involve private financing through real estate investment firms and financing through the governments of foreign countries via G-to-G (Government-to-Government) models. Some examples of such financing models include the new capital city of Afghanistan funded by Japan; Amaravati in Andhra

Pradesh, with financial help from Singapore; the capital city relocation in Egypt that will be financed by UAE's Capital City Partners (CCP) and Chinese Construction Company; and the construction of the new capital city of Zimbabwe financed by the Chinese firms.

There are also problems associated with the evaluation of performance of capital cities and criteria identifying their success.

So far there is no consensus regarding these questions, and some of them are not even properly formulated. Undoubtedly, the answers will depend on particular circumstances and local specifics. It is also clear that more efforts – both theoretical and practical – are expected to develop the concept of a new capital city to ensure its successful implementation.

Selected bibliography

Adama, Onyanta. 2012. "State, Space and Power in Postcolonial Africa: Capital Relocation as a State Building Project in Nigeria," *Hemispheres: Studies on Cultures and Societies*, no. 27, 35–39.
Adebanwi, Wale. 2011. "Abuja." In: *Capital Cities in Africa: Power and Powerlessness*, Ed. by G. Therborn & S. Bekker (Pretoria & Dakar: HSRC & CODESRIA), pp. 84–102.
Ades, Alberto & Glaeser, Edward. 1995. "Trade and Circuses: Explaining Urban Giants," *Quarterly Journal of Economics*, vol. 110, 195–227.
Akam, Simon. 2011. "Not Such a Capital Idea after All," *Independent*, February 24.
Aksakov, Konstantin. 2000. "Znachenie stolitsy." In: *Moskva-Petersburg: Pro et Contra. Dialog kultur v istorii natsionalnogo samosoznania* (Saint-Petersburg: Russkii khristianskii gumanitarnii institut).
Alimbekova, Gulzhan. 2008. "Otnoshenie astanchan i almaatintsev k perenosu stolitsy: resultaty sotsiologicheskogo issledovania." In: *20yi vek: perenosy stolits* (Astana: Elorda).
Al Sultani, Abdullah. 2009. "Muharraq City: A GIS-Planning Strategy for Its Ancient Heritage," Ph.D. Dissertation, University of Portsmouth, 2009.
Ambedkar, B.R. 1955. "India and the Necessity of a Second Capital: A Way to Remove Tension between the North and the South." In: *Thoughts of Linguistic States* (Bombay: Ramkrishna Printing Press).
Anandan, Sujata. 2012. "Make Mumbai Second Capital of India, City Forum Petitions PM," *Hindustan Times*, June 26.
Anderson, Benedict. 1991. *The Imagined Community* (London: Verso).
Anna, Timothy. 1998. *Forging Mexico, 1821–1835* (Lincoln: Nebraska University Press).
Aristotle. 2013. *Politics*. Translated by Carnes Lord (Chicago & London: University of Chicago Press).
Ata-Meken. 2010. "Perenos stolitsy Kyrgyzstana v Osh nevozmozhen i neeffektiven—eksperty," July 9.
A.T. Kearney Global Cities Index and Global Cities Outlook, Global Cities. 2015. www.atkearney.com/research-studies/global-cities-index/2015#sthash.vt5INT7Y.dpuf
Atkinson, David & Dodds, Klaus (eds.). 2004. *Geopolitical Traditions: Critical Histories of a Century of Geopolitical Thought* (London: Routledge), p. 416.
Averchenko, Tatiana. 2011. "Tadzhikistan pomeniaet stolitsu?" *Pravda*, July 22–25.
Averianov, Y. 1993. "Moskva—natsionalnyi tsentr russkogo naroda," *Rossiiskii etnograf*, no. 3.

Selected bibliography 279

Bae, Se-Young. 2004. "The Effects of Capital City Relocation in Korea Based on Total Factor Productivity Analysis," *Japan Economic Policy Association Annual Conference*, Tokyo, November 11.
Baldussi, D. 2010. "Brasilia, 50 Years as the Capital," *Rio Times*, January 12.
Bangkok Post. 2011. "PT MPs Propose New Capital City," November 15.
Barani, Luca. 2011. "Fiscal Federalism and Capital Cities: A Comparative Analysis of Berlin and Brussels," *L'Europe en Formation*, vol. 1, no. 359, 21–45.
Barnstone, Deborah. 2014. *Nomina sunt Omina—Capital City Bonn: Inventing an Image for the Federal Republic of Germany* (Oxford: Oxford University Press).
BBC News. 2003. "Make Liverpool UK Capital, Says MP," January 7.
BBC News. 2009. "Taking the Capital Out of a City," November 3.
Benjamin, Walter. 2002. "Paris, Capital of the Nineteenth Century." In: *Walter Benjamin: Selected Writing, Volume 3, 1935–1938*, Ed. by Howard Eiland & Michael W. Jennings (Cambridge: Harvard University Press), p. 462.
Berger, Stefan & Miller, Alexei (eds.). 2014. *Nationalizing Empires* (Budapest: Central European University Press).
Berges, Wilhelm. 1953. "Das Reich ohne Hauptstadt." In: *Das Hauptstadtproblem in der Geschichte*, Ed. by Friedrich-Meinecke-Institut (Tübingen: Max Niemeyer Verlag), pp. 1–30.
Berry, Brian. 2008. "Urbanization." In: *Urban Ecology. An International Perspective on the Interaction between Humans and Nature*, Ed. by John Marzluff et al. (New York: Springer), pp.25–48.
Bertaud, Allen. 2004. *The Spatial Organization of Cities: Deliberate Outcome or Unforseen Consequence?* (Institute of Urban and Regional Development: Berkeley, University of California at Berkeley).
Best, A.C. 1970. "Gaberone: Problems and Prospects of a New Capital," *Geographic Review*, vol. 60, 1–14.
Bettencourt, L.M.A., Lobo, J., Helbing, D., Kuhnert, C. & West, G.B. 2007. "Growth, Innovation, Scaling, and the Pace of Life in Cities," *Proceedings of the National Academy of Sciences*, vol. 104, no. 17, 7301–7306.
Bhardwaj, Surinder. 1994. "The Concept of Sacred Cities in Asia with Special Reference to India." In: *The Asian City: Processes of Development, Characteristics and Planning*, Ed. by Ashok Dutt (Dordrecht: Kluwer Academic Publishers).
Bianchini, Annik. 2009. "The Ten 'Grand Paris' Projects for the Coming Decades," *Actualité en France*, no. 15 (April).
Bilham, Roger. 1999. "Millions at Risk as Big Cities Grow Apace in Earthquake Zones," *Nature*, vol. 401, no. 6755, 738–740.
Bird, Julia & Staub, Stéphane. 2014. "The Brasília Experiment: Road Access and the Spatial Pattern of Long-Term Local Development in Brazil," *World Bank Research Working Paper*, Report Number WPS6964, July.
Blair, Sheila. 1986. "The Mongol Capital of Sulṭāniyya, 'The Imperial'," *Iran: Journal of the British Institute of Persian Studies*, vol. 24, 139–151.
Boiy, T. 2004. *Late Achaemenid and Hellenistic Babylon* (New York: Peeters Publishers).
Borgatti, Stephen & Everette, Martin. 2006. "A Graph-Theoretic Perspective on Centrality," *Social Networks*, vol. 28, no. 4, 466–484.
Borgstede, Simone Beate. 2011. *All is Race: Benjamin Disraeli on Race, Nation and Empire* (Berlin: Lit Verlag).

Borisov, G. 2012. "Perenos stolitsy Irana—tekhnicheskie, ekonomicheskie i politicheskie aspekty," *Regnum*, December 17. www.regnum.ru/news/polit/1723028.html
Bosworth, Clifford Edmund. 1990. "Capital Cities, II: In Islamic Times." In: *Encyclopedia Iranica*, Ed. by Ehsan Yarshater, vol. 4 (New York), pp. 770–774.
Boucaud, André et Louis. "Paranoïa, Répression et Trafics en Birmanie," *Le Monde Diplomatique*, Novembre, 2006.
Boucheron, Patrick (ed.). 2006. *Les villes capitales au Moyen Âge. XXXVIe Congrès de la SHMES (Istanbul, 1–6 juin 2005)* (Paris: Sorbonne).
Bowring, B. 2005–2006. "Moscow: Third Rome, Model Communist City, Eurasian Antagonist—and Power as Power," A London Metropolitan University Research Institute, *Polis*.
Bozdoğan, Sibel. 2001. *Modernism and Nation Building: Turkish Architectural Culture in the Early Republic* (Seattle & London: University of Washington).
Brade, Isolde & Rudolph, Robert. 2004. "Moscow, the Global City? The Position of the Russian Capital within the European System of Metropolitan Areas," *Area*, vol. 36, no. 1, 69–80.
Brakman, Steven, Garretsen, Harry & Van Marrewijk, Charles. 2001. *The New Introduction to Geographical Economics* (Cambridge: Cambridge University Press).
Braudel, Fernand. 1974. *Capitalism and Material Life, 1400–1800* (New York: HarperCollins).
Braudel, Fernand. 1977. *Afterthoughts on Material Civilization and Capitalism* (Baltimore & London: John Hopkins University).
Braudel, Fernand. 1992. "The Function of Capital Cities." In: *Civilization and Capitalism, 15th-18th Century: The Structure of Everyday Life* (Berkeley: Berkeley University Press), pp. 527–563.
Braudel, Fernand. 2001. *Memory and the Mediterranean* (New York: Knopf).
Braun, Dietmar. 2011. "How Centralized Federations Avoid Over-Centralization," *Regional & Federal Studies*, vol. 21, no. 1, 35–54.
Brenner, Reuven. 1994. *Labyrinths of Prosperity: Economic Follies, Democratic Remedies* (Ann Arbor: University of Michigan Press).
Brenner, Reuven. 2001. *From the Force of Finance: Triumph of the Capital Markets* (New York: Texere).
Butler, Catherine. 2014. "Want to Save the United Kingdom? Move the Capital to Glasgow," *Independent*, June 19.
Callaci, Emily. 2015. "'Chief Village in a Nation of Villages': History, Race and Authority in Tanzania's Dodoma Plan," *Urban History*, vol. 43, no. 1 (2015) 96–116
Callegari, Lope. 2009. "La Geopolítica Aconseja Trasladar la Capital de la República a la Sierra Central," *Eco Andino. Revista de Cultura*, 17 de octubre.
Campante, Filipe & Do, Quoc-Anh. 2013. "Isolated Capital Cities, Accountability and Corruption: Evidence from US States," NBER Working Paper No. 19027, May.
Campante, Filipe, Do, Quoc-Anh & Guimaraes, Bernardo. 2012. "Isolated Capital Cities and Misgovernance," Harvard Kennedy School of Government, *Working Papers Series*, RW12–058.
Campbell, Scott. 2000. "The Changing Role and Identity of Capital Cities in the Global Era," *Paper presented at the Association of American Geographers*, Pittsburgh, p. 27.

Campbell, Scott. 2003. "The Enduring Importance of National Capital Cities in the Global Era," University of Michigan, *Working Papers Series*, p. 32.
Campos, Thai. 2011. "Brasilia—The Mystical Capital of Brazil," http://suite101.com/article/brasilia-the-mystical-capital-of-brazil-a367914
Carlstrom, Gregg. 2011. "Juba: East Africa's Economic Boom Town," *Al Jazera*, July 7.
Carmichael, J. 1967. *The Shaping of the Arabs* (New York & London: Macmillan).
Carr, S., Francis, M., Rivlin, L.G. & Stone, A.M. 1992. *Public Spaces* (Cambridge: Cambridge University Press).
Carrol, Glenn & Meyer, John. 1982. "Capital Cities in the American Urban System: The Impact of State Expansion," *American Journal of Sociology*, vol. 88, no. 3 (November), 565–578.
Cavour (Benso), Camillo. 1906. "Rome as the Capital of United Italy." In: *The World's Famous Orations. Continental Europe (380–1906)*. vol. 7, Ed. by William Bryan (New York & London: Funk and Wagnalls Company).
Cerutti, Furio & Lucarelli, Sonia (eds.). 2008. *The Search for a European Identity: Values, Policies and Legitimacy of the European Union* (London & New York: Routledge).
Chanco, Boo. 2015. "Decongest Metro Manila," *Philippine Star*, August 12.
Charle, Cristophe & Roche, Daniel (eds.). 2002. *Capitales culturelles, capitals simboliques. Paris et les expériences européennes,* XVIIIe-XXe *siècles* (Paris: Publications de la Sorbonne).
Chase-Dunn, Christopher & Willard, Alice. 1993. "Systems of Cities and World-Systems: Settlement Size Hierarchies and Cycles of Political Centralization, 2000 BC-1988 AD," *Paper presented at the International Studies Association Meeting*, March 24–27 (Mexico: Acapulco).
Chevrant-Breton, Marie. 2007. "Selling the World City: A Comparison of Promotional Strategies in Paris and London," *European Planning Studies*, vol. 5, no. 2, 137–161.
Chocrane, Allan & Jonas, Andrew. 1999. "Reimaging Berlin: World City, Capital City or Ordinary Place," *European Urban and Regional Studies*, vol. 6, no. 2, 145–164.
Choe, Sang-Hun. 2010. "City's Evolution Offers Lessons in Korean Politics," *New York Times*, March 3.
Chubashenko, Dmitry. 2012. "Chetvertaia Moldavskaia respublika," *Regnum*, April 9.
Çinar, Alev. 2007. "The Imagined Community as Urban Reality: The Making of Ankara," In: *Urban Imaginaries: Locating the Modern City*, Ed. by Alev Çinar & Thomas Bender (Minneapolis: The University of Minnesota Press), pp. 151–181.
Clark, Peter & Lepetit, Bernard. 1996. *Capital Cities and Their Hinterlands in Early Modern Europe* (Cambridge: Scholar Press), p. 249.
Clarke, John. 1971. "The Growth of Capital Cities in Africa," *Africa Spectrum*, vol. 61, no. 2, 33–40.
Claval, Paul. 2000. "The European System of Capital Cities," *GeoJournal*, vol. 51, no. 1, 73–81.
Cohen, Gary & Szabo, Franz (eds.). 2008. *Embodiments of Power: Building Baroque Cities in Europe* (New York & Oxford: Berghan), p. 320.
Cohen, Saul. 2009. *Geopolitics: The Geography of International Relations* (Ianham, MD: Rowman & Littlefield).

Corey, Kenneth. 2004. "Relocation of National Capitals," *International Symposium on the Capital Relocation*, Seoul, September 22, pp. 43–107.

Corey, Kenneth. 2011. "Planning and Implementing Capital Cities—Lessons from the Past and Prospects for Intelligent Development in the Future: The Case of Korea." In: *Engineering Earth: The Impacts of Megaengineering Projects*, Ed. by Stanley Brunn (London & New York: Springer).

Cornish, Vaughan, 1921. "London as an Imperial Capital," *Scottish Geographical Magazine*, vol. 37, no. 3, 164–171.

Cornish, Vaughan. 1923. *The Great Capitals: An Historical Geography* (London & New York: Methuen).

Cotterell, Arthur. 2008. *Imperial Capitals of China* (Woodstock, NY: Overlook Press).

Coulanges, Fustel de. 2001. *The Ancient City. A Study on the Religion, Laws, and Institutions of Greece and Rome*. (Kitchener: Batoche Books).

Cox, Wendell. 2010. "Unmanageable Jakarta Soon To Lose National Capital?" *New Geography*, September 13. www.newgeography.com/content/001767-unmanageable-jakarta-soon-to-lose-national-capital

Cross, Samuel & Sherbowitz-Wetzor, Olgerd P., trans. and ed. 1953. *The Russian Primary Chronicle: Laurentian Text*. (Cambridge: Massachusetts).

Curl, James. 2011. *Freemasonry & the Enlightenment: Architecture, Symbols, & Influences* (New York: Historical Publications).

Dagron, Gilbert. 1974. *Naissance d'une capitale. Constantinople et ses institutions de 330 à 451* (Paris: Presses universitaires de France).

Dale, E. 1961. "The West Indies: A Federation in Search of a Capital," *The Canadian Geographer*, vol. 5, no. 2, 44–52.

Dascher, Kristof. 2000. "Are Politics and Geography Related? Evidence from a Cross-Section of Capital Cities," *Public Choice*, vol. 105, 373–392.

Daum, Andreas & Mauch, Christof (eds.). 2009. *Berlin-Washington. 1800–2000: Capital Cities, Cultural Representations, and National Identities* (New York: Cambridge University Press).

Davies, David. 2007. "Nottingham: The New Capital of England?" *Britology Watch: Deconstructing 'British Values'*, November 6.

Denicke, Lars. 2011. "Fifty Years' Progress in Five: Brasilia—Modernization, Globalism, and the Geopolitics of Flight." In: *Entangled Geographies: Empire and Technopolitics in the Global Cold War*, Ed. by Gabrielle Hecht (Boston: MIT Press), pp. 185–208.

Dieye, Yatma. 2013. "Faut-il déplacer la capitale sénégalaise?" *Assirou.Net*, 22 mai. http://www.seneweb.com/news/Economie/faut-il-deplacer-la-capitale-senegalaise_n_96236.html

Dijkink, Gertjan. 2000. "European Capital Cities as Political Frontiers," *GeoJournal*, vol. 51, no. 1, 65–71.

Dijkstra, Lewis. 2013. "Why Investing More in the Capital Can Lead to Less Growth," *Cambridge Journal of Regions, Economy and Society*, vol. 6, no. 2, 251–268.

Dikshit, Ramesh. 1975. *Political Geography of Federalism: An Inquiry Into Origins and Stability* (London & Delhi: Macmillan).

Dikshit, Ramesh. 2000. *Political Geography: The Spatiality of Politics* (New Delhi: McGraw Hills), pp. 85–94.

Djament, Géraldine. 2005. "Le débat sur Rome capitale," *L'Espace Géographique*, Tome 34, no. 3, 369–380.

Djament, Géraldine. 2009. "Le débat sur Rome capitale (1861–1871): choix de localisation et achèvement de la construction nationale italienne," *Revue historique*, no. 1, 99–118.
Djament-Tran, Géraldine. 2010. "Les scénarios de localisation des capitales, révélateurs des conceptions de l'unité nationale," *Confins. Revue franco-brésilienne de géographie*, no. 9. http://confins.revues.org/6414
Dogan, Mattei. 2004. "Four Hundred Giant Cities Atop the World," *International Social Science Journal*, vol. 56, no. 181, September, 347–360.
Donahue, Bill. 2005. "The Believers," *Washington Post*, September 18.
Dorling, Danny. 2014. "The London Problem: Has the Capital Become too Dominant?" *New Statesman*, September 4.
Dorling, Danny. 2015. "Should Parliament Move Out of London?" *The Guardian*, March 7.
Dunnet, James. 2011. "Great Britain—The Case for a New Capital City," *The Architectural Review*, November 26.
Dunnet, James. 2015. "This House Moves to Move: The Case for Relocating Parliament," *The Architectural Review*, May 7.
Du Preez, P. 1995. *One Nation: One Capital, the Case of Pretoria* (Pretoria: Adams & Adams).
Durand-Guédy, David. 2013. *Turko-Mongol Rulers, Cities and City Life* (Leiden & Boston: Brill), p. 452.
Eaton, Jonathan & Eckstein, Zvi. 1994. "Cities and Growth: Theory and Evidence from France and Japan," *Regional Science and Urban Economics*, vol. 27, August 4–5, 443–474.
The Economist. 1998. "Who Says Brasilia Does Not Work?" June 20.
The Economist. 2004. "The Pros and Cons of Capital Flight," August 13.
The Economist. 2006. "Ani, a Disputed City: The Ruins of a Contested Capital Are Still Hostage to Geopolitics," June 15.
The Economist. 2010. "Sing a Song of $40 Billion," July 22.
The Economist. 2012a. "The Capital: Removal Time," December 15.
The Economist. 2012b. "The City Roars Back," July 21.
The Economist. 2012c. "The Laws of the City," June 23.
The Economist. 2012d. "On a High. London: Special Report," June 30.
Egreteau, Renaud & Jagan, Larry. 2013. *Soldiers and Diplomacy in Burma: Understanding the Foreign Relations of the Burmese Praetorian State* (Singapore: NUS Press).
Egyptian Street. 2014. "Egypt to Build a 'New Administrative Capital City'," July 18.
Eisenstadt, Shmuel. 1986. *The Origins and Diversity of Axial Age Civilizations* (New York: SUNY Press).
Eisenstadt, Shmuel N. & Shachar, Arie. 1987. *Society, Culture, and Urbanization* (Newbury Park: Sage), p. 391.
Elazar, D.J. 1987. *Exploring Federalism* (Tuscaloosa: University of Alabama Press).
Eldredge, Hanford. 1975. *World Capitals: Toward Guided Urbanization* (Garden City, NY: Anchor Press).
Emet, Chad. 1996. "The Capital Cities of Jerusalem," *Geographical Review*, vol. 86, no. 2, 233–258.
Encyclopedia Iranica. "Erevan". www.iranicaonline.org/articles/erevan-1
Epstein, David. 1973. *Brasilia from the Plan to Reality: A Study of Planned and Spontaneous Urban Development* (Berkeley: University of California Press).

284 Selected bibliography

Ernst, Carl. 2003. *Eternal Garden: Mysticism, History, and Politics at a South Asian Sufi Center* (Minneapolis: Lerner Publications).
European Commission & Belgian Presidency. 2001. Brussels, Capital of Europe. Final Report, October.
Evanson, Norma. 1973. *Two Brazilian Capitals: Architecture and Urbanism in Rio de Janeiro and Brasilia* (New Heaven: Yale University Press).
Evered, Kyle. 2008. "Symbolizing a Modern Anatolia: Ankara as Capital in Turkey's Early Republican Landscape," *Comparative Studies in South Asia, Africa, and the Middle East*, vol. 28, no. 2, 326–341.
Eyinla, B.M. 2000. "From Lagos to Abuja: The Domestic Politics and International Implications of Relocating Nigeria's Capital City." In: *Hauptstädte und Global Cities and der Schwelle zum 21*, Ed. by A. Sohn & H. Weber (Bochum: Winkler Verlag), pp. 239–266.
Falola, Toyin. 2003. *Power of African Culture* (Rochester, NY: University of Rochester Press), p. 354.
Farrar, Margaret. 2008. *Building the Body Politic. Power and Urban Space in Washington, D.C.* (Champaign, IL: University of Illinois Press).
Fields, Gary. 1999. "City Systems, Urban History, and Economic Modernity," *Berkeley Planning Journal*, vol. 13, 102–128.
Fiévé, Nicolas & Waley, Paul. 2003. *Japanese Capitals in Historical Perspective: Place, Power and Memory in Kyoto, Edo and Tokyo* (London: Routledge).
Flanagan, James. 1979. "The Relocation of the Davidic Capital," *Journal of the American Academy of Religion*, vol. 47, no. 2, 223–244.
Flanders, Stephanie. 2013. "Should Britain Let Go of London?" *BBC News*, March 25. www.bbc.com/news/business-21934564
Florida, Richard. 2005. *Cities and the Creative Class* (New York: Routledge).
Fortenbaugh, Robert. 1948. *The Nine Capitals of the United States* (New York, PA: Maple Press Co.).
Frank, Andre. 1969. *Latin America: Underdevelopment or Revolution?* (New York: Monthly Review Press).
Frey, R. Scott & Dietz, Thomas. 1990. "The Growth of Capital Cities in the World Economic System," *Sociological Spectrum*, vol. 10, no. 2, 271–281.
Fuccaro, Nelida. 2009. *Histories of City and State in the Persian Gulf: Manama since 1800* (Cambridge: Cambridge University Press).
Gabuev, A. 2004. "Formirovanie regionalnoi identichnosti politii v Kitae III-II vv. do n. e. (po materialam *Shǐjì*)" In: *Put Vostoka. Kulturnaya, etnicheskaya i religioznaya identichnost*. Ed. by P. Neshitov, Seria "Symposium", Vol. 33 (Saint-Petersburg: Sankt-Peterburgskoe filosofskoe obschestvo), pp. 71–74.
Galiani, Sebastian & Kim, Sukkoo. 2008. "The Law of the Primate City in the Americas," *Proceedings of a Conference Honoring the Contributions of Kenneth Sokoloff*, UCLA, Los Angeles.
Gao, Jing. 2010. "Discussion on Relocating China's Capital Resumes after Beijing is Deemed Unlivable," *China News*, December 18. www.ministryoftofu.com/2010/12/discussion-on-relocating-chinas-capital-resumes-after-beijing-is-deemed-unlivable/
Garnett, Alice. 1928. "The Capitals of Morocco," *Scottish Geographical Magazine*, vol. 44, no. 1, 31–41.
Geertz, Clifford. 1973. *The Interpretation of Cultures: Selected Essays* (New York: Basic Books).

Geil, William Edgar. 2005. *Eighteen Capitals of China* (Philadelphia: Lippinkot Co). Originally published in 1911.
Gerasimov, Ilia. 2004. *Novaia imperskaia istoria postsovetskogo prostranstva* (Kazan: New Imperial History).
Ghurye, G.S. 1962. *Cities and Civilization* (Bombay: Popular Prakashan).
Giblin, Béatrice, Papin, Delphine & Subra, Philippe. 2001/2. "Paris/London: Geopolitical Challenges of Capital Cities," *Hérodote*, no. 101, 26–56.
Gilbert, August. 1989. "Moving the Capital of Argentina: A Further Example of Utopian Planning?" *Cities*, vol. 6, 234–242.
Gibson, Lay James. 1996. "Some Thoughts on a New Capital for Japan, on Capitals in General, and on Sustainable Cities," *Studies in Regional Science*, vol. 27, (1996–1997) no. 1, 267–273.
Goethem, Ellen von. 2008. *Nagaoka. Japan's Forgotten Capital* (Leiden: Brill NV).
Goma, Daniel. 2010. "Naypyidaw vs. Yangon: The Reasons Behind the Junta's Decision to Move the Burmese Capital." In: *Burma or Myanmar? The Struggle for National Identity*, Ch. 7. Ed. by Lowell Dittmer (Singapore: World Scientific Publishing), pp. 185–204.
González, Javier & Ríos, Alberto. 2009. "La Ciudad de Mexico y el Districto Federal: Un Analisis Politico-Constitucional," *Estudios constitucionales*, vol. 7, no. 2, Santiago, 207–239.
Gordon, David & Seasons, Mark. 2009. "Administrative and Financial Strategies for Implementing Plans in Political Capitals," *Canadian Journal of Urban Research*, June, 94–117.
Gordon, I.R. 2006. *Capital Needs, Capital Growth and Global City Rhetoric in Mayor Livingstone's London Plan*, Research paper (London: LSE).
Gottmann, Jean. 1985. "The Study of Former Capitals," *Ekistics*, vols. 314/315 (Sept./Oct.–Nov./Dec.), 541–546.
Gottmann, Jean. 1990. "Capital Cities." In: *After Megapolisis: The Urban Writings of Jean Gottmann* (Baltimore: Johns Hopkins University), pp. 63–82.
Graan, Andrew. 2013. "Counterfeiting the Nation? Skopje 2014 and the Politics of Nation-Branding in Macedonia," *Cultural Anthropology*, vol. 28, no. 1, 161–179.
Gravier, Jean-François. 1947. *Paris and the French Desert* (Paris: Portulan), p. 418.
Grief, Avner & Tabellini, Guido. 2010. "Cultural and Institutional Bifurcation: China and Europe Compared," *American Economic Review*, vol. 100, no. 2, 1–10.
Griffiths, Ieuan. 2005. *The African Inheritance* (London: Routledge), p. 232.
Grygiel, Jakub. 2006. *Great Powers and Geopolitical Change* (Baltimore: John Hopkins University).
Gupta, Harsh. 2015. "Pataliputra: The New Capital?" *Swarajya*, June 1. http://swarajyamag.com/ideas/pataliputra-the-new-capital/
Gurund, Anand. 2012. "Maoists to Propose Chitwan as Federal Capital of Nepal," *Nepal News*, April 25.
Hall, C. Michael. 2002. "Tourism in Capital Cities," *Tourism: An International Interdisciplinary Journal*, vol. 50, no. 3, 235–248.
Hall, John W. 1968. "The Castle Town and Japan's Modern Urbanization." In: *Studies in the Institutional History of Early Modern Japan*, Ed. by John W. Hall & Marius Jansen (Princeton, NJ: Princeton UP), pp. 169–188.
Hall, Peter. 1980. *Great Planning Disasters* (Berkeley: University of California Press).

Hall, Peter. 1993. "The Changing Role of Capital Cities: Six Types of Capital City." In: *Capital Cities/Les Capitales: Perspectives Internationales/International Perspectives*, Ed. by J. Taylor, J.G. Lengelle & C. Andrew (Ottawa: Carleton University Press), pp. 69–84.

Hamdan, Gamal. 1964. "Capitals in the New Africa," *Economic Geography*, vol. 40, 239–253.

Hansen, Niles, Higgins, Benjamin & Savoie, Donald. 1990. *Regional Policy in a Changing World* (New York: Plenum Press).

Hardoy, Jorge. 1993. "Ancient Capital Cities and New Capital Cities of Latin America." In: *Capital Cities: International Perspectives*, Ed. by J. Taylor, J. Lengelle & C. Andrew (Ottawa: Carleton University Press), 99–128.

Hardy, Dennis. 2006. "Capital Matters: Reflecting on a Recent Meeting of the Capital Alliance Network of Capital Cities. Lessons for the UK in the Function and Organization of Capital Cities Elsewhere in the World," *Town and Country Planning*, January.

Harris, Chauncey. 1970. *Cities of the Soviet Union* (Chicago: Chicago University Press).

Harvey, David. 2012. *Rebel Cities: From the Right to the City to the Urban Revolution* (London: Verso).

Haushofer, Karl. 2013. *Geopolitik des Pazifischen Ozeans: Studien über die Wechselbeziehungen zwischen Geographie und Geschichte* (Bremen: Dogma).

Hawkins, Don. 2014. "No, D.C. Isn't Really Built on a Swamp," *Washington Post*, August 29.

Heike, Monogatari. 1918. *Transactions of the Asiatic Society of Japan*, vol. XLVI, Part II (Tokyo: Keiogijiki, Mita).

Hein, Carola (ed.). 2006. *European Brussels: Whose Capital? Whose City?* (Brussels: La Lettre Vole), p. 313.

Henderson, Vernon. 2003. "The Urbanization Process and Economic Growth: The So-What Question," *Journal of Economic Growth*, vol. 8, no. 1 (March), 47–71.

Henderson, Vernon. 2005. "Urban Primacy, External Costs and Quality of Life," *Resource and Energy Economics*, vol. 24, nos. 1–2, 95–106.

Henrikson, Alan. 1983. "A Small, Cozy Town, Global in Scope: Washington, D.C.," *Ekistics*, vol. 50, no. 299 (March/April), 123–145.

Herrick, Bruce. 1962. "Internal Migration, Unemployment, and Economic Growth in Post-War Chile." unpublished Ph.D. thesis, Massachusetts Institute of Technology.

Hiromi, Otsuka. 1999. "A Study on the National Capital City: Relocating Capital City Functions: The Significance in Japan and Other Countries," *City Planning Review*, no. 218, 25–28.

Hirst, Paul. 2005. *Space and Power: Politics, War and Architecture* (Cambridge: Polity).

Hitler, A. *Hitler's Table Talk, 1941–1944*. 1988. H.R. Trevor-Roper (intro), (Oxford: Oxford University Press).

Hitti, Philip. 1973. *Capital Cities of Arab Islam* (Minneapolis: University of Minnesota Press).

Ho, K.C. 2005–2006. "Globalization and Southeast Asian Capital Cities," *Pacific Affairs*, vol. 78, no. 4, 535–541.

Hohenberg, Paul & Lees, Lynn. 1985. *The Making of Urban Europe, 1000–1950* (Cambridge: Harvard University Press).

Holston, James.1989. *The Modernist City: An Anthropological Critique of Brasilia* (Chicago: University of Chicago Press).
Horvath, Ronald J. 1969. "The Wandering Capitals of Ethiopia," *The Journal of African History*, vol. 10, no. 2, 205–219.
Hoselitz, Bert. 1955. "Generative and Parasitic Cities," *Economic Development and Cultural Change*, vol. 3, no. 3 (April), 278–294.
Hosking, Geoffrey. 1998. *Russia: People and Empire, 1552–1917* (Cambridge: Harvard University Press).
Hosking, Geoffrey. 2001. *Russia and the Russians: A History from Rus to a Russian Federation* (London: Allen Lane).
Hsu, Shengi. 2004. "From Pingcheng to Luoyang—Substantiation of the Climatic Cause for Capital Relocation of the Beiwei Dynasty," *Progress in Natural Sciences*, vol. 14, no. 8, 725–729.
Iannaccone, Laurence, Haight, Colleen & Rubin, Jared. 2011. "Lessons from Delphi: Religious Markets and Spiritual Capitals," *Journal of Economic Behavior & Organization*, vol. 77, 326–338.
Ikoku, Goomsu. 2004. "The City as Public Space: Abuja—The Capital City of Nigeria," *Forum*, vol. 6, no. 1, 34–45.
Illés, Iván. 2011. "Transformation of the Territorial Structure in South-Eastern Europe," *Schriftenreihe des Europa Institutes Budapest, Band*, vol. 27, 105–119.
Inwood, Stephen. 1998. *A History of London* (London: Carroll & Graf Publishers).
Isserman, Andrew. 1995. "Comments on 'Urban Concentration' by Krugman," *Proceedings of the World Bank Annual Conference on Development Economics*, Los Angeles.
Izazola, Haydea. 2004. "Migration to and from Mexico City, 1995–2000," *Environment & Urbanization*, vol. 16, no. 1.
Jacobs, Jane. 1984. *Cities and the Wealth of Nations: Principles of Economic Life* (New York: Random House).
Jahn, Friedrich-Ludwig. 1833. "An Essay on Capital Cities." In: *Essai sur les Moeurs, la Littérature, et la Nationalité des peuples de l'Allemagne* (Paris: J.B. Nichols & Son, 1832). The Gentleman's Magazine, vol. 103, no. 2 (July–December), pp. 226–229.
Joffe, Alexander. 1998. "Disembedded Capitals in Western Asian Perspective," *Society for Comparative Study of Society & History*, vol. 40, no. 3, 549–580.
Johnson, Gary. 2011. "The Drivers of Dehsabz: Who Is Building New Kabul City?" *Family Security Matters*, July 14. www.familysecuritymatters.org/publications/id.9940/pub_detail.asp
Jun, M.J. 2007. "Korea's Public Sector Relocation: Is It a Viable Option for Balanced National Development?" *Regional Studies*, vol. 41, no. 1.
Kacar, Duygu. 2010. "Ankara, a Small Town Transformed to a Nation's Capital," *Journal of Planning History*, vol. 9, 43–65.
Kaganov, Grigory. 2003. "Jerusalem on the Neva," *Rossica International Review of Russian Culture*, Spring/Summer, 38–51.
Kaganov, Grigory. 2004. *Sankt-Peterburga: Obrazi prostranstva* (Moscow: ID Ivana Limbakha).
Kallis, Aristotle. 2014. *The Third Rome, 1922–43: The Making of the Fascist Capital* (New York: Palgrave Macmillan), p. 352.
Karamzin, Nikolai. 1991. *Zapiska o drevnei i novoi Rossii v eyo politicheskom i grazhdanskom otnosheniakh* (Moscow: Nauka).

Karapetyants, Artemiy. 2000. "Kitaiskaia tsivilizatsiia kak alternative Sredizemno-morskoi," *Obschestvennie nauki i sovremennost*, no. 1, 132–138.
Kearns, K.C. 1973. "Belmopan: Perspective on a New Capital," *Geographic Review*, vol. 63, 147–169.
Keating, Michael. 1983. "Decentralization in Mitterrand's France," *Public Administration*, vol. 61, 237–225.
Kedourie, Elie. 1984. "Foreign Policy: A Practical Pursuit." In: *The Crossman Confessions and other Essays in Politics, History, and Religion* (London: Mansell), pp. 133–136.
Kern, Iara & Pimentel, Ernani Figueiras. 2001. *The Secret Brasilia: Enigmas of Ancient Egypt* (Brasilia: Porfiro), p. 64.
Keyes, Sean. 2012. "How Capital Cities Can Turn Into Parasites?" *Money Week*, March 13.
Kezer, Zeynep. 1992. "The Making of a National Capital: Ideology and Socio-Spatial Practices in Early Republican Ankara," Ph.D. dissertation. University of California at Berkeley.
Khaldun, Ibn. 1967. *The Muqaddimah: An Introduction to History*. Translated by Franz Rosenthal (Princeton, NJ: Princeton University Press).
Khayutina, Marina. 2007. "Zur Konstruktion der imperialen Hauptstadt im frühen China." *Workshop "Metropolen" of the Interdisciplinary Project "Comparison of Empires" at the Ruhr-University Bochum*, Bochum, February 2.
Khayutina, Marina. 2008. "Did the First Kings of the Zhou Dynasty Relocate their Capital? The Topos of the *Central Place* in Early China and its Historical Contexts," *XVII Conference of the European Association of Chinese Studies*, Lund, August 6–10.
Kim, Yeong-Hyun & Short, John. 2008. *Cities and Economies* (New York: Routledge).
King, Ross. 2010. "Re-Writing the City: Putrajaya as Representation," *Cities*, vol. 27, no. 4 (August), 285–297 **OR** King, R. 2007. "Re-writing the city: Putrajaya as representation," *Journal of Urban Design*, vol. 12, no. 1, 117–138.
Kinoshita, Yusuke & Kiyotani, Kohei. 2011. "Post-Earthquake-Disaster Reconstruction and Dispersion of Risks Associated with Capital City Functions," *Quarterly Journal of Public Policy & Management*, vol. 4.
Kirkup, James. 2008. "Londoners' £2000 Tax Subsidy for Rest of UK," *The Telegraph*, September 30.
Kironde, J.M. Lusugga. 1993. "Will Dodoma Ever be the New Capital of Tanzania?" *Geoforum*, vol. 24, no. 4 (November), 435–453.
Knight, D. 1991. *Choosing Canada's Capital: Conflict Resolution in a Parliamentary System* (Ottowa: Carleton University Press).
Ko, Chiu Yu, Koyama, Mark & Sng, Tuan-Hwee. 2014. "Unified China and Divided Europe," *SSRN*, December 5. http://eh.net/eha/wp-content/uploads/2014/05/Koyama.pdf
Koch, Natalie. 2013. "Why Not a World City? Astana, Ankara, and Geopolitical Scripts in Urban Networks," *Urban Geography*, vol. 34, no. 1, 109–130.
Kolbe, Laura. 2006. "Helsinki: From Provincial to National Centre." In: *Planning Twentieth-Century Capital Cities*, Ed. by David Gordon (London: Routledge), pp. 73–87.
Konovalova, Irina (ed.). 2013. *Perenosi stolits. Istoricheskii opit geopoliticheskogo proektirovania* (Moscow: Institut vseobschei istorii).

Kotarumalos, Ali. 2010. "Indonesia Mulls Plans to Relocate Capital City," *Huffington Post*, September 30.
Krugman, Paul. 1995. "Urban Concentration: The Role of Increasing Returns and Transport Costs," *Proceedings of the World Bank Annual Conference on Development Economics*, Washington, D.C.
Kudriavtsev, Mikhail. 2007. *Moskva—Tretii Rim. Istoriko-gradostroitelnoe issledovanie*. Second Edition (Moscow: Troitsa).
Kumar, Niraj. 2009. "Decapitate *Capital* Tag from *Delhi* Commemorating Century of Coronation," *Perspectives on Pan-Asianism*, August 29. http://ariseasia.blogspot.sk/2011/12/shift-indias-political-capital.html
Kühnhardt, Ludger. 2010. *Region Building* (Oxford, NY: Berghahn Books), p. 490.
Kuper, Herbert. 1972. "The Language of Sites in the Politics of Space," *American Anthropologist*, vol. 74, no. 3, 411–425.
Landau-Wells, Marika. 2008. "Capital Cities in Civil Wars: The Locational Dimension of Sovereign Authority." In: *Crisis States Occasional Papers* (London: School of Economics, April), pp. 1–24.
La Prensa. 2014. "¿La capital a otra parte?" April 27. www.laprensa.com.ni/2014/04/27/reportajes-especiales/192104-la-capital-a-otra-parte
Lara, Fernando & Nair, Stella. 2007. "The Brazilianization of Brasilia," *The Journal of the International Institute*, vol. 14, no. 2. http://quod.lib.umich.edu/j/jii/4750978.0014.214/--brazilianization-of-brasilia?rgn=main;view=fulltext
Large, David. 2000. *Berlin* (New York: Basic Books).
Lee, Man-Hyung, Choi, Nam-Hee & Park, Moonseo Park. 2005. "A Systems Thinking Approach to the New Administrative Capital in Korea: Balanced Development or Not?" *System Dynamics Review*, vol. 21, no. 1, 69–85.
Lee, Richard & Pelizzon, Sheila. 1991. "Hegemonic Cities in the Modern World-System." In: *Cities in the World-System: Studies in the Political Economy of the World-System*, Ed. by Reşat Kasaba & Immanuel Wallerstein (New York: Greenwood Press), pp. 43–54.
Le Maître, Alexandre. 1682. *La métropolitée, ou De l'établissement des villes capitales, de leur utilité passive et active, de l'union de leurs parties, de leurs anatomie, de leurs commerce* (Amsterdam: B. Boekholt).
Leroi-Gourhan, André. 1965. *L'espace humanisé. Préhistoire de l'art occidental* (Paris: Mazenod).
Levine, S. 2006. *What if Nelson Had been Made the Capital of New Zealand?* (Wellington: Victoria University Press).
Lewis, Mark Edward. 2006. *The Construction of Space in Early China* (New York: SUNY Press), 238.
Lindsay, Greg. 2010. "Can Port-au-Prince be Saved, or Should Haiti Move the Capital?" *Fast Company*, February 8.
"Liberia: President Sirleaf Unveils Plan for a New Capital City." In African Press International on January 25, 2011. https://africanpress.wordpress.com/2011/01/25/liberia-president-sirleaf-unveils-plan-for-a-new-capital-city/
Lilly, I. (ed.). 2002. *Moscow and Petersburg: The City in Russian Culture* (Nottingham: Astra Press).
Lin, Pai. 2006. "Options Are Plentiful for the Capital's Relocation," *Taipei Times*, October 26.
Logan, William S. 2005. "The Cultural Role of Capital Cities: Hanoi & Hue, Vietnam," *Pacific Affairs*, vol. 78, no. 4 (Winter), 559–575.

Selected bibliography

Lohausen, Heinrich Jordis von. 1992. "Wien und Belgrad als geopolitische Antipoden," *Staatsbriefe*. Heft 12.

London, Bruce. 1977. "Is the Primate City Parasitic? The Regional Implications of National Decision Making in Thailand," *The Journal of Developing Areas*, vol. 12, no. 1 (October), 49–68.

Gordon, Ian, Traverse, Tony, Whitehead, Christine & Scanlon, Kathleen. *London's Place in the UK Economy, 2009–2010* (London: London School of Economics).

Lowenthal, David. The Inferior Capital City: An American Phenomenon (Berkeley: MS).

Lowenthal, David. 1958. "The West Indies Chooses the Capital City," *Geographical Review*, vol. 48, no. 3, 336–364.

Luneva, Galina. 2013. "Stolitsa pereedet v Chayok?" *Slovo Kyrgyzstana*, July 3.

Lungu, Julius. "What about moving the capital city?" *Zambia Daily Mail*, March 11, 2015.

Mabin, Alan. 2011. "South African Capital Cities." In: Bekker, S & Therborn, G. (eds.), *African Capital Cities: Power and Powerlessness* (Cape Town & Dakar: HSRC Press), pp. 168–197.

Mabogunje, Akin. 1968. *Urbanization in Nigeria* (London: University of London Press).

Machiavelli, Nicolo. 2009. *The Prince*. Translated by J.G. Nichols (London: Alma Classics).

Madaleno, Isabel Maria. 1996. "Brasilia: The Frontier Capital," *Cities*, vol. 13, no. 4, 273–280.

Magutt, Joseph. 2009. "Need to Relocate the Capital City," November 10. www.josephmagutt.com/social-development/need-to-relocate-the-city/

Maitland, Robert. 2014. *Tourism in National Capitals and Global Change* (London: Routledge).

Maizlish, 2013. "V konkurentsii s Parizhem: Burgundskie goroda v borbe za rol politicheskogo tsentra." In: *Perenos stolitsi*, Ed. by I. Konovalova (Moscow: Institut vseobschei istorii).

Makas, Emily. 2010. "Shaping Central and Southeastern European Capital Cities in the Age of Nationalism." In: *Capital Cities in the Aftermath of Empires*, Ed. by Emily Gunzburger Makas & Tanja Damljanovic Conley (London: Routledge), pp. 1–28.

Makas, Emily & Conley, Tanja (eds.). 2010. *Capital Cities in the Aftermath of Empires: Planning in Central and Southeastern Europe* (London: Routledge).

Mammadova, Sama. 2014. "Iran's Capital Relocation Threatens Azerbaijani Minorities," *Harvard Business Review*, January 8.

Mangabeira da Vinha, Daniel. 2014. "Brasília through British Media," *Vitruvius*, ano. 14.

Mango, Cyril. 2005. "Constantinople: Capital of the Oikoumene?" Presented at *'Byzantium as Oecumene' Conference*, Athens, Greece 2001. Published by the Institute for Byzantine Research, Athens.

Manning, Clarence. 1952. *The Forgotten Republics* (New York: Philosophical Library).

Marchand, Bernard. 2009. *Les ennemis de Paris* (Rennes: Presses Universitaires de Rennes), p. 397.

Marchand, Bernard. 2010. "The Image of Paris in France Since Two Centuries: From Good to Bad to Worst." http://halshs-00527779

Markusen, Ann. 1999. *Second Tier Cities: Rapid Growth Beyond the Metropolis* (Minneapolis: University of Minnesota Press), p. 403.

Marlow, Jeffrey. 2011. "Relocation: The Pros and Cons of Plans in South Sudan," *Geographical Magazine*, December.
Masha'allah. 1994. *Book of Nativities*, Translated by Robert Hand (Berkeley Springs: Golden Hind Press).
Matsikh, Leonid. 2011. "Metafizika Severnoy Stolitsy, a Lecture in a Series 'Akademia' in the 'Kultura' Channel," January 19.
Maul, Stefan. 1997. "Die altorientalische Hauptstadt—Abbild und Nabel der Welt." In: *Die Orientalische Stadt: kontinuitat. Wandel. Bruch. 1 Internationale Colloquium der Deutschen Orient-Gesellschaft. 9.-1 0. Mai 1996 in Halle/Saale* (Saarbrücken: Saarbrücker Druckerei und Verlag), pp. 109–124.
McDonnell, Patrick & Ordonez, Oscar. 2007. "Plan to Move Capital Seen as Step to Divide Bolivia," *Los Angeles Times*, August 12.
McGee, Terence. 1967. *The Southeast Asian City: A Social Geography of the Primate Cities of Southeast Asia* (London: Bell & Sons).
McKinsey Global Institute. 2011. "Urban World: Mapping the Economic Power City," March. www.mckinsey.com/insights/urbanization/urban_world
McLynn, Frank. 1997. *Napoleon: Biography* (New York: Arcade Publishing).
Mechnikov, Lev. 1995. *Tsvilizatsiya i velikie istoricheskie reki* (Moskva: Progress).
Meining, Donald. 1956. "Heartland and Rimland in Eurasian History," *The Western Political Quarterly*, vol. 9, no. 3 (September), 553–569.
Melman, Yossi. 2009. "Israel Should Give Up Jerusalem as Its Capital," *Haarez*, December 6.
MercoPress. 2014. "Argentine Idea to Move the Capital to North of the Country Closer to Pacific Basin," January 9.
Metcalf, Thomas. 1989. *An Imperial Vision: Indian Architecture and Britain's Raj* (London: Faber and Faber).
Meyer, Jeffrey F. 1976. *Peking as a Sacred City* (Taipei: Chinese Association for Folklore).
Miller, James M. 1963. *Lake Europe: A New Capital for a United Europe* (New York: Books International).
Minkenberg, Michael (ed.). 2014. *Power and Architecture: The Construction of Capitals and the Politics of Space* (Berghahn Books: New York), p. 320.
Mommsen, Theodor. 1941. *Istoria Rima: Vol. 3. Ot smerti Sully do bitvy pri Tapse*. Translated by I. Masyukov (Moskva: OGIZ).
Montesquieu, Charles. 2012. *My Thoughts (Mes Pensées)*. Translated, ed., and with an Introduction by Henry C. Clark (Indianapolis: Liberty Fund).
Moomaw, Ronald & Alwosabi, Mohammad. 2004. "An Empirical Analysis of Competing Explanations of Urban Primacy: Evidence from Asia & the Americas," *The Annals of Regional Science*, vol. 38, 149–171.
Moore, Jonathan. 1984. "The Political History of Nigeria's New Capital," *The Journal of Modern African Studies*, vol. 22, no. 1 (March), 167–175.
Morrill, John. 2000. *Stuart Britain: A Very Short Introduction* (Oxford: Oxford Paperbacks).
Morshed, Adnan. 2011. "A Post-Dhaka Bangladesh," June 16. http://opinion.bdnews24.com/2011/06/16/a-post-dhaka-bangladesh/
Moser, Gary, Rogers, Scott & Van Til, Reinhold. 1997. "Nigeria: Experience with Structural Adjustment." In: *IMF Occasional Papers* (Washington D.C.: International Monetary Fund, 1997), March, pp. 106.
Moser, Sarah. 2010. "Putrajaya: Malaysia's New Federal Administrative Capital," *Cities: The International Journal of Urban Policy and Planning*, vol. 27, no. 3, 285–297.

292 Selected bibliography

Mosha, Aloysius. 2004. "The Planning of the New Capital of Tanzania: Dodoma, an Unfulfilled Dream," www.etsav.upc.es/personals/iphs2004/pdf/148_p.pdf

Mukherjee, Rudrangshu & Singh, Malvika. 2009. *New Delhi: Making of a Capital* (New Delhi: Lustre Press, Roli Books).

Mumford, Louis. 1968. *The City in History: Its Origins, Its Transformations, and Its Prospects* (New York: Harvest Books).

Murphey, Rhoads. 1957. "New Capitals of Asia," *Economic Development and Cultural Change*, vol. 5, no. 3 (April), 216–243.

Musavat. 2014. "Novyi grandioznii proekt Alieva," October 10.

Musgrove, Charles. 2013. *China's Contested Capital: Architecture, Ritual, and Response* (Honolulu, HI: University of Hawai'i Press; Hong Kong: Hong Kong University Press), 316 p.

Myers, David. 2002. "The Dynamics of Local Empowerment: An Overview." In: *Capital City Politics in Latin America: Democratization and Empowerment*, Ed. by David J. Myers and Henry A. Dietz, (Boulder, CO: Lynne Riener), pp. 1–27.

Myers, David & Dietz, Henry (eds.). 2002. *Capital City Politics in Latin America: Democratization and Empowerment* (Boulder, CO: Lynne Riener).

MyTexro. 2006. "Ministrul Hardau vrea capitala la Brasov," www.mytex.ro/component/content/article/540-texpert/422321-propunere-ministrul-hardau-vrea-capitala-la-brasov.html

Nagel, Klaus-Jürgen. 2011a. "Capital Cities of Federations: On the Way to Analysing the Normative Base of Their Asymmetrical Status," *Working Paper*, Universitat Pompeu Fabra, Barcelona.

Nagel, Klaus-Jurgen. 2011b. "Der Status der Bundeshauptstädte: Plädoyer für eine vergleichende Hauptstadtforschung." In: *Europäisches Zentrum für Föderalismus-Forschung Tübingen*, Ed. by Jahrbuch des Föderalismus (Nomos Verlagsgesellschaft: Föderalismus, Subsidiarität und Regionen in Europa, Baden-Baden), pp. 57–66.

Nagel, Klaus-Jürgen (ed.). 2013. *The Problem of the Capital City: New Research on Federal Capitals and Their Territory* (Barcelona: Collecció Institut d'Estudis Autonòmics), p. 86.

Naipaul, V.S. 1984. "The Crocodiles of Yamoussoukro." In: *Finding the Center: Two Narratives by V. S. Naipaul* (New York: Alfred A. Knopf), pp. 149–150.

NCC (National Capital Commission). 2000. *Planning Canada's Capital Region* (Ottawa: National Capital Commission).

Nieuwkoop, Renger von. 2012. "City Size and City Growth," Lecture, November 2, Department of Management, Technology and Economics, ETH Zurich www.cepe.ethz.ch/education/UrbanSpatial/L07

Neal, Zachary. 2011. "Differentiating Centrality and Power in the World City Network," *Urban Studies*, vol. 48, no. 13, 2733–2748.

Nedrebø, Tore. 2012. "City-Belt Europe or Imperial Europe? Stein Rokkan and European History," *Europæus norvegicus*, 30. mars 2012 (originally published in Nervegian at *Nytt Norsk Tidsskrift*, no. 3, 2012).

Neue Zürcher Zeitung. 2002. "Russland heimliche Hauptstadt. Neue Debatten um den alten Status St. Petersburgs," März 5.

Nwafor, J.C. 1980. "The Relocation of Nigeria's Federal Capital: A Device for Greater Territorial Integration and National Unity," *GeoJournal*, vol. 4, no. 4, 359–366.

Nyrko, V. 2003. "Gorod razdora," *Sovershenno sekretno*, January 15.

Olsson, Ola & Hansson, Gustav. 2011. "Country Size and the Rule of Law: Resuscitating Montesquieu," *European Economic Review*, vol. 55, no. 5, 613–629.
Orr, A. 2012. "Move Over Eastern States—Perth Could be Moving on Up," *WAToday*, October 26.
Ortega y Gasset, José. 1967. *La redención de las provincias y La decencia nacional. Articulos de 1927 y 1930* (Alianza: Madrid).
Osathanon, Prapasri. 2015. "Action Required to Stop Sinking of the Capital," *Nation*, July 23.
Ovason, David. 2002. *The Secret Architecture of Our Nation's Capital: The Masons and the Building of Washington, D.C.* (New York: Harper), p. 528.
Ovsená, Blažena. 2010. "Na obranu Svätopluka a o potrebe tieňového hlavného mesta Slovenska," *Sclabonia*, August 8.
Pacione, Michael. 2002. *The City in Global Context* (London & New York: Routledge).
Palatino, Mong. 2013. "Will ASEAN Countries Move Their Capitals?" *The Diplomat*, July 18.
Parker, Geoffrey. 2014. *Power in Stone: Cities as Symbols of Empires* (London: Reaktion).
Parkinson, John. 2012. "Symbolic Representation in Public Space: Capital Cities, Presence and Memory." In: *Democracy and Public Space* (Oxford: Oxford University Press).
Pegrum, Roger. 1983. *Bush Capital: How Australia Chose Canberra as Its Federal City* (Sydney: Hale & Iremonger).
Perception Survey on Quality of Life in European Cities. Analytical Report. 2009. "Conducted by the Gallup Organization, Hungary, for European Commission."
Perrot, Jean. 1998. "Birth of a City: Susa." In: *Capital City: Urban Planning and Spiritual Dimensions*, Ed. by Joan Goodnick Westenholz (Jerusalem: Bible Lands Museum), pp. 83–97.
Petty, William. 1984. "Sir William Petty on the Causes and Consequences of Urban Growth," *Population and Development Review*, vol. 10, no. 1, 127–133, reprint.
Philippou, Styliane. 2008. *Oscar Niemeyer: Curves of Irreverence* (New Haven & London: Yale University Press).
Philippou, Styliane. 2010. "Brasília, Capital of the Highways and Skyways," *Greek Architects*, April 30. www.greekarchitects.gr/en/degrees/bras%C3%ADlia-%E2%80%98capital-of-the-highways-and-skyways%E2%80%99-id3005
Pingree, David. 1989. "Classical and Byzantine Astrology in Sassanian Persia," *Dumbarton Oaks Papers*, vol. 43, 227–239.
Pinto, Christian. 2007. *Riddles in Stone: The Secret Architecture of Washington DC* (USA).
Pipes, Daniel. 2001. "The Muslim Claim to Jerusalem," *Middle East Quarterly*, September, 49–66.
Plekhanov, Sergey. 2003. *Reformator na trone* (Moscow: Mezhdunarodnie otnoshenia).
Polèse, Mario & Denis-Jacob, Jonathan. 2009. "Staying on Top: Why Cities Move Up (or Down) the Urban Hierarchy: An International Comparison Over a Hundred Years," *Working Paper no. 2009–02*.
Poliszuk, Joseph. 2004. "Ciudad Libertad," *El Nacional*, Jueves 29 de Julio.
Potts, Deborah. 1985. "Capital Relocation in Africa: The Case of Lilongwe in Malawi," *Geographical Journal*, vol. 151, no. 2, 182–196.

Prakoso, Hananto. 2012. "Moving Capital City to Improve Transport Conditions? The Case of Jakarta." In: *Colloque international La fabrique du movement* (Paris), Mars 26–27.
Preecharush, Dulyapak. 2009. *Naypyidaw: The New Capital of Burma* (Bangkok: White Lotus), p. 181.
Przeworski, Adam, Alvarez, Michael E., Cheibub, Jose Antonio & Limongi, Fernando. 2000. *Democracy and Development; Political Institutions and Well-Being in the World, 1950–1990* Ed. by Adam Przeworski (New York: Cambridge University Press).
Proudfoot, Peter. 1994. *Secret Plan of Canberra: Masonic Architecture of Australia's Capital* (Kensington: University of New South Wales Press), p. 120.
Quistorff, Brian. 2015. "Capitalitis? Effects of the 1960 Brazilian Capital Relocation," March 30. Available at SSRN: http://ssrn.com/abstract=2588620 or http://dx.doi.org/10.2139/ssrn.2588620
Raafat, Hassan. 2008. "UAE to Get New Capital," *The National*, April 17. www.thenationalae/article/20090311/NATIONAL/786098729/1010
Rabinovich, Itamar & Shaked, Haim (eds.). 1987. *Middle East Contemporary Survey*, vol. XI (Boulder, San Francisco & London: Westview Press), p. 546.
Radović, Srđan. 2008. "From Center to Periphery and Vice Versa: The Politics of Toponyms in the Transitional Capital," *Bulletin of the Institute of Ethnography*, vol. 56, no. 2, 53–74.
Rappoport, Amos. 1993. "On the Nature of Capitals and Their Expansion." In: *Capital Cities/Les capitales*, Ed. by John Taylor, Jean G. Lengellé & Caroline Andrew (Ottawa: Carleton University Press), pp. 30–45.
Rawat, Rajiv. 2006. "Capital City Relocation: Global-Local Perspectives in the Search for an Alternative Modernity," *Annual Meeting of the Association of American Geographers*, Chicago, IL, March 8.
Read, Justin. 2005. "Alternative Functions: Oscar Niemeyer and the Poetics of Modernity," *Modernism/modernity*, vol. 12, no. 2 (April), 253–272.
Rehman, Abdul. 2009. "Doxiadis Dynapolis and What Went Wrong in the Development of Islamabad?", *Proceeding of the Fourth Seminar on Urban and Regional Planning, NED University Karachi*, Karachi.
Rehmat, Adnan. 2010. "50 Years of Islamabad 1960–2010: Capital Crown," *Pak Tea House*, January 11. https://pakteahouse.wordpress.com/2010/01/11/50-years-of-islamabad-1960-2010-capital-crown/
Reichart, Thomas. 1993. *Städte ohne Wettbewerb* (Bern: Haupt).
Richardson, H.W. 1981. "National Urban Development Strategies in Developing Countries," *Urban Studies*, vol. 18, 267–283.
Richardson, H.W. & Bae, Chang-Hee Christine. 2003. "The Location and Relocation of National and State Capitals in North America and the Rest of the World," *The International Symposium on a Planning Policy for Korea's New Capital City*. Seoul: Korea Planners Association.
Richardson, H.W. & Bae, Chang-Hee Christine. 2009. "Options for the Capital of a Reunified Korea," *SAIS Review of International Affairs*, vol. 29, no. 1, 67–77.
Richter, Darmon. 2012. "Astana: The Illuminati Capital of Kazakhstan," bohemianblog, December. www.thebohemianblog.com/2012/12/dark-tourism-illuminati-capital.html
Rigg, Jonathan. 2003. "Exclusion and Embeddedness: The Chinese in Thailand and Vietnam." In: *The Chinese Diaspora: Space, Place, Mobility, and Identity*, Ed. by

Laurence J.C. Ma & Carolyn L. Cartier (Lanham, NY: Rowman & Littlefield), pp. 97–115.

Ringrose, David. 1973. "The Impact of a New Capital City: Madrid, Toledo, and New Castile, 1560–1660," *The Journal of Economic History*, vol. 33, no. 4 (December), 761–791.

Ringrose, David. 1983. *Madrid and Spanish Economy: 1560–1850* (Berkeley: University of California Press), p. 405.

Ringrose, David. 1998. "Capital Cities, Urbanization and Modernization in Early Modern Europe," *Journal of Urban History*, vol. 24, no. 2 (January), 155–183.

Röber, Manfred & Schröter, Eckhard. 2004. "Governing the Capital—Comparing Institutional Reform in Berlin, London, and Paris," *Working Paper PRI-8*.

Robertson, James. 2001. "Stuart London and the Idea of a Royal Capital City," *Renaissance Studies*, vol. 15, no. 1, 37–58(22).

Roche, Daniel. 1997. *France in the Enlightenment* (Cambridge: Cambridge University Press).

Rodrigues, Charlene. 2015. "Yemenis Divided Over Capital: Can Aden Replace Sanaa?" *Middle East Eye*, March 19. www.middleeasteye.net/news/yemenis-divided-over-capital-can-aden-replace-sanaa-1498766749#sthash.ZUxeNDLx.dpuf

Rogachev, Sergey. 2008. "Naypyidaw—novaia stolitsa Myanmy," *Geografia*, no. 19.

Rogers, David. 2015. "Why Mongolia is Considering a German Plan for New Eco-Capital," *Global Construction Review*, April 21.

Rokkan, Stein. 1973. *Building State and Nation*. Ed. by Stein Rokkan & Shmuel Eisenstadt (Beverly Hills: Sage).

Rokkan, Stein. 1976. "Dimensions of State Formation and Nation Building: A Possible Paradigm for Research on Variations Within Europe." In: *The Formation of National States in Europe*, Ed. by Charles Tilly (Princeton: Princeton University Press).

Rokkan, Stein. 1980. "Territories, Centers and Peripheries: Toward a Geoethnic, Geoeconomic, Geopolitical Model of Differentiation Within Western Europe." In *Centre and Periphery. Spatial Variations in Politics*, Ed. by Jean Gottman (Beverly Hills: Sage).

Rokkan, Stein. 1999. *State Formation, Nation-Building, and Mass Politics in Europe*. Ed. by Peter Florida (Oxford: Oxford University Press).

Rossman, Vadim. 2008. "Misteria tsentra: Identichnost i organizatsiya sotsialnogo prostranstva v sovremennykh i traditsionnikh obschestvakh," *Voprosy filosofii*, no. 2, 42–57.

Rossman, Vadim. 2013. "In Search of the Fourth Rome: Visions of a New Russian Capital City," *Slavic Review*, vol. 72, no. 3, 505–527.

Rossman, Vadim. 2014. *V poiskakh Chetvertogo Rima* (Moskva: Vysshaia shkola ekonomiki).

Rousseau, Jean-Jacques. 1913. *The Social Contract* (London & Toronto: JM Dent & Sons).

Rowland, Daniel. 1996. "Moscow—The Third Rome or New Israel," *Russian Review*, vol. 55, no. 4, 591–614.

Rowley, Storer. 1987. "Argentina Wants to Grow a New Capital," *Chicago Tribune*, February 8.

Ruble, Blair. 1990. *Leningrad. Shaping a Soviet City* (Berkeley: University of California Press).

Sakyi, Kwesi Atta. 2011. "Does Ghana Need a New Capital City?" *GhanaWeb*, October 21.
Salimpur, Mirzoi. 2012. "Dushanbe—stolitsa tadzhikov Movarounnakhra," *Radio Odzi*, April 21.
Sarmiento, Domingo. 2007. *Argiropolis: O la Capital de los Estados Confederadus del Rio del Plata* (Buenos Aires: Biblioteca Quiroga Sarmiento).
Sassen, Saskia. 2011. *Cities in a World Economy* (Thousand Oaks, CA: Pine Forge Press) updated 4th ed.
Schatz, Edward. 2003. "What Capital Cities Say About State and Nation Building," *Nationalism and Ethnic Politics*, vol. 9, no. 4, 111–140.
Schlögel, Karl. 1988. *Jenseits des Grossen Oktober, Das Laboratorium der Moderne, Petersburg 1909–1921* (Berlin: Siedler).
Sellers, Jeffrey. 2005. "Re-Placing the Nation, an Agenda for Comparative Urban Politics," *Urban Affairs Review*, vol. 40, 419–445.
Semenov-Tian-Shansky, V.P. 1989. "Tsentr Rossii, yego osobennosti i znachenie dlya strany." In: *Geografiya i khozyaistvo, no. 3. Tsentrograficheskiy metod v ekonomicheskoy geografii* (Leningrad: Izdadelstvo Geograficheskogo obschestva SSSR).
Sharymov, Aleksandr. 2004. Predistoria Sankt-Peterburga. Kniga 1 i 2 (Sankt-Peterburg: "Zurnal Neva")
Shatkin, Gavin. 2005–2006. "Colonial Capital, Modernist Capital, Global Capital: The Changing Political Symbolism of Urban Space in Metro Manila, The Philippines," *Pacific Affairs*, vol. 78, no. 4, 577–601.
Shevryev, A. 2003. "The Axis Petersburg-Moscow: Outward and Inward Russian Capitals," *Journal of Urban History*, vol. 30, no. 1, 70–84.
Shmidt, C. 2013. "Argentina's Cuestión Capital." In: *Latin American Modern Architectures: Ambiguous Territories*, Ed. by Patricio del Real & Helen Gyger, (London: Routledge), pp. 170–191.
Shrestha, Hari. 2011. "Nepal Needs New Capital City: With Reference to Some Capital Cities Transfer," *American Chronicle*, October 1.
Siegenthaler, Peter. 1999. "Japanese Domestic Tourism and the Search for National Identity," *The CUHK Journal for Humanities*, no. 3, 178–195.
Şimşir, Bilâl. 2007. "Ankara: The Republic's Capital—to be or Not to be!," *The Guide Ankara Magazine*, 192078.
Slack, Enid & Chattopadhyay, Rupak. 2009. *Finance and Governance of Capital Cities in Federal Systems* (Montreal: McGill-Queen's University Press).
Smith, Anthony D. 1995. *Nations and Nationalism in a Global Era* (Cambridge: Polity Press).
Smith, Anthony. 2003. *Chosen Peoples: Sacred Sources of National Identity*.(Oxford: Oxford University Press)
Smith, Carol. "Theories and Measures of Urban Primacy: A Critique." In: *Urbanization in the World-Economy*, Ed. by Michael Timberlake (London: Academic Press, 1985), pp. 87–116.
Sohn, Andreas & Weber, Hermann (Hg.). 2000. *Hauptstädte und Global Cities and der Schwelle zum 21. Jahrhundert* (Bochum: Verlag Dr. Dieter Winkler).
Southhall, Aidan. 1998. *The City in Time and Space* (Cambridge: Cambridge University Press).
Spate, O.H.K. 1942. "Factors in the Development of Capital Cities," *Geographical Review*, vol. 32, no. 4, 622–631.

Spurek, Milan. 1996. *Praga Mysteriosa: The Secret of the Prague Solstice* (Prague: Eminent:).
Stahl, Jörg. 2014. "Capital Gain: The Returns to Locating in the Capital City." www.econ.upf.edu/gpefm/jm/pdf/paper/JMP%20Stahl.pdf
Statham, Pamela (ed.). 1989. *The Origins of Australia's Capital Cities* (Cambridge: Cambridge University Press).
Stephenson, Glenn. 1970. "Two Newly-Created Capitals: Islamabad and Brasilia," *The Town Planning Review*, vol. 41, no. 4 (October), 317–332.
Stratfor. 2000. "A Shift in Asia as Mongolia Stirs," *Global Intelligence Update*, May 19.
Stratfor. 2012. "The Geopolitics of Brazil: An Emergent Power's Struggle with Geography," May 13.
Svetliakovskii, E. & Ills, U. 1989. "Tsentrograficheskii metod i regionalnii analiz." In: *Geografia i khoziaistvo. Vol.3. Tentrograficheskii metod v ekonomicheskoi geografii*, Ed. by Sergey Tarkhov (Leningrad: Izdatelstvo geograficheskogo obschestva SSSR).
Tache, Catalin. 2015. "Klaus Iohannis, impins de la spate sa mute Capitala la Alba Iulia," *National*, October 2. www.enational.ro/dezvaluiri/klaus-iohannis-impins-de-la-spate-sa-mute-capitala-la-alba-iulia-457987.html/#ixzz3tjGmv4Kf
Takamura, Yoshiharu & Tone, Kaoru. 2003. "A Comparative Site Evaluation Study for Relocating Japanese Government Agencies Out of Tokyo," *Socio-Economic Planning Sciences*, vol. 37, 85–102.
Tarkhov, Sergey. 2007. "Perenosy stolits," *Geografia*, nos. 5–6.
Tarling, Nicholas (ed.). 1999. *Cambridge History of South-East Asia* (Cambridge: Cambridge University Press).
Taylor, Peter. 1985. *Political Geography: World Economy, Nation-State and Locality* (New York: Longman).
Taylor, Peter. 1995. "World Cities and Territorial States: The Rise and Fall of Their Mutuality." In: *World Cities in a World-System*, Ed. by Paul L. Knox & Peter J. Taylor (Cambridge: Cambridge University Press), pp. 5–32.
Taylor, Peter & Derudder, B. 2014. "Tales of Two Cities: Political Capitals and Economic Centres in the World City Network," *Glocalism*, no. 3.
Taylor, P.J. & Ben, Derudder (eds). 2007. *Cities in Globalization: Practices, Policies and Theories* (London: Routledge), pp. 287–297.
The Telegraph. 2011. "Afghanistan: New Kabul to be Built North of War Torn Capital," Apr 1.
Țene, Ionuț. 2009. "C. Noica și mutarea Capitalei României," *Frontpress*, December 14. www.napocanews.ro/2009/12/c-noica-%C8%99i-mutarea-capitalei-romaniei.html
Therborn, Göran. 2002. "Monumental Europe: The National Years: On the Iconography of European Capital Cities," *Housing Theory and Society*, vol. 19, no. 1, 26–47.
Therborn, Göran. 2006a. *Capitals and National Identity* (European Variants). https://ecpr.eu/Filestore/PaperProposal/26673996-3b0c-4ece-b8c6-e13b29169627.pdf
Therborn, Göran. 2006b. "Eastern Drama: Capitals of Eastern Europe, 1830s-2006: An Introductory Overview," *International Review of Sociology—Revue Internationale de Sociologie*, vol. 16, no. 2, 209–242.
Therborn, Göran. 2008. "Identity and Capital Cities: European Nation and European Union." In: *The Search for a European Identity: Values, Policies and*

Selected bibliography

Legitimacy of the European Union, Ed. by Furio Cerutti & Sonia Lucarelli (New York: Routledge), pp. 59–74.

Therborn, Göran. 2011. "Why and How Place Matters." In: *The Oxford Handbook of Political Science*, Ed. by Robert E. Goodin (Oxford: Oxford University Press).

Therborn, Göran & Bekker, Simon (eds.). 2011. *African Capital Cities. Power and Powerlessness* (Cape Town and Dakar: HSRC Press).

Therborn, Göran & Ho, Kong Chong (eds.). 2009. "Capital Cities and Their Contested Roles in the Life of Nations," *City*, vol. 13, no. 1, 71–79.

Tilly, Charles. 1992. *Violence, Capital and European States. 990–1992* (Cambridge: Cambridge University Press).

Toby, Ronald P. 1985. "Why Leave Nara? Kammu and the Transfer of the Capital," *Monumenta Nipponica*, vol. 40, no. 3 (Autumn), 331–347.

Tocqueville, Alexis de. 1856. *The Old Regime and the Revolution* (New York: Harper & Brothers).

Toma, Adriana. 2008. "Ce-ar fi daca am muta Capitala Romaniei in Ardeal?", *Ziare*, May 25. www.ziare.com/politica/stiri-politice/ce-ar-fi-daca-am-muta-capitala-romaniei-in-ardeal-317255

Toynbee, Arnold. 1970. "Capital Cities: Their Distinctive Features and Capital Cities: Melting-Pots and Powder-Kegs." In: *Cities on the Move* (New York & London: Oxford University Press), pp. 67–78, 143–152.

Toynbee, Arnold. 1987. *A Study of History. Abridgement of Volumes VII-X by D.C. Somervell* (New York & Oxford: Oxford University Press).

Traugott, Mark. 1995. "Capital Cities and Revolution," *Social Science History*, vol. 19, 147–169.

Turchin, Peter. 2009. "A Theory for Formation of Large Empires," *Journal of Global History*, vol. 4, no. 2 (July), 191–217. www.eeb.uconn.edu/people/turchin/PDF/JGH-A-Turchin5.pdf

Turner, Sidney & Turner, Richard. 2011. "Capital Cities: A Special Case in Urban Development," *Annals of Regional Science*, vol. 46, 19–35.

Twain, Mark. 1869. *The Innocents Abroad* (Hartford: American Publishing Co).

Tynyanova, Olga. 2011. "Tekuschaya gosudarstvennaya politika i model Rossii i ekstrapolatsionnyi prognoz eyo srednesrochnykh rezultatov v mirovykh koordinatakh," *Nauchnyi ekspert*, no. 4, 36–67.

Tyrwhitt, J. & Gottmann, Jean (eds.). 1983. "Capital Cities," *Ekistics*, vol. 50, (March/April) [Oslo, Warsaw, Rome, Tokyo, & Washington D.C.].

UNESCO World Heritage Sites List. 2012. "Capital Cities and Tombs of the Ancient Koguryo Kingdom," http://whc.unesco.org/en/list/1135

Vale, Lawrence. 1992. *Architecture, Power, and National Identity* (Yale: Yale University Press), p. 350.

Vale, Lawrence. 2006. "The Urban Design of 20th Century Capitals." In: *Gordon D. Planning 20th Century Capital Cities*, Ed. by David Gordon (London: Routledge), pp. 15–38.

van Ginneken, Sophie. 2015. "The Burden of Being Planned: How African Cities Can Learn from Experiments of the Past: New Town Dodoma, Tanzania." In: *New Towns on the Cold War Frontier* (Rotterdam: Crimson Architectural Historians), www.newtowninstitute.org/spip.php?article1050.

Vedder, Richard. 1996. "Capital Crimes, Political Centers as Parasite Economies," *Cato Policy Analysis*, no. 250 (February 28). http://object.cato.org/sites/cato.org/files/pubs/pdf/pa250.pdf

Vernon, Christopher. 2012. *Capital Connections: Australia, Brazil and Landscapes of National Identity*, 15th International Planning History Society Conference, Sao Paulo.
Vilkovsky, Mikhail. 2012. "Simvolicheskaia geografiia arkhitekturi gorodskogo prostranstva na primere Washingtona, Moskvi i Sankt-Peterburga." In: *Materialy konferentsii Simvolicheskoe i arkhetipicheskoe v culture i sotsialnikh otnosheniakh* (Prague: Sotsiosfera).
Vogel, Ronald K. 2001. "Decentralization and Urban Governance: Reforming Tokyo Metropolitan Government." In: *Urban Governance Around the World*, Ed. by Blair A. Ruble, Richard E. Stren & Joseph S. Tulchin (Washington D.C.: Woodrow Wilson International Center for Scholars), pp. 114–148.
Voloshin, Dmitry. 2014. "Zachem Ukraine nuzhen perenos stolitsy," *Khvilia*, December 28.
Vorobiov, M. 1968. "Sistema piati stolits zhurzhenei." In: *Doklady otdelenii i komissii Geograficheskogo obschestva SSSR*, vol. 5 (Leningrad).
Vries, Jan de. 1984. *European Urbanization, 1500–1800* (London: Methuen).
Vries, Jan de. 2002. "Great Expectations: Early Modern History and the Social Sciences" In: *Testing the Limits of Braudel's Mediterranean*, Ed. by John Marino (Kirksville, MO: Truman State University Press).
Wagenaar, Michiel, 2000. "Townscapes of Power," *GeoJournal*, vol. 51, 1–2.
Wagenaar, Michiel. 2001. "The Capital as a Representation of a Nation." In: *The Territorial Factor: Political Geography in a Globalizing World*, Ed. by Gertjan Dijkink & Hans Knippenberg (Amsterdam: Vossiuspers).
Wallace, Jeremy. 2013. "Cities, Redistribution, and Authoritarian Regime Survival," *Journal of Politics*, vol. 75, no. 3, 632–645.
Wang, Jenn-hwang & Huang, Shuwei. 2009. "Contesting Taibei as the World City," *City*, vol. 13, no. 1, 103–109.
Weber, Max. 1978. *Economy and Society: An Outline of Interpretive Sociology* (Berkeley: California University Press). Originally published in 1925.
Wellhofer, E.S. 1989. "Core and Periphery: Territorial Dimensions in Politics," *Urban Studies*, vol. 26, 340–355.
Westenholz, Joan G. (ed.). 1996. *Royal Cities of the Biblical World* (Jerusalem: Muzeon artsot ha-Mikra), p. 334.
Westenholz, Joan G. (ed.). 1998. *Capital Cities: Urban Planning and Spiritual Dimensions* (Jerusalem: Bible Lands Museum).
Wheatley, Paul. 1971. *The Pivot of the Four Quarters: A Preliminary Enquiry Into the Origins and Character of the Ancient Chinese City* (Chicago: Aldine Publishing House).
Wheatley, Paul & See, Thomas. 1978. *From Court to Capital: A Tentative Interpretation of the Origins of the Japanese Urban Tradition* (Chicago & London: University of Chicago Press). p. 242. See also *Journal of the Royal Asiatic Society*, vol. 111, no. 2, 181–200.
Williams, Richard. 2005. "Modernist Civic Space and the Case of Brasília," *Journal of Urban History*, vol. 32, no. 1, 120–137.
Wise, Michael. 1998. *Capital Dilemma: Germany's Search for a New Architecture of Democracy* (New York: Princeton Architectural Press).
Wise, Michael. 2002. "A Capital of Europe?" *New York Times*, March 2. www.nytimes.com/2002/03/02/arts/think-tank-a-capital-of-europe-brussels-is-primping.html

Wolfel, R.L. 2002. "North to Astana: Nationalistic Motives for the Movement of the Kazakh Capital," *Nationalities Papers*, vol. 30, no. 3, 485–506.
World Bank. 2005. *From Transition to Development. A Country Economic Memorandum for the Russian Federation*, Report No. 32308-RU, March.
Wusten, Herman van der. 2000. "The Cityscapes of European Capital Cities," *GeoJournal*, vol. 51, 129–133.
Wusten, Herman van der. 2001. "Dictators and Their Capital Cities: Moscow and Berlin in the 1930s," *GeoJournal*, vol. 52, no. 4, 331–352.
Yahye, Mahamud. 2005. "Move the Capital from Mogadishu?" *wardheernews.com*, May 30.
Ye, Longli. 1979. *Istoria gosudarstva kidanei*. Translated by V. Taskin (Moskva: Nauka).
Yoon, Duncan. 2011. "The Rationalization of Space and Time: Dodoma and Socialist Modernity," *Ufahamu: A Journal of African Studies*, vol. 36, no. 2, 1–27.
Yoon, Hong-Key. 2006. *The Culture of Fengshui in Korea: An Exploration of East Asian Geomancy* (Lanham: Lexington Books), p. 332.
Zadverniuk, L. & Kozirenko, N. 2002. "Migratsia stolits v Kitae I fenomen pustogo goroda." In: *Rossia i Kitai na dalnevostochnih rubezhah*, Ed. by A. Zabiyako. Issue 6 (Blagoveschensk: Izdatelstvo AmGu), pp. 154–159.
Zanetta, Cecilia. 2004. *The Influence of World Bank on Housing and Urban Policies: The Case of Mexico and Argentina in the 1990-s* (Burlington, VT: Ashgate).
Zenn, Jacob. 2011. "New Capital Ambitions in Indonesia," *Asia Times*, August 4.
Zhai, David & McGown, Simon. 2013. "Hypercapital. A backup city for Tokyo," *Applied Research in Practical Architecture (ARPA)*, no. 1.
Zimmerman, Horst. 2010. "Do Different Types of Capital Cities Make a Difference for Economic Dynamism?" *Environment and Planning C: Government and Policy*, vol. 28, 761–767.
Zoback, Mary et al. 2009. "Seismic Vulnerability of South American Capital Cities," *2nd International Workshop on Earthquake Casualties*, June 15–16, University of Cambridge, UK.
Zubarevich, N. "Agglomeratsionnii effect ili administrativnii ugar," *Rossiiskoe ekspertnoe obozrenie*, no. 4–5 (2007), 11–13.
Zurga, Guillermo. 2011. "Cambio de Capital: Una solución estratosférica," *Analitica.com*,1deagosto.www.lahistoriaparalela.com.ar/2011/08/03/cambio-de-capital-una-solucion-estratosferica/

Appendices

Table 1 Major capital city relocations in the past 100 years

Country	From	To	Year	Distance (km)
Russia	Saint-Petersburg	Moscow	1918	633
Albania	Durrës	Tirana	1920	39
Turkey	Istanbul	Ankara	1923	351
Australia	Melbourne	Canberra	1927	472
Zambia	Livingston	Lusaka	1935	484
Guinea-Bissau	Bolama	Bissau	1941	40
China	Nanjing	Beijing	1949	1219
Mauritania	Saint-Louis	Nouakchott	1957	303
Senegal	Saint-Louis	Dakar	1958	265
Brazil	Rio de Janeiro	Brasília	1960	754
Botswana	Gaborone	Mafikeng	1961	138
Rwanda	Butare	Kigali	1962	80
Uganda	Entebbe	Kampala	1962	35
North Yemen	Ta'izz	Sana'a	1962	198
Pakistan	Karachi	Islamabad	1966	1144
Libya	Bayda/Benghazi	Tripoli	1969	1000
Belize	Belmopan	Belize City	1970	68
Malawi	Zomba	Lilongwe	1974	227
Côte d'Ivoire	Abidjan	Yamoussoukro	1983	228
Libya	Tripoli	Sirte	1988	463
Chile*	Santiago	Valparaiso	1990	98
Nigeria	Lagos	Abuja	1991	541
Tanzania	Dar es Salaam	Dodoma	1996	571
Kazakhstan	Almaty	Astana	1997	974
Germany	Bonn	Berlin	1999	604

(Continued)

Table 1 (Continued)

Country	From	To	Year	Distance (km)
Malaysia**	Kuala Lumpur	Putrajaya	1999	47
Myanmar	Yangon	Naypyidaw	2005	330
UAE	Abu Dhabi	Khalifa City	2012	30
Georgia*	Tbilisi	Kutaisi	2012	230
Afghanistan	Kabul	New Kabul	2013	25

*Legislative only **Executive only

Note: This list does not include temporary relocations, relocations in smaller states, and those within the same metropolitan area (<10 km).

Table 2 Temporary or smaller-scale capital city relocations in the past 100 years

World Region	Country	From	To	Year
South Asia	Sri Lanka	Colombo	Kotte	1982
	Bhutan	Punakha	Thimphu	1952
SEA	Philippines	Manila	Quezon City	1976
	Laos	Luang Prabang	Vientiane	1975
	Indonesia	Yogyakarta	Jakarta	1949
	Philippines	Quezon City	Manila	1948
Middle East	Oman	Salalah	Muscat	1970
	Israel	Tel Aviv	Jerusalem	1949
	Oman	Muscat	Salalah	1932
	Bahrain	Muharraq	Manama	1923
	Jordan	Salt	Amman	1921
Africa	Guinea-Bissau	Bolama	Bissau	1941
	Guinea-Bissau	Bissau	Madina do Boe	1973
	Guinea-Bissau	Madina do Boe	Bissau	1974
Oceania	Palau	Koror	Ngerulmud	2006
	Federated States of Micronesia	Kolonia	Palikir	1989
	Marshall Islands	Jabor	Majuro Atoll	1944
	Solomon Islands	Tulagi	Honiara	1942
Southern Europe	Montenegro	Cetinje	Podgorica	1946

Table 3 Countries with active public debates on capital city relocation

Region	Country	Present Capital	Proposed Capital(s)	Year Debate Began
Africa	Egypt	Cairo	Al-Fayoum	2005
	Equatorial Guinea	Malabo	Oyala	2012
	Ghana	Accra	Kintampo	2007
	Kenya	Nairobi	Gigiri	2009
	Liberia	Monrovia	Bentol	1982
	Senegal	Dakar	Lompoul	2007
	Somalia	Mogadishu	Hargeisa, Baidoa	2004
	South Sudan	Juba	Ramciel	2010
	Uganda	Kampala	Karuma	2011
	Zimbabwe	Harare	Hampden	2011
East Asia	China	Beijing	Chongqing	2010
	Japan	Tokyo	Hokuto	1995
	Mongolia	Ulan Bator	Kharkhorin	2005
	South Korea	Seoul	Sejong City	2002
	Taiwan	Taipei	Kaohsiung	2006
Post-Soviet States	Azerbaijan	Baku	Gyandzha/Alyat	2010
	Georgia	Tbilisi	Sukhumi	2010
	Kyrgyzstan	Bishkek	Osh	2006
	Russia	Moscow	Novosibirsk	2005
	Tajikistan	Dushanbe	Danghara	2012
	Ukraine	Kyiv	Baturin	2005
Southeast Asia	Indonesia	Jakarta	Palangkaraya	2010
	Philippines	Manila	Cebu City	2011
	Thailand	Bangkok	Nakhon Nayok	2011
South Asia	Bangladesh	Dhaka	Trishal	2010
	Nepal	Kathmandu	Chitwan	2012
Americas	Argentina	Buenos Aires	Santiago del Estero	2014
	Bolivia	La Paz	Sucre	2008
	Haiti	Port-au-Prince	Cap Haitien	2010
	Nicaragua	Managua	Estelí	2014
	Peru	Lima	Huancayo	1983
	Venezuela	Caracas	Ciudad Libertad	2005
Middle East	Iran	Tehran	Qom, Isfahan, Tabriz	2003
	Yemen	Sana'a	Aden	2014

(*Continued*)

Table 3 (Continued)

Region	Country	Present Capital	Proposed Capital(s)	Year Debate Began
Europe	Romania	Bucharest	Alba Iulia	2010
	Slovakia	Bratislava	Martin	2009
	UK	London	Liverpool*	2003

Note: This table does not list all the candidates for the role of a new capital city. For example, in Iran, Tabriz, Parand, Shahroud, Isfahan, and Qom have been proposed; in Indonesia, Palangkaraya, Banjarmasin, and Jonggol; in Russia, Ekaterinburg, Tver, Vladivostok, and other cities; in Egypt, 6th of October City, Alexandria, Suez, and Port Said; in China, Zhengzhou, Lanzhou, Wuhan, Linxi, Xiangyang, Liaocheng, Changsha, Anyang, and several others. For the sake of brevity, this table lists only the most popular candidates for new capitals.

*In the UK, in 2003, Plaid Cymru party MP Adam Price proposed moving the capital of the UK to Liverpool. In 2012, MP John Mann proposed relocating the headquarters of most government departments to different cities outside of London. In 2014, MP Graham Stringer called for England's government to be moved to Manchester, Lord Adonis suggested moving the House of Lords to the North, and trade unionists suggested designating Glasgow the capital of the UK, as an alternative to Scottish independence. Other contenders for this role in England include Middlesbrough, Lichfield, and Nottingham.

Table 4 Recent subnational capital city relocation debates and moves

Country	Region	From	To	Year
India	Andhra Pradesh	Hyderabad	Seemandhra	2014
	Telangana	Hyderabad (shared capital with Andhra Pradesh)	Hyderabad (capital of Telangana only)	
Russia	Yamal Autonomous Republic	Salekhard	Noyabrsk	ongoing debate
	Karelia	Syktyvkar	Ukhta	
	Ingushetia	Nazran	Magas	2000
Indonesia	Maluku	Ambon	Masohi	2012
	Banggai Island	Banggai	Salakan	2008
United States	Alaska	Juneau	Anchorage	ongoing debate

* Since 1956, 16 new states and union territories with new capitals have been created in India: Gujarat and Maharashtra in 1960; Nagaland in 1963; Haryana in 1966; Himachal Pradesh, Manipur, Meghalaya, and Tripura in 1971; the Kingdom of Sikkim in 1975; Arunachal Pradesh, Goa, and Mizoram in 1987; Chhattisgarh, Uttarakhand, and Jharkhand in 2000; and Telangana in 2014.

Table 5 The relationship between four normative concepts and six strategies

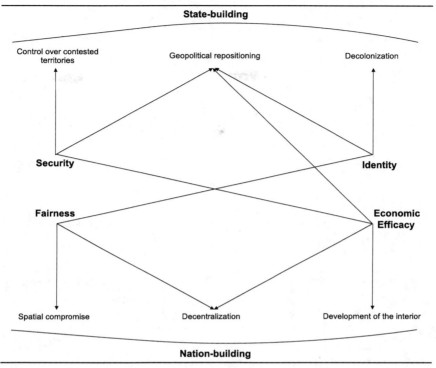

Table 6 Pairs of the opposing types of capital cities

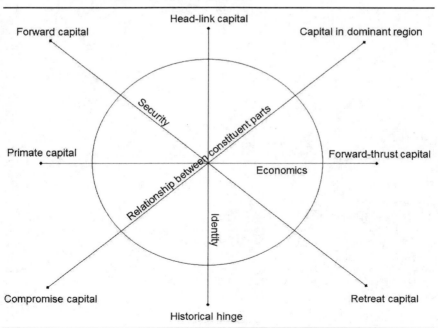

(*Continued*)

Table 6 (Continued)

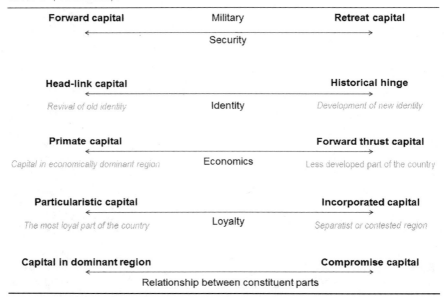

Table 7 Capital city relocation costs/budgets by country

Country	From	To	Total Budget in billions	Alternative Estimates	Total GDP in current USD*	%GDP**
Germany	Bonn	Berlin	16	11	1800	0.8%
Kazakhstan	Alma-Ata	Astana	12		22	54.5%
Malaysia	Kuala Lumpur	Putrajaya	8.1		79.1	10.2%
Brazil	Rio de Janeiro	Brasília	19.5		137.5	14.2%
Nigeria	Lagos	Abuja	13		72.4	18.0%
Tanzania	Dar es Salaam	Dodoma	0.144		3.3	4.4%
Malawi	Zomba	Lilongwe	0.12		0.84	14.3%
Myanmar	Rangoon	Naypyidaw	5		83.9	6.0%
Afghanistan	Kabul	New Kabul	34	50	15	280.0%

* GDP is quoted in the year the project was started. E.g., Kazakhstan's GDP is quoted based on 1997, and the GDP of Malaysia based on 1999.
** % GDP represents the average between the suggested budget and alternative estimate when applicable.

Suggested capital city relocation budgets/estimates in a sample of countries

Country	Old Capital	New Capital	Suggested Budget	Alternative Estimate	GDP	% GDP
Japan	Tokyo		144	350	4400	3.3%
Indonesia	Jakarta		11		695	1.6%
S Korea	Seoul	Sejong	38.5–45		1000	3.9%
S Sudan	Juba		10		2	500%
Iran**	Tehran		29–43		417	7.2%
Russia	Moscow		150	300	1300	17.3%
Argentina	Buenos Aires	Viedma	4.7		115	4.1%
Egypt	Cairo	New Cairo	45		287	15.7%

* GDP is quoted in the year when the proposal was made. E.g., Indonesia's GDP in 2010, and Japan's GDP in 1999.
** % GDP represents the average between the suggested budget and alternative estimate when applicable.

Sources:
Malawi. GDP in 1975: Gross Domestic Product (GDP) of Malawi, 1970–2010 http://kushnirs.org/macroeconomics/gdp/gdp_malawi.html#t2_1 The amounts spent significantly exceeded the original budget of $60–70 million (50–60 million MWK) (Potts, 1985: 189). Moreover, some expenses, notably the construction of the airport and of the new transportation routes were not included in the expenses. $120 million is a more realistic estimate.

Tanzania. The appraisal as of 1993 was 4.9 billion TZS (Kironde, 1993: 448). GDP in 1974: Gross Domestic Product (GDP) of Malawi and its neighbors, billions dollars, 1970–2010. The exchange rate in 1993 год is found in Krichene, N. "Purchasing Power Parities in Five East African Countries," *IMF Working Paper*, October 1998

Brasília. The appraisal is done in 2010 dollars. Baldussi, D. "Brasilia, 50 Years as the Capital," *Rio Times*, Jan 12, 2010. Accordingly, GDP in 1957 ($17.6 billion) is converted to 2010 USD ($137.5 billion). Pessoa, M. "Fiscal Policy in Brazil and Japan: what can be learned" (Tokyo, 2004: 47).

Nigeria. $10 billion was spent in 12 years, from 1985 to 1997. The economists have estimated in 1997 that $2–4 billion will be necessary to finish the project. Moser, G., Rogers, S. & Van Til, R. 1997. "Nigeria: Experience With Structural Adjustment," *IMF Occasional Papers* (Washington D.C.), March, 37. In 1985–1992 the GDP of Nigeria has significantly increased. The average GDP throughout these seven years годах was $244 billion. Accordingly, 5–6 percent of GDP was spent on the construction of a new capital.

Russia. The first estimate was cited by the mayor of Moscow Нгкш Luzhkov (2002), and the second one by Iosif Diskin, the co-Chair of the Council for National Strategy (Babaian, 2011).

Myanmar. This estimate was provided by an expert in Burmese economy Sean Turnell, Professor at Macquarie University in Sydney, Australia. "Built to Order: Myanmar's New Capital Isolates and Insulates Junta," *The New York Times*, June 24, 2008.

Kazakhstan. According to the official estimates, originally $2 billion were spent by the government and $2 billion by the private companies.

Afghanistan. State budget ($11 billion) and private funds ($23 billion).

Table 8 Selected countries ranked by economic dominance of capital city (2014)

Country	GDP/capita	People (%)	GDP (%)	Capital City
Brazil	3.05	1	4	Brasília
Russia	2.33	9	21	Moscow
Thailand	2.30	13	29	Bangkok
China	2.27	2	3	Beijing
Indonesia	2.17	6	13	Jakarta
Italy	2.08	4	9	Rome
India	1.90	2	4	New Delhi
Iran	1.88	16	30	Tehran
Egypt	1.85	19	35	Cairo
Spain	1.70	7	12	Madrid
UK	1.69	13	22	London
France	1.67	18	30	Paris
Argentina	1.47	32	47	Buenos Aires
Venezuela	1.35	10	14	Caracas
Mexico	1.32	17	22	Mexico City
Austria	1.30	20	26	Vienna
Sweden	1.23	26	32	Stockholm
Japan	1.14	29	33	Tokyo
South Korea	1.10	21	23	Seoul

Table 9 Zipf plot for cities in a sample of countries

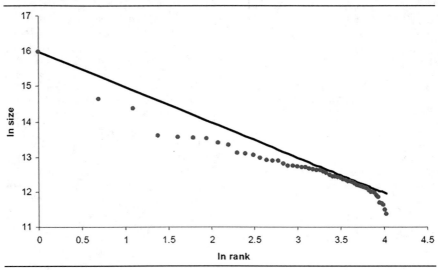

Graph Cl 5(a) Size distribution of cities in the UK

Source: Overman, H. "Are Britain's 'Second Tier' Cities too Small," Spatial Economics Research Center. 2012. October 12.

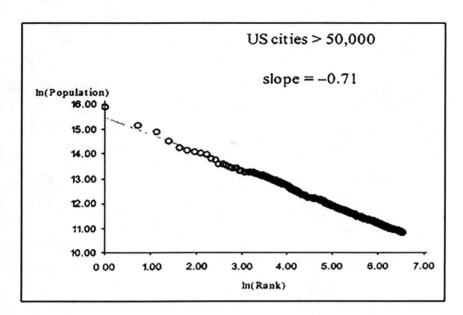

Graph C1 5(b) US

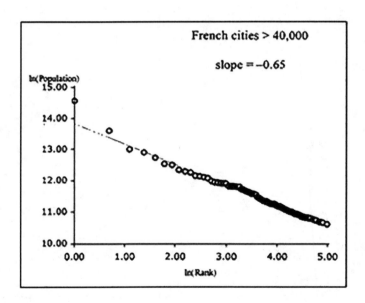

Graph C1 5(c) France

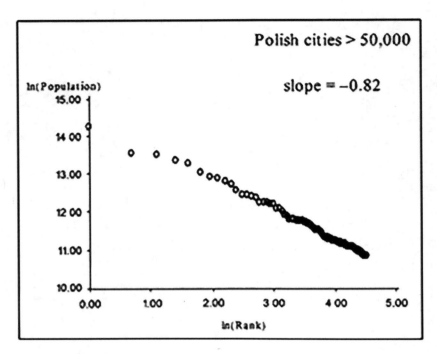

Graph C1 5(d) Poland

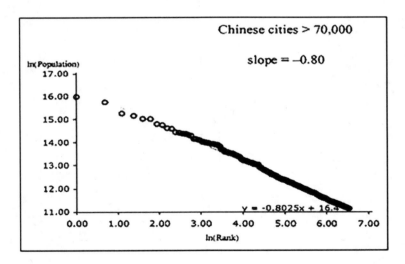

Graph C1 5(e) China

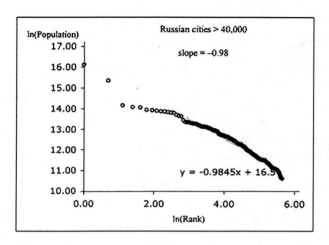

Graph C1 6 Size distribution of Russian cities
Source: World Bank. *From Transition to Development: A Country Economic Memorandum for the Russian Federation*. Report no. 32308. March

Table 10 Economic dominance: second cities compared to capital cities

Country	GDP/capita	People (%)	GDP (%)	Capital City
China	2.27	1.5	3.4	Beijing
	2.24	1.7	3.8	Shanghai
Italy	2.08	4.3	9.0	Rome
	2.70	2.0	5.4	Milan
India	1.90	2.0	3.8	Delhi
	3.62	1.7	6.2	Mumbai
Pakistan	1.25	0.8	1.0	Islamabad
	2.00	10.0	20.0	Karachi
Spain	1.70	6.9	11.7	Madrid
	3.48	3.6	12.5	Barcelona
Brazil	3.05	1.3	4.0	Brasília
	2.17	5.3	11.5	São Paulo
	1.61	3.1	5.1	Rio de Janeiro
USA	0.92	0.7	0.6	Washington D.C.
	2.66	2.6	7.0	New York
Russia	2.33	9.0	21.0	Moscow
	1.03	3.7	3.8	Saint-Petersburg
UK	1.69	13.0	22.0	London
	1.75	0.8	1.4	Manchester
France	1.67	18.0	30.0	Paris
	2.89	0.8	2.2	Lyon
Japan	1.14	29.0	33.0	Tokyo
	1.95	2.0	3.9	Osaka

Index

Abidjan 86, 88
Abu Dhabi 125, 243, 261
Abuja 83, 88–91, 165, 179, 195, 197, 212, 214, 254, 272
administrative capital 26, 27, 67, 75, 79–80, 93, 95, 99, 100, 118, 122, 124, 148, 150, 162, 169, 183, 188, 192, 203, 206, 265
Alexander the Great 21, 47, 53, 59, 67
Alexandria 21, 28, 47, 64–5, 262
Alexandrine model 20–1
Almaty 41, 145, 214
Amman 124–5
Amsterdam 45, 78, 179
Ankara 17, 84, 119–20
Aristotle 21–2
Astana 79, 84, 141–5, 176, 185, 203, 212, 214, 253–4
Ataturk 119–20, 182, 218–19
Athens 78–9, 182, 254, 261, 264
Auckland 161, 179

Babylon 13, 21, 24–5, 27, 48, 53, 59, 67–8, 70, 182
Baghdad 15, 19, 59, 69, 71, 178, 209, 265, 274
Baltoscandia 157, 185
Bangkok 81, 103–4, 174
Barcelona 259–60
Bayda 94
Beijing 18, 54, 56–7, 59, 114, 147, 174, 226, 240, 259, 274
Belgrade 61, 82, 179, 185, 228
Belize City 139–40
Belmopan 139–40
Berlin 13, 17, 23, 32, 58, 78–9, 83, 152–4, 182, 186, 189, 199–200, 214, 218, 239, 244, 261, 263, 270
Bern 19, 79, 178–9, 261

Bishkek 82, 146
Bismarck, Otto von 78, 199–200
Bonaparte, Napoleon 160, 172, 251–2
Bonn 152–3, 186, 220, 239
Brasília 17, 84, 102, 128–33, 137, 140, 153, 160, 166, 170, 175–6, 186, 188, 206, 212, 214, 217, 239, 242, 248–9, 251–4, 261, 272
Bratislava 63, 79, 152, 165
Braudel, Fernand 32–3, 48, 263
Brussels 16, 19, 23, 47, 79, 102, 176, 178, 244, 262
Bucharest 64, 79, 82, 154–6, 164
Buda 63, 82
Buenos Aires 127, 135–6, 203, 235, 257
Butare 86

Cairo 18, 60, 123–4, 209
Calcutta 79, 105–7, 195, 228
Canberra 17, 153, 162–3, 176, 179, 185, 202, 248, 252–4, 261, 272
capital city goods 204–5
capital city clause 5
Caracas 136–7, 173
centrality 25, 27, 51, 64, 74, 180, 185–6, 192, 231–2, 247
centrography 226–7, 232
centroid 192
cerrado 129, 133
Ciudad Constitution 137
Ciudad Libertad 136–7
clan politics 192
cleavages 89, 126, 142, 244, 272
clientalism 116, 175
colonial politics and capitals 43, 79–81, 272, 274
Connectivity 103, 129, 158, 261
consensus-making method 156, 191, 198, 213, 216, 232

Constantinople 18–19, 21, 28, 59–61, 64–7, 209, 265
core-periphery relationship 229–30
Cornish, Vaughan 53–7
corrupt state 234–6
Ctesiphon 56, 59, 67, 178
culture *vs.* nature 175–6

Dakar 79, 93–4, 183
Damascus 19, 57, 75, 125, 178, 261
Dar es Salaam 91–3, 202
Daulatabad 72–3
decentralization 95, 98–9, 107, 112, 113, 134, 140, 161, 163, 174, 177, 187–9, 190
Delphi 26–8
designed capital 17, 70, 99, 108, 128, 135, 209, 249, 254–5
devolution 161, 188
Dhaka 107, 110–11, 173
differential urbanization theory 151
disembedded capital 48, 67–74, 198, 247, 274
distributed capital 17–18, 179–81
divide 66, 89, 105, 114–15, 158–9, 186–7
doctrine of the forward position of the capital 16, 55–6
Dodoma 91–4, 254
Doxiadis, Konstantinos 108, 254
dual capital system x, 17–18, 126
Durrës 154
Dushanbe 59, 73, 82, 146–7

Eco, Umberto 19, 41, 130
Ecumene (*oecumene*) 192
Elazar, Daniel 247
empire-building 58, 61
engineered cities 206
entrepôt 80, 85, 105
Eurasianism 144–5, 149–50

Falola, Toyin 195
federalism 7, 111, 153, 241–6
federalist capitals 242–8
Fez 195, 261
fixed and peripatetic capitals 23
former capital 47, 59, 85, 188, 198, 201, 216
forward capital 16, 55–6
forward-thrust capital 16, 187, 229
frontier capital 53–4, 56, 58, 62

Gaborone 85–6, 272
Geertz, Clifford 25, 48, 262
geomancy 55, 224–7
geopolitical positioning 227–9
geopolitics 2, 227–9, 232, 272–3
Germania 13, 218
global cities 255–62
Gravier, Jean-Francoise 160, 229
great power 55, 57, 73
growth pole theory 9, 93, 129, 132, 135, 186–7, 214, 228–30

The Hague 13, 19, 45, 78, 179, 180, 210
hard capitals *vs.* soft capitals 19
Haushofer, Karl 228
Haussman, Georges-Eugène 20, 31, 194–5
head-link capital 184
heartland 103, 105–6, 119, 128, 133, 192
hegemony 159, 198, 239
Helsinki x, 17, 63, 79
Henderson, Vernon 240
hinge 66, 110, 181, 258
hinterland 16, 79, 112, 114–15, 127, 129, 135, 137, 148, 186, 188, 193, 207, 215, 232, 257
Hitler, Adolf 13, 157, 218
Holy Roman Empire 23–4, 47, 67, 178, 265
hypercentralization 159, 209, 276
hypercephalism 205, 233

iconography 83, 120, 130, 163, 197, 218, 233, 248–9, 255–7, 272
imperial capital 16–17, 53, 56, 58, 64, 87, 196, 249
inclusivity (inclusive *vs.* exclusive capital cities) 91, 177, 198, 248–51, 274
incorporated capital 59–60
infrastructure 80, 86–7, 89, 92, 97–8, 100, 104–5, 108, 110–12, 114, 117, 121–4, 136, 146–9, 151, 161, 184, 188, 201, 212, 215–16, 219, 235, 240–1, 271, 273, 276
inland capital *vs.* coastal capital 262
insular *vs.* continental capital 22, 134, 136
interim/transitional capital 19, 107
inward and outward capital 16, 252, 258
irredentism 142, 155, 189
Islamabad 107–8, 195, 206, 212, 254, 272
isolated capital 205–8, 210–12
Istanbul 119–20, 164, 185, 218, 261

Jacobs, Jane 263
Jahn, Friedrich Ludwig 61, 78, 223
Jakarta 81, 101–3, 173, 240
Jerusalem 28–9, 59, 62, 75, 177, 182, 247, 251–2, 254, 261
joint capital xv, 47

Kabul 18, 21, 59, 123, 147, 272
Karachi 79, 107–8, 147, 195
Karakorum 59, 118, 182
Kathmandu 16, 111, 173
Khaldun, Ibn 58
Khalifa City 126
Khan, Ayub 107–8, 197
Khartoum 85
Kiev 150–1
Kigali 84
Königsberg 58
Kotte 111–12, 182–3, 197
Kragujevac 79, 185, 264
Kraków x, 29, 156, 178, 196
Kuala Lumpur 13, 79, 81, 99–101
Kubitschek, Juscelino 128–9, 132–3, 217, 219, 252–3
Kyoto 19, 29, 71–72, 113, 184, 225, 261

Lagos 79, 86, 88–91
landlocked country 85–6, 259
La Roche-Guyon 160–1, 188
Le Maître, Alexandre 40
L'Enfant, Pierre Charles 254
Lilongwe 86, 93
Lima 137–8, 173, 186
Lisbon 16, 32, 178
London 14, 16–17, 19–20, 30, 32–3, 42, 60, 158–9, 229, 231, 236, 237–40, 257–8, 262–3

Machiavelli, Niccolò 61, 235–6
Madrid 17, 19–21, 31, 32, 37, 57, 177–8, 209–10, 257, 259, 260
Mafeking 86
Manama 125, 176, 261
Masonic symbols 252–3
Mecca 27, 29, 75, 125
mega-region 83–4, 105, 173, 183–6, 192–3, 236, 271, 273, 275
Melbourne 179, 231
Memel 19, 78, 83, 157, 184, 189
Memphis 28, 68–9, 177, 251–2
metanarratives 248, 251, 255
metropole 63–4, 79, 80–1, 93, 106, 128, 161, 230

Index 315

metropolitanism xii, 64, 113, 116, 175, 188, 195, 216, 235, 238
Mexico City 176, 243, 244
misgovernance 234–5
mobile capital 22–3
modernist urban planning/architecture 101, 130–2, 169–70, 220, 251–2
Mohamad, Mahathir bin 100–1
monocephality 104, 151, 156, 188
Montesquieu, Charles-Louis 50, 73–4, 267, 269
Moscow 13–14, 16, 21, 28, 52, 149–50, 156, 184, 187, 196, 204, 206, 218, 230, 235, 238, 240, 248–9, 251, 254, 257, 259–60, 264
Muscat 60, 127
Mussolini, Benito 218

Nanjing 57, 114, 226
Naples 196
Nara 19, 24, 29, 63, 71, 225
nation 5–7, 13–16, 35–8, 43, 58, 77–8, 81, 120, 176, 182–3, 189, 192, 196, 198
nationalism 4, 35, 38–9, 77–8, 81, 100, 106, 151, 275
nation-building xiv, 4, 6–9, 19, 35, 37, 43, 78, 84–7, 94, 96, 99, 117–18, 120, 124, 127, 143, 176, 183, 185, 187, 197, 209, 233, 272–5
nation-state xi, xiv, 8, 12, 17, 28, 31, 34–6, 44, 77, 80, 83, 85, 255, 257–8, 274–5
nativization 120, 151
Naypyidaw vii, 108–10, 183, 212, 214
Niemeyer, Oskar 128, 130, 132–3, 242
Nippur 26–7
nodality 53, 103, 125, 256
node 251, 257–8
Nouakchott 85
Nyenschatz 74, 176
Nyerere, Julius 91–2

Ottawa vii, 161, 179, 244–5, 250
outward capital 16
overcentralization 8, 208, 227

Pakštas, Kazys 157
Palermo 196
Paris 17, 19, 20, 23, 30, 32, 33, 40–1, 52, 160–1, 194, 205, 212, 216, 229, 231, 236–7, 239, 252, 257, 263
particularistic capitals 193, 197
performativity 249

Index

Perroux, François 228–9
Persepolis 24–5, 27, 48, 182
Philadelphia xix, 19, 78, 246
planned cities 101
polycephality (polycephalous urban systems) 19, 262
Port-au-Prince 140
primate city xv, 233, 236, 240, 245, 266–7
protest movement 105, 174, 193–5, 198, 275
provisional capital 19, 67
public policy objectives 9, 192, 207–8, 213, 215
pull and push factors 173
Putrajaya vii, 84, 99–102, 188, 251, 253–4, 272

Qixia 27, 249

Rabat 87, 195, 261
Rangoon 108, 195
Rawalpindi 107–8
regional planning 161
region-building 99, 185, 186, 193, 273
Rio de Janeiro 19, 129–30, 169, 231
Rokkan, Stein 41–2
Rome vii, xi, xvii, 13, 17–20, 23, 28, 30, 32, 56, 57, 64–7, 78–9, 88, 129, 182, 199, 218, 247, 251–2, 254, 259–60, 262
Rousseau, Jean-Jacques 40–1, 160
roving and wandering capitals 23, 67
royal capital 20, 24, 29–30, 31, 45, 100, 178, 225
retreat capital and frontier capital 16, 62

sacred capital 18, 24–7, 29, 38, 47–8, 124, 149, 250, 253
Saint-Petersburg 7, 13, 17, 60, 74, 164, 176, 184, 196, 206, 231, 251, 252, 259, 260, 270
Salalah 127
Samarkand 59, 60, 82–3, 140, 146–7, 253, 262
Sana'a 126, 174
satellite city 123, 150
Schatz, Edward 43, 143, 145, 176
seasonal capitals (winter/summer/monsoon) 18, 24, 111
seats of power xiv, 106, 196, 205, 274

Sejong City 115–18, 204, 272
Seoul 115–18, 204, 225, 227
separatist movements 39, 140, 143, 145, 152
Sirte 95, 197
spatial compromise 163, 177, 179, 188, 190
spatial economics 2–3, 9, 211, 233
split capital 115, 180, 204
Stalin, Josef 140, 151, 156, 218
state-building xiii, 6, 41, 43, 51, 61, 142, 192, 214, 233
Suli 6, 4 24
supracapital 16, 17
symbolic inclusivity 248–9
symbolism 2, 4, 26–7, 107, 112, 120, 130, 144, 183, 250, 251–7
system dynamics 227

Tabriz 122, 182, 189, 261
Taipei 64, 115, 173
Târgovişte 64, 155
Taylor, Peter 230
Tbilisi 148, 149
Tehran 63, 121–2, 173–4, 195, 204
Tel Aviv 182, 261
Terra irredenta 189
Thebes 28, 64, 68, 177
Therborn, Göran 83
Thessaloniki 182
Tirana 79, 154
titular nation 81, 122, 142, 157, 183, 189, 193, 196–8
Tokyo 7, 16–17, 112–13, 173, 184, 203–4, 231, 236, 257
Toledo 23, 29–31, 177
Toronto 161, 179, 245
Toshiaki, Honda 61
Toynbee, Arnold 9, 55–7, 128, 193
Tripoli 94–5
Turin 78, 199, 262
Twain, Mark 194

Ulaanbaatar 24, 81, 118, 145
urban planning 2, 3, 20, 85, 87, 109, 124, 194, 203, 217, 271
urban primacy 9, 42, 86, 104, 127, 205, 234, 240, 255, 266

Vienna 7, 23, 32, 52, 60, 61, 78, 185, 228
Vienna system 78
Vilnius 82, 157

Wallace, Jeremy 194
Warsaw 82, 156, 178, 274
Washington DC 14, 16, 17, 19, 70, 83, 112, 161, 163, 176, 179, 210, 220, 244–8, 250, 252, 254, 272
Wellington 181, 174, 179, 261
Westphalian system 22, 42–3, 78

world-system analysis 9, 229–30

Yamoussoukro 88

Zimmerman, Horst 238–9
Zipf law/plots 236
Zomba 86, 93